WILDLIFE INDIA @ 50

WILDLIFE INDIA @ 50

Saving the Wild, Securing the Future

Edited by MANOJ KUMAR MISRA

RUPA

First published by
Rupa Publications India Pvt. Ltd 2022
7/16, Ansari Road, Daryaganj
New Delhi 110002

Sales Centres:

Allahabad Bengaluru Chennai
Hyderabad Jaipur Kathmandu
Kolkata Mumbai

ISBN: 978-93-5520-557-5

First impression 2022

10 9 8 7 6 5 4 3 2 1

Printed in India

To my parents, Ramesh Kumar Misra 'Siddhesh', an artist, and Dr Padma Siddhesh, a teacher, for those Sunday excursions along the river Kho, and for the freedom to explore the wilds, in my 'wow' years as a child.

CONTENTS

PART TWO

PREFACE

I had been a forester for a large part of my professional life. Little past midway of what would have been a normal bureaucratic lifespan of 35 years, I chose to change track, opt out of government employment and explore the secrets of rivers instead. But I never lost touch with that part of my life—the, wildlife and people in that sector. This came in handy as I worked on putting this book together.

Sometime in the latter half of 2021, as I lay convalescing after a major surgery, I realized that the following year, 2022 would mark the fiftieth anniversary of India's wildlife legislation, namely the Wildlife (Protection) Act, 1972. This deserved suitable commemoration, stocktaking and a reality check. But my first instinct was that there might already be several people working on a project of this magnitude and prestige. I began to sound some friends informally; even put out a tweet about it, receiving hardly any response or traction on the thought. It seemed as if a general dulling of senses by the Covid-19 pandemic had taken a toll on our alertness to prepare for such anniversaries. Ultimately, I decided to take the plunge and put this book together as a fitting commemoration of the event.

I knew from day one that such a book could not be the enterprise of a single author, since the field of wildlife conservation is too vast and beyond one person's scope of understanding or experience. Moreover, for an individual to relive and recount events spread over half a century is not only difficult but also risks glossing over quite a few key elements of the complete story.

It was only logical and, not to mention, easier to collate a thorough critique of wildlife legislation by a select group of subject matter experts and a few practitioners. Many suggested that I follow this time-tested recipe for its audience—readymade in lawyers, jurists, judges, law colleges, forest and wildlife training institutions, and field practitioners. But I wondered if there was some other way to put this book together that would appeal to and yet go beyond a niche audience. Was there a genre to capture not just the strengths and weaknesses of wildlife legislation as it has panned out over the last 50 years? Can we document different shades of processes, institutions and experiments that it has spawned over its long life and, more importantly, in a manner which would interest not just the practitioners but even a layperson?

Aware that stories about and by people appeal to us the most, I chose storytelling as the style for this book and reached out to several people to write about their own 'lived' wildlife stories. Accordingly, my opening e-mail to a select group said, 'I am putting together a book on 50 years of India's wildlife journey...The idea is to take a reader along on a personal journey in a story format that informs as well as enlightens... Please use "first-person" as the mode of narration.'

So, if you find a lot of 'I' in here, this is by design, for you can't write your own 'lived' tale without bringing in the 'I'. But you will find that the 'I' here is not the showy type, for many writing these tales have been self-effacing 'doers' and hence not famous in the traditional sense of the term. Even H.S. Panwar, perhaps the most celebrated amongst the list of chapter authors, is self-effacing to a fault. So is Usha Rai, a remarkable career journalist who began her reporting in the 'ancient' 1960s. As octogenarians, they constitute the senior-most contributors to this book. There are more similarly interesting and accomplished individuals as authors in this book.

Here, you shall find stories about making of legislation; need of inviolate habitats; intractable man–animal conflicts and dilemmas around hunting; ground realities of law implementation; opportunities in making parks and people, friends; illegal wildlife trade; zoos; wildlife research, documentation and tourism; saving species like crocodiles, lions, tigers, elephants, barasinghas and the great Indian bustard (GIB); conservation challenges in Arunachal Pradesh, Gulf of Mannar in Tamil Nadu, conservation reserves in Uttarakhand and private sanctuaries in Rajasthan; people, institutions and wildlife non-governmental organizations (NGOs); the impact of climate change and a potential picture of wildlife legislation after another 50 years in 2072. A lot packed into a single book? Not really, as you will find on its perusal.

It is hoped that our endeavour to commemorate five decades of India's wildlife journey in short personal stories is found worthwhile.

INTRODUCTION

India's natural history stretches back more than 2,500 years, when the emperor Chandragupta Maurya (322–297 BC) created *hasti vanas* as instructed in Vishnugupta or Kautilya's Arthashastra. This predates by many centuries the Yellowstone National Park, the first nature reserve in the modern world, which is celebrating its 150th anniversary this year.

For ages, the Indian subcontinent has attracted outsiders and visitors. Of its many attractions, wild animals, birds, reptiles, insects and plants have held a place of pride. Writing about Babur (sixteenth century), the ornithologist and naturalist Dr Salim Ali said, 'of the larger mammals of Hindustan, the rhinoceros was one that must have seemed altogether strange and unnatural…'[1] Babur's memoirs are replete with mention of the animals, fruits and flowers he encountered in Hindustan. They were so numerous that shikar became a popular royal pastime all through the medieval period and continued as a sport during the British period (1858–1947) and even much later, in independent India, at least for the first few decades.

The process of state control over wildlife harvests began with the Madras Elephant Protection Act of 1873 and the Wild Birds Protection Act of 1887, later revised in 1912 to the Wild Birds and Animal Protection Act. The Act of 1912 as amended in 1935, led to the creation of 'sanctuaries' and 'national parks', where hunting of wild animals was not permitted. For example, the Jim Corbett National Park was first declared Hailey National Park in 1936. Princely India, too, had its own version of wildlife preserves.

At the widely participated Tenth General Assembly of International Union for Conservation of Nature (IUCN) held in 1969 at New Delhi from 24 November to 1 December, a wake-up call on the wildlife front in the country was sounded. As an iconic wild animal, the tiger, had begun to lose ground to hunting pressure and habitat loss; Asiatic cheetah had already gone extinct, and several other wildlife species were in trouble. Large-scale conversion of forests into farmlands and other land uses, and runaway hunting of wildlife had taken a heavy toll. It all pointed to a dire situation, necessitating urgent ameliorative measures.

One such measure was a national wildlife legislation which could ensure uniformity of purpose, institutions and governance all over the country. The Indian Board of Wildlife (IBWL), created in 1952, had also appealed for such legislation.

Taking heed of the above, the 1970s and 1980s became brave new decades for the nation's wildlife when wild species and spaces came to be protected with a missionary zeal. A national law, the Wild Life (Protection) Act (WLPA),1972, opened up opportunities and avenues for firm action on the ground. The launch of Project Tiger in 1973 was a major national-level initiative. So were the efforts to save the crocodilians. New wildlife protected areas (PAs) in the form of national parks and sanctuaries, were created all over the country. The Wildlife Institute of India (WII), Dehradun, was established as a premier institution in 1982, and a few sections of the WLPA underwent enabling amendments from time to time in 1977, 1980, 1982, and 1986.

AD 1991: Economic hardships had led India to open up its economy and adopt the western market-driven model for faster economic growth.

AD 2000: Here onwards, there was a sudden brake put on the missionary zeal to promote wildlife conservation in the country.

AD 2022: India @ 75 is trending as 'Azadi ka Amrit Mahotsav (The Celebration of Everlasting Freedom)'. It is time to both celebrate and introspect. There are many achievements that India, as a mature nation, can be proud of, including its democratic credentials. Its greatest asset is the young and aspirational demographic, with 65 per cent of its population below the age of 35 years. But the same cannot be said of its wildlife, wild spaces, climate and natural assets, which are all under grave threat despite being the very foundation of a strong, healthy and happy nation. It is not that there are no success stories on the wildlife front to share, but they are few and far between. To understand all this and more, we need to travel back in time. Some five decades, actually! This book is about that journey and more.

It is a book of short stories with a difference. These are not fictional but 'lived' tales told by people who have played long or short innings in India's 50-year-long journey to protect its wildlife and wild spaces.

While preparing a short list of potential authors for this anthology, I looked for a distinctive quality in each of them. As a result, here you will find pioneers such as Usha Rai (wildlife reporting), Dr Asad R. Rahmani (wildlife research), Joanna Van Gruisen (wildlife filmmaking and tourism), Sharad Gaur (wildlife volunteering), Lala Aswini Kumar (A.K.) Singh (crocodilian research), Vinod Uniyal (co-opting people in conservation), Aparajita Datta (discovering mammals in Arunachal Pradesh), Ritwick Dutta (wildlife jurist) and Aditya 'Dicky' Singh (private properties as wildlife havens).

Then there are field practitioners who have excelled in their craft by walking that extra mile. These include H.S. Panwar (builder of institutions), Vishwas B. Sawarkar (teacher par excellence), Suresh Chandra (S.C.) Sharma (Government of India [GoI] veteran), Harbhajan Singh (H.S.) Pabla (out-of-the box thinker), Suhas Kumar (innovative approaches), Arvind Kumar

Jha (out-of-the box doer), Rabindra Kumar Singh (experimenter of repute) and R. Sreenivasa Murthy (never-say-die attitude).

Many have shared their experiences with specialized assignments. These include Prerna Singh Bindra (National Board for Wildlife [NBWL]), Saket Badola (wildlife trade), Sudha Ramen (zoos), Koustubh Sharma (researching chausingha), Sumit Dookia (saving the great Indian bustard [GIB]) and Faiyaz A. Khudsar (Kuno National Park as second home for the Asiatic lion).

Finally, there are enthusiasts who have worked for wildlife conservation, whether it matched or not their core profession. These include Ananda Banerjee (journalist and artist), Stella James (advocate), Nayana Udayashankar (advocate), Bhuvana Balaji (development professional), Ghazala Shahabuddin (researcher and academic), Anjali Bhartari (natural and cultural heritage enthusiast), Ishan Kukreti (journalist), Ishan Dhar and Dharmendra Khandal (wildlife biologists), Nivedita Khandekar (journalist) and Neha Sinha (wildlife biologist and author).

What you will not find here are stories from some of the famous wildlife advocates, researchers, activists etc., for their tales and views are already in the public domain in the form of articles and books.

This book has been divided into two parts. In Part 1 are those that reflect directly on matters that relate to the WLPA, while those in Part 2 deal with it indirectly through personal tales about people, projects and institutions. The final two chapters look forward to the future of wildlife in India and the WLPA and hence are good takeaway for the future.

Part I

The book opens with S.C. Sharma sharing in 'The Changing Shades of Wildlife Legislation in India' his incredible journey as an insider with government of India for 15 long years during which he participated in and witnessed the process and politics of law making in general and of the two major amendments made to the WLPA in 1991 and 2003.

H.S. Panwar, the doyen of Indian wildlife practitioners, highlights the necessity of inviolate wild spaces, recalling his decade-long Kanha days marked by a remarkable recovery there, of the threatened barasingha. That India requires a series of Kanha-like PAs all over to safeguard its wildlife is the subject matter of his seminal work in collaboration with W. Alan Rodgers, on planning a national network of PAs, produced during his second decade-long assignment as the founder-director of the Wildlife Institute of India at Dehradun. His tale 'Securing Habitats for Ecosystem Revival' is about these and more.

Hunting—more appropriately, poaching—had been identified as the bane of and behind the sharp decline in wildlife numbers in the country even at the time when WLPA was enacted in 1972. Reason, why the national wildlife act, has 'protection' written all over it? H.S. Pabla, a practitioner of long standing dwells deeper into this question and presents a rather provocative hypothesis in his 'Hunting for Answers'.

A law is just a piece of paper without its effective implementation. Arvind Kumar Jha is one such practitioner who ensured that violators of the provisions of the WLPA were pursued with the doggedness they deserved. His tale, 'How Fair: Long Arms of the Law' with a twist in its tail, raises an important point, how legislation removed from its socio-economic implications proves counterproductive in the long run.

Local people, especially forest-dwelling tribal communities, have often been at the receiving end of the creation of wildlife-protected areas. A change in this equation where both people and wildlife flourish has been tried time and again since the 1980s. Vinod Kumar Uniyal has been involved in three such efforts with commendable results. His story 'Building Bridges: Protected Areas and People' is about them.

In 2002–2003 a major amendment to the WLPA amongst other things took a bold futuristic step. It created two new categories of PAs namely community reserves and conservation reserves. These were to recognize and account for people's voluntary wildlife protection efforts and enable such wild spaces to receive the state's legal protection. How this move has panned out on the ground is what academics and researchers Ghazala Shahabuddin and Anjali Bhartari narrate in 'Conserving with People: Challenges and Opportunities of Conservation Reserves'.

The trade of wildlife and wildlife products has been seen as a key driver of the sharp reduction in wildlife numbers. Saket Badola shares in 'Commerce Most Foul: Illegal Trade in Wildlife' his learnings and fears from the vantage seat of head of Trade Record Analysis of Flora and Fauna in Commerce (TRAFFIC) India about the course of wildlife trade nationally and internationally over the last few decades and where it could potentially end up in a click of a button-'connected' world.

Zoos are as much loved as reviled, depending on whether they are seen as saviour or exploiter of the natural world. Sudha Ramen, a sensitive practitioner shares in 'Managing Wildlife in Captivity' her fond and fruitful experiences over three years as the curator of the zoo at Chennai.

Researching wildlife is no child's play. But it can be life-changing in so many ways, is what Koustubh Sharma reminiscences in his personal tale on 'Unravelling the Unknown: Researching Chausingha in the Wild'. He spent five years deep within the Panna Tiger Reserve chasing chausingha, the only wild animal with four horns.

Filming wildlife has been much fulfilling and often celebrated profession for a practitioner. Wildlife viewing in the natural setting by a visitor to a national park or sanctuary is now much valued. Joanna Van Gruisen is a veteran filmmaker who now runs a small but compact eco-resort with her partner. Her tale

'A Life in the Jungles: Wildlife Documentation to Tourism' is about a quantum leap over the years in the art and equipment of filming and the challenges and opportunities in wildlife tourism.

Two notable conservation initiatives began in 1970s; one was the Project Tiger to revive tiger numbers, while the other was focused on crocodilians, namely the gharial, mugger and marsh crocodile. The crocodile project interestingly began as a commercial project to soon take to conservation since initial surveys found that the crocodile numbers had plummeted alarmingly all over the country. Lala A.K. Singh was one of the earliest crocodilian researchers who spearheaded the conservation saga. 'From Commerce to Conservation: Saving Crocodiles' is his tale.

The reintroduction of locally extinct wildlife species into habitats with a known history of past occurrence is a legitimate human-assisted effort at wildlife conservation. 'Saving Endangered Wild Mammals: Reintroduction Stories from Madhya Pradesh' by Suhas Kumar is an experiential narrative of several such reintroductions of herbivores like gaur, blackbuck, chital and barasingha in different PAs in the state of Madhya Pradesh.

In almost the same vein but with frustrating outcomes is the story of lion reintroduction in Kuno National Park in northwest Madhya Pradesh. Supported actively by the central government and the WII, Dehradun, Kuno was painstakingly developed as a second home for the highly endangered Asiatic lion. But to no avail. Faiyaz A. Khudsar, in 'Betrayed Locals and Lions: Story of Kuno National Park', shares his experiences of Kuno spread over some 20 years.

In law, it is often the fine print that overrides what seems apparent. The WLPA is no exception to this adage, is what the Right Livelihood awardee Ritwick Dutta's 'Wildlife Law and Institutions in Fine Print: Vignettes from My Diary', seems to suggest. His story also lays bare the blunders that happen when provisions of the law are either ignored or misread by design or default.

The NBWL is the apex statutory body in the land charged with upholding the cause of wildlife protection and conservation in the country. With long years on the board and its Standing Committee (SC), Prerna Singh Bindra is scathing in her tale 'NBWL: National Board for(?) Wildlife' about its slide as an institution over the years.

Part II

Dr Salim Ali was perhaps the tallest name in the game, in the period leading to and following the promulgation of WLPA. Dr Asad R. Rahmani, no less celebrated than his guru, in his 'The Incredible Salim Ali' pens an inspirational tale of his meeting and the time he spent with him and other stalwarts at the Bombay Natural History Society (BNHS), Bombay (now Mumbai).

Reporting, wildlife was not her own choice. It came Usha Rai's way since she lived close to the zoo in Delhi, and her male colleagues had already cornered the important beats like political reporting at *The Times of India*, where she had joined as its first-ever female reporter. In her tale, 'In the Wilds: Reporter at Large', Usha Rai shares her long experiences in wildlife and nature reporting since the early 1960s.

The WII has been in the vanguard of wildlife conservation movement in the country. V.B. Sawarkar narrates the story of the making of the Institute as only he could have told on account of his rare privilege of having been part of the journey much before the WII was even conceptualized. While his story ends on a wishful note, sharpness of language and wit form the hallmark of Sawarkar's tale titled 'More than Bricks and Mortar: Making of the Wildlife Institute of India, Dehradun'.

In 1972, World Wide Fund for Nature-India (WWF-India) was perhaps the only national-level NGO in the country which set the trend for others to follow. Yes, the BNHS is much older than WWF, but it has always been primarily research-focused and is not a nationwide organization in the same sense. Volunteerism and nature education was WWF's forte in its formative years, and, as a result, it has spawned thousands of naturalists in the country. Sharad Gaur, a long time and one of the earlier staffers at WWF-India harkens back in 'Spawning a Generation of Conservationists: Reminiscences of WWF-India' about the organization, its achievements and its evolution—which has not always been smooth or desirable—over the decades since 1969.

Reports of a fall in tiger numbers at the Ranthambore Tiger Reserve and the disappearance of all its tigers at Sariska and Panna Tiger Reserves during the first decade of the twenty-first century brought home to a jolted nation that all was not well on the wildlife front in the country. Poaching was identified as the main cause, and rearguard action was taken to improve protection measures and reintroduce tigers into these areas. 'Paradise Regained' by R. Sreenivasa Murthy is the story of tiger revival in Panna Tiger Reserve told by the man who led it from the front.

Eastern Himalayas, in particular, the state of Arunachal Pradesh, is among the prominent biodiversity hotspots in the country. But till late, not much was known about it in terms of its biodiversity richness and even the presence of some wild animals there. Aparajita Datta, a celebrated researcher has been one of the pioneers in the area and 'Journeys in Arunachal Pradesh' is her tale about it.

Not many are aware that there are some 128 protected areas in the country under the marine protected areas (MPAs) category. Even less are aware of 18 types of winds that locals claim to blow in the Gulf of Mannar Marine National Park in Tamil Nadu. In 'Shifting Sands: Diaries from the Gulf of Mannar National Park, Tamil Nadu', Stella James, Nayana Udayashankar and Bhuvana Balaji narrate a touching tale of people and park interactions and tensions.

Ishan Kukreti's 'Boomerang: When Success Begins to Breed Contestation', is a take on challenges that have begun to confound local voluntary efforts at wildlife conservation and an urgent need for the state to design policies and realign the WLPA to address increasing instances of human-wildlife conflicts.

Similarly, increasing instances of man-animal conflict reported from different parts of the country have emerged as a key roadblock in ensuring a safe future for wild animals and the locals. Elephants are often at the centre of these skirmishes. R.K. Singh in 'Elephant in the City' weaves a fascinating tale about these incidents within the eastern state of Chhattisgarh and what the future holds in its bosom on this front.

There was a time when the majestic great Indian bustard (GIB) vied with the peafowl for adoption as India's national bird. Today it is struggling for survival. Sumit Dookia, a GIB researcher of note, traces the GIB story and its current predicament in his comprehensive tale, 'Survival: The Existential Threat Facing the GIB'.

Few conservationists in Rajasthan are engaged in developing private properties as wildlife havens. Interestingly at least two gaushalas (cow shelters) are also playing host to local wildlife within their campuses. This private conservation initiative is path-breaking in India and is a possible way forward in the future. 'Four Conservancies Silently Protecting Wildlife in Rajasthan' by Ishan Dhar, Dharmendra Khandal and Aditya 'Dicky' Singh is all about such initiatives.

A large number of people preparatory to and after the promulgation of the WLPA championed the cause of wildlife conservation as a personal mission. Many of them made a name for themselves, while others worked in the wildlife field and related disciplines behind the scenes. Ananda Banerjee, an artist and journalist rubbed shoulders with quite a few of them. In his tale about 'Conservation Champions', he talks of them and provides a rather incomplete list of them.

Similarly, beginning with a few notable NGOs that were active when the WLPA became operational, their number and geographical presence in the country has since increased. 'NGOs in Wildlife Conservation' is my personal tale about them and their vision, mission and priorities. Like the one before, this story needs to be considered an 'incomplete' narrative since the number of wildlife NGOs in the country is too large to fit within a single chapter in a book.

It is now well established that anthropogenic climate change has begun to transform land, air, water and life on earth. Adaptation to this change would be the difference between extinction and survival for various life forms extant on earth. Nivedita Khandekar in 'WLPA in a Climate-Altered India' highlights the emerging ground realities that any future wildlife policy and legislation must consider.

More specifically, is it possible to gaze into the crystal ball and visualize wildlife in India and an appropriate WLPA, 50 years hence in 2072? Neha Sinha took up the challenge and, true to her mastery in her craft, created 'Looking into the Crystal Ball—The WLPA of 2072', a scenario which might even turn out to be just the soothsayer's jackpot. She discusses how the proposed WLPA amendment bill of 2021 can benefit from attention to climate change and creating a climate-conscious policy for wildlife.

This 'story' book seeks to offer you insights into varied aspects of wildlife conservation as it has unfolded in India over the last fifty years and a peep into what could unfold in the next fifty years. We hope you are well informed, entertained and enlightened as you read it.

Notes

1. Ali, Salim, 'The Moghul Emperors of India as Naturalists and Sportsmen', *A Century of Natural History*, J. C. Daniel (ed.), Bombay Natural History Society, 1983.

PART ONE

CHANGING SHADES OF WILDLIFE LEGISLATION IN INDIA

SURESH CHANDRA SHARMA

The mention of the words 'fifty years of wildlife conservation' takes me down memory lane to the fateful day of the last week of September 1972. I reached the headquarters of the Uttar Pradesh Forest Department and met the Chief Wildlife Warden (CWLW), who warmly welcomed me and said, 'Now you need not worry with the drafting of the state legislation on wildlife protection. The Government of India (GoI) has already enacted wildlife legislation for the whole country.' He continued, 'Now, we have to start the work of effective implementation of the Wild Life (Protection) Act (WLPA), 1972, in our state.' This was exciting news to me and I was overjoyed. By then, I had been working as a wildlife warden for more than four years and had had a tough time dealing with the cases of illegal hunting due to the absence of an effective wildlife law with deterrent punitive measures.

The existing Wild Birds and Animals Protection Act, 1912, lacked the provisions to prosecute poachers effectively. To make matters worse, the forest officers could not initiate action on their own and were required to lodge a complaint with the police for any offence committed under the Wild Birds and Animals Protection Act, 1912, and only the police were authorized to take cognizance of violations under the said Act. Moreover, as per Section 3 of the Act, hunting birds and animals specified in the schedule was prohibited only during the closed season. Hunting outside the 'close period' was not an offence. Further, any offence against the provisions of this Act was punishable with a penalty of maximum ₹50 only.

We were forced to resort to the use of provisions of the Indian Forest Act (IFA), 1927, especially sections 26 and 33, which prohibit, among other activities, any person from hunting, shooting, fishing or poisoning water or setting traps in contravention of any rules made by the state government for the said purpose. It may sound strange, but even a tiger was treated as forest produce, and poaching, killing or maiming tigers resulted in the same punishment as illegally removing forest produce (like firewood/dry leaves) from a reserved forest (RF). The maximum penalty prescribed in both these sections was six months in jail or a fine of ₹500 or both. The courts also treated these offences as petty, and the cases dragged on for years. Poachers were let off with minor penalties. Also, there was no protection for animals and birds outside the notified forest areas. We were utterly helpless.

When we read the WLPA, it gave us new hope. We worked hard to ensure that the rules and regulations prescribed under the new Act were notified by the government so that it quickly came into force, which, for the state of Uttar Pradesh, happened on 1 February 1973.

Overcoming the Constitutional Hurdle

It may be worthwhile to note that the subject 'protection of animals and birds' was listed at number 20 in the State List (List II) of the Seventh Schedule of the Constitution of India. The Constitution thus allocated the powers and the responsibility to make laws on the subjects mentioned in List II only to the state legislatures and not the national Parliament. To overcome this hurdle, Article 252 of the Constitution of India was introduced, which provides that if two or more state legislatures pass a resolution empowering Parliament to legislate upon a subject that falls on the State List, Parliament, with such consent, can legislate on that subject. In this case, several state legislatures had passed resolutions empowering Parliament, and as a result, the WLPA, came into existence. This had happened at the urging of the then prime minister, Indira Gandhi.

New Enthusiasm

The WLPA infused a fresh enthusiasm in the officers and field staff of the wildlife conservation wing. I do remember that in my capacity as the wildlife warden (central region) Lakhimpur Kheri (Uttar Pradesh), I apprehended a poaching party led by the Sub Divisional Magistrate (SDM) and realized a composition amount from him. I also had a tiff with a police inspector who was passing through Dudhwa Wildlife Sanctuary on duty in a jeep with a gun in his hand. My successor had one forester dismissed for his connivance with a poaching party. Statistics are hard to come by, but there was definitely a significant spurt in the number of cases detected by the wildlife staff consequent to the enactment of the WLPA.

At the time of the Act's enactment, the country had only five national parks and 36 wildlife sanctuaries extending over just about 5,566 sq. km of forest area. A large number of national parks and sanctuaries were now being notified by the state governments, which was a heartening sign, and the protected areas (PAs) network saw a significant increase.

Even though we had a more comprehensive legal remedy, its implementation remained a challenge due to grossly inadequate numbers of trained staff, acute shortage of funds and indiscriminate diversion of forest areas by the state governments for various developmental activities resulting in the PAs being honeycombed.

Fortunately, the central government realized the problem and began to provide financial assistance to states to improve the management of the PAs. However, the emphasis in the PAs was more on anti-poaching work. The prime wildlife habitat in the PAs—the valleys—continued to be occupied either by villages or by plantations of exotic species like eucalyptus. Commercial monoculture plantations were replacing the natural forests. The animals that inhabited open grassy patches were driven away from the PAs, often into the surrounding agricultural lands, where they were looked upon as threats or pests, and were mercilessly slaughtered.

By this time, it was realized that another major issue required urgent attention: the trade in wildlife products, particularly elephant ivory products; export of fur and skins of endangered animals, including tigers and leopards; and huge quantities of snake skins. The WLPA, was, therefore, amended in 1986, and Chapter VA was inserted, which provided for a total ban on dealings in all the animals specified in Schedule I and Part II of Schedule II. Dealing in parts of these particular animals or articles made therefrom was also prohibited. Although this amendment established a total ban on trade in Indian elephant ivory and articles made therefrom, incendiary dealings continued in the garb of 'imported' ivory. As such, a ban on trade in imported ivory and ivory items was also very much required.

Getting Acquainted with the GoI System

In August 1987, I was posted as joint director (wildlife) in the Ministry of Environment and Forests (MoEF) (which was renamed the Ministry of Environment, Forest and Climate Change [MoEFCC] in 2014). I was keen to do my bit to stem the rot. With Dr M.K. Ranjitsinh, joint secretary (JS) (Wildlife), as my boss, the going became easy and interesting.

Dr Ranjitsinh was the main architect of the WLPA and a man with an encyclopaedic knowledge of wildlife and a passion to boot. He had been handling wildlife matters in the ministry for many years, first as deputy secretary (DS) and then as JS. As such, he was fully conversant with the issues involved in the implementation of the provisions of the WLPA. Rajiv Gandhi was the prime minister and T.N. Seshan, the secretary, MoEF. Both of them accorded high priority to issues relating to wildlife conservation.

The Process to Amend the WLPA Begins

It is well known that the first major amendment to WLPA was made in 1991. But not many know that the process began in earnest in 1987. Under Dr Ranjitsinh's able guidance, we got off to a flying start. The first priority was to protect the habitat of the PAs, which included national parks and sanctuaries. This required a change in Section 29, which, in the original legislation, had only prohibited hunting within the limits of a sanctuary. The draft amendment to this section read, 'No person shall destroy, exploit or remove any wild life including forest produce' unless such exploitation or removal 'is necessary for improvement and better management of wildlife'[1].

Other amendments proposed in various sections to ensure expeditious declaration and better management of sanctuaries were:

i. Section 26A[3]: No alteration in the boundaries of a sanctuary shall be done without the approval of the legislature of the state concerned.
ii. Section 33A: Immunization of livestock within 5 km of the sanctuary made mandatory.
iii. Any RFs where all rights have already been settled and the parts of territorial waters where no individual rights existed could be notified as a national park/wildlife sanctuary under

Section 26A and subsection 4 of Section 35. Going through the process of settlement of rights would not be necessary in such cases.

iv. Section 26A(1)(a): In the interest of the exercise of the rights of the local people, till the same has been settled, declaration of a sanctuary was made a two-stage process in respect of areas other than the areas covered by the previous point. The first notification would be of the *intent* of constituting an area as a sanctuary and the second notification would be constituting that area a sanctuary.
v. Section 26A(3): No person shall damage the boundary marks of a sanctuary by way of altering, destroying, removing or defacing such boundary marks.
vi. Section 34(3): No new arms licences shall be issued within 10 km of the boundaries of a sanctuary without the prior concurrence of the CWLW.
vii. Activities that were proposed to be made punishable offence by inserting new provisions under Section 27 included:

    a) damaging or removing the boundary pillars of a sanctuary;
    b) molesting and teasing of wild animals and littering the grounds of a sanctuary; and
    c) ban on entry of unimmunized livestock in a sanctuary.

Amendments were also proposed in Chapter V, which deals with trade or commerce in wild animals, animal articles and trophies with the intention to regulate the possession of and trade in imported ivory and articles made therefrom.

The following were also proposed:

i. appointment of honorary wildlife warden;
ii. state wildlife boards to be empowered to advise the state governments in the formulation of policy on protection and conservation of wildlife and matters regarding amendment of schedules of the Act;

iii. enhancement of penalties for offences; and power to alter entries in the schedules to vest in central government only.

The Tortuous Journey of the Amendment Bill

Dr Ranjitsinh forwarded the draft proposals for approval to the secretary, T.N. Seshan. He directed that the proposed amendments be submitted in a tabular form with the existing provision of each section, amendment proposed, the objective being served by the amendment and how the amended section would read. The compliance with these directions was both time-consuming and tiring, but it yielded good results. Seshan made invaluable inputs and made the proposals quite pinpointed and legally sound.

The proposed Bill was placed for approval before the Indian Board of Wildlife (IBWL) headed by Prime Minister Rajiv Gandhi. The board authorized the Standing Committee (SC) of the board for a detailed examination of the proposals and taking a final view in the matter. The SC, after a detailed examination, endorsed the draft proposals. The same was then circulated to various ministries that were concerned with the Bill for their views. Getting the views of the ministries was a time-consuming process in itself.

By the time the comments from various ministries were received and the revised draft Bill could be submitted to the law ministry for its vetting, general elections were held in the country, followed by a new government headed by V.P. Singh taking charge on 2 December 1989. Maneka Gandhi became the new minister of environment and forest. As such, the draft Bill was submitted for her approval. She almost revolutionized the entire Bill by proposing a total ban on hunting, regulating the exploitation and trade of endangered species of plants, and providing a mechanism for overseeing and regulating the management of zoos in the country. The revised draft Bill was prepared and sent to the law ministry for vetting. She pursued the matter with utmost conviction and got the vetting done by the law ministry in record time. The Cabinet note seeking the Bill's approval by the Cabinet was submitted to the office of the Cabinet Secretary. The note could not get the approval of the Cabinet in the first instance, due to opposition from the Union ministers Ram Vilas Paswan and Sharad Yadav on the grounds that the it was against the interests of fishermen and the poor craftsmen who thrive on making and selling decorative articles from peacock feathers. They also argued that the Bill did not address the interests of the tribal communities that depend on the forest and forest products for their livelihood. The Cabinet, therefore, referred the Bill to the Cabinet Secretariat for the consideration of the Committee of Secretaries (CoS). The CoS, after detailed discussions on the draft Bill, suggested following changes in it:

i. Restrictions applicable to sanctuaries should not apply to the areas notified under Section 18, where the settlement of rights had not been completed.
ii. As the boundaries of marine sanctuaries are not demarcated, fishermen could inadvertently enter inside a sanctuary. The fishing net and boat of such fishermen would not be impounded.
iii. The limits of territorial waters to be included in a sanctuary would be decided in consultation with the chief naval hydrographer of the central government, after taking adequate measures for the safety of the local fishermen.
iv. No trade restrictions would apply to the dealers in peacock feathers and articles made therefrom.
v. Permission shall be granted for hunting snakes for the extraction and dealings in snake venom.
vi. The SBWL should be made responsible for harmonizing the needs of the tribals and other forest-dwellers with the protection and conservation of wildlife.

A revised Cabinet note was prepared, incorporating the suggested changes, and submitted for consideration. The Cabinet approved the revised Bill and granted permission to introduce the Bill in Parliament. The law ministry then gave final shape and added a few finishing touches to it. The Bill was introduced in Rajya Sabha by Maneka Gandhi in the Monsoon Session of Parliament in 1990. But before the Bill could come up for consideration, the V.P. Singh government fell, and Chandra Shekhar Singh became the new prime minister. Hence, Cabinet approval was sought and obtained anew. The Chandra Shekhar government was also short-lived; hence the Cabinet's approval was sought for a third time. In this rigmarole, the enactment of the Bill was delayed by about 18 months. The Bill was ultimately passed both by the Rajya Sabha and the Lok Sabha in the tenure of Prime Minister P.V. Narasimha Rao in the month of September 1991, and was presented to the President for his assent, which was duly obtained. Thereafter, it was notified as Act No. 44 of 1991 on 20 September 1991.

The Wild Life (Protection) Amendment Act, 1991, brought a paradigm shift in the approach towards protecting and conserving wildlife in the country. It also, for the first time, brought the endangered species of flora (plants) within its ambit.

Post-1991 Scenario

India liberalized its economy in 1991, which was followed by a period of rapid economic development. Often this development came at the cost of the environment, including wildlife areas and the people who depended on them. The GoI, in the Eighth Five-Year Plan (1992–1997) launched a scheme for 'Eco-Development of Areas Around National Parks and Sanctuaries' by providing financial assistance to villagers for carrying out activities that would reduce their dependence on the bioresources of the national parks and sanctuaries as well as for activities that would augment their income.

Another scheme titled 'Beneficiary-Oriented Scheme for Tribal Development Around Tiger Reserves' was also launched. The funds under the scheme were to be used to relocate the tribal villages inside the tiger reserves to the areas outside the reserve and bring them into the mainstream of development. The tribals of Nagarahole Tiger Reserve and Bhadra Wildlife Sanctuary, in Karnataka, were amongst the first beneficiaries of the scheme.

In 1996, a World Bank-funded scheme, 'India Eco-Development Project (IEDP)', was launched with an outlay of $74 million (₹262 crore). The project aimed at the inclusive development of seven wildlife PAs, namely the Buxa Tiger Reserve (West Bengal), Nagarahole Tiger Reserve, Palamau Tiger Reserve (Bihar), Periyar Tiger Reserve (Kerala), Ranthambore Tiger Reserve (Rajasthan), Gir National Park (Gujarat) and Pench National Park (Madhya Pradesh). The project's main component was the development of the local communities, for which 54 per cent of the funds were earmarked. The second priority of the project was the infrastructure development of the PAs. Here also, the priority was taking up such activities that created livelihood opportunities for the landless locals. The Project Tiger Directorate spearheaded the project.

In the year 1987, India had 59 national parks and 254 wildlife sanctuaries, which extended over an area of 1,32,000 sq. km. At that point of time, there were 15 tiger reserves with an area of 25,000 sq. km. Considerable progress was being made on the front of enhancing the network of the national parks and wildlife sanctuaries. By 2001–2002, there were 89 national parks and 417 sanctuaries in the country, extending over an area of 1,56,000 sq. km. These figures indicate a significant increase in area under the PA network since 1987, when the process of amending the Act was initiated. The area under tiger reserves was also rising. In 2001–2002, there were 27 tiger reserves extending over an area of 37,761 sq. km. The budget allocation under both the schemes, namely the 'Development of National Parks and Sanctuaries' and 'Project Tiger', was also enhanced significantly.

With the objective of providing better protection to elephants, 'Project Elephant' was launched in 1992–1993. A new scheme to control poaching and illegal trade was also launched. On the ex situ conservation front, the performance of the Central Zoo Authority (CZA) was notable. More than 200 substandard and dingy zoos were closed down. Funding was provided to the CZA-recognized zoos to improve their infrastructure and carry out planned breeding of endangered species.

Wildlife Protection Takes a Nosedive

Sadly, state governments failed to take advantage of the new initiatives of the central government and achieve their projected goals. They often failed to utilize the allocated funds because of their inability to provide the state's matching share. Not only that, no action was taken to fill the vacant field staff posts—the number of vacancies in various tiger reserves, national parks and wildlife sanctuaries had risen to as high as 40 per cent. In many states, salaries and wages were not being disbursed in a timely fashion. This situation began to work against the interest of wildlife conservation.

Poaching of wild animals and illegal trade in parts and products became rampant. The sales tax barrier officials accidentally seized a consignment of three tiger skins and 50 panther skins in Ghaziabad, Uttar Pradesh, on 19 December 1999. On the basis of the intelligence gathered from this case and the spade work done by Trade Record Analysis of Flora and Fauna in Commerce (TRAFFIC) India, a raid was conducted on campus in a locality near Khaga in Fatehpur district (Uttar

Pradesh) on 12 January 2000, where four tiger skins, 70 panther skins, 221 otter skins, and a huge quantity of tiger and panther claws were seized. In May 2000, 80 panther skins were seized at Haldwani (Uttarakhand). Subsequently, tiger skins were also seized at Nagpur and Coimbatore.

Concurrently, there was a major downwards trend in the population of tigers in the country. In Sariska Tiger Reserve (Rajasthan), in 2005, and later, the Panna Tiger Reserve (Madhya Pradesh), there was not one tiger to be seen. Alarmed with the situation, people started challenging the authenticity of the tiger population figures being reported by the state governments. Hence, in 2003, the task of estimating the tiger population in the country was assigned to the Wildlife Institute of India (WII), Dehradun. The institute carried out the census in a scientific manner. The census report that was published in the year 2006 showed that the country had only 1,411 tigers. This was against the then official figure of 3,500.[2]

Intervention by the Supreme Court

The management of national parks and sanctuaries began to grow worse with each passing year. There were many sanctuaries where most of the habitat was either under mining or some non-forest use. State governments were keen to reduce the area of the sanctuaries to accommodate the non-forestry activities. Ultimately, the Supreme Court, on the basis of a submission made by the MoEF in response to an intervention application filed by one non-governmental organization (NGO) in the T.N. Godavarman Thirumulpad case, intervened in the matter and passed orders on 13 November 2000 to the effect that no area of national park and sanctuaries would be denotified without the approval of the apex court. For one-and-a-half decade years, the Supreme Court took on the responsibility of deciding on every case for the diversion of areas within national parks and sanctuaries. This intervention saved thousands of hectares of wildlife habitat from destruction. Finally, in May 2015, the court delegated this power to the National Board for Wildlife (NBWL).

There were several cases where, under the garb of habitat improvement, commercial disposal of trees/bamboo from sanctuaries and national parks went unnoticed. To safeguard against such instances, the Supreme Court, vide its order of 14 February 2000, directed that no dead and dying trees, grasses and driftwood shall be removed from a national park or a sanctuary.[3]

There was a silver lining to the regulation of trade in ivory. Ivory traders had filed a public interest litigation (PIL) in the apex court, challenging the provisions made in Chapter VA of the Act of 1991. The PIL was dismissed, and the trade in animals and articles made therefrom, as mentioned in the Schedule I and Part II of Schedule II, was banned once and for all. Since the WLPA did not apply to Jammu and Kashmir, shahtoosh continued to be sold and bought. It was finally banned by the High Court of Jammu and Kashmir. The Supreme Court also banned the trade in deer antlers. Since the subject of fishing fell under the jurisdiction of the Department of Fisheries, GoI, wildlife officials refrained from regulating fisheries. But when the massive slaughter of whale sharks and other elasmobranches was brought to the notice of MoEF, these species were brought under Schedule I of the WLPA, and trade and hunting of both were prohibited.

Wild Life (Protection) Amendment Act, 2002

The MoEF, in the year 1995, taking into consideration the increasing number of wildlife crimes and the growing alienation of local communities from wildlife conservation, appointed a committee consisting of experts, representatives of state governments, ministry officials and other wildlife enthusiasts under the chairmanship of Dr Ranjitsinh to review the existing provisions of the Act and suggest necessary amendments therein. The committee, in its report, made the following suggestions:

i. The public perception that wildlife conservation is an elitist activity has to be done away with. Instead, the role of wilderness areas in maintaining the ecological and environmental security of the country should be highlighted.
ii. There is a need to bring greater transparency in the management of national parks and sanctuaries. To achieve this objective, a provision would be made in the Act for every national park and sanctuary to have an advisory committee comprising a member of state legislature, a representative of panchayati raj institutions, NGOs and individuals active in the field of wildlife conservation, and the honorary wildlife warden. The officer-in-charge of the sanctuary/national park is to be the member secretary and the CWLW or their nominee to be the chairman of the advisory committee.
iii. The committee also suggested the creation of 'conservation reserves and community reserves' to act as buffers around national parks and sanctuaries. Conservation reserves would have minimal restrictions and greater involvement of local people in their management. Provision is made for the creation of 'community reserves' on the community land/private land on a specific resolution from the community/request from the landowner.
iv. To provide greater sanctity to the decisions of the IBWL, it should be given a statutory status as 'National Board for Wildlife (NBWL)'.
v. The committee suggested that provision should be made in the Act for the forfeiture of the property derived from illegal hunting and trade in wildlife, on the lines of the Narcotics Control Bureau. This will help tackle

the problem of the rich and influential persons who have become the kingpins of organized illegal trade in parts and products of wild animals.

vi. The states to constitute the State Board of Wildlife (SBWL) within six months of the amendment Act coming into force.

vii. Under the powers vested under Section 11 of the Act that no Schedule I animal shall be killed unless the CWLW is satisfied that the same cannot be tranquillized or translocated. No animal so captured shall be kept in captivity unless CWLW is satisfied that the animal cannot be successfully rehabilitated in the wild. Tranquillization or the translocation of the animals shall be done in a manner that creates the least trauma to the animals.

viii. To safeguard against gregarious animals raiding the crops, the authorized officer should be empowered to permit hunting groups of animals, as well.

ix. It should be mandatory for the state government to appoint the collector under the Act within 60 days of the issue of the notification under Section 18 of the Act. The process of settlement of rights must be completed within a period of two years.

x. To safeguard against the degradation of wild animal habitats, sections 27–33 to come into force in the area that is proposed to be constituted as a sanctuary on the day of issue of notification under Section 18. During the period of settlement of the rights, the state government shall make alternative arrangements required for making available the fuel, fodder and other forest produce to the right holders.

xi. No construction of commercial tourist lodges, hotels, zoos and safari parks shall be done inside a sanctuary without prior approval of the NBWL.

xii. Provision should be made in Section 38H of the Act that no new zoo shall be established without prior approval of the CZA. Further, no zoo shall acquire, sale or transfer any wild animal except to and from a recognized zoo.

xiii. Provision should be made in Section 40 of the Act that no person shall acquire any wild animal specified in Schedule I or Part II of Schedule II except by way of inheritance.

xiv. A large number of persons, in possession of parts and products of wild animals specified in Schedule I and Part II of Schedule II, could not make declaration of the same under Section 39 of the Act within prescribed time, because of their being unaware of the said legal obligation. Another chance should be given to them to comply with the legal requirement of getting a certificate of ownership.

The above recommendations of the committee were considered by the IBWL. The board authorized the SC to examine the recommendations in detail and to take a final view. The SC, being satisfied, endorsed the recommendations. The Bill, after due formalities, was passed by Parliament and, after President's assent, became Act No. 16 of 2002. This was notified by the legislative department on 17 January 2003.

I superannuated from government service in September 2002. So, while I had the satisfaction of doing all the groundwork for the new amendment, it came into effect only after I had handed over my charge after spending some 15 eventful and satisfying years in different capacities with the GoI.

Wildlife (Protection) Amendment Act, 2006

To tackle the challenging problem of organized poaching of wild animals, the GoI created the Wildlife Crime Control Bureau (WCCB). For the legal empowerment of both the WCCB and the NTCA, necessary provisions were made in the WLPA through the 2006 amendment. There was also an impulse to further empower the Project Tiger Directorate by making it an autonomous statutory authority. The amendment of 2006 dealt exclusively with these two issues.

Moving Forward

It is crucial that while drafting amendment Bills, the status of compliance with the existing provisions of the Act be evaluated before planning the amendments. There are many existing provisions of the WLPA on which the state governments have not taken any action. For example, the final notification of several PAs is still pending, as is the formation of the advisory committee to many sanctuaries. This situation must be addressed.

Honest implementation of the provisions of the WLPA is crucial for effectively conserving wildlife and its habitat. For this, a requisite number of trained field staff, who not only have technical skills for wildlife management but also the communication skills for getting the support of the people living around wildlife reserves, is the foremost requirement. Further expeditious settlement of rights and redressal of the problems of loss of life and property from man–animal conflicts is also crucial. No amount of legislation and enforcement can protect wildlife and its habitat from the aggrieved and deprived local communities living around the wildlife habitats.

Notes

1. *The Wild Life (Protection) Act, 1972*, Parliament of India, https://bit.ly/3mPOtnO. Accessed on 15 June 2022.
2. Project Tiger Directorate, *Evaluation Reports of Tiger Reserves in India*, MoEF, 2006, https://bit.ly/3ufcR6C. Accessed on 29 June 2022.
3. 'T.N. Godavarman Thirumulpad vs Union of India and Ors', Writ Petition (Civil) No. 202 of 1995, https://bit.ly/3I7AZxv. Accessed on 29 June 2022.

SECURING HABITATS FOR ECOSYSTEM REVIVAL

H.S. PANWAR

Greenhorn

Before my promotion to the deputy conservator of forests (DCF), I was posted as the assistant conservator of forests (ACF) in the forest department's head office that had moved from Nagpur to Rewa following the 1956 linguistic reorganization of states. I had just completed my probation of two years, including a training range charge in the then Umaria division, most of which is now Bandhavgarh Tiger Reserve. I was lucky to have been initiated into the religion of nature, first, by a king-size leopard terrorizing me as I cycled down alone on a forest road, only to melt away into the forest. Then, shortly thereafter, my tryst with nature had its placid confirmation from a huge male tiger regaling in the middle of Umaria–Rewa road. Our team of four was accessing the road to board a bus. While we stayed put and remained observant, the otherwise-nonchalant tiger was disturbed by an approaching lorry—his ears perked up. As the lorry drew near, he arose lazily and turned to look at us, his eyes furrowed in what I could only assume was annoyance at the lorry trespassing noisily upon his territory. He walked majestically across the road and into the grasses on the other side and got lost in the forest. During my two-year-long stint in Umaria, I would often see sambhar, barking deer, chital and chinkara on field tours. My interest, thus, consistently energized, and I felt wildlife had already crannied an early but well-snuggled nook in my professional life.

A posting in the head office was unusual for a probationer. But that was none of my concern, and I devoted myself to my work as assistant forest utilisation officer (FUO). There were three changes at the level of my superior, the FUO, during my four-and-a-half-year tenure. First, because the incumbent—although a gentleman—had been ailing for long, and sadly, passed away within six months of my posting. This required me to do most of the work from the outset, as he was mostly on leave. His successor, S.S. Srivastava was a considerate and knowledgeable officer, and in my view, a guru-incarnate. I enjoyed my work and learnt a lot from him. But early in his second year, he was charged with a task that was his own brainchild—the nationalization of the trade of tendu leaf, which had, thus far, been monopolized by bidi-industry magnets. He took on them successfully with his indomitable skills and finesse. I toiled and did my best as the proverbial bearer of the cross, both at my desk and during occasional tours. The last of my three bosses was on the verge of promotion to conservator of forests (CF) and had come alone, leaving his family behind. Upon joining, he told me clearly to continue doing as I was, presuming his approval. There seemed to be tacit approval from the bigger bosses as well, and I kept carrying the cross.

I must have done well because in my interaction with every top officer, I was told that it was high time I moved and gained experience as an sub divisional officer (SDO) to some division before becoming a DCF/DFO. But this lip service did not bring any change, and eventually, in May 1966, when my promotion was due, I got posted as divisional forest officer (DFO), North Mandla. This posting was usually reserved for very senior DCFs—maybe it was a reward for keeping the trust of the Chief Conservator of Forests (CCF). A year later, I had to hold the concurrent charge of South

Mandla, including the Kanha National Park; once again, in order to relieve an ailing colleague who did not want to get a midterm transfer. But sad to say, his condition got worse and he went on a long medical leave. Thereafter, I was moved from North Mandla to South Mandla, putting me in regular charge of Kanha National Park. Thus, my period of looking after Kanha in my first stint was a little under two years in June 1969, when I got transferred as DFO, Dewas. This was preceded by my conversation with K.N. Mishra, then CCF of Madhya Pradesh, who, apparently having noted my interest in wildlife and, in particular, my efforts for the branderi barasingha (including the first-ever amicable relocation in the country for wildlife of a village named Sonf), asked me if I would like to continue as DFO, South Mandla.

I responded to him with a proposition: if the 128 sq. km of the Mukki range of North Balaghat was added to Kanha National Park's 318 sq. km, I was prepared to continue with the park's full-time independent charge. But in those times, there was little scope of placing a DFO in charge of just 446 sq. km of forest, particularly if it was a national park having no forestry operations. Yet, one late afternoon in the last week of June 1969, standing in the rain of the pre-monsoon showers on the edge of Sonf—with cattle and people gone—I saw about 25 barasingha foraging on the new flush of grass, their bodies glinting in the evening sun. I had a premonition that I would return to Kanha—and, I did, just two years later, in 1971.

Every person with a modicum of interest in wildlife would know that in the mere two years following the 1969 Delhi International Union for Conservation of Nature (IUCN) General Assembly, there was a sea change in the importance given to wildlife conservation. While I kept abreast, CCF K.N. Mishra, the department head, was certainly better aware of the significant major steps taken—a countrywide ban on tiger hunting, stronger legislation being formulated and a special major project on the anvil for saving tigers. I had a firm belief that the government of Madhya Pradesh would like to have the primacy of Kanha National Park fortified for the park to be a part of Project Tiger upon its inception. So, in concert with CCF K.N. Mishra, I wrote up a scheme to enlarge Kanha National Park by adding 128 sq. km of Mukki area from Balaghat with an independent DCF in charge and also some additional field and office staff. This time, the scheme was not only met with the approval of the government but also with my posting as its director, despite strong opposition by the then boss of mine, CCF-II in charge of a special initiative of nationalization of timber trade, who had chosen and got me posted as a key executive. That's how my second and unbroken innings of 10 years at Kanha began in June 1971.

My Kanha Experience

In one sentence, my experience of 12 years in two phases at Kanha instilled in me a conviction that inviolate habitats were essential to conserving the diverse associations of floral and faunal communities.

I had planned and executed the relocation of the village Sonf downstream of Kanha along river Sulkum in 1967–1969 with the full awareness that availability of extended inviolate habitat was the key to saving the barasingha immediately and in the long run. Such inviolate spaces were essential not just for barasingha but also for the full range of ungulate prey and, hence, for tigers, leopards and other predators. The presence of villages strewn all over the park meant heavy livestock grazing, rampant fires and even poaching. With Sonf relocated, habitats had recovered rapidly between Kanha and Sonf, allowing barasingha to disperse wider, breed successfully and raise fawns, as reflected in a verifiable increase in their numbers. In April

1969, I had moved the lone tiger-baiting site that existed since the famed American scientist Dr George B. Schaller studied tigers in the central meadows to deep inside the forest, thereby putting an end to excessive predation of the barasingha, which also contributed to the increase in barasingha numbers. It was evident that the full range of ungulates—also, tigers and other predators—gained from the release of productive habitat by availing this bonanza of nature. Our monitoring of barasingha numbers from 1971 onward confirmed this in my second innings, motivating me to envision larger.

Barasingha Saved

In my management plan, villages based in valleys that, upon relocation, had the potential to come up as extensive grassy forage-bearing habitats having pockets of tall grass areas suitable for fawning, were preferred targets for relocation. Upon implementation, this strategy proved itself, and among the 22 villages proposed for relocation, many in Kanha, Kisli, Sarahi and Mukki ranges were developed into model habitats for the barasingha. The combination of woodland-grassland habitats in these extensive tracts also suited the entire ungulate spectrum and, concomitantly, all major predators. There was wide-ranging dispersal and phenomenal population increase in prey and the predators. Mass congregations of animals typical of central Kanha in early 1970s yielded to their much larger populations well-dispersed all over the park, individual species ranging through and utilizing their favoured habitats.

In their breeding season in winters, dominant barasingha stags are a treat to watch; once their multitined antlers are fully grown, they pull out tufts of grass from the ground and wear these tufts as crowns. With a slight tilt in his neck, a large crowned stag is an image of elegance. One can see numerous dominant stags so adorned displaying to woo the females in a large spread-out barasingha herd. Lo and behold, one stag wallows in a pool of muddy water secreting a smelly fluid and returns to the herd, raises its head and muzzle and releases a fluctuating bellow—'eeinoien'. The forest rings with his call as he repeatedly bugles to draw the attention of receptive females.

Often, there is a duel between two dominant stags—a spectacle to watch. The duellists first go around in a shrinking circle with an inward and watchful tilt in the neck and then suddenly engage in a duel by locking their antlers and pushing one another with savage strength. On a dry afternoon, their hooves kick off clouds of dust as one pushes the other as far as 20–30 metres. The one nearing loss, counters in aggression and pushes the rival back. This ritual can go on for as long as 15–20 minutes until the vanquished reneges and, chased by the victor, gallops to avoid being pierced in his flank. The victor recedes too, to a fresh wallow to cool off and cover his body in mud, now steaming and smelling of the odour of his own secretion, a telling signal to receptive females and also to lesser stags to distance away—the victor will have his spoils. In this way, nature ensures that only the best genes pass to the progeny.

With Kanha's candidature as one of the nine tiger reserves under Project Tiger affirmed in 1972, I prepared my big-vision management plan for the 10-year (1973–1983) period for a much-enlarged Kanha Tiger Reserve. The plan targeted a core segment of 940 sq. km with a buffer zone of 1,005 sq. km that proposed the relocation of 17 out of over 35 villages in the first five-year period. I contemplated this large-scale relocation of villages out of my self-acquired conviction that this alone could revive the natural ecosystem comprising inviolate habitats, thereby saving the tiger and all constituents of the biological pyramid it headed, barasingha included. To my happiness, the plan was sanctioned both by the state and central governments. My plan proposals provided for an increase in the staff to work towards effective protection against poaching and forest fires as well as for the amelioration of habitats, including strategic facilitation of water. Notably, I also proposed that the forestry operations be postponed in the recently added 500 sq. km of Supkhar Sanctuary for 10 years, as there was no such ipso facto closure in sanctuaries under the Wild Life (Protection) Act (WLPA), 1972, back then. The added core area of Supkhar–Bhaisanghat forests had valuable sal and other timber trees besides extensive bamboo-bearing areas. The forestry operations were already statutorily closed in the national park segment, and I felt the need for tranquillity in the large 500 sq. km added to the core zone. The logic presented in my plan was that a five-year period was far too short for habitats to recover. I further argued that with village relocations, effective control over livestock grazing, woodcutting and forest fires, alongside concerted amelioration measures under the project, the overall growth—including in timber trees—would far exceed the deficit in the annual loss of revenue from non timber forest produce (NTFP). In those formative years, the Government of India's (GoI's) initial commitment to Project Tiger funds was only for five years. I was delighted that the government of Madhya Pradesh agreed with my proposal while forwarding my management plan to the Centre. As I am aware, Kailash Sankhla, the first director of Project Tiger, welcomed this as a rare gesture only from Kanha. With approvals from both governments, our field operations started in 1973–1974.

My well-conceived process of village relocation anchored on the active participation of the affected villagers bore fruit. Well before the five-year budget cycle ended, we warmly embraced residents of seven more villages, who, impressed by the well-being of the relocated villagers at new sites, readily volunteered. This speaks volumes of the sincere effort of the Kanha team that ensured every opportunity of mutual benefit to the people as well as the park was wisely and perceptively harnessed. This happy situation was as eloquent as eloquence can be, not just for all the floral and faunal elements of the Kanha ecosystem but equally for the people of the 22 (against the targeted 17) villages at new rehabilitation sites. The resulting accrual of vast, secure and productive habitats within the park was a cardinal milestone in Kanha's march as a constituent of Project Tiger, untarnished by even a single case of deprival of the affected people. Elements of all-around recovery comprised widespread amelioration of habitats and phenomenal growth in diverse prey bases and predators, led by the tiger. While my faith in inviolate habitats as the architect and implementer of this vast-scale development was reaffirmed into a conviction, I must allude to the larger environmental dimension of such an epochal transformation of wild habitats. Forest floor humus and decaying leaf litter above it retard the surface flow of rainwater, enhancing stream flows and recharging subterranean aquifers. This amelioration, while supporting the park and its wildlife, leads to sequestered carbon, optimized air quality and augmented water availability through canals and bore wells in a vaster tract around, if unknown to people in villages and towns tens of kilometres away.

It is necessary to recount here my learning success as the leader of the Kanha team since 1964–1965, when Schaller studied the deer and tiger in central Kanha meadows. Based on his data, there was an 'excessive predation of barasingha by tiger aided by two other likely causes'. Let me first deal with the two causes. The first that the disease brucellosis could be responsible for the in vivo death of fawns in advanced pregnancy was ruled out with the help of a competent veterinarian. The second and more important cause, alleging fawns succumbed to predation by small predators soon after birth, was also overcome as I located and fostered potential patches of tall grass that females then used in the rainy season to drop fawns. Each nascent mother would make and keep two to three fawn beds ready by frequently sitting on growing grass and allowing the canopy to close above the beds. She would forage around and suckle the fawn until it was grown enough to trail her to join the herds and, with it, the benefit of herd security led by matriarchs.

As for Schaller's recorded excessive predation of the barasingha, suggestive of the predator decimating one of its wholesome prey species, it militated against my ecological sense as both the tiger and the branderi barasingha had been coexisting in Kanha for millennia before Schaller set foot in here. Also, it was a known fact that the two other subspecies of barasingha had been coexisting with the tiger and thriving in Terai areas of Uttar Pradesh and Assam since times immemorial. That the excessive predation and resulting decimation of the barasingha had continued since 1964–1965 was confirmed by me in April 1969 from a duel between two tigresses in which one succumbed to grievous injuries. This rebutted my initial sense of the ecological incongruity of the thought that the tiger could have a 'paw' in the barasingha debacle. The debacle indeed was due to the extranormal congregation of tigers induced by baiting to facilitate year-round data collection by the scientists. Mercifully, this duel between tigresses was the proof, if needed at all, of excessive predation. I moved the baiting site away from meadows and into the forest in April 1969, well before my transfer in June at the end of my first innings. This put an end to extranormal congregation of tigers and excessive predation of barasingha once and for all; their population grew steadily thereafter.

During my second innings in 1971, my first step was to stop baiting in the park altogether. As already mentioned, the greatly augmented habitat from large-scale village relocations did the rest. Thus, we successfully saved the barasingha with our concerted conservation follow-up that kept the graph for several years at 30 per cent accretion, which is acknowledged as the maximum for monoestrous deer. I recorded these findings in my paper, 'Decline and Restoration Success of the Central Indian Barasingha *Cervus duvauceli Branderi*' presented to the IUCN Species Survival Commission (SSC) Deer Specialist Group in Longview Island, USA, in 1977, cheering the global group. With extensive habitats being revived through the implementation of my management plan, aided by the steady effort of the Kanha team, the present population of branderi barasingha has risen to 1,000.

Kanha Strategy: Save the Ecosystem to Save the Tiger

To understand the sound strategy adopted by Kanha Tiger Reserve, it is necessary to know how its plan evolved based on sound management, envisioning and zoning. My goal was to reduce the dependence of people on the 'core zone' (the sanctum sanctorum of the park) through viable alternatives that also included the villagers' worthwhile suggestions. Implemented with the Kanha team, in participation with the people, this established a working model in park planning and management. In the decades that followed after I left Kanha in 1981, the Kanha team did not relent and continued with the same thrust, adjusting operations to augment tranquil areas as one village after another was relocated. By 2017, all the 38 targeted villages had been relocated from Kanha National Park, in addition to Sonf, the only Indian pioneer of the pre-Project Tiger days. Sajalagan, the lone village in the Phen Wildlife Sanctuary, which was Kanha's satellite mini-core, was relocated in 2012–2013, and the other villages, namely Ajanpur and Sukdi, by 2017. The real challenge to habitat overcome, the vast tract is now tranquil and is a safe high potential abode of diverse multitude of Kanha wildlife.

Kanha Tiger: Shining Bright

The first-ever countrywide tiger estimation was done in 1972. I conducted this in Kanha and found that the park had no less than 30 tigers. The all-India tiger estimation 2018 results says the number was 108 tigers using Kanha and 88 as within Kanha, including, the 'breeding surplus dispersants'. The all-India tiger estimation results recognize that Kanha is home to a cardinal 'source population' within the Central and Eastern Ghats mega landscape between Odisha and Maharashtra. This outcome bears out projections in my management plan, including 'breeding surpluses' of tigers dispersing wider. The all-India tiger estimation results have confirmed Kanha dispersants were reaching as far southwest as the Nawegaon-Nagzira Tiger Reserve. It has also shown tigers from Kanha are radiating through its functional satellite mini-core Phen Wildlife Sanctuary into Chhattisgarh's Bhoramdev Wildlife Sanctuary.

I mention from my Kanha experience just one example of response to the tiger's ability to exploit the increasing populations of a prey species. In 1976, gaurs were inflicted by rinderpest contacted from the cattle grazing in the buffer zone. We disposed of 69 gaur carcasses when the total population was around 250. But the gaur population—initially slowly, but later, energetically—rose to over 500 in 1981. Now, of course, their number is over 1,000, and this plenty is cleverly exploited by the smart and strong predator—the tiger.

Expect a surprise: the large tiger males now do not chase so much after the gaur herds but, indeed, stalk the dominant bulls that, in overconfidence of their strength and sharp-tipped horns, seem oblivious of the proneness of their hind legs. The tiger, a master predator and stalker, stealthily closes in behind a foraging bull and pounces, with pinpoint accuracy, on the rear legs, hamstringing the bull that cannot but fall to the ground. Holding his strong bite from behind, safe from the bull's dagger-sharp horns, the tiger starts tearing away at the rump of the live bull. Helpless against the clever predator, the big gaur bulls become an added quantum source to the tiger's diet. Subadult tigers and adult tigresses continue to go after younger gaur bulls and cows from the herds. In this way, nature ensures a trilateral balance between habitat productivity on the one hand and smaller and larger ungulates on the other—the tiger, nature's chosen executant.

This overall strategy consolidated Kanha's management by providing viable and acceptable alternatives to the affected people. Pulling the branderi barasingha back from the brink of extinction to over 1,000 in population has led to an increase in tiger numbers from 30 to well over 100, the latter achieving the status of a vital 'source population' for the Central and Eastern Ghats landscape. People from relocated villages and those in the vicinity have been availing increased income opportunities in the park works as well as others in the park-based tourism sector.

Other Tiger Reserves

Nine parks had initially been chosen as tiger reserves under Project Tiger. These were Bandipur National Park (Karnataka), Jim Corbett National Park (erstwhile Uttar Pradesh, now Uttarakhand), Kanha National Park (Madhya Pradesh), Manas National Park (Assam), Melghat Wildlife Sanctuary (Maharashtra), Palamau Wildlife Sanctuary (erstwhile Bihar, now Jharkhand), Ranthambore National Park (Rajasthan), Similipal National Park (Odisha) and Sundarbans National Park (West Bengal).

I left Kanha in 1981 to take over as director, Project Tiger. As for the other tiger reserves, during my 1981–85 tenure at

Project Tiger, the project had already had a successful run for a decade. Besides, tiger reserves have always had either a national park or a sanctuary as the statutory keel since the project's inception. Every tiger reserve also considered neighbourhood protected areas (PAs) and visualized the forest land and inhabited areas in between to serve as a buffer. So, the WLPA has been the sheet anchor since the inception of Project Tiger.

The number of tiger reserves has now grown from nine to 53 and, ingeniously, some small tiger reserves have been set up only to enhance contiguity and adequately protect transiting and settling tigers in such small reserves. In these small reserves, a tiger may choose to remain, while others may move on using movement spaces between sub-landscapes. For example, the main objective of setting up Navegaon-Nagzira Tiger Reserve, with a movement link with two other small PAs was to offer a potential corridor linking Kanha–Pench tiger reserves with Tadoba Andhari Tiger Reserve. The latter has links with Melghat and Satpura tiger reserves in the west and with PAs in Bastar's Indravati and Udanti tiger reserves in the east.

Biogeographic Basis of the National PA Network

In India lies the junction of three of the seven global biogeographic realms—Indomalayan, Eurasian (Palaearctic) and Afrotropical. Diversity of bioclimatic regimes, of the lie of the land and terrain, are manifest in the vast subcontinent, from the mighty Himalayas to Central and Eastern Ghats and from the Western Ghats mountain ranges to the Great Indian Peninsula thrusting into the sea. Interspersion of hills and dales within mountain ranges and extensive plateaus define India's terrain and, in turn, its bioclimatic, floral and faunal diversity. Coasts of Odisha sheltering olive ridley and other sea turtles are also rich in fisheries, and are bolstered by a low to moderate salinity gradient actuated by freshwater flushed by several sea-bound rivers. The courses of these rivers, in their final stretch, feature this salinity spectrum for a rich diversity of fishes to thrive. With a unique eco-development-inspired package, the Chilika Lake Bird Sanctuary involves the fisherfolk of the neighbourhood in sharing fish productivity without undermining habitat features, and thus, is a classic example of a well-managed coastal PA. The incredible estuaries of the Ganga and the Brahmaputra sport the Sundarbans mangroves that straddle West Bengal in India and Bangladesh; these are among the world's largest complexes of mangroves. On the west coast, extensive beaches and gulfs, for example, the Gulf of Kutch and the Little Rann of Kutch, have unique attributes; the latter, a salty marsh hosting Indian wild ass (khur) in the dry season and productive prawn fisheries when inundated during monsoon. The Gulf of Kutch is also marked by varying salinity gradients that are supportive of shrimps and varied fishes. The Gulf of Mannar on the east coast, just above the southern tip of the peninsula, is rich in coral reef attributes that shelter pretty coral fish and other aquatic fauna, besides edible fish much in demand in the country and overseas. The Gulf of Mannar Marine National Park also successfully employs a wise eco-development package involving local fishermen to share a sustainable harvest of shrimps and fish.

India's Biogeographic Classification System

The National Wildlife Action Plan (NWAP) was released at the tenth-anniversary function of Project Tiger in 1983. The first item of the NWAP was, 'Establishment of a representative network of protected areas' with the intent to rationally plan and implement a comprehensive network of PAs. In 1984, the GoI asked the Wildlife Institute of India (WII) to formulate plans for such a network. From Project Tiger, I took the reins of WII as its director, in 1985.

I, as director of the WII, and the late W. Alan Rodgers, the Food and Agriculture Organisation (FAO), United Nations Development Programme (UNDP) consultant at the WII, engaged a large number of knowledgeable individuals from different parts of the country having a fair idea of existing PAs and the biological communities and endangered species covered within them. We also looked at more potential sites to enhance representation. Based on the reports of these consultants (Erach Bharucha, V.B. Sawarkar, B.C. Choudhury, Manoj Misra and J.C. Daniel, among them) and the knowledge of the authors (W. Alan Rodgers and H.S. Panwar) the first report was produced in 1988 and covered four aspects[1]:

i. the preparation of a biogeographic classification of India designed to facilitate conservation planning. This included the classification of the identified and defined biogeographic zones, and within each zone, the sub-units or 'provinces' with subregional diversity, including maps;
ii. consideration of important biologically diverse areas;
iii. a review of existing protected areas; and
iv. the recommendation of new protected areas to ensure an adequate network, as far as possible, representing the range of Indian diversity.

During the WII's interaction, most states cooperated, enabling consultants to work in the field and file useful reports. Alan and I got on well and closely worked together on this task of caring for the country's biologically diverse habitats. We, received the reports from the states and the consultants retained by us and were happy to find that the positively responsive states set up even more PAs than those suggested in the 1988 report. We, accordingly upgraded and updated our earlier report. With more extensive feedback from states, experts and individuals, and by including data of new PAs up till 1998, the WII published a final report in 1999 with Vinod Mathur joining Rodgers and me in authorship. This report has since been used extensively in PA planning matters and is widely quoted in scholarly articles.

I reckon that ever since the biogeographic planning work was undertaken with countrywide consultation, there has been a better recognition of the importance of a representative PA network as the best means of protecting the county's habitat and faunal diversity, indeed biodiversity. This system of network planning in India's PAs is considered suitable, mutatis mutandis, for most Asian countries.

According to the database maintained at the WII, in 2021, there were 987 PAs, including 106 national parks, 564 wildlife sanctuaries, 99 conservation reserves and 218 community reserves covering, in all, some 5.26 per cent of the country's geographic area.[2]

PAs Face New Challenges

PAs and the wildlife they sustain face multifaceted challenges in India. Most of these challenges are at the field level, among the protection and administrative hierarchy and politicians. People dwelling within on fringes and outside, claim that the productivity of wild habitats ranging from livestock grazing to fuel wood for cooking to timber and bamboo for housing, not to mention the diverse NTFP that they also collect. Then there is the claim even for hunting and eating venison as a traditional and cultural practice, usually by stealing from predator kills and not so unusually by poaching—helped by the wantonly weakened protection—of live animals. Local politicians provoke and promote these claims, right up to those at the helm who turn a blind eye, making a mockery of not only the PA status but even tiger reserves in some states. Use of the Scheduled Tribes and Other Traditional Forest Dwellers (Recognition of

Forest Rights) Act (FRA), 2006, which was originally intended to be responsible legislation, has been progressively and wantonly corrupted by rules going beyond the parameters set by the Act. Its implementation is a loose gun in the hands of the intentionally irresponsible. Indeed, the locally powerful thugs favoured by the top power are usurpers, while the intended Adivasis remain deprived and swindled.

The Future of Habitats

At the national and regional levels, it is the wild habitats in the PAs, in forests around and in other non-forest biomes whose life support services, including aquifer recharge, are essential for all wildlife and humans—near and far, in villages, towns and cities. Despite the ups and downs, India has fared the best in Asia insofar as conservation of wild habitats and wildlife is concerned. Given this attribute and the essential values cited in the foregoing, there is enough hope that habitats, in the future, shall hold and continue to host a wide diversity of plants and animals that India has been known for, for ages, notwithstanding the pressures of rapid economic growth that these seem to be facing presently.

Notes

1. Rodgers, W. A., and H.S. Panwar, *Planning a Wildlife Protected Area Network in India*, FAO, 1988.
2. 'Protected Areas-Subject Area: Wildlife Institute of India, Ministry of Environment & Forests', ENVIS Centre on Wildlife & Protected Areas, https://bit.ly/3AyH0ll. Accessed on 1 July 2022.

HUNTING FOR ANSWERS

HARBHAJAN SINGH PABLA

I think I am one among the rare Indian foresters who believe hunting and tourism are critical to the success of wildlife conservation in India. At least, I am the only one who openly talks and writes about it. Obviously, I am both hated and loved for my beliefs. I have become the darling of the scions of the formerly feudal families who often go abroad on hunting trips. Some of them are also occasionally invited to hunt man-eating tigers or leopards in India. The ecotourism industry also wonders why other foresters are not like me despite coming from the same school. My colleagues usually accept my logic but end up saying that all this is not for India. Some also think that I am spreading some kind of poison and have become professional foes. This is my world now!

But I was not always like this. Like others of my generation, I, too, believed for a long time, that killing and conservation could not go together. Almost the same went for wildlife tourism, although some positives were also attributed to it. For nearly 20 years into my service, I had had no second thoughts about this conviction. Yes, I was vaguely aware of conservation and hunting going hand in hand in other countries but never wondered why we were different.

However, it all changed one day when I got a request in late 1996 from a local non-governmental organization (NGO) to write an article for their newsletter on human–wildlife conflict (HWC). This was probably the first time I had looked at wildlife conservation through such a prism. After a few days of contemplation, the conclusion was stark and clear: HWC cannot be managed without managing populations of wild animals, and the animals cannot be saved without mitigating HWC. Population management requires hunting (capturing or killing) of wild animals.

I was deeply tormented by these thoughts for several days. When I finally accepted that there was no alternative, the next question was whether mitigation of HWC through hunting would be enough to make the conservation of dangerous animals sustainable. Finally, everything fell in place beautifully: *If hunting produced incomes (and food) for the suffering communities and also kept their crop losses tolerable, wild animals would be seen as a resource rather than a menace. That would be a win–win situation both for people as well as for animals.*

I was still worried to the core for coming up with these apparently stupid thoughts. But my conviction grew with every day of pondering over the issue. My piece was published in the April 1997 issue of *Vacham*[1], the journal of the National Centre for Human Settlements and Environment (NCHSE), an NGO set up by M.N. Buch, an environmentally conscious civil servant in Bhopal. Apart from suggesting that hunting of crop-raiding animals was necessary to reduce HWC, I wrote that this could generate considerable incomes for rural communities if hunting licences were commercially sold instead of allowing a free-for-all or paying hunters to cull animals. I also mentioned that hunting was a part of Indian culture, as many gods in our pantheon are believed to have hunted.

Perhaps not many read this article. However, J.J. Dutta, one of the most revered foresters of our generation, under whom I had started my service, called to congratulate me for writing a 'wonderful' article. Encouraged by his endorsement, I began to speak up about my ideas in meetings and conferences. In the beginning, I spoke hesitantly but saw people nodding heads in approval, probably also in disbelief. I gave a few talks at the Wildlife Institute of India (WII), where I heard people saying, 'After a long time, we have heard something new about wildlife conservation in India.' As the word spread on the internet, the hunters of the world got excited. Although I have never had a chance to handle a gun in my life, Indians for Guns, an association of gun-loving hunters, invited me to become its member. Someone also sent me an email from the US that he would like to bring his clients to hunt crop-raiding blackbucks in India. Someone else put me on the mailing list of *African Indaba*, a journal reporting on hunting in Africa, and my understanding of the concept of sustainable use of wildlife started growing further.

As my conviction grew, I tried to introduce community-based hunting of crop-raiding species in Madhya Pradesh but without success. The Wild Life (Protection) Act (WLPA), 1972, had been amended to change its colour and contours by 1991, and the system of hunting permits, which was present in the 1972 Act, had been removed. But the provision for hunting dangerous animals remained, which could be used to generate sustainable community benefits while reducing crop losses. Incidentally, the idea appealed to every forest minister I worked with, but my efforts remained futile. Either the bureaucracy stalled the proposals or the ministers developed cold feet due to impending elections. Thus, 25 years since my 'enlightenment', nothing has changed on the ground.

Hunting in Contemporary India

The hunting framework and definitions provided in the WLPA have been continually changing since its inception in 1972. In its current form, hunting means killing, capturing, driving or baiting animals for any purpose, and every attempt to do so. At present, hunting can be permitted in the following situations:

i. when animals, other than notified vermin, become dangerous to human life or property, including standing crops (Section 11);
ii. for education and scientific research (Section 12);
iii. for scientific management (only capture and translocation) (Section 12);
iv. collection of specimens for zoos and museums (Section 12);
v. for 'improvement and better management of wildlife' in protected areas (PAs) (sections 29 and 35); and
vi. when a species is declared a vermin (Section 62).

No permit is required for killing an animal in self-defence or in defence of another person (Section 11).

Out of these, permissions under Section 11 are regularly granted by the states. Section 12 is occasionally used to allow animal capture and translocation for management purposes. The provision for hunting in PAs, under sections 29 and 35, has never been used so far. Even when animals are captured in PAs for any purpose, permission is granted only under Section 12 (scientific management). Section 62 has recently become popular to declare wild pigs, nilgai and rhesus monkeys as vermin in states like Uttarakhand, Bihar and Himachal Pradesh.

Many states allow the hunting of crop-raiding pigs and nilgai. But none except Punjab allows the consumption of the meat of the hunted animal. The carcass has to be burnt or buried. Thus, other than a few enthusiasts who occasionally hunt for fun, there are no takers for hunting licences anywhere except in Punjab. Sometimes, states like Bihar engage paid hunters to kill crop-raiding animals after having them notified as vermin by the central government. Although their numbers run into lakhs in most states, only a few dozen or a few hundred animals are culled through these initiatives. For example, hired hunters had killed just about 250 nilgais in Bihar in 2015 before the hue and cry by animal rights activists stopped the activity.[2]

The policy of not allowing the consumption or sale of wild meat is usually justified to ensure that hunting does not result in creating a demand for venison. However, despite this policy, wild animals continue to be snared and electrocuted by farmers to protect their crops, and by poachers for profit. Poaching is rampant all across the country. For example, Dr M.K. Madhusudan and Dr K. Ullas Karanth reported that every village around Kundremukh and Nagarhole national parks of Karnataka did 216 man-days of illegal hunting every month.[3] Wild meat was sold in many big cities of south India. It is also well-known that everybody hunts in Arunachal Pradesh and other northeastern states—some regularly and some occasionally. The meat of wild birds and animals is openly sold in the markets of the Northeast.[4] Mass hunting in the name of akhand shikar or paradh is a well-known annual ritual among most tribal communities in the country.

Apart from meat and local trade, a great deal of poaching also happens to feed the huge international market for pets and traditional medicine, particularly in Southeast Asia. While tortoises, turtles and birds are the favourite pets across the world, almost every animal has some imagined medicinal value. The local market for wildlife-based remedies is also not insignificant. Ritesh Sarothia, the head of Madhya Pradesh State Tiger Strike Force (STSF) and an intrepid pursuer of wildlife poachers, once told me that nearly 30 per cent of tiger poaching in India was instigated by tantrics promising 'sons and riches' to gullible folks.

States also permit hunting man-eating leopards and tigers as and when necessary. The National Tiger Conservation Authority (NTCA) has directed that such hunting should be done only by departmental staff. However, most of the hunting is still done by private hunters engaged by the states, as most foresters carry no weapons and have no experience in hunting. Such incidences are most common in Uttarakhand (for leopards) and Maharashtra (for tigers). Uttarakhand reportedly ordered the killing/capture of 55 leopards and tigers in 2019 and 75 in 2020.[5] Translocation of problem leopards is a common practice in many states, particularly in Gujarat, Karnataka and Maharashtra. Most such animals, however, are known to return to their former homes sooner or later or become a problem in their new habitats.

Thus, despite the ban on hunting wild animals for consumption and trade, a great deal of hunting goes on in the country. Hunting is perhaps like alcohol: prohibition only pushes the practice underground and everybody is happy.

The Changing Colours of Hunting

Hunting has been around as long as man has existed on earth. The early man hunted animals for food and pelts, as illustrated in the ancient cave paintings around the world. While hunting for food continues till today, the advent of settled living, agriculture and animal husbandry nearly 10,000 years ago added a new dimension to the need for hunting. Now animals were captured for domestication or killed to eliminate crop raiders. As agricultural crops acted as a lure for herbivores, it became easier to shoot (with stone weapons, arrows or spears) or snare them. Hunting of crop-raiding herbivores established a kind of symbiosis between men and animals, as both provided food for each other. The livestock as well as wild herbivores lured by crops brought their predators closer to human settlements, although humans were perhaps not on the main menu of any predator at least since humans began to use fire. The elimination of such threatening predators must have been a part of the early hunting culture of man. As the predators proliferated unchecked, assisted by plenty of food, and became an impediment to human spread and safety, their extermination became the responsibility of the community leaders and rulers.

Over time, the pursuit of dangerous animals became a means of showcasing one's strength, courage and valour to fellow beings and hunting came to be treated as a sport. Hunters began to call themselves sportsmen, and animals became game. In India, hunting by the bigwigs was called *shikar khelna*.

As occupations and livelihoods diversified, human dependence on hunting as a primary means of sustenance and survival decreased. Most communities remained only partially dependent on hunting for food, although some continue to follow this ancient occupation full-time till today. Traditional hunting communities like Pardhis, Mogias, Bawarias, Bahelias, etc., are examples of the latter, although now, even they have begun to diversify occupations. While the affluent and ruling classes were never dependent on hunting for food or survival; they hunted merely for recreation and continue to do so.

The demand for fashionable furs and pelts in fourteenth- and fifteenth-century Europe, fuelled heavy hunting of small carnivores like minks and beavers in the Americas. Now, the demand for tiger skins and bones, rhinoceros horn, bushmeat, traditional medicine and pets is fuelling poaching.

Large predators were once so numerous in India that rewards were given for their killing. John Hewett (1938), a British Imperial Civil Service (ICS) officer in India at the turn of the twentieth century, wrote: 'Tigers infested certain parts of the country up to the beginning of the nineteenth century to such an extent as to make it almost uninhabitable.'[6] Due to this, killing tigers and other predators was considered a noble deed. Apart from the British and the local nobility killing tigers for fun, local shikaris hunted predators for rewards announced by the government, resulting in enormous annual bags. Hewett says that in a five-year period around 1916, rewards were paid for nearly 9,000 tigers and 27,000 leopards. He further observes, 'in spite of the continuous destruction of so many, they hold their own in the backward and wild parts of the country.' As the British ruled only about two-thirds of India directly, this picture is, obviously, only partial.

As the human ability to hunt grew with the advent of firearms and motor vehicles, wildlife populations started to decline visibly. Primarily to ensure continued supply of game for the rich and powerful, hunting regulations were developed by the princely states by the middle of the nineteenth century. They started creating their private preserves, where the public was not allowed to hunt. When the British created reserved forests (RFs), they restricted hunting only to those who held permits. As wildlife continued to deplete despite these measures, further restrictions were imposed. This culminated in a complete ban on recreational and consumptive hunting of animals in 1991, although many state governments had already declared the entire state as a 'closed area' and the entire year as 'closed season' soon after the promulgation of the WLPA in 1972.

While India decided to save wildlife by progressively increasing restrictions on hunting, African countries took to a new kind of hunting, called conservation hunting (CH), about the time WLPA was enacted. Contrary to the traditional motives for hunting, namely exploitation and eradication of wildlife, CH aims to strengthen its conservation by generating sustainable benefits for the public. CH is built on the premise that wild animals are a natural resource that can be sustainably utilized for human welfare. If society sees wild animals as a resource, there will be no need to exterminate them. CH can introduce wildlife-based public benefits in many ways. One, it produces jobs in the hunting industry and ancillary businesses. Second, if communities have ownership of wild animals, as is the case in most African countries, the hunting fees also go to them. Thirdly, in the 'trophy hunting' practice, most of the meat is given to the local communities. CH also produces revenues for the governments, which are often ploughed back into the conservation of wildlife, directly or indirectly.

The tag of CH is generally reserved for trophy hunting or tourist hunting. It is also called recreational hunting, sport hunting and safari hunting. Those who practise it are more interested in the adventure, the thrill of the chase rather than the goods. The hunter takes home only the 'trophy' for display, which generally is the head but can also be the skin of a predator. Only overmature males, which are past their breeding age, are hunted as trophies. As their number is minuscule, trophy hunting has no impact on the population of the hunted species. As most of the trophy hunters in Africa are foreigners, hunting tourism is a major source of foreign exchange for many African nations. These hunters come from wealthier sections of the population and tend to spend and donate more liberally than budget tourists, thus contributing more to the local economies. Trophy fees for the big five of Africa generally run into thousands, even lakhs of dollars for each animal. Pakistan recently sold just four Chitral markhor (*Capra falconeri*) permits in the Khyber Pakhtunkhwa area for $57,550. With local communities deriving benefits from trophy hunting of markhor, its population in the area has increased to 3,500–4,000 from 1,500–2,000 in 2001.[7]

Although trophy hunters claim that the selective hunting of trophy animals has no impact on the species' gene pool, their opponents vehemently contest this notion. Many people consider killing beautiful animals for fun an unethical and repugnant practice. However, it is widely agreed that community-based trophy hunting reduces poaching by locals and smugglers, leading to a fast recovery of populations, as seen in many conservancies in Pakistan, Namibia, Zimbabwe and elsewhere.

Although hunting for meat or culling for habitat protection is usually not considered CH, perhaps this notion is also debatable. Hunting for meat (which is then dried and cured is called *biltong* in Africa) confers value on animals that would otherwise be considered useless or troublesome, thus deserving elimination. Millions of hectares of wild lands are being conserved in the name of biltong hunting areas in Africa. Culling overgrown populations can also be considered conservation hunting because it is done primarily to improve the health of the ecosystem that supports local wildlife.

Killing wild animals only to protect human life and property would perhaps not qualify as CH unless it leads to increased acceptability of the species to the society and reduced poaching. This can happen only if the hunting income goes to the local people or to the conservation agencies, preferably to both. This is the kind of hunting I had in mind when I wrote the article mentioned before. The goal of such hunting is the creation of human–wildlife symbiosis, not just coexistence. 'Coexistence' indicates an uncomfortable compromise, while 'symbiosis' is a dream relationship: *made for each other*, as the cliché goes.

Hunting in Wildlife Laws in India

Although references to wildlife conservation regulations are also available in ancient Indian texts, modern conservation laws began with the advent of British rule in India. The first British intervention to stop free-for-all hunting came in the form of the The Indian Forest Act (IFA), 1865, the 1927 version of which still applies in most of India. This law empowered the government to convert any forest into government property (RFs and protected forests) and defined wildlife as 'forest produce'. Wildlife, like any other forest produce, could be taken out of the government forests only with the permission of a forest officer.

The next important legal milestone came in the form of the Elephant Preservation Act, 1879, which provided, among other things, that:

> No person shall kill, injure or capture, or attempt to kill, injure or capture, any wild elephant unless—

(a) in defence of himself or some other person;
(b) when such elephant is found injuring houses or cultivation, or upon, or in the immediate vicinity of, any main public road or any railway or canal; or
(c) as permitted by a license granted under this Act.

By the end of the nineteenth century, princely states as well as the British provinces began to come up with their own hunting regulations. For example, the Rules for the Mysore Game and Fish Preservation, under Regulations II of 1901, authorized the state to 'prohibit absolutely the killing or capture of any specified kinds of animals or birds'.[8] It also empowered the government to declare closed seasons and closed areas for the hunting of game or other animals if the government had reason to believe that they were 'being largely destroyed for the sake of their skins, horns or plumage for commercial or other uses'. The Indore Game Act, 1907, and the Central Provinces Game Act, 1935, also had similar provisions. The Indore Game Act also provided for the designation of hunting 'preserves' for permit-hunting and 'protected areas' where no hunting was permitted.

The British government promulgated the Wild Birds and Animals Protection Act, 1912, for its territories. This law empowered the government to declare 'closed time' for killing or capturing of scheduled or any other animals or birds in whole or a part of the state. This law also provided that it was unlawful 'to sell or buy, or offer to sell or buy, or to possess, any such bird or animal which has not been captured or killed before the commencement of such close time, or the flesh thereof'. It also provided for the creation of sanctuaries where no hunting was to be permitted.

The United Provinces National Parks Act, 1935, and The Madhya Pradesh National Parks Act, 1955, created the templates for modern-day national parks. These laws primarily provided that no capturing or killing of animals shall be done in a national park, except 'for the purpose of scientific study or protection of human life and property'.

Thus, wildlife management, as expected, was all about the regulation of hunting. States controlled hunting using the rules made under various wildlife laws operating there. The last of the hunting rules made in Madhya Pradesh under these laws were the Madhya Pradesh Game Rules, 1962, under the Madhya Pradesh Game Act, 1935, and the Madhya Pradesh Forests (Hunting, Shooting, Fishing, Poisoning Water and Setting Traps or Snares in Reserved or Protected Forests) Rules, 1963, under the IFA, 1927. Hunting in government forests was managed through the 1963 rules, while outside forests, it was done through the 1962 rules. However, the situation was a bit confusing as The Wild Birds and Animals Protection Act, 1912, was also operational in the country. To make things even worse, states were also empowered to make rules to regulate hunting in the villages under the Land Revenue Code (LRC) (e.g., Section 249 of the Madhya Pradesh LRC). Similar situations existed in all states.

Thus, most states had a fairly well-established shikar system when the WLPA combined all the existing laws into a single national statute in 1972. Under the then prevailing system, the rich could have their shooting blocks reserved for recreational hunting; the general public could hunt either in their croplands or in forests outside the shooting blocks, except during the closed seasons. Virtually, the same scheme was imported into the WLPA with perhaps the only difference that now a permit was required for hunting even crop-raiding animals. Further, unlike before, self-defence was limited to the defence of human life alone, not crops or other property.

However, most features of the WLPA related to hunting were deleted in 1991. Chapter III (Hunting of Wild Animals), which provided for issuing and management of hunting licences, was denatured entirely. In 2003, the definition of hunting was modified to include even driving and baiting.

Wildlife Without Hunting?

Protection of dangerous and harmful wild animals without the option of hunting (sustainable use) seems to make little sense as it falls foul of several constitutional, legal, moral, ecological and economic parameters.

As the state protects wild animals, their impact on the people's lives and livelihoods is also the state's responsibility. Despite being a constitutional obligation, the protection of wild animals in the present form violates Article 21 (Right to Life) and Article 300A (Right to Own Property) of the Constitution of India. As per the Constitution, no citizen of India can be deprived of these rights without following the process prescribed by law. However, protected animals take away these rights every day. Killing or injuring people and destruction of property by wild animals also amounts to crimes committed by the state, like culpable homicide, theft and mischief, etc., under the Indian Penal Code (sections 289, 299, 321, 322, 336, 337, 338, 378 and 425). By that measure, even conservation professionals and NGOs also become abettors in this crime against humanity.

No doubt, the conservation of all life, including wild animals, is our moral responsibility. However, protecting vulnerable people against wild animals is also the state's moral duty. Destruction of people's lives and livelihoods through the agency of *protected* wild animals is any day more immoral than the killing of animals. Letting poor people die or become impoverished at the hands of wild animals is not only criminal and immoral but it also smacks of classism on the part of the elite who are happy to sacrifice the poor tribals for their love of animals, morality or profits.

However, despite all these questions and doubts, we must protect wild animals for their intrinsic and heritage value. Without them, India would not be India. But their conservation is impossible so long as they are seen as a threat by the majority and have no economic value of their own. That is where hunting and tourism come in as strategic conservation tools. While both can lend economic value to wild animals, hunting can also reduce their threat to human lives and livelihoods. This would strengthen conservation rather than impair it. If a few animals pay for the assured survival of their species, such hunting cannot be immoral.

Conservation of wildlife can conform to our Constitution and criminal law only if it has an economic dimension. If animals produce jobs and income, any damage caused by them shall be equivalent to civilizational risks as in any other economic endeavour.

The truth is that hunting will exist as long as people and wild animals live together. We may call it poaching instead of hunting. If the population of herbivores in our forests have not exploded despite the absence of authorized removals for half a century, it means that poachers are having a good time. If wildlife has virtually disappeared from 75 per cent of our forests (PAs constitute the other 25 per cent), it means that somebody is killing the animals. The only thing we need is a system to regulate it and channelize the returns into visible benefits for men and animals. That would put conservation on a solid footing.

Putting Hunting to Work for Conservation of Wildlife in India

While we can take our time discussing and debating whether we should introduce trophy hunting of iconic species or not, we do not have the luxury of time where wild animals are in serious conflict with people. Two kinds of situations are eminently suitable for conservation hunting in India. These are:

i. crop-raiding species like wild pigs, nilgai, blackbuck, elephants, etc.; and

ii. overpopulation of predators in the close vicinity of towns and cities.

While the former category needs no elaboration, examples of the latter are the leopards of Mumbai, tigers of Bhopal and the lions living in over 1,500 villages adjoining Gir. These animals present a clear risk to the people in cities and villages and have no value in conservation terms. Therefore, there is no point in letting them proliferate in these environs. Thirty-four persons were killed by wild animals (29 by tigers) in 2021 in the Chandrapur district of Maharashtra alone.[9] It does not get more serious than this. There is no alternative to killing these animals, as putting them in cages and feeding them for decades would be even more inhuman and wasteful.

As mentioned before, many states have already crossed the moral red line by allowing the hunting of wild pigs and nilgai in croplands. Man-eating predators are also being killed on a regular basis. Now, it is just a question of making these systems sustainable and ensuring positive conservation and social outcomes. This can be done by commercializing the hunting of crop-raiding ungulates and predators living in dangerous situations on a sustainable-use basis, and distributing the returns to the victim communities. If rural people benefit from wildlife, its conservation would be more sustainable, socially, economically as well as politically.

Conclusion

We all spend our lives seeking answers to questions that guide our actions. These questions may arise in our own heads or may be posed by others. After a month of field training in Kanha National Park in 1980, I remember asking the then director, Mr H.S. Panwar, at the rounding-off session, to explain to me why dangerous animals like tigers should be saved. I also remember villagers in Panna shaking their heads in disbelief when I myself tried to dispense the same arguments in defence of some harsh measures that we had to take in 1982–1983 after the area became a proposed national park. Most telling was the reaction from my own mother, who had never seen wild animals in her life. When I tried to explain my job to her, she said, 'Kaka, I am unable to understand why you should save tigers that can eat someone's child or buffalo someday.' Buffalos were as dear to her as her children.

It took me almost 20 years to find some justification for the apparently illogical stuff I was doing. I could now say that wild animals should be saved because they could also be used for human welfare. However, the country had outlawed any form of wildlife utilization by the time I attained this enlightenment. Later, efforts were also made to outlaw even wildlife tourism, which is known to create wildlife-based jobs. Fortunately, those crazy efforts did not succeed fully, and we can still go out and watch wild animals in our PAs. However, the country has still not realized the stupidity of abandoning hunting as a wildlife management tool. The WLPA is totally confused on this issue, as it allows trade but not the production of wildlife-based goods. I tried to use some chinks in the law to turn vermin into blessings but could not go far. Despite having spent nearly 45 years pondering the issue with an open mind, I have not found a stronger justification for saving wild animals than their potential economic value. To realize this potential, we need to use our heads despite the distractions caused by clouded minds and vested interests.

My hunt for answers continues...

Notes

1. Pabla, H.S., 'Human Wildlife Conflict around Protected Areas', *Vacham, NCHSE*, April 1997.
2. Priyadarshi, Ashok, and Rahul Noronha, 'The Unholy Cow',

India Today, June 2016, https://bit.ly/3aGSV65. Accessed on 21 June 2022.

3. Madhusudan, M. D., and K. Ullas Karanth, 'Local Hunting and the Conservation of Large Mammals in India', *AMBIO: A Journal of the Human Environment*, Vol. 31, No. 1, Royal Swedish Academy of Sciences, February 2002, pp. 49–54, *bioone.org*, https://doi.org/10.1579/0044-7447-31.1.49. Accessed on 21 June 2022.
4. Aiyadurai, Ambika, 'Hunting in a Biodiversity Hotspot: A Survey on Hunting Practices by Indigenous Communities in Arunachal Pradesh, Northeast India', *Nature Conservation Foundation*, 2007, https://bit.ly/39DM64G. Accessed on 21 June 2022.
5. Pabla, H.S., *Besides Loving the Beasts: Wildlife Conservation in India*, 1st edn., 2021.
6. Hewett, John, *Jungle Trails in Northern India*, Natraj Publishers, UK, 2021.
7. 'Markhor Trophy Hunting Permit Auctioned at Record Price', *GeoTV*, 5 Nov 2021, https://bit.ly/3QDy9Es. Accessed on 21 June 2022.
8. Government of Mysore, *Papers Relating to Draft Rules under the Mysore Game and Fish Preservation Regulation, II of 1901*, 1901, https://bit.ly/3zNo6ql. Accessed on 21 June 2022.
9. Ali, Mazhar, 'Farmer Killed in Predator Attack in Tadoba Buffer', *The Times of India*, 11 November 2021, https://bit.ly/3n4Oogb. Accessed on 21 June 2022.

HOW FAIR: LONG ARMS OF THE LAW

ARVIND KUMAR JHA

Bihar

The first time I heard the roar of a tiger in the jungle was on a day in 1961. I, a five-year-old boy, was enjoying ripe ber (*Zizyphus*) with my friends, just on the other side of a forest colony's barbed-wire fence. My father was posted as a range officer in Hazaribag (the name Hazaribag comes from 'thousand tigers') in the erstwhile Bihar state, and we lived in a transit accommodation near Canary Hill. We heard the roar of a tiger from somewhere close by and, as if struck by a whip, we ran towards the wooden ladder resting on the fence and scrambled back into the residential area in no time, pledging never to cross the fence again. A few days later, a cow belonging to one of the villagers was reportedly killed by a tiger. The villagers considered the whole incident quite usual, and it was regarded as an inevitable hazard of living in a forest area. They shared the surroundings with wild animals, and that was it—no revenge was planned against the tiger, no ire expressed against my father as the 'custodian' of that tiger!

I was witness to the 'protection' duties of forest bureaucracy at close quarters much before I joined the Indian Forest Service (IFS) in 1980. The year was 1970 when I went from Vikas Vidyalaya, my residential school in Ranchi, to spend the holidays with my parents. My father was posted at Chhipadohar near

Betla National Park in the Palamau district. Chhipadohar village fell on the annual migration route of elephants that would cross the village at night, following a route between the same two huts every year. The occupants of the neighbouring huts would count their numbers and take pride in reporting the same to the range office the following day. My father owned a double-barrel gun that he carried on his patrols occasionally. The local-level control systems rested more on the fear of a rarely exercised 'authority' of the government or Sarkar that existed to a great extent, only in the people's subjective perception than in the rule books. And yes, this worked very well in most cases. The gun was meant to scare the elephants, poachers and outsiders who came to tempt the members of the local hunting community for assistance.

The small hunting community played an essential role in the village as the supplier of protein-rich food, primarily in the form of a variety of birds, hares and small animals. The Bihar Forest Hunting, Shooting and Fishing Rules, 1958, framed under the Indian Forest Act (IFA), 1927, for the reserved and protected forests, comprised of 19 simply stated rules. It provided permission for tribal and customary hunts, and to licensees once a year in any government forest. The permits for these hunts were issued for restricted hunting in designated shooting blocks. The entire year was considered a 'close' season for 15 specified species, indicating that their hunting was prohibited. Wildlife was seen as abundant; forest officers were strict, considerate, effective and had large jurisdictions. There was a fear of the law, and local people were simple and honest. Cases of offences were very few and far between. There hardly emerged issues such as the unavailability of a person to sign a panchnama or a witness becoming hostile in court. The penalty prescribed in the Wild Birds and Animals Protection Act, 1912, was a fine of ₹50 for first-time offenders, while subsequent offences attracted one-month imprisonment or a fine of ₹100 or both.

With hardly any formal linkages of wildlife trade with the outside world, the proverbial arm of the law didn't perhaps need to be too long in these remote areas!

One evening, in 1970, an adult spotted deer was killed in a road accident on the Daltonganj–Chhipadohar road at a point that fell neither in the reserve nor the protected forest. The animal had run into a truck on a blind turn and was killed instantly by the impact. The truck driver lifted the carcass with the help of a few manual labourers and brought it to the range office. The hunting community experts promptly and neatly skinned the deer, and distributed the meat in the village. The hide was sent for tanning to be preserved as a trophy by the forest department. Back then, there were no rules mandating cremation or burial to destroy the carcass. Since the location of the accident was neither inside the sanctuary nor in the reserve/protected forest or a shooting block, the inferences drawn by simultaneous consideration of the Bihar Forest Hunting, Shooting and Fishing Rules, 1958, and the definition of wild animal, parts and articles therefrom in the IFA, 1927, did not appear to contradict the traditional practices embedded in the cognitive environment of the villagers and the actual operational environment as defined by the statutory framework. The institutions and the arm of law, thus, rested for a while!

Historically, along with the spread of knowledge about the statutes and institutions that deal with wildlife cases, came a silent transition in the world view of locals from being a 'violator' of unwritten customary practices to becoming a 'criminal' under a state-enacted law for the same action. The pace of transition was obviously slower in remote areas, where people's free access to forests to meet their daily needs, fight hunger or sustain livelihoods—though devoid of any criminal intent as defined by mens rea—was gradually being subjected to regulations. Muscles of the enforcement machinery were building up with the cognizance of each new wildlife offence. The 'permit system' as provided under the hunting rules favoured those who had access to the authorities; were equipped with weapons; used fast-moving vehicles and hunted for pleasure—the locals, of course, were blatantly ignorant and far from aware of these rules. The illiterate local hunting communities were hesitant but skilled; they hunted with handmade equipment, moved on foot, followed their traditional hunting rules and closed seasons, often captured live animals only and hunted for livelihood and sustenance. Needless to say, the formal regulatory system was monopolized and exploited by the so-called 'civilized' and powerful, ultimately causing a decline in wildlife populations and the consequent depletion of the resource base on which the local hunters depended for livelihood and survival. Ironically, the National Forest Policy, introduced in 1952, took note of just the 'decline' and not the 'depletion'.

The Wild Life (Protection) Act (WLPA), 1972, became the first legislation at the national level prescribing control on the exploitation of wildlife and management of habitats. In 1972, it was indeed conservation-oriented, as it had a 'utilization' component. The concern about the decline was addressed by introducing hunting licences; categorizing species into special game, big game, small game etc.; and designating specific areas for hunting. Through an amendment in 1991, categorization of the severity of offences with corresponding quanta of penalties was attempted to keep pace with the growing importance of wildlife conservation; increased returns from the hunting of wildlife for parts and products; and the development of networks of poachers and markets, global trade and smuggling. With a complete ban on hunting, it truly became an Act that provides the 'protection' it so promises, albeit in total disregard for the concerns of the village community.

Gadchiroli

I was posted in the Gadchiroli district of Maharashtra as deputy conservator of forests (DCF) in 1990. This district, mostly known for the presence of infamous left-wing extremists, had more than 70 per cent of its area under forest cover and was once swarming with a good wildlife population.

One early morning, I received a written complaint that the Additional Collector (AC) was smuggling a tiger skin in his vehicle to Nagpur and then to Mumbai. I alerted my Assistant Conservator of Forest (ACF) who resided in the same colony as I did, and asked him to immediately reach the forest checkpost on the Gadchiroli–Nagpur Road. As a precaution, I called the Deputy Conservator of Forest (DCF), Wadsa, and DCF, Brahmpuri, and asked them to send a few senior officers to their division's checkposts that were on the same road. Realizing that the AC might take an alternate route through Chandrapur, I alerted the DCF, Chandrapur, as well.

After about half an hour, the informant came to tell me that the AC didn't take his own vehicle and was travelling with the Collector, Gadchiroli. The tiger skin was allegedly being transported in the Collector's vehicle, fitted with the usual amber light. My ACF confirmed that the Collector's vehicle had indeed crossed the division's checkpost. Wadsa and Brahmpuri divisions were intimated that even vehicles with amber light be searched. The DCF, Wadsa, informed me after a while that with no barrier on his division's checkpost, the Collector's vehicle had sped past the forest staff despite being signalled to stop. The next checkpost at Kanpa Tempa, in the Brahmapuri division had a barrier, which was instructed to be kept lowered.

The Collector's car had to stop at this checkpost. The Range Forest Officer (RFO) saluted the Collector and informed him of my instructions to search all vehicles. The self-absorbed

AC interrupted him, stepped out of the vehicle in anger and asked the RFO whether he was aware the car was the official vehicle of the Collector. The RFO replied that he had orders to search every vehicle regardless of the status or standing of its owner. The driver was asked to open the boot, wherein a green holdall was discovered. The AC followed the RFO to the back of the car and stood by his side. The RFO simply touched the bag but did not open it. After that, the RFO saluted the Collector and allowed the vehicle to pass the barrier. On sharing information about a green holdall in the car, the informer said that the tiger skin was in the same bag. As the Collector was on his way to the Commissioner, Nagpur, for a meeting, the Nagpur Forest Division was requested to intercept and search the car. The Nagpur forest staff searched the car once it was on the premises of the Commissioner's office but did not find the bag. An enquiry was made at the Nagpur airport but to no avail. The AC did not board the plane to Bombay that day. Similarly, the Geetanjali Express train that had left Nagpur for Bombay was searched at the Bhusaval junction by the Jalgaon divisional staff, but they returned empty-handed as well.

Now was the time for action at Gadchiroli itself. The AC's jeep was seized and sealed for a detailed search and panchnama. As he lived alone, his residence was also sealed. The Collector wrote two letters to me requesting that the searches be carried out only after the AC returned. The vehicle, however, was unlocked and searched in the presence of panchas. In the search, 71 hairs of what we could safely assume was a wild animal were found in the vehicle. A preliminary offence report (POR) was registered against the AC. From his residence, a diary with several mentions of village-wise availability of various types of trophies and animal skins, along with the names of the persons who stored them for him, was recovered. The diary also contained a record of the assurances he had given to some for jobs in lieu of the skins/trophies. His secret linkages were thus unearthed. The sample of hairs seized from the jeep was sent to the Wildlife Institute of India (WII), Dehradun, for forensic examination and identification.

News of the incident gained traction and soon found mention in print media. After a Member of Legislative Assembly (MLA) threatened to go on a hunger strike demanding suspension of the accused AC, the Collector wrote to me in his official capacity as the district magistrate (DM), asking me to explain why I should not be proceeded against for creating a law and order problem in the district. I replied to the DM quoting the two letters I had received and mentioned that the District Collector was, in fact, interfering in the enquiry and that was causing a delay in bringing out the truth, which, I thought, was the reason for the problem, if at all there was any. I requested him to inform the Collector appropriately and handle the issue of law and order, which was his subject as the district's DM. After that, no letters came from the Collector/DM. The AC, as was expected, expertly absconded.

I appointed the RFO (Vigilance) as an enquiry officer to take further action in the matter. Raiding teams were formed to simultaneously search the premises of persons named in the diary. A large number of trophies/skins were seized from their properties. The enquiry went on, but new stories started getting fabricated to vitiate the process. Some quarters publicized it as a tiff between the Indian Administrative Service (IAS) and the Indian Forest Service (IFS). Some also began to spread that I, a person coming from another state into the Maharashtra cadre, was biased against the local officers. After about two months of the incident, my immediate boss, the Conservator of Forests (CF), asked me to explain why I had not approached him for guidance before acting on the complaint. He changed the enquiry officer and assigned the enquiry to the DFO (Vigilance) attached to his office.

Meanwhile, the WII, Dehradun, confirmed that the sample was indeed of the *Panthera* species, making it clear that the crime pertained to a Schedule I wild animal under the WLPA. The statement of the persons whose premises were raided corroborated the involvement of the accused in multiple crimes.

A variety of versions about me and my work style started doing rounds in the state and reached the Chief Secretary, Maharashtra, who called me to present the whole case before him. At the mantralaya, I first met the Joint Secretary (JS) (Forests), who was a senior forest officer. Considering the fact that I was raw, with just 10 years of service experience, he offered to accompany me to the Chief Secretary's chamber.

The Chief Secretary was quite patient and began to read the case file, carefully absorbing each page before moving on to the next. An eerie silence prevailed as I waited for him to speak. Suddenly, he stopped, picked up the intercom and addressed the Home Secretary, 'Hey, come, I'll show you a piece of literature.' When the Home Secretary arrived, he was shown my reply to the DM's letter on the law and order issue. While he read the letter, the Chief Secretary asked me some questions about the case. He then assured me that the strongest action would be taken against the culprits, including the Collector, who might as well have abetted. The Home Secretary, apparently displeased at this statement, said that action should instead be taken against the RFO at Kanpa Tempa checkpost for his failure to carry out a thorough search of the Collector's vehicle. I responded to him by saying that, in fact, considering the level and general morale of the foresters in the field, the RFO should be rewarded for having shown the courage to stop and search the Collector's vehicle. The Chief Secretary supported my stand by asking the Home Secretary whether any police officer on the mantralaya gate would have the temerity to search his briefcase on the basis of an oral complaint. He further said that the Collector should have complied and stepped out of the car and allowed the RFO to search the vehicle properly rather than sitting inside in an egotistical display of his authority. He went on to quote many instances when he had allowed himself to be frisked at the airport in contrast to some other senior officers who, assisted by local police, took pride in avoiding frisking as if it was part of their official privilege. Further, he was kind enough to clarify that some people had complained about my high-handed approach in the case, but having met with me, he was convinced that this was not so and that it was, indeed, a serious case. I returned with a sigh of relief.

The public prosecutor vetted the entire case and its documents before filing a complaint case in the Gadchiroli Court to ensure that no legal loopholes could be taken advantage of. I was transferred from Gadchiroli in June 1992. After some 15 years, one day, I received a call from my old office, the Gadchiroli Forest Division. The caller asked, 'Do you still have the original copy of the hair sample's examination report given by the WII, Dehradun?' Apparently, the original forensic report was missing from the records! It simply shocked me, for it was a perfect example of the arm of the law getting amputated.

Bombay

In 1992, I was posted in Bombay as the Regional Deputy Director (RDD) (Wildlife), Western Zone, on deputation to the Government of India (GoI). The job included working as a management authority under the Convention on International Trade in Endangered Species of Flora and Fauna (CITES) for India's western region. Working closely with the customs authorities, my wildlife inspectors examined consignments at the cargo complex, Bombay airport, and also at the export-import hubs at the Bombay Port Trust and the Jawaharlal Nehru Port Trust. Despite the fact that officers of the RDD office had statutory authority under the WLPA, the airport authorities issued them a 'blue' pass that allowed entry only up to the security gate. Customs officers, on the other hand, had 'red' passes (allowing entry to all areas of cargo and airport). The RDD vehicle was not deemed worthy of a pass, while the Customs Department's vehicles were issued a 'red' pass that allowed entry into the airport tarmac area. Compared to the size of the customs office, the RDD office had hardly any presence. That seemed to be the yardstick for considering the importance of various offices, so my request letter for the requisite passes did not work. I wrote to the airport authorities that in case of the occurrence of any wildlife offence in the areas out of bounds for the staff of RDD office, they would be made a party to the offence. Lo and behold, 'red' passes were promptly issued to the RDD office staff and the enforcement staff of the DCF (Wildlife) office, Thane. An entry pass was also issued for the RDD's vehicle. This, obviously, facilitated and improved our day-to-day movement and enforcement work. The provision of secret funds for informers was often utilized to receive timely information and tips regarding illegal wildlife trade. Raids were conducted in coordination with the Thane Wildlife Division staff, for my office had just two inspectors, who were already burdened with the task of examination of consignments. The offence cases were handed over to the Thane Wildlife Division for further action.

One day, on being informed about a clandestine sale of recently banned ivory items, the DCF (Wildlife) and I visited a shop behind the Taj Hotel in Colaba and enquired about ivory plate paintings—incognito, of course. The DCF (Wildlife) posed as my local acquaintance, while I assumed the role of a Middle Eastern businessman. After a bit of reluctance, the owner took us upstairs and showed us his stock. We left the shop under the pretence that we would compare his prices to those of the other shopkeepers' and return. On the date fixed for the raid, we approached some members of the gentry to accompany us as witnesses. They had attended my recent lecture on wildlife trade organized by the Bombay Natural History Society (BNHS). On the issue of poor prosecution and conviction rate in wildlife cases, they had opined that the reason was the enforcement agency's unwillingness to involve knowledgeable people such as them as witnesses. When asked to walk the talk, they wriggled out and made excuses that those who were involved in illegal businesses behind the Taj Hotel probably had connections with criminals and the underworld. We reached the ivory shop to find that the owner was yet to arrive. When asked to show some samples, the man in the shop emphatically denied having any ivory articles. When the owner arrived, he also denied the presence of any contraband; however, when asked to take us upstairs, he surrendered. The entire stock was seized and a prosecution was launched by the DCF (Wildlife).

During our survey, we noticed some vendors selling trinkets on the pavement behind Taj Hotel—articles made of camel bone being passed off as ivory items, fake musk pods (goat-hide pouches filled with sawdust and synthetic perfume) in large numbers and even imitation tiger claws made from animal horns. Some vendors were ready to supply any number of 'tiger claws' within a fortnight for a hefty advance. One could also find goat hides with stripes painted on them to pass off as tiger skins. They were kept hidden to assert their genuineness. From another perspective, the business of counterfeit animal products, such as the one behind the Taj Hotel, although not illegal per se, always provided an alibi for selling the contraband. The counterfeit dupes, discernible only to a keen eye, were kept for display by those who were perhaps involved in the illegal wildlife trade.

One day, I received a complaint on the phone about a jeweller engaged in the sale of tiger-claw lockets in the South Bombay area. His was a big and well-known shop. We promptly raided the shop and seized the tiger claw, which was duly sealed and brought to my office. Interestingly a call was received in my office the same afternoon from someone claiming to represent Godrej Group. The caller said that Mr S.P. Godrej, chairman of the Godrej Group, himself wanted to speak to me. Young and presumptuous then, I immediately suspected the call was meant to pressure me into giving up. I had already been briefed by one of my subordinates that the jewellery shop's owner was on good terms with Mr S.P. Godrej. I instructed my staff not to connect me to Mr Godrej if he called my office again. The very day, when my assistant was on a break, the telephone rang loudly. Whoever wanted to reach me could not wait and called repeatedly despite the lack of an answer. Hearing the continuous ring, I took the call and heard a very soft and feeble voice—Mr Godrej was on the other end, speaking with the characteristic pauses between his sentences. I regret, even today, the fact that I could have been more receptive at the beginning of our conversation that day.

Mr Godrej said, 'The owner of the jewellery shop raided the other day is my good friend, who is aware that I have excellent relations with the senior wildlife authorities…' I listened and waited for him to request me to downplay the issue. Mr Godrej went on to say that he was, in fact, worried about his friend using his name to affect the legal process for a lenient view in the matter, and so, he requested me to go strictly by the rule book, as he did not want me to be influenced in any way by the fact of his friendship with the accused. I was dumbstruck and taken aback. Something sank inside me—I had deliberately ignored his calls the last few days because I had thought the worst of Mr Godrej. I gathered myself and simply thanked him for his advice. Though I revealed to him my presumptions about the call in a later meeting with him, I still regret my failure to apologize to him at the right time.

Regarding the tiger claw seizure, I received a call from office of the joint director (Wildlife), from the Ministry of Environment and Forests (MoEF), GoI, while the enquiry was underway. I was directed to send the tiger claw seized by us to his office to verify if it was real. The tiger claw had already been sealed in the presence of the accused and some witnesses; hence I was hesitant to send it, but he was my reporting officer, so I relented. The sample was sealed once again in the presence of witnesses and sent. After a few weeks, the sample was returned to our office via post without sealing or drawing a panchnama. The defence lawyer used this lapse of opening the sample and returning it without the panchnama to allege that the sample seized during the raid and the one submitted to the court were different. The outcome of the prosecution, in this case, is anybody's guess. Thus, although the WLPA provided for the severest punishment in this case involving a Schedule I animal trophy, the proverbial arm of the law was made to loosen its grip by inept handling of the evidence material.

My tenure as the RDD (Wildlife), Western Zone, in Bombay provided me with a unique opportunity to be part of a process that demanded the coordinated application of the provisions of the WLPA, CITES, Export Import (EXIM) Policy and the Customs Act, 1962. Consistent efforts to integrate various legal provisions and development of common understanding amongst the participating agencies had to be made for day-to-day handling of operational issues, with the limited availability of just two wildlife inspectors working very hard and often beyond their call of duty. They could detect cases, to name a few, of smuggling of walrus tusk, ivory articles, banned sea shells, antler items, crocodile skin articles, sea horses, Schedule VI items under the WLPA, parakeets, Indian star tortoise and banned medicinal plant species that had been attempted to be exported/imported under the wrong declaration. Even after bringing the offices of the then RDD

(Wildlife) under the Wildlife Crime Control Bureau (WCCB) in 2006, with an enhanced role, only 10 wildlife inspectors in the whole country are engaged in carrying out the physical examination of consignments, while an online system created for 'ease of business' has apparently increased the porosity of our export points so far as parts and produce of our natural resources are concerned. Western Zone office still has only two wildlife inspectors despite all the new international airports and the five ports that have come into existence recently in its jurisdictional area.

Nasik

I was posted as chief conservator of forests (CCF) (Wildlife) in the Nasik circle in June 2006. The Yawal Wildlife Sanctuary in Maharashtra's Satpura Range faced a serious problem of habitat destruction by encroachers from bordering Madhya Pradesh. Any resistance by the field staff (a poorly equipped contingent of just 10 people) was met with violent reactions. There were many instances of assault on forest staff with bows and arrows and sling stones, snatching away of personal weapons and damage to government property. Till mid-2006, the staff could somehow monitor the encroachments, but after the enactment of the Scheduled Tribes and Other Traditional Forest Dwellers (Recognition of Forest Rights) Act, 2006, popularly called the FRA, these encroachments—supported mostly by local leaders and some NGOs—increased considerably in anticipation of their regularization. Most of the offence reports recorded the offender as 'unknown', as the arrest of culprits was difficult.

The reduction in the effectiveness of the WLPA in containing the destruction of habitat post the FRA's enactment has been quite conspicuous. From the beginning, the FRA's implementation primarily promoted 'intensive' use of forest land for 'personal gains' by emphasizing individual forest rights. Almost all forests face the same fate, but the integrity of habitats of PAs and even tiger reserves is under serious threat also due to recognition of community forest rights despite non-fulfilment of criteria stipulated under Section 3(1)(i) and Section 4(3) of the FRA. Using the WLPA to create many PAs while failing to implement the regulatory provisions to check habitat destruction therein, and keeping quiet on the illegal recognition of forest rights is nothing but a demonstration of the de facto derogation of the Act itself.

Duly encouraged by the above, the notorious 'Navad Patils' of the area used to invite gangs of 200–300 people from Madhya Pradesh to cut the trees, and clear and prepare the land overnight. Such land was then clandestinely sold to the people who could afford it, including the tribals who were advised by some NGOs to promptly submit claim to the Forest Rights Committee/gram sabha and take shelter of Section 4(5) of FRA that prohibited their eviction till the final decision on claims. Pendency of such claims at various levels became the order of the day. Completely trapped in the whirlpool of grossly insufficient budget, poor staffing, inadequate mobility, seclusion from the mainstream, pitiable facilities, infrequent support of state reserve police, fear of the Scheduled Caste and Scheduled Tribe (Prevention of Atrocities) Act, 1989, and isolated and demonized as 'anti-tribal' for its attempt to remove encroachments, the sanctuary management could hardly show any courage to use the WLPA to stop the ongoing habitat destruction in the Yawal Wildlife Sanctuary.

The development of a strategy was in progress when, in 2007, I was posted out as commissioner, Tribal Research Training Institute, at Pune. Nasik's post was upgraded and an additional principal chief conservator of forests (APCCF) joined in 2013. After sensitizing the revenue, police and forest departments of the Jalgaon district on the issue of encroachment and habitat destruction in Yawal Wildlife Sanctuary, he scheduled a meeting with encroachers in January 2014. While requesting them to vacate, he declared the possibility of deploying a strong contingent comprised of Pal forest school trainees, state reserve police, and wildlife wing staff to reverse the damage done to the sanctuary. Perhaps this worked as a show of strength, after which the encroachers from Madhya Pradesh agreed to leave. In all, 865 persons with no application under the FRA vacated, and the department began habitat restoration activities at the relevant sites. Interestingly, the reversal of large-scale habitat destruction began without invoking the penal provisions under the WLPA!

'Your Tiger' Throws a Challenge

In 2013, in the Dhakna range of Melghat Tiger Reserve in Amravati, there were reports of a case of tiger poaching. An impressive combination of the latest technology, local villagers' cooperation, a professional job by the enforcement team, the coordination of police and foresters of various states, the law officer's dedication, and sensitivity and promptitude of the judiciary resulted in exemplary punishments to the culprits within three to four years. The severity of the punishment and the long arm of the law amply demonstrated that poaching would not be tackled with any leniency. In May 2016, however, it was reported that a tiger was killed by poisoning in Melghat!

In fact, the use of successive amendments of the WLPA as the primary tool for protecting wildlife has resulted in a change in the cognitive environment of the local traditional hunting communities. The government's enthusiasm to protect wildlife using legal instruments unrelated to the local socio-anthropological context has changed people's perceived relationship with the wildlife and its habitat. The process of alienation from the wildlife resource that supported their means of survival started with the resource turning first into 'public property' monopolized by the licence-holder hunters and was completed when it was declared as 'government property', whether it was in the forest or captured/hunted outside. This culmination resonated with the criminalization of their livelihood caused by a total ban on hunting in 1991, which simultaneously made their marginalization and the inability to utilize their skill and indigenous knowledge a fait accompli. In the overall atmosphere that has built up, revenge-oriented behaviour and/or prioritization of financial gains over the risk of getting caught is not surprising. The obduracy observed in the increasingly audacious attacks on foresters and the forest department's property after unfortunate incidents of crop-raiding, cattle lifting and attacks on humans by wildlife indicate a gross alienation that has taken root in the villagers in and around forests. Resultantly, the villagers, while talking to foresters, refer to the tiger as 'your tiger' and not 'our tiger'. It's not surprising that considering the relative placement of species in various schedules of the WLPA's successive amendments as an indicator of its accomplishment, one hardly finds any examples of a shift of species from 'higher protection level' schedules to 'lower protection level' schedules.

The moot question now is whether we, in the background of all the issues mentioned above, are ready to rewrite the WLPA to conserve our wildlife and its habitat, and ensure the simultaneous reversal of wildlife-dependent forest dwellers' current slide towards becoming ecological refugees?

BUILDING BRIDGES: PROTECTED AREAS AND PEOPLE

VINOD KUMAR UNIYAL

Walking the Miles

On a pleasantly warm afternoon in September 1999, the meeting concluded with *pal payasam* on banana leaves. The venue of the meeting was close to the river Azhutha that emerges from the forests of Periyar Tiger Reserve, flowing westward to the Arabian Sea. About 50 men and women, both uniformed foresters and colourfully dressed villagers, had assembled to finalize the arrangements for managing pilgrim facilities along the 13-km-long Azhutha–Pamba forest track, which takes millions of pilgrims to the sacred shrine of Sabarimala in Kerala from November to January every year.

The track passes through one of the last remaining low evergreen forests of the southern Western Ghats, which harbours an amazing amalgamation of countless signatures of life. Repositories of unique biodiversity, these forests are reverently spoken of as Poonkavanam, for it is here that Lord Ayappa rests in the Sabarimala temple and roams on the back of a tiger, the idiom for conservation of the Periyar Tiger Reserve. In a legally constituted wildlife area, the pilgrimage presents two mutually opposing objectives—it necessitates the movement of many people in an otherwise restricted area.

The movement of Sabarimala pilgrims through the Periyar Tiger Reserve is not a new phenomenon. The phenomenal rise in numbers of pilgrims amplified collateral ecological consequences due to the convergence of multiple interests of politico-religious dimensions of the sacred landscape on the one hand and unregulated use of priceless ecosystems on the other.[1] For barefoot devotees, walking through the Poonkavanam, resting places would be set up along the route, which entailed unauthorized occupation of the waysides, littering and illegal removal of forest produce for construction of facilities. Thousands of temporary stalls and hawkers operated along the route without any control over their activities, generating a huge amount of waste defiling the forest. Elephant dung, encountered after the season along forest roads, contained plastics, and annually, about 2,00,000 poles of various tree species would be cut down without authorization to construct makeshift resting places.[2]

For decades, the temple administration, vested in the Travancore Devaswom Board (TDB), managed pilgrimage facilities along the forest routes. The TDB would auction out waysides for setting up temporary facilities, where the successful bidders would establish temporary sheds, mostly using forest materials. Increasingly penetrating markets generated substantial revenues to TDB and incomes to businesspeople but tended to convert the wilderness into a space of trade and commerce.

In 1895, Periyar Lake was formed on the completion of the Mullaperiyar Dam, and areas around the lake were reserved as hunting grounds of the king of Travancore. In 1934, these areas were declared a game sanctuary, and post Independence, the size of the sanctuary was increased and it was notified as Periyar Wildlife Sanctuary. Owing to its high conservation value, the sanctuary was brought under the Project Tiger umbrella in 1978. The upgradation of Periyar to a tiger reserve placed it among the most important wildlife areas in the country with better technical and financial support coming to it from the Project Tiger Directorate in New Delhi. Consequently, a 'Management Plan' was prepared for the Periyar Tiger Reserve, which flagged the unregulated Sabarimala pilgrimage as an issue of concern.

Until 1997, the Sabarimala pilgrimage was conducted by the TDB, with the Periyar Tiger Reserve administration supporting it only by supplying fuel wood and maintaining the pilgrimage routes. Pilgrimage management was not considered feasible, for the massive requirement of men and material needed to set up facilities was beyond the Periyar Tiger Reserve's financial and technical capability. But the pilgrimage management by the TDB without appropriate conservation-friendly controls resulted in the development of an unregulated, temporary marketplace in the forest, which contravened the prevailing forest and wildlife laws. The problem appeared intractable until it was realized that the involvement of local people living in and around the Periyar Tiger Reserve could be the way forward to manage the disparate demands of pilgrimage in a wilderness area.

Mostly small farmers and only a few local villagers owned temporary stalls on the forest routes, and many worked there as manual labour helping outsiders who ran the business of pilgrim facilities. Most of them were not able to buy wayside spaces in the auctions, but all of them were skilled enough to manage the facilities. If only the villagers could be given the responsibility to manage pilgrim facilities in a framework of participatory management, unauthorized use of the forest could be prevented. This idea of community-centric arrangement required legal, administrative and financial backing for implementation, for it was a departure from the traditional approach of wildlife management, which usually did not involve people in management.

The support came in the form of the India Eco-Development Project (IEDP), a World Bank-sponsored conservation project in selected tiger reserves, Periyar Tiger Reserve being one of them. Launched by Project Tiger in 1996, it advocated a management process that encouraged negotiations between wildlife managers and local people based on shared trust, entitlements and responsibilities. Recognizing the conflicts that had resulted from the creation of resource-rich conservation areas in impoverished human surroundings, eco-development was suggested as a strategy of managing such conflicts and it was incorporated in the first National Wildlife Action Plan (NWAP) in 1983. The idea emphasized that people and parks need to be *with* each other and not *against*. The wildlife areas must provide incentives to proximate communities, through sustainable land use in their community spaces and alternative means of livelihoods, to elicit their support. This idea was a transformative departure from the founding principles of wildlife management in India, which relied on excluding human presence from the wildlife areas.

With the launch of the IEDP, participatory management of the Periyar Tiger Reserve with the local communities got underway. Ecological and socio-economic characteristics associated with the pilgrimage were analysed and consultations were held with local people to understand their concerns, expectations and commitments vis-à-vis the conservation efforts. The forest staff was trained in participatory methods, and joint workshops with local stakeholders were held to reinforce the new idea of inclusive management. The premise that the local people bear the cost of conservation necessitated that they first be compensated through financial incentives. The market associated with pilgrimage offered this opportunity.

Legal and administrative justifications for entrusting pilgrimage management to local communities were made emphasizing the historical existence of the temple and the inevitability of the use of forest routes by pilgrims. It was argued that a controlled temporary market run by the locals under the supervision of wildlife staff would increase the stake of people in the Periyar Tiger Reserve, improving its protection and habitat conditions. In a quid pro quo arrangement, local villagers were assured of wayside spaces free of cost with part financing to establish their small businesses. In return, the villagers would stop using forest material for construction and fuel, maintain a proper system of garbage collection and disposal, run responsible businesses with officially agreed costs and quality, and assist the Periyar Tiger Reserve staff in protecting the area from fires, illegal occupation and removal of forest produce/material.

Initially, the villagers familiar with pilgrimage business were organized into an Eco-Development Committee (EDC), named Swami Ayyappa Poonkavanam Punarudharana (SAPP) EDC, authorized to receive project funds and implement activities as identified in the mutually agreed micro-plans. For the pilgrimage season of 1998, six sites were identified along the traditional route for allocation to the EDC. The objections raised by the TDB for this arrangement were settled through administrative and judicial processes, freeing a large part of the forest route from unauthorized economic activities. Necessary official approvals for implementation came fast, as this was an activity under the IEDP, approved both by the governments of India and Kerala.

The SAPP EDC was supported with a project investment of ₹44.17 lakh to buy construction material for creating temporary facilities. The funds were placed in their account, and social sector consultants were engaged to aid them in group work and record keeping. Forest staff was directed to diligently work with the EDCs. At the end of the season, each family, among the 441 families involved in this enterprise, made a net profit of about ₹30,000.[3] By the 2002 season, 32 such EDCs were managing pilgrimage in the Periyar Tiger Reserve, grouped under a well-structured confederation of the EDCs, which procured and managed a liquefied petroleum gas (LPG) agency and oversaw issues related to sociopolitical and financial nature. Illegal removal of forest material had stopped and defiling of the forest had reduced. The pilgrimage management was mutually beneficial, as it helped the Periyar Tiger Reserve build a supportive sociopolitical constituency and improve its protection, whereas, for the local communities, the project not only extended financial support but helped them grow into an alternative institution capable of undertaking socio-economic development through group work.

Jayan and Aneesh: The Natural History Gurus of Periyar

1998: About 12 boys belonging to the Mannan tribe approached the Periyar Tiger Reserve officials with a proposal to form a Tribal Trekker EDC. The boys would be trained in natural history and conduct tourists on an early morning walk of about 3 km through the forests of Periyar Tiger Reserve. For giving the national and international tourists a glimpse of the ants and elephants, birds and butterflies, herbs and trees, and the land and people of the area, the boys would receive an officially agreed honorarium from the tourists in return. Free from conducting the tourists, they would accompany the Periyar Tiger Reserve staff on protection duties as part of their quid pro quo obligation under the IEDP. Attired in an olive-green uniform, complete with leech-proof footwear, with a binocular dangling over their chests and a field notebook held in hand, the boys would grow into the nature interpreters of the Periyar Tiger Reserve. Exemplifying people's participation in wildlife management, this group of tribal trekkers would bring laurels to the Periyar Tiger Reserve management, simultaneously giving themselves the opportunity to lead a respectable life.

2000: The IEDP organized tribal groups into efficient management institutions, and many culture-conscious tourists visited tribal hamlets, farms and households close to the town of Kumily. Always looking for new livelihood opportunities for local people, the innovative team of the Periyar Tiger Reserve officials hit the jackpot by creating a Tribal Heritage EDC with a tribal museum designed and maintained by the EDC. A paid visit to the museum would provide the visitors with experiential learning on tribal culture and art. A group of about 15 young tribal boys and girls were identified as members of the EDC, trained in the art of communication and natural history to guide the visitors through their living places and stories.

Jayan Ponnappan was then a 23-year-old, slightly built young man with a class 10 education but an uncertain future. Within a couple of years of joining the EDC, Jayan had become an avid watcher of wildlife and a capable communicator on natural history. The Periyar Tiger Reserve management encouraged and supported the boys through language learning and natural history courses, and their self-motivation continued to improve their abilities. Recognizing their role in the Periyar Tiger Reserve protection and nature education, the EDC was awarded the David Shepherd Wildlife Award in 2008. Jayan, one of the brightest, is now a permanent employee of Periyar Tiger Reserve and is a walking encyclopaedia on natural history. He can, in his own words, 'identify 250 species of birds, nearly 50 species of dragonflies, 250 species of butterflies, and many amphibians and plants'. His most spectacular growth is in the field of arachnids, as he can identify about 200 species of spiders and is a highly sought-after resource person for students, researchers and natural history lovers.

R. Aneesh, a 15-year-old, schoolgoing Mannan boy, joined the Tribal Heritage EDC in 2000 and began attending capacity-building courses conducted by the Periyar Tiger Reserve management in his free time. By the time he graduated from class 12, he had become like his tribal elder Jayan, a competent natural history observer, confidently interacting with visitors, students and officials. Aneesh, in his own words, 'can identify 230 species of butterflies, more than 80 species of dragonflies, and a host of birds, amphibians, reptiles, and trees of the Periyar Tiger Reserve.' Awarded the Sanctuary Asia Young Naturalist Award in 2007, Anish is now a permanent employee of the Periyar Tiger Reserve and is a valuable resource person for nature education programmes.

Walking many miles along with my committed colleagues, the agenda of coexistence was formally placed on the ground, testimony to which was the pal payasam completing the Malayali *sadya*, representing an evolving relationship between the Periyar Tiger Reserve staff and people, in which protecting the Periyar Tiger Reserve's values and improving livelihoods of local people have fused as complementary interests of both the parties. Together, we were embarking on a journey that would 'make people stakeholders in the conservation of the park'[4] and usher in a new chapter of participatory stories in wildlife conservation.

Citizens as Partners in Management Planning

In 2009, I was invited to the inaugural function of the declaration of Parambikulam Tiger Reserve, the second tiger reserve in Kerala after Periyar. The upgradation of Parambikulam Wildlife Sanctuary to a tiger reserve filled me with immense joy and pride, for it was at Parambikulam that I had begun my professional career as a young forester in 1985 and had participated in its management planning involving its transition from a timber-producing area to a wildlife sanctuary.

Located immediately south of the Palghat gap and shielded by the Nelliampathy and Anamalai hills, the wide amphitheatre consisting of Thunacadavu and Parambikulam valleys drains southwestward to Kerala midlands. Wrapped in timber-rich tropical evergreen and deciduous forests, the hill slopes and valleys enclose large reservoirs; are criss-crossed by several streams and punctuated intermittently by grass and sedge-dominated small swampy landforms, the *vayals*.

Before being notified as a wildlife sanctuary in 1984, Parambikulam was managed since 1961 as a timber production area under a specially constituted teak plantation division with a Divisional Forest Officer (DFO) in charge of planting and harvesting teak. In 1972, under an agreement between the governments of Kerala and Tamil Nadu on water use and sharing, the government of Tamil Nadu had constructed three dams in the valleys, which began attracting some visitors. A major source of timber revenue to the government of Kerala, Parambikulam also began to be highlighted as a 'good wildlife area' for large mammals such as elephants, gaurs, deer; sometimes, even leopards and wild dogs would be seen around the reservoirs and along the roads. In 1933, Dr Salim Ali visited and, henceforth, Parambikulam came to be seen as a birdwatching spot as well. The resident tribal groups Muduvar, Malasar and Kadar attracted social scientists and anthropologists.

In 1984, a wildlife wing was created within the forest department led by the Chief Wildlife Warden (CWLW). Consequently, the DFO was redesignated as Wildlife Warden, Parambikulam, reporting to the Field Director (FD), Project Tiger, in the new hierarchy of wildlife wing. With administrative arrangements in place, the Wildlife Warden was tasked to prepare a plan to realize the objectives of wildlife management. Occupying about 90 sq. km area in the valleys, the teak plantations, hitherto managed as revenue resource, presented the challenge of managing them as wildlife habitats. My predecessor, who was himself trained in the field of wildlife and was a highly respected officer had overseen the administrative transfer of the area to the wildlife sanctuary and initiated the planning process by setting priorities and strategies of management.

The first strategic step towards managing teak plantations as wildlife habitats was to stop clear-felling of plantations that were due to be harvested. My predecessor had obtained the necessary departmental authorization to stop clear-felling by putting up robust scientific and legal justifications, supported strongly by the senior officers of the wildlife wing.

Following the principle that 'forestry operations do not destroy habitats, they alter them'[5], the fieldwork on management planning began from September 1986. For the first time in Kerala, the planning process was made participatory, involving sanctuary staff, forestry students, local scientists, naturalists, photographers and the local tribals. Before being deployed for fieldwork, the teams were briefed on the purpose and methodology to collect statistically testable field information on habitats and animal abundance. Derived from the consultations and field results, the objectives and strategies of management were finalized. The draft plan was initially handwritten, then typed, sent to the Wildlife Institute of India (WII) and the FD for their review, and after incorporating suggestions received, the management plan was printed in FD's office on the newly purchased electronic typewriter.

Applicable for 10 years, the plan prescribed selective extraction of teak trees at rotation age in place of clear-felling to allow growth of the suppressed natural regeneration. The prescription assumed that such removal of teak trees would create enough openings for miscellaneous trees to grow in the vacated space. Additionally, the low-intensity forestry works would continue to generate employment for the tribal people, who had been depending on plantation activities for many decades. This was perhaps the first time that silviculture was being used for habitat management, with timber as a by-product. Though sketchy and data deficient, the management planning process, nevertheless, laid the foundation of participatory, scientific planning for wildlife management in Kerala.

The central valley of the wildlife sanctuary with teak plantations and tribal settlements was categorized as the buffer zone for permitting limited forestry, feasible tribal development and nascent tourism activities. The natural forests of the wildlife sanctuary surrounding the buffer abutted the neighbouring forests of Tamil Nadu and Kerala, contributing to the formation of an ecologically significant landscape of about 3,000 sq. km. Visualizing the expansion of Parambikulam in future, the surrounding forests were identified as the core zone for strict protection and scientific monitoring. The plan engendered a new perspective, to shift the orientation from managing a 'timber space' to an 'ecological space'.

The new perspective also helped to stop the entry of a few development projects that would have changed the ecological character of Parambikulam. A proposal from the tourism department came in 1988 to build a double-storeyed tourist lodge. Similarly, converting an old forest track in the western part of the wildlife sanctuary to a public road was an old public demand. Both these issues had high political stakes. The management, however, vehemently argued against these proposals, citing existing forest and wildlife laws prohibiting non-forestry activities in PAs, and mobilized scientific as well as public opinion to highlight the irreplaceable loss of biodiversity, should these projects be allowed. Supported steadfastly by senior officials, the projects were halted.

I left Parambikulam in September 1989, but not before a proposal was submitted to the FD to include the proximate areas of the neighbouring forests into the wildlife sanctuary to maintain ecological contiguity and long-term conservation of the landscape. The declaration of the Parambikulam Tiger

Reserve in 2009 consisting of the wildlife sanctuary and the outlying forests, realized the two-decades-old dream of the conservation community. Many people who participated in the first management planning exercise attended the inaugural function as lifelong friends of Parambikulam and as an influential conservation constituency.

In Support of Inclusive Management

The WLPA has been amended several times to become more inclusive, reinforcing the dynamic nature of conservation. The evolution of inclusiveness can be understood from the various government policy pronouncements, guidelines, strategy papers and action plans. Notwithstanding the consistent vigil and concern, and rightly so, against the manifold threats to wildlife, the management progression towards inclusiveness is also a realization of the situation at ground zero. Over the years, a gradual opening of a conversation, albeit slow and sometimes frustrating, has commenced between the State actors and the stakeholders to build a partnership to protect precious pockets of rich biodiversity while simultaneously helping local partners in building a better future for themselves.

However, the practice of participation is not niggle-free for several reasons. One, such programmes continue to be project-based and target-driven external initiatives, and two, a systemic reluctance in accepting the necessity of an inclusive approach in management appears to be too stubborn to go away. Project-based participation has its limitation of a fixed duration, beyond which, the sustainability of the programmes and institutions created during the project period becomes problematic. Post-project hand-holding of institutions appears necessary to allow internalization of the participatory processes in the behaviour and conduct of all partners. To continue engagement with the EDC, the Periyar and Parambikulam managements are using the business model of sharing revenues generated from innovative programmes developed around tourism, pilgrimage, and tribal arts and crafts. Elsewhere, opportunities are being explored to enable community organizations as implementing agencies of the local panchayats and various government departments to execute public works. Aided by efforts on social capital building and appropriate technical inputs, such committees could become active participants in conservation and development programmes, sustaining themselves and the participatory processes.

For about five years, from 2005, I worked in Attappady, the only tribal block of Kerala, on a participatory eco-restoration and social development project launched by the rural development department with financial assistance from the Japan International Cooperation Agency (JICA). For project implementation, an autonomous special delivery vehicle named Attappady Hill Area Development Society (AHADS) was created under the department. Beginning with project planning in 1997, the project investments continued until 2011, spending about ₹225 crore through more than 300 watershed- and tribal hamlet-level institutions, collectively called people's institutions (PI). With PIs, mutual agreements were formalized by the AHADS that defined the roles, responsibilities and accountability of all participants. Checks and balances required to maintain transparency in spending public funds and quality control were recorded in governance rules.

The professional team of the AHADS worked on social capital building and enhancement of technical capabilities of participating individuals, especially the tribals, to empower them to plan, execute and supervise the project works within the framework of the mutually agreed implementation arrangements. The project generated about 4.5 million man-days of employment over the project period, regenerating thousands of hectares of degraded forest and agricultural wastelands, and creating physical assets related to social development. The implementation of the project made measurable positive impacts on the ecology and socio-economic development of Attappady.

Attappady: A River Rejuvenates

Following the watershed-based resource management approach, the Attappady eco-restoration and social development project was implemented by the AHADS using participatory methodology. The geographical area of Attappady block is 745 sq. km, which includes 444 sq. km of forest lands. Based on geographical, cultural and professional attributes, 93 micro-watershed-based user associations, 54 joint forest management committees (JFMCs) and 166 tribal development committees (TDCs), were constituted, involving about 20,000 people, with tribals contributing more than half the numbers. After joint field visits and transparent consultations, professionals of the AHADS helped each PI to develop micro-plans and, through various capacity-building training, enabled them to implement and monitor the planned activities.

In about 10 years, the massive people's action brought 1,554 ha of agricultural wasteland under the plow, raised agro-forestry plantations of over 5,347 ha and promoted traditional crops and sericulture over 664 ha and 72 ha, respectively. On forest lands, tree plantations of over 3,776 ha were raised and natural regeneration was assisted in 8,061 ha. About 9,000 ha of forest land and 6,700 ha of private lands were treated with the soil and moisture conservation works by constructing staggered trenches, gully plugs, check dams, groundwater recharging wells, open wells, rainwater harvesting structures, drainage lines, etc. In addition, several infrastructure works were undertaken by PIs, the most talked about being a 40-bed hospital, a bridge facilitating vehicular traffic across two major panchayats, a drinking water scheme benefitting 2,700 families, and 1,288 tribal houses completed and handed over to the beneficiaries by March 2010.

The works helped in the greening of Attappady, reflected in forest cover improvement and improvement in social development indices. The most significant gain was the improvement of the water regime that saw many rivulets and streams running perennially again. The rejuvenation of river Kodungarapallam, a tributary of river Siruvani, became the face of the ecological success of the project, which was widely covered in media. In recognition of the cooperative approach, JICA presented a certificate of appreciation to AHADS on 19 October 2009.[6]

For post-project sustainability, the AHADS was proposed to be linked with the Kerala Institute of Local Administration (KILA), a state training institute for people's representatives. The government of Kerala was also requested to issue enabling orders for the recognition of PIs as implementing agencies of the panchayats and other government agencies. The proposal took some time to materialize, by which time most of the professionals had left the AHADS for secure jobs elsewhere. About 90 tribal boys and girls working in AHADS were appointed permanent government employees and left AHADS. Today, the infrastructure of the AHADS is used by KILA and various government departments for official capacity-building programmes; however, with far less vibrancy and communication with PIs compared to the project period. Despite the enabling executive orders, the PIs could not elicit significant public works from the panchayats or other government departments due to age-old politico-financial and cultural interests involved in the use of public funds.

The Future

It stands to reason, therefore, that systemic adoption of participatory processes will continue to challenge the protagonists. The challenges inherent in the complex sphere of the political economy of conservation demand appropriate actions built around the equitable distribution of resources, social justice and respect for common citizens. Conservation, being a political argument laden with socially determined values, will benefit from more voices coming in its support. Inclusive management is one way of reaching that goal.

The inclusion of local people in the management of the Sabarimala pilgrimage and at Attappady or the involvement of civil society in the management planning of the Parambikulam Wildlife Sanctuary helped in building an inclusive narrative on nature conservation, which was sensitive to the welfare of both—the wildlife and the civil society. In the case of protected area (PA) management, which is now synonymous with biodiversity or nature conservation, the forest departments bear greater responsibility to internalize this notion of inclusiveness, for they have been lawfully mandated to ensure the ecological security of the nation, which necessarily includes humans and non-humans in its management archetype.

While working, I had often encountered very concerned voices arguing against foresters' involvement in community-centric projects, for such opinions find various line departments mandated with social development works and consider foresters' core function to be the protection of forests and wildlife through policing. I had countered that by saying that the notion of command- and control-based protection emerged in the colonial context of property, superior knowledge and racial discrimination, evolving into exclusivist management. By including local people in management, the core function only gets strengthened, as extra hands and minds become available to forest and wildlife managers. It also offers an opportunity to the forest managers and various agencies of the government to break their silos and work in an integrated environment for the security of the nature and culture of the nation. Streaming from all over the country, the encouraging stories of the integration of science and social science in conservation and human welfare activities keep the flame of my optimism alive. We may occasionally see a weakening of institutions and faltering individuals, but there is always light at the end of the tunnel.

Notes

1. Sivadas, S., *Conservation, Development and Incompatibilities: Transition of a Sacred Geography*, MPhil thesis, School of Social Sciences, Mahatma Gandhi University, 2001.
2. Veeramani, A., and Joju P. Alappatt, *Ecological Impact and Regeneration Status Assessment of Sabarimala Pilgrim Routes Report*, India Eco-development Project, 2003.
3. *Financial Sustainability – A Study of the Village Ecodevelopment at Periyar Tiger Reserve*, Mahatma Gandhi University, 2003.
4. *Joining the Dots: The Report of The Tiger Task Force*, Union Ministry of Environment and Forests (Project Tiger), 2005, p. 139, https://bit.ly/3Icfqfe. Accessed on 22 June 2022.
5. Thomas, Jack Ward (ed.), 'Wildlife Habitats in Managed Forests the Blue Mountains of Oregon and Washington', *Agriculture Handbook: U.S. Department of Agriculture, Forest Service*, Vol. 553, 1979, https://bit.ly/3yD8PXZ. Accessed on 22 June 2022.
6. *Status Report (2010)*, AHADS, Rural Development Department, Government of Kerala, 2010.

CONSERVING WITH PEOPLE: CHALLENGES AND OPPORTUNITIES OF CONSERVATION RESERVES

GHAZALA SHAHABUDDIN
AND ANJALI BHARTARI[1]

Forest, Birds and People

It was a salubrious spring evening in March 2015 when we reached the picturesque village of Pawalgarh, located near the Corbett Tiger Reserve, along with our conservationist colleagues. Preparations were afoot for hosting the Uttarakhand Spring Bird Festival. Naturalists, trainers, tourists, senior government functionaries and even tourism entrepreneurs had arrived for the event. Five nature trails had been identified in the lush sal forests, villages and streams near the historic forest rest house (FRH) of Pawalgarh and the valleys beyond. The stage was set for three days of birding in this biodiversity hotspot, along with numerous other activities planned for nature tourists, such as workshops and cultural performances.

Interestingly, the Uttarakhand Spring Bird Festival in 2015 represented a rare collaborative effort across a diverse set of stakeholders: non-governmental organizations (NGOs), scientists, the village community, entrepreneurs and the Uttarakhand Forest Department. The value of this collaboration became evident during the festival. Local village homestays, food stalls, cafes and resorts were being used by birdwatchers, providing business to local people. Scientists and professional guides were volunteering as trainers for novice guides. As trainers ourselves, we could see productive links being forged during the festival: entrepreneurs hobnobbed with professional guides and tourists, while aspiring guides benefitted from talks with scientists and tourists.

Thus, when Pawalgarh and its surrounding areas were declared a conservation reserve under the Wild Life (Protection) Act (WLPA), 1972, in December 2012, the move was hailed as a progressive step by all of us who were associated with the area. Giving legal recognition and support to what was already a dynamic and productive process of nature-linked tourism could only be beneficial to conservation.

Yet, almost 10 years after its declaration, the Pawalgarh Conservation Reserve has yet to be operationalized. The first step of notifying the conservation reserve management committee has not yet been taken, nor has any public consultation been initiated for this purpose. Further, much of the existing bird tourism by locally trained guides has been curtailed due to the retraction of permission to access the nature trails. The Pawalgarh Conservation Reserve, sadly, exists only in name today.

There are other biologically significant conservation reserves in Uttarakhand that are yet to take off; they require organized impetus to ensure community participation and institutional support from the state government. Some of these include the Asan Conservation Reserve, Jhilmil Jheel Conservation Reserve and Naina Devi Himalayan Bird Conservation Reserve. Already, several local guides have been trained in these areas by Titli Trust, Nature Science Initiative and other collaborating NGOs and individuals.[2] However, the functioning of all these conservation reserves remains stalled by all accounts; further, no additional conservation reserves have been established in Uttarakhand despite the considerable potential, particularly in high-altitude areas.

Importance of Conservation Reserves

The WLPA largely came about intending to create inviolate spaces—spaces from which people would be excluded for the benefit of nature, such as national parks and wildlife sanctuaries. Yet, even such strictly protected areas, ironically, continue to benefit from local expertise and labour, which is used to track poachers, tourism activities, infrastructure maintenance and habitat management. The role of local communities, thus, continues to be important in protected areas (PAs) in India, though it often goes unrecognized.

It has been observed that inviolate PAs alone are simply not adequate for ensuring the viability of either ecosystems or species in the long term. With increasing fragmentation, retaining biodiversity-friendly land uses in the larger landscape around PAs has become exceedingly important, including multiple-use forests, fields and orchards that can allow foraging, breeding and dispersal of wild species.[3] It is important to note that despite varied tenurial regimes, agrarian landscapes do provide for many endangered species: leopards that breed in cultivation areas in Junnar, Maharashtra, and great hornbills that nest in coffee plantations in the Anamalai Hills, Tamil Nadu, come easily to mind.

Given the observable need to enhance the conservation value of multiple-use landscapes, most conservationists welcomed the 2003 amendment in the WLPA that provided for community and conservation reserves.[4] Conservation reserves are defined as 'protected areas established on government lands that are typically uninhabited but used for subsistence by local communities'.[5] The equivalent of a conservation reserve on village land was proposed as a community reserve in the Act. The enunciated aim of such PAs was to create viable buffer zones, connectors or even migration corridors between PAs such as national parks and wildlife sanctuaries. The rationale for their creation was 'the reduced protection in and around existing or proposed protected areas due to private ownership of land, and land use.'[6]

In both cases, the law calls for co-management committees that include village representation and the conservation reserve management committee, in case of conservation reserve, or the community reserve management committee, in case of community reserves. These committees, once formed, are envisioned as the 'competent authority to prepare and implement management plans for the reserve and to take steps to ensure the protection of the wildlife and its habitat in the reserve'. The representatives in these committees are to be nominated from the local village panchayat or gram sabha. The decentralized nature of such committees is supposed to be pivotal to localized management plans that could be more suited to the local conditions around individual PAs. Today there are 97 conservation reserves covering 4,483 sq. km, and 214 community reserves covering 1,302 sq. km[7] across India.

The Case of Pawalgarh Conservation Reserve

Ghazala Shahabuddin

I had been visiting the incredibly diverse landscape of Pawalgarh, comprising tall sal forests, shisham stands, fields, orchards and mountain streams, since 2006. Over 380 species of birds have been recorded in this area.[8] The backdrop itself is spectacular, with the emerald-green forest-covered Shivaliks in the background lording over the village lands. The Pawalgarh Conservation Reserve abuts six villages in addition to Pawalgarh, covering an area of 58.25 sq. km, where the majority of the population work as cultivators and service providers to tourists or are employed in towns nearby, such as Ramnagar.

My first visit to Pawalgarh in November 2006 was to scope out possibilities of research on woodpeckers, a bird group represented by an astonishing 16 species in the Corbett area. The abundance and diversity of birds thriving in the midst of fields and villages within the forest matrix were also of interest. On this trip, I realized how community involvement could have so much potential for conservation, given the observably easy coexistence between birds and humans.

While birdwatching and other research remained a primary objective of my visits even after 2006, my interactions with a local environmentalist and the homestay owner, Manohar Singh Manral, and his son, Vicky Manral, have led to fascinating insights about people, birds and biodiversity governance over time. His homestay was initially promoted by the erstwhile Director of Corbett Tiger Reserve in a far-sighted move to create more tourism sites across the reserve, as the core area of the reserve was becoming increasingly crowded with tourists.

Over the years, Manral's home has become a hub for nature education and conservation activities in the Pawalgarh area. Apart from commercial activities, he also hosts nature programmes for local children and cultural events for the villages. Most importantly, he has been responsible for the largely organic growth of a local youth group called Pawalgarh Prakriti Prahari (PPP), which works towards conservation and nature tourism in the area. The PPP[9] is a not-for-profit organization formed in December 2015, shortly after the aforementioned Uttarakhand Spring Bird Festival in March 2015. The PPP's main objective is to 'support nature conservation, environment protection and sustainable living by promoting alternate livelihoods such as ecotourism through village homestays, nature tours with experienced guides and promoting local produce and cuisine in the landscape of the Pawalgarh conservation area'.[10] Sanjay and Anchal Sondhi of Titli Trust, Dehradun, have played important roles as trainers and mentors for the village youth, particularly through their nature guide training programme, which began in 2015. While the emergence of the PPP and the guide training programmes were instrumental in creating local support for and involvement in the Pawalgarh Conservation Reserve, they were localized home-grown activities that grew from strength to strength since 2015, providing potential for community-based conservation in the area. When I visited Pawalgarh for birdwatching, members of the youth group took me on the birding trails within the village and along the river Dabka where one could easily observe a range of woodland and aquatic species. My most memorable experiences have been the sighting of a rare white-naped woodpecker, pin-tailed green pigeon, the striking-looking green magpie and the great slaty woodpecker. During this time, the training of guides by Titli Trust in Pawalgarh continued and was even encouraged by the Ramnagar Forest Division, which manages the Pawalgarh Conservation Reserve, although the conservation reserve management committee had still not been formed.

In the summer of 2016, I revisited the Pawalgarh Conservation Reserve and stayed in Manral's homestay, eager to learn more about how the reserve was shaping up. While local support and involvement in the area had grown, mainly due to the enthusiasm of the PPP members, on the other hand, developments on the governance side did not deem well for the Pawalgarh Conservation Reserve. Ramnagar Forest Division managers had inexplicably cut off walking access to local guides in late 2015. At the same time, virtually unregulated jeep safaris focusing on wildlife viewing were allowed into the same forest areas, with little control on numbers of jeeps.

In an interview in 2021, the founder of Titli Trust, Sanjay Sondhi, explained to me the repercussions of these new restrictions for the local guides. All their training had come to nought: the guides were now forced to keep to the village areas and could not take tourists on foot into the nature trails within the Pawalgarh Conservation Reserve—trails that are key for birdwatching. In 2016 itself, the Ramnagar Forest Division committed to the Titli Trust that if 30 guides were trained, they would officially make guiding compulsory on the jeep safaris operating inside Pawalgarh Conservation Reserve. This would mean that the guides from the local villages could be gainfully employed. However, Sanjay Sondhi also told me that, as of December 2021, there had not yet been any appointments from the first cohort of trained guides.

In late 2016, I spent a few days in Camp Hornbill, Kyari, where Naveen Upadhyay runs a campground and resort creatively designed for environmental learning and birdwatching activities. A native of Kyari village, he was the first local entrepreneur to commercially take up bird-based nature tourism. Being an accomplished birder, he has developed a committed following of birdwatcher tourists. A few walks along the stream upstream of his resort, where the Shivaliks steeply meet the plains, revealed the diversity in this landscape. One evening, walking in the dense sal forests close to his camp, we chanced on one of the rarest owls in India—a large spot-bellied eagle-owl—quietly observing us in the rapidly gathering evening gloom.

Back at the camp, Upadhyay related to us the difficulties he faces in creating an environment and market for nature tourism in the area, based on low-impact hiking and birdwatching activities. He said, 'The government doesn't have a clear policy that works on the principles of ecotourism or nature tourism. Although this is an area abundant in wildlife, little is done to stop loud music, parties and crowding of village roads by tourists.' He had asked the other village homestays and community members to sign a letter petitioning the government to take action against resorts flouting ethical guidelines, but so far, nothing has come of this. The resorts are disposing of their waste in the open and continuing to pollute the forest and local water sources. Upadhyay averred, 'Since Kyari is on the periphery of Pawalgarh Conservation Reserve, such disturbances and pollution can adversely impact wildlife. While no action has been taken on this front, we ourselves face restrictions on movement and birding in the nearby forest areas.'

Recognizing the role of the locals in conservation is essential. There are crucial benefits for conservation: local communities can and do assist the forest department in monitoring these ecosystems and watch out for any illegal forest incursions such as timber theft or encroachments, particularly in places with insufficient ground staff. During interviews in early 2021, the PPP members told me that the forest department sometimes calls upon them to help in awareness sessions during Wildlife Week (and other similar events), in stopping the spread of forest fires and controlling the invasive plant *Lantana camara*.

If the vision of Pawalgarh Conservation Reserve has to be realized, forest managers need to encourage low-impact nature tourism and further regulate the more disruptive safari-type operations. Clearly, a functioning Pawalgarh Conservation Reserve with local involvement will be critical for conservation in the Corbett landscape.

A Ramsar Site: Asan Conservation Reserve

Anjali Bhartari

As a person working on the management of heritage sites and having mentored a few such projects in Uttarakhand too, Asan has always been of special interest to me. I see community involvement as a key component in the conservation of a PA. This may be attributed to traditional knowledge, more working hands in the forest, and emotional and traditional association with the forests. However, my experiences there show that there is certainly a structure in place for the conservation reserve—what lacks in the governance is accountability. There is also a lack of technical inputs and skills required to successfully involve the community in conservation.

The Asan Conservation Reserve is a freshwater wetland at

the confluence of the Asan River and the Yamuna River near village Dhalipur in the Dehradun district. It covers an area of only 444.4 ha, most of which comes under the state irrigation and forest departments. The Asan Conservation Reserve has the distinction of being declared the first conservation reserve of the country on 5 August 2005 in view of its high biodiversity, particularly riverain grasslands. In addition, it is an Important Bird Area (IBA) and was also declared the first Ramsar site of the state in 2020, a thrilling moment for Uttarakhand, which had documented its wetlands back in 2012.[11] The reserve is known for its biodiversity, particularly the avifaunal diversity of 358 species[12], which includes nine threatened and seven near-threatened bird species. In addition, many rare birds are frequently spotted in the area, due to which the reserve has become a popular destination for birdwatchers. The Asan Conservation Reserve includes three small villages—Kulhal, Kunja Grant and Dhalipur—which harbour 770 households with an approximate population of 4,600, including tribal communities such as Gujjars and Buxas.

My recent interactions with the community revealed that the local people had very little association with the conservation reserve. The governance of the conservation reserve is carried out through a management plan (2009–2010 to 2013–2014), which has been subsequently revised. A management committee has been set up along with the executive committee and has developed micro-plans. However, further research reveals that not much has happened in executing these micro-plans, and the committees are almost inactive due to lack of funding. Overall, there has been negligible participation of the community in the meetings.

The main tourism facility at the Asan Conservation Reserve was given over to the tourism department in 1994 and is run by the Garhwal Mandal Vikas Nigam (GMVN). The facility on the banks of the wetland has paddle boats, water skiing, kayaking, canoeing and rowing boats, of which currently only paddle boats are functional. There is also accommodation available here. However, the local community is not employed in any of these tourist facilities. This is quite a ironic situation wherein another government agency (GMVN) has become the prime stakeholder, though it contributes minimally to the biodiversity of the reserve. Of late, people from the community have set up small food kiosks along the highway on their own. However, these shops need to be a part of the larger planning process for livelihood generation. One can see that waste management around the shops will soon become an issue in the areas surrounding the reserve. A small area of 5 ha in the Rampur Mandi forest, which includes a children's park, deer park, forestry training centre, the Rampur Mandi FRH and a few tourist huts that are a part of the facilities at the conservation reserve, falls under the forest department. However, these facilities do not draw tourists, as they are located away from the main wetland.

The forest department trained the local youth and women as birdwatching guides to increase community participation from 2012 to 2015. I was told that small livelihood initiatives such as running the canteen at the forest training centre by the community, were also initiated for a short span. A few interactive multi-stakeholder workshops were organized with the community, forest department, irrigation department and even the forest department of the neighbouring state of Himachal Pradesh. However, any further plans soon faded out with a change in leadership and without an accountability process.

The conservation reserve management has little control over tourist traffic, as the reserve is accessible from Uttarakhand and Himachal Pradesh, with National Highway 72 skirting it. There is no way to check if the tourists are passing by or stopping at the wetland, making it difficult for the visitors to engage with the nature guides. This has also demotivated the trained nature guides, as their income is not only sporadic but also seasonal. While they engaged with the conservation reserve after their training, local nature guides have sought employment elsewhere, as the conservation reserve did not sustain their livelihoods.

Though the community indulges in fishing when the water recedes and collects some amount of non-wood products for cattle and household needs, the significance of the wetland, visiting migratory birds or the heritage value of the conservation reserve is lost on them. The fact that the conservation reserve is the first Ramsar site of the state matters very little to them. Needless to say that these villages have the potential to build positive linkages for the protection and management of the conservation reserve, as they do associate on a voluntary basis with the forest department for forestry activities such as forest fire control, human–wildlife conflicts (HWCs) and tree plantations.

The main challenge before the management is to put in place a system of providing some supplemental livelihood opportunities for the local communities and to link these benefits to the protection/management of the Asan Conservation Reserve. The management plan did suggest the formation of the Conservation Reserve Management Committee as a part of the institution-building process. This could support and facilitate conservation-related activities of the reserve and the various programmes of eco-development committees (EDCs). In addition, it could also be responsible for research and monitoring, and training and conservation awareness programmes in this area. This initiative has, however, not been implemented as planned. Developing a completely new approach to associate the community with the conservation reserve through tourism is eminently required. As discussed, considering the lacunae vis-à-vis tourism, a detailed site management plan needs to be developed.

With my experience in managing heritage sites, I feel that there need to be multiple facilities[13] apart from birdwatching, such as nature trails in the forest, cycling paths, birdwatching hides/towers, machans, homestays, cultural experiences or even heritage trails to nearby sites. For example, the Buxa and the Gujjar tribes who inhabit the conservation reserve could contribute to the cultural experience.

The first bird festival of Uttarakhand was organized at Asan on 5–9 February 2014. The subsequent bird festivals, in 2016 and 2018, did explore options like nature walks and heritage walks; however, in the absence of an institutional structure to promote ecotourism for the conservation of the reserve, these remained limited to discussion and display in the festivals.

All in all, more significant efforts are required to fulfil the hopes of various organizations and the people for the Asan Conservation Reserve. Previous efforts in this field have laid the foundation; now, new strategies need to be developed to deal with the problems that have been encountered. The Asan should be brought back into focus and developed with an imaginative vision that includes local interests.

Complementarities and Synergies

Soon after the WLPA amendment on community and conservation reserves was passed, conservationists raised several concerns with respect to their usefulness and effectiveness.[14] In particular, conservationists felt that the rules were incomplete and fragmentary, and feared that their implementation might affect the future access of local people to forest goods and sites. In that case, the incentives for long-term conservation may, in fact, be weakened rather than strengthened by the imposition of conservation reserves[15] on existing informal structures. In the case of the Pawalgarh Conservation Reserve, this eventuality has definitely come to pass. While there have been no efforts to clearly lay out the rules and conditions of co-management by local communities in this conservation reserve, home-grown vitality has been sapped by the arbitrary changes in laws and rules.

It has been pointed out that in many such cases, continued anthropogenic use by local communities may pose a problem, causing forest and wetland degradation in the long term.[17] However, local use can be managed through licencing systems and autonomous monitoring, as in numerous community-managed systems in India. Some examples are Devalsari forest[18], Khonoma Nature Conservation and Tragopan Sanctuary (Nagaland) and Singchung Bugun Village Community Reserve (Arunachal Pradesh).

Conservation reserves in India can be seen as an unprecedented opportunity via the amended WLPA to not only involve local communities in the conservation of wildlife but also provide benefits to them. Adopting a participatory approach in multiple-use landscapes in and around established PAs is clearly critical for the effectiveness of biodiversity conservation. Such modalities are highly overdue in the state of Uttarakhand and elsewhere, where poorly planned infrastructure development, suburban sprawl and climate change threaten to overwhelm the gains made for biodiversity due to the WLPA during the twentieth century.

Notes

1. We are grateful to Sanjay Sondhi, Manohar S. Manral, Naveen Upadhyay and others in the Pawalgarh area for freely sharing their thoughts, which made this article possible. Arushi Parmar compiled discussion points from interviews with several respondents in Pawalgarh area, carried out in February 2021.
2. Guide-training activities have been carried out by a consortium of NGOs since 2012, with support from the Uttarakhand Forest Department. These NGOs include Titli Trust, Nature Science Initiative, Rainbow Friends of Nature and numerous individual scientists and birdwatchers.
3. Rangarajan, Mahesh, et al., (eds.), *Nature Without Borders*, Orient Blackswan, 2017.

4. Dutt, Bahar, 'Are Community Reserves the Answer to Conservation?', *Down to Earth*, 15 August 2003, https://bit.ly/3R9mI7w. Accessed on 22 June 2022.
5. 'Community Reserves', Wildlife Institute of India, https://bit.ly/3RnfSvB. Accessed on 22 June 2022.
6. Ibid; 'Conservation Reserves', ENVIS Centre on Wildlife & Protected Areas, https://bit.ly/3NHkARM. Accessed on 22 June 2022.
7. 'Conservation Reserves', ENVIS Centre on Wildlife & Protected Areas, https://bit.ly/3NHkARM. Accessed on 22 June 2022.
8. Sondhi, Sanjay, and P. Kumar, *Checklists of the Birds, Butterflies and Moths of Pawalgarh Conservation Reserve Dehradun, India*, Uttarakhand Forest Department, 2020.
9. 'Conservation at Pawalgarh', Pawalgarh Prakriti Prahari, https://bit.ly/3OKNCBe. Accessed on 23 June 2022.
10. Ibid.
11. *Wetlands of Uttarakhand: A Documentation*, Uttarakhand Forest Department and WWF India, 2012, https://bit.ly/3PlnEnV. Accessed on 22 June 2022.
12. Mohan, D., et al., *A Checklist of the Birds of Asan Conservation Reserve*, 2nd edn., Uttarakhand Forest Department and Titli Trust, 2021.
13. Ravi, Anjali Bharthari, 'Community Based Tourism: Chhoti Haldwani', *Context*, Vol. 8, No. 1, Spring/Summer 2011, pp. 71–76, https://bit.ly/3acXTqK. Accessed on 22 June 2022.
14. Rangarajan, Mahesh, et al., (eds), *Nature Without Borders*, Orient Blackswan, 2017; Pathak, N., and S. Bhushan, 'Community Reserves and Conservation Reserves: More Reserve and Less Community!', *The Hindu Survey of Environment*, 2004.
15. Rangarajan, Mahesh, et al., (eds), *Nature Without Borders*, Orient Blackswan, 2017; Sondhi, Sanjay, 'The Devalsari Story Unfolds', Vikalp Sangam, 22 June 2015, https://bit.ly/3yjNnWz. Accessed on 22 June 2022.

COMMERCE MOST FOUL: ILLEGAL TRADE IN WILDLIFE

SAKET BADOLA

The day was sunny and the river was relatively calm. Sitting behind the wheel of the fast-moving speedboat procured recently to strengthen the anti-poaching efforts of the tiger reserve, I was spellbound, as always, by the vastness of the waterbody and the grandeur of the forests that surround it. In the last four years of my posting, I had probably sailed across this water innumerable times, but there hadn't been a single day when I wasn't overwhelmed by the magnificence of the landscape, which undoubtedly is one of the best surviving habitats for wildlife in the country.

I, along with my teammates, was returning from a special patrol and was navigating through the Kalagarh Dam reservoir on river Ramganga in Uttarakhand, inside the famous Corbett Tiger Reserve. The patrol was organized to scan the sensitive areas of the reserve, which were best accessed through the water channels and were once the preferred hideouts of wildlife poachers operating in the area. With improved resources, new technologies, better-trained staff, a stronger political will and greater support of local communities towards conservation, things have certainly improved in recent times. But certain threats to wildlife still remain.

The recent incident of tiger poaching in the nearby forest area, had once again underscored the fact that the future of wildlife in the country cannot be secured merely by securing its habitat. The ever-persistent demand for wildlife products in the national and international markets coupled with the greed of humans who are ready to supply them has the potential to shatter decades of dedicated conservation efforts in no time. How poachers wiped out all the resident tigers from the famous Sariska Tiger Reserve in Rajasthan and the Panna Tiger Reserve in Madhya Pradesh is a testament to the damaging impact of such threats.

While moving out of Corbett for my next assignment, I was determined that since the threat to wildlife extended far beyond its natural habitat and if given a chance, I would prefer to contribute at those levels as well.

As destiny would have it, I didn't have to wait for long. Within a year of leaving Corbett, I was offered the position to lead the Trade Record Analysis of Flora and Fauna in Commerce's (TRAFFIC's) India office in World Wide Fund for Nature-India (WWF-India).

TRAFFIC, an international organization headquartered in Cambridge (the United Kingdom [UK]), has a tremendous reputation globally for its sustained and quality work on wildlife trade-related issues. Since its inception in the early 1970s, TRAFFIC has firmly established itself as a leading international wildlife trade monitoring network, working through its several country offices spread across the globe. In India, it began operating in the early 1990s and is hosted by WWF-India.

A sudden change in work is not easy to undertake, as it pushes us out of our comfort zone. However, driven by Rabindranath Tagore's prophetic guidance, 'Life should not be the infinite elongation of a straight line', I decided to take the plunge to quench my desire to explore the nuances of illegal wildlife trade; little aware, what an exciting learning experience it was going to be.

Soon after I joined the organization, I was overwhelmed by multiple mentions of weird-sounding words like Ambergris, *hatha-jodi*, shahtoosh, 'yarsa gumbo', *siyaar-singhi*, etc., and found myself trying to make sense of certain oft-repeated code words such as 'double engine', 'scooter', 'rope' and 'chaadar'. If you are as clueless about these terms as I was during my initial days or are wondering how they're connected to the big and murky world of illegal wildlife trade—which today, purely on financial terms, is the fourth largest criminal activity globally, and is pushing several species towards extinction—then allow me to elaborate.

Ambergris, for easy understanding, can be best described as 'vomitus of whales'; hatha-jodi is the dried genital organs of the monitor lizard; siyaar-singhi is the cranial bone of the golden jackal; while yarsa gumbo is a unique combination of the moth caterpillar with a fungus; and shahtoosh is a premium quality wool obtained by slaughtering Tibetan antelope, a critically endangered species endemic to the Himalayas. All these are highly sought-after products in the wildlife market.

Similarly, 'double engine' is the code used in clandestine trade to refer to of the red sand boa snake, while 'scooter' is used to indicate turtles; 'rope' is used for pythons and 'chaadar' refers to tiger or leopard pelts. What is more concerning is that this list is by no means exhaustive. The actual list of wildlife articles traded and demanded globally would fill pages and would include even more weird-sounding names and even more unique products.

Presently, the Convention on International Trade in Endangered Species of Wild Fauna and Flora (CITES)—an agreement signed by more than 180 countries to regulate international wildlife trade—enlists more than 37,000 species of wild fauna and flora in its various appendices to prohibit or regulate international trade in them.

The Passion for Collection

To understand the drive behind the trade of wild animals and their products and to comprehend its impact on wild animals as well as humans in a better way, we need to travel slightly back in the past because this in not a recent human endeavour. The demand for food and medicine coupled with the intrinsic human desire to own anything that is considered beautiful and exclusive has driven this trade ever since humans started bartering their surpluses. Further, the discovery of intercontinental trade routes and the development of long-distance transport facilities led to the rapid expansion of this erstwhile local-level trade into a highly profitable international business endeavour.

The major surge in this trade as a truly global phenomenon came during the Victorian era when, following the acceptance (and popularity) of Darwin's theory of evolution, collecting samples of wild fauna and flora became a widely practised hobby, finding justification even in Biblical texts. In Genesis, the Victorians happily read that God formed every living thing on Earth and then commanded Adam to name them. It was hence postulated that 'humanity has a duty to inventory', which resulted in a spree of activities related to collecting and naming the various creations of God, not just from one's surroundings but also from faraway places. It became an approved endeavour even in cultures where outdoor sports had been frowned upon till that time. While this undoubtedly led to rapid advancement in the science of taxonomy, it also had some not-so-desired consequences for wildlife. For a few individuals, this benign hobby transformed into an addiction as they started employing every possible trick, legal or illegal, to acquire, smuggle or steal unique wildlife samples to 'enrich' and 'diversify' their personal collections that they could proudly display to demonstrate their wealth, passion or interests.

This addiction, often exhibited under the guise of scientific studies ranged from certain individual venturing out to collect specimen to more elaborate and systematic exercises carried out at the intercontinental level. The famous (or infamous) Smithsonian–Roosevelt African Expedition of 1909–1910 is often cited as an example of one such effort to collect samples of wildlife for purportedly scientific purposes. A well-organized, large-scale operation was undertaken to collect species of different continent and which resulted in more than 11,000 faunal specimens being collected. To date, this expedition cited as an upsetting example of excessive killing and waving off of local laws on the part of the elite, while others view it as the most elaborate exercise to collect samples for scientific study.

India, at that time was ruled by the mighty British Empire, and couldn't afford to remain untouched by this growing European fad. Our country, with its vast expanse of rich tropical forests, full of unique and often endemic biological diversity, offered an exciting treasure for enthusiastic collectors from the West. While this passion, led by colonial officers, did enrich the systematic taxonomy of wild flora and fauna of the subcontinent, it simultaneously made destructive activities like recreational hunting an accepted signature sport of the elite. As the fashion for shikar grew in the region, the wildlife of the subcontinent withered. This continued even after the imperial powers had left the shores of the country, and the new breed of nouveau elite rose up the societal ladder.

Stopping the Slide

By the late 1960s, however, it was clear that driven by hunting and international trade, several wild animals in India were facing an existential threat. The last surviving Asiatic cheetah, once a widely prevalent big cat in the country, had already been shot to local extinction by the early 1950s. Apparently, the cheetah was not alone to be subjected to such threats. Under the then prevailing scenario, several other species appeared to be heading the same way. Though the skin of the tiger was the ultimate trophy sought by the visiting tourist-hunters, several other wild animals, such as snakes, monitor lizards, crocodiles, etc., were also hunted in large numbers for their skin and other products.

While the products made of shahtoosh and ivory constituted premium-quality export items of that era, the bulk of export from the country was of birds, trapped for their feathers or sold in cages; of monkeys and langurs, demanded for animal trials; and of frogs, fancied for the flesh of their legs.

As an outcome of this unchecked onslaught against wildlife species, the wild population several species crashed. While tigers reached a precariously low number, other species, such as the crocodiles were almost on the verge of extinction. To the conservationists and the policymakers, it was becoming abundantly clear that if India wished to protect her precious wildlife, then something had to be done, and that too quite urgently. The decision was, however, not an easy one to make. Revenues generated from the export of these wildlife products were an important source of foreign exchange for the newly independent country still trying to find a foothold in the international market. This trade also ensured livelihood for thousands of artisans, bird and animal trappers, taxidermists, and exporters. However, considering the vastly deleterious impact such trade had on its wild heritage, India decided to put a near-total stop to the unregulated exploitation of its wildlife. The fact that hunting and the practice of making money by killing innocent animals wasn't part of the cultural ethos of a largely non-violent nation also helped the country to bring about these changes rather smoothly. In 1968, the export of furs of wild animals from the country was officially banned, and during the International Union for Conservation of Nature's (IUCN) triennial meeting held in New Delhi in 1969, Prime Minister Indira Gandhi made the intent of the country clear when she said, 'We need more foreign exchange but not at the cost of the life and liberty of some of the most beautiful species in our country.'[1] The complete ban on tiger-hunting, the enactment of the Wild Life (Protection) Act, 1972, and the launch of Project Tiger followed in quick succession.

The WLPA and Teething Troubles

Soon after the IUCN meeting and the United Nations Conference on the Human Environment held in Stockholm in 1972, the push to legislate a comprehensive national law for the protection of wildlife reached its peak. As forests and wildlife at that time fell under the State List of Schedule VII of the Indian constitution, the central government's powers to legislate on these subjects were restricted. To overcome this obstacle, a relatively less-used provision of the Constitution, viz., Article 252 that empowered Parliament to legislate on a State List subject if two or more states of the Union passed a resolution to this effect in their respective state assemblies, was used to enact the WLPA as a central Act. The Act was passed by Parliament during its Winter Session in 1972 and became the prime legal instrument to protect the country's wild flora and fauna. In its present form, this 'special' Act covers almost everything from the procedure to declare a protected area (PA) to provisions for combating the trafficking of fauna and flora, enlisted in its various schedules. Ever since its enactment, it has been the bedrock of wildlife management and protection in the country.

During its enactment in 1972 and soon thereafter, it did attract criticisms from certain expected quarters. For example, provision to put a complete ban on hunting of wildlife, which included the practice of traditional hunting by some indigenous communities, was fiercely debated. However, the strongest pushback against the Act came from the affluent and economically strong lobby of traders of wildlife products and from the supremely resourceful hunting companies.

Under such pressures, initially, it took a while for the WLPA to be fully implemented, especially in the state of Jammu and Kashmir, where it was opposed strongly by the artisans and traders of wild furs. In areas like Andaman and Nicobar Islands, reasonable relief was granted to accommodate the traditional rights of indigenous groups. However, driven by the strong political will and the ingrained cultural ethos of the country towards conservation, the Act became operational without any major dilution in its original provisions. In the years that followed, the unsustainable and unregulated commercial exploitation of wildlife in the country gradually came to a near complete halt, attesting to the value of a timely and well-conceived piece of legislation.

But no legislation can deal with a dynamic issue for perpetuity. Though the Act, as amended from time to time, dealt with the issue of wildlife crime and had a structure to tackle it, the tiger debacle at Sariska and Panna forced the country to revisit the issue once again and ensure a more robust mechanism to stop the crime against wildlife. As a result, a dedicated multi-agency enforcement body, coordinated under a single command was established via an amendment to the WLPA in 2006. Operating under the Ministry of Environment, Forest and Climate Change (MoEFCC), the Wildlife Crime Control Bureau (WCCB) is staffed with officers from forest, police and customs department, all working under a single command. This agency has also been given the role to manage quotas and permits for legal international trade of wild animals through a mechanism established under CITES and to strengthen wildlife crime investigation and detection capabilities in the country.

Regulating International Trade

When India initiated its legal journey to protect its wildlife it was not alone in realizing the negative impacts of commercial trade on wildlife. At the global level as well, the concerns due to unprecedented growth in international trade in wildlife and their products had gained prominence, and by the late nineteenth and early twentieth century, it was already identified as the prominent driver of biodiversity loss across various regions of the world.

Beavers had already gone extinct from the northern Great Plains of Canada due to horrific large-scale fur trade to Europe. Similarly, the trappers across the world were cleaning forests of birds to supply feathers for making fashionable ladies' hats that were quite popular in the West. In fact, the fashion-led plume trade had become so lucrative that, by 1914, bird feathers fetched up to 28 times their weight in silver. The ongoing mass trapping of birds for their feathers resulted in the near extinction of few widely targeted species, such as ostriches, in their natural distribution range and certain species of targeted birds species, like the Carolina parakeet—the only parrot species in the USA—ultimately failed to survive this fashion-driven trade.

Realizing that controlling the trade-led threat to the survival of sought-after species was beyond any single country's jurisdiction, international efforts to control this cross-boundary activity gained momentum. Incidently, the initial efforts towards controlling rampant hunting and unregulated trade were led by the very beneficiaries of such businesses who, in their quest to protect their business interests in the longer run, advocated better regulations. However, soon, the focus of international efforts shifted to more sincere, desperate and conservation-driven efforts.

A major milestone in the journey of global efforts towards this came when several earlier efforts culminated in the adoption of the Resolution 5 on 'Illegal Traffic in Wildlife Species' at the Eighth General Assembly of the IUCN held in Nairobi in 1963. This resolution triggered the process of establishment of an 'international convention on regulation of export, transit and import of rare and threatened wildlife species or their skin and trophies'.[2]

In 1969, during IUCN's General Assembly meeting held in New Delhi, the first list of species proposed to be controlled was presented. Following this, in 1972, the United Nations Conference on Human Environment in Stockholm adopted Recommendation 99.3, which led to the presentation and discussion regarding a draft convention at the Plenipotentiary Conference in Washington DC in early 1973.

On 3 March 1973, 21 countries signed CITES, which came into force on 1 July 1975. The day of signing of the convention is commemorated now as the World Wildlife Day.

India's Relationship with CITES

India became one of the earliest parties to join the convention when Parliament ratified it in 1976 to become the twenty-fifth country in the world to do so. The country also played an active role in the formative phase of the convention when it hosted the third meeting of CoP in 1981, and upon election, served as the chair of the SC for three consecutive terms from 1981 to 1987. Incidentally, the existing logo of CITES was initially drawn as the logo of the third Conference of Parties (CoP) held in India in 1981. But this logo was so much appreciated by the parties that it was accepted as the official logo of the convention itself.

However, India's initial active role at CITES lost its steam in subsequent years. This is best reflected in India's failure to integrate the provisions of the convention in its national wildlife law for the longest possible time, even though it is expected from all the signatories of the convention to do so, and in spite of the repeated nudges regarding this from the CITES Secretariat.

Today, though the legal import and export of species listed in Appendix I and II of CITES require permission from the CITES Management Authority in the country, such trade falls out of the purview of the WLPA. Though such trade is partly regulated at the entrepôts, under the provisions of the Customs Act and as per various Export Import (EXIM) policies, the lack of CITES integration in the prime wildlife legislation of the country poses enforcement challenges in regulating trade in exotic species.

As a result of this legal loophole, India has recently emerged as a major destination market for certain exotic wildlife species, which are actively regulated under CITES. A recent study by TRAFFIC India shows that in the last 10 years, various consignments belonging to over 153 species of exotic animals have been seized across various entrepôts of the country. Such unregulated trade of exotic wildlife not only threatens the survival of the traded species in their natural habitats but also poses the risk of zoonotic disease outbreaks and the spread of invasive species in the country. The invasion of exotic red-eared slider turtles, one of the most widely imported turtle species, into Chandigarh's Sukhna Lake is an example of such threats.[3]

It is thus crucial to harmonize the WLPA with the provisions of CITES, as this will not only empower wildlife law enforcement agencies to stop the trade of exotic wildlife in the country but will also prevent the emergence of India as a consumer market of globally threatened species.

The Emerging Threats

Despite criticism related to certain provisions and its effective enforcement, the fact remains that the WLPA has been fairly successful in arresting the depletion of Indian species of wildlife.

The Act has also served as an inspiration for enactment of similar legislation in several countries in our immediate neighbourhood, and India may rightfully be proud of enacting such a legislation.

However, as the conditions around us are changing at a fast and unprecedented speed, the Act needs to evolve at a matching pace to address the current and emerging threats to the country's biodiversity.

Illegal wildlife trade has also entered new realms in recent times, which were earlier unimaginable, but quite in tune with the ongoing developments in the world. For example, the astronomical growth of cyberspace and the global transport infrastructure are posing newer threats to the country's biodiversity by acting as facilitators of wildlife trafficking.

In today's internet-connected world, wildlife traders sitting in the comfort of their homes can connect to an unimaginably vast pool of potential global sellers and buyers with relatively less risk of enforcement action. A mind-boggling number of internet-powered social media platforms, instant messaging apps, video-sharing websites, blogging sites, etc., facilitate this interaction between the buyers and sellers, often using the end-to-end encrypted technology, which is extremely difficult for law enforcement agencies to monitor, detect and track.

The level of ongoing transactions over cyberspace can be visualized by the fact that between 2018 and 2021, the Coalition to End Wildlife Trafficking Online, a joint coalition of three leading conservation organizations (TRAFFIC, WWF and International Fund for Animal Welfare [IFAW]), along with 47 leading internet-based companies, helped detect and remove more than 11.6 million illegal wildlife trade-related post from their platforms. This group of highly influential and extremely committed internet-based companies, however, represent a minuscule number of those operating in the vast expanse of the cyber world. Stopping similar clandestine transactions on the dark web and through one-to-one messenger service pose an even higher and more complex challenge.

Being one of the fastest-growing markets of the internet in the world, the use of cyberspace for illegal wildlife trade has started bothering the wildlife law enforcement agencies in India as well. In one study where TRAFFIC monitored eight public groups on a popular social media platform for just 40 days, it found records of sale and purchase offers for a total of 24,267 birds belonging to 43 species of prohibited or regulated species, listed under the WLPA or CITES. Another such study to track the sale of sea fans and trochus shells over cyberspace showed 139 traders openly offering to sell these prohibited marine species over 30-odd popular e-commerce platforms. The use of digital payments further eases and facilitates such internet-supported transactions.

Similarly, the rapid expansion of long-distance transportation infrastructure is also being exploited by the wildlife traffickers for rapid transport of prohibited wildlife articles across the globe. A partnership forged among various stakeholders to disrupt the use of the transport sector for wildlife trafficking, called Reducing Opportunities for Unlawful Transport of Endangered Species (ROUTES) partnership, carefully documented and demonstrated the increasing use of international shipping and airline facilities for such illicit activities. A global analysis[4] placed India amongst the top 10 countries where airlines are widely used for trafficking of prohibited wildlife products. With ever-expanding air transport infrastructure at national and international levels, this abuse of the sector is likely to increase further unless timely preventive actions are taken.

Relaxation in customs scrutiny processes in order to promote speedier trade of goods and commodities is also being exploited by the wildlife traffickers. Similarly, increasing penetration of national and international courier services also facilitates door-to-door delivery and pick-up of the traded products even to and from the remotest corners of the globe. These developments have eliminated even the need for one-to-one interaction among buyers and sellers, posing an even higher challenge for the law enforcement agencies to combat such activities.

Moving Forward

Considering the existing and emerging challenges and to continue the centrality of the WLPA in India's commitment towards protecting its wildlife, the Act will have to urgently incorporate certain eminent changes to keep pace with this fast-transforming sector. While the latest set of amendments introduced in the Parliament in late 2021 seems to address the need to harmonize the provisions of CITES and proposes other provisions to pre-empt the spread of invasive species in the natural habitat, the new-age challenges mentioned above will also need to be addressed. This might require steps to be taken even outside the purview of the WLPA, such as bringing relevant changes in the Information Technology Act, 2000, to prevent the use of the internet as facilitator of illegal wildlife trade or in the Customs Act, 1962, to prevent the use of fast-developing trading infrastructure for the trafficking of prohibited wildlife articles. Even the threat of the spread of zoonotic diseases via illegally trafficked wild animals and their products can only be minimized by employing better quarantine and hygiene regulations for animals crossing international borders and may require building capacities in animal husbandry departments to respond to this. We will also have to work to ensure foolproof traceability of the products passing even the legal trade chain to prevent the mixing of legally procured articles with the illegally procured ones.

As international trade is a transborder activity, even a national-level effort to regulate it will only yield limited success.

It can not be stopped completely unless the demand for these products remain in the international market. Hence, enhancing the capacities of border police, customs officers, airport and seaport enforcement agencies, and staff of private airlines, shipping and courier companies will have to be undertaken to orient, train and equip them to stop any such act of trafficking.

At the international level, intergovernmental organizations and multi-country collaborations will have to be strengthened and sufficiently resourced to tackle the transboundary issues. International organizations (government and non-government) working closely with national law enforcement agencies will have to play a significant role in minimizing trade-linked threats to wildlife and in reducing the demand for wildlife products in the consumer countries.

In short, only local-level conservation actions cannot ensure the complete protection to wildlife. A global effort that starts from local-level action and goes upto the highest decision-making bodies, such as CITES CoP and the United Nations, will have to come together to be undertaken to ensure a secure future for wildlife on this planet. I sincerely hope that our combined efforts lead to this.

Notes

1. Ramesh, Jairam, *Indira Gandhi: A Life in Nature*, Simon & Schuster India, 2017, p. 90.
2. *Eighth General Assembly: Proceedings*, IUCN, 1963, p. 130 https://bityl.co/DAsX. Accessed on 11 July 2022.
3. Badola, Saket, Dr, 'Tortosies and Freshwater Turtle Trade in India 2009–2019', TRAFFIC, p. 4, https://bit.ly/3Ayno0r. Accessed on 22 June 2022.
4. *From Take Off to Touch Down*, The ROUTES Partnership, January 2022, https://bit.ly/3nFV2cS. Accessed on 6 July 2022.

MANAGING WILDLIFE IN CAPTIVITY

SUDHA RAMEN[1]

After completing my tenure as divisional forest officer (DFO) at Thiruvannamalai (Tamil Nadu), I was posted as deputy director cum curator at the Arignar Anna Zoological Park (AAZP), Vandalur, in Chennai, in 2017. On joining, I was shocked to see how badly the December 2016 cyclone Vardah had affected the zoo. Many trees were uprooted and the zoo, which was once lush green, looked barren. I was worried about the animals housed there and understood the enormous responsibility on my shoulders as the zoo's new curator.

Perhaps the first in the country, the zoo dates back to the year 1855, when the state was called Madras. In 1854, Edward Green Balfour, the then director of the Central Museum (now known as the Government Museum) at Madras, persuaded the Nawab of Carnatic to donate his entire animal collection to the museum. This attracted large crowds and became the nucleus of the Madras zoo. Within a year, it had over 300 animals, including mammals, birds and reptiles. In 1861, the expanding zoo, which was under the charge of the Madras Municipal Corporation, was moved to People's Park near Chennai Central Railway Station at Park Town. It occupied one end of the 116-acre park and remained open to the public, free of cost.

In 1976, about 512 ha of forest land at Vandalur was chosen as the new site for the zoo because the previous site had become cramped and unhygienic. Thanks to the visionary planners who had a clear thought of the probable expansion of the zoo in the later years, a large area had been set aside for zoo operations. This made the AAZP the largest zoological garden not only in India but in entire Southeast Asia. In the beginning, the area was nothing more than a scrub jungle, with practically no tree cover. The zoo authorities and people from surrounding villages collected seeds of different trees from neighboring areas and planted the zoo premises with mostly native tree species. It provided an environment similar to the natural wilderness, which helped to meet the biological and psychological needs of the animals and birds. The existing landscape was utilized and different animals were exhibited in a large open-moated island-type enclosure with a simulated natural environment. The zoo, in its new premises, was officially opened to the public on 24 July 1985 by the then Chief Minister of Tamil Nadu. In 2001, 92.45 ha (228.4 acres) of land next to the park was acquired to build a rescue and rehabilitation center for confiscated and abandoned wild animals.

I thoroughly enjoyed my three-year tenure at the AAZP as its curator. Apart from everyday zoo operations, we made the existing system more efficient, introduced new facilities, and enhanced the services to animals and the visitors.

Management of Zoos

In 1991, the amended Wild Life (Protection) Act (WLPA), provided for a Central Zoo Authority (CZA) to set up, monitor and regulate captive animal facilities. The CZA then came up with the Zoo Rules, which serve as the standard by which zoos are inspected and requested to improve if certain requirements are not met. By 2002, more than 120 facilities were closed, as they did not meet these basic standards. Zoos that are permitted to operate by the CZA are called recognized zoos. They are not 'recognized' in perpetuity and are subject to inspections by experts who suggest improvements, if any, every three years. Compliance with the recommendations made by the expert members who carry out the inspection is mandatory for all recognized zoos.

The number of zoos increased from 21 at the time of Independence to 145 known zoos in 1987 and to 300 by the time the CZA put together its list. After the CZA announced that all zoos, including new ones, had to register with the government, the mushrooming growth of zoos came to a screeching halt. All zoos need to have units such as animal management, veterinary care, administration, rescue and rehabilitation, feed management, education and awareness, visitor management, visitor services, conservation breeding and disaster management for their regular and routine functioning.

Gradually, I began to understand how these different units functioned and how crucial they were for the overall zoo management. The important factor here is that coordination and effective communication between these units ensure proper management of the plethora of activities that takes place in a zoo. Overseeing and coordinating these activities are major duties of a zoo manager. Zoos never have a holiday—they may be closed to the visitors on one particular day in a week for management purposes, but the units that take care of the feed supply, animal house maintenance and veterinary care continue to work round the year. The zoo staff does not have the privilege to avail leave on public holidays or festivals, as their work is an essential service to all the animals in the zoo. Not many would be aware of this fact, but my tenure at the zoo required me to be present every day of the year—including weekends, holidays such as Diwali, Pongal, Christmas, New Year, Independence Day, etc. One can easily guess the reason behind this—a holiday would call for many to plan a visit to the zoo. So, all your holidays are our working days, and I thoroughly enjoyed working on those days. Seeing the happy faces of people with their families and friends made me content, and I felt happy to work in such an institution.

Animal Management

Animals in the zoo being the primary stakeholder of the zoo, I would start my day by going around the zoo and visiting important animal enclosures. Slowly, I learnt that interacting with the animal keepers was important, as they are the primary source of information with respect to the status of the animal. For each animal that they oversee, animal keepers maintain a record of all their observations, such as feed quality, animal cages, squeeze cages, enclosure yards and animal mating, and about the young ones, if any. I would spend about two to three hours a day visiting various animal enclosures and interacting with the staff on the ground. This helped me immensely to understand each animal, their needs and the grievances of the zoo staff. Decision-making became easy, as I was aware of the ground situation.

Animal Exchange

Animal exchange is a standard practice wherein the surplus and single-sexed animals are exchanged between the zoos to balance their sex ratios and sustain the zoo's population. Inbreeding among the zoo population is an important problem, which results in depression of genetic vigour. Hence, new bloodlines are regularly required.

During my tenure, we were able to carry out the animal exchange programme with various zoos in the country, including the Thiruvananthapuram Zoo, the Pilikula Biological Park, the Bannerghatta Zoo, the Mysuru Zoo, the Nehru Zoological Park in Hyderabad, the Madras Crocodile Bank Trust (MCBT) and Centre for Herpetology, the Nandankanan Zoological Park, the Patna Zoo, the Udaipur Zoo, and many more. Building a good network in the zoo community helps in the exchange of information about animal collections, best practices, innovations, etc. It also helps to carry out animal exchange programmes. I fondly remember the animal exchange with the zoos in Patna and Hyderabad, which helped us get two rhinoceros to Tamil Nadu after 30 long years.

Ramu and Rhine Come to the AAZP

In 2014, the state government desired the AAZP to possess the great Indian one-horned rhinoceros. This was realized only in 2019. Attempts were made to identify zoos housing rhinoceros for a potential animal exchange programme with them. A young female rhinoceros was identified at the Sanjay Gandhi Biological Park in Patna, and a surplus male was located at the Nehru Zoological Park in Hyderabad. Discussions were held, and exchange agreements were reached. The CZA was approached for formal permission for the exchange.

Once CZA approval came through, a travel plan for the animals was charted for the exchange. A team, including a veterinarian, biologist and forest staff, visited the Nehru Zoological Park and stayed there for a few days to identify and observe the selected rhinoceros named Ramu. The animal was trained for two days to familiarize him with the crate in which it would complete his journey.

Ramu was the first rhinoceros to reach the AAZP. The zoo team was happy, excited and ready to receive him with a special feed. We ensured that his animal house was comfortable and there were adequate layers of safety. Ramu was successfully removed from the crate and was monitored round the clock till the time he felt at home in his new enclosure.

Greater care and caution during travel and transport of the animals were called for, since the female rhinoceros from Patna was to travel some 2,000 km, crossing six different states. The forest officials and the zoo's staff en route were informed about this transit with a request to render all possible assistance in case of any emergency. Little Rhine reached the AAZP after a two-day-long road journey and was quarantined for a few days. She was on watch round the clock during this period. We ensured that Ramu and Rhine were kept in isolation till the time they adjusted to each other's presence. This was planned in advance, and their enclosures were created to mimic their natural habitat, with waterbodies and slushy soil. A sprinkler shower was installed for them in their animal yard. Slowly, they started to feel at home in their new enclosures, and the animal keeper also successfully established a good relationship with both Ramu and Rhine.

The Birth of Black Tigers

Any animal birth in a zoo is a matter of celebration, more so if it happens to be a tiger. I was happy and excited on 9 January 2019 when animal keeper Chelliah called to inform us that our white tigress, Namrutha, had given birth to one male and two female cubs. She had mated with Nagula, a Bengal tiger from a white mother. On visiting the animal enclosure to ensure that the arrangements were in place to prevent visitors from disturbing the mother and cubs, I was informed by the animal keeper that out of the three, two cubs had unusually dark stripes. It turned out to be a case of melanism. A tiger with broader black stripes is a rare colour variant but is not a distinct species. Such 'black' tigers exhibit pseudomelanism, in which thick stripes are formed close together with the tawny background barely visible between the stripes. The other cub was white, just like her mother. Within months, these three little ones grew up into handsome and bold subadults.

Beating the Summer Heat

Summer temperatures in Chennai can be daunting for anyone, especially wild animals from foreign locales. Extreme temperatures can cause significant stress to them. An innovative summer management plan is prepared in advance for all the zoo mammals, birds and reptiles. Arrangements of sufficient shade and adequate water are a priority. Large herbivores are provided with water showers and sprinklers. Bird enclosures are usually covered with gunny bags that are sprayed with cool water during the hot hours of the day. Carnivores are provided with frozen meat, while primates and bears are given frozen fruits and ice cubes. These small interventions also help break their daily routine, and animals begin to excitedly explore when a new kind of feed is given to them differently.

Zoo e-Eye

Another innovation during my tenure at the zoo was the Zoo e-Eye. About 150 surveillance cameras were strategically placed to monitor the health and safety of the animals and for effective crowd control and zoo security.

Surveillance cameras made it easy for staff to ensure that visitors did not tease or misbehave with animals and that the latter were safe and secure in their respective enclosures. Timely veterinary care also became possible through Zoo e-Eye, which helped us provide stress-free monitoring of sick animals, reduce the animal death rate and improve neonatal care.

A dedicated control room operating round the clock was established, making AAZP a pioneer in the field of 'digital' zoo management.

Veterinary Care

The veterinary unit of a zoo is as critical as the heart in the human body. As the curator, I was responsible for ensuring periodic animal health checks at the zoo. We maintained a health card for each in the zoo that was updated regularly after check-ups. The zoo hospital had three veterinary doctors and two lab assistants. Periodic health evaluation and biometrics of the animals were carried out to determine growth rate, which includes factors like intercanine length, tail length, foot circumference, etc. These references act as standards and help estimate the age of animals of unknown origins.

The veterinary hospital at the AAZP is fully equipped with essential medical and surgical equipment. A lab for sample analysis was also established and is operational at the zoo. Our working team, which included veterinary doctors, biologists and the range officers, met every day to share updates about the daily happenings at the animal houses. Any decision regarding the animals would only be taken after discussion and deliberation within the working team; this way, we would have an opportunity to hear various perspectives from each team member. We discussed feed quality, animal keeping, enclosure enrichments, animal exchange, captive breeding, animal health and many more issues related to animal management. Any important decisions would be made only after discussing with the zoo Director. During one such discussion, the veterinarians expressed the need for advanced medical devices that would help in early diagnosis and treatment. We decided to procure a portable ultrasound scanner and X-ray unit. These two machines have been put to good use and have simplified the process of tranquilizing large animals and moving them to the hospital for scanning and monitoring after the reversal. With the high-end, totally mobile and portable digital radiography unit, Vandalur became the first zoo in the country to use the same. As the entire unit can be operated with inbuilt battery backup, it can be used in any animal enclosure or field-level operations for rapid diagnosis of conditions that demand radiography.

Saving a Day-Old Tiger Cub

In August 2018, early one dawn, the tigress Uthra gave birth to two cubs, a male and a female. The mother and cubs were continuously monitored through remote surveillance cameras (Zoo e-Eye) and we noticed that while the cubs did attempt to suckle for the colostrum, the mother did not cooperate much. This continued for another 24 hours, but there was no improvement in the situation, and soon, the mother began to push them away. The cubs were retrieved immediately, and it was decided that they would be hand-reared. They were then brought to the intensive neonatal care centre at the zoo veterinary hospital.

The cubs were dehydrated and had poor to no suckling reflexes. We soon lost the female cub despite continued rehydration and oxygen therapy efforts. The male cub was then intubated, and a milk replacement was provided, but he resisted feeding through the bottle. A total quantity of 20 per cent of body weight was calculated, and feed was divided into eight to 10 parts at intervals of one to three hours. Meconium was excreted within 24 hours after we fed him the first batch of milk replacement. He opened his eyes on the eleventh day and began inspecting his environment inquisitively. As milk replacer alone could induce constipation, diluted goat milk was also added to his diet, which soon gave him some relief. Till he was one month old, the cub was handled with great care and fed only by the veterinarians with high precaution. His diet management protocol was followed in earnest, and his growth rate was quite good. He was dewormed after 30 days and vaccinated on the sixtieth day.

On the fortieth day, he began to consume chicken soup via feeding bottle. Twenty days after that, we began his transition to solid food with great care and struggle, and gave him cooked and minced meat. He could eat and digest chopped-up pieces of meat from the seventieth day. When he turned four months old, he began to eat fresh meat chunks with bones. At about six months, he was released into the animal enclosure under our watchful eye. Today, he is a handsome adult male tiger in the zoo.

Covid Times

During the Covid-19 pandemic in 2020, a designated protocol was developed for the zoo. Our main concern was the sanitization of animal feed. While the vegetable feed could be easily sanitized in a potassium permanganate ($KMnO_4$) solution and hot water, the real challenge was sanitizing the meat. The veterinary doctors and the range forest officers visited the Chennai corporation slaughterhouse to ensure that Covid protocols were scrupulously followed there to rule out the chances of the viral load spreading through the meat. However, as the meat gets handled by many human hands before reaching the zoo feed store, it was planned to develop a system of irradiation at the zoo feed store. A (UV) irradiation chamber was created for meat disinfection. UV-C rays can inactivate all microorganisms, including viruses on the surface of the meat, rendering it safe as well as without the problem of residual odour or taste, that are the side effects of surface disinfection with chlorine or $KMnO_4$. This was carried out on the suggestion of experts from Tamil Nadu Veterinary and Animal Sciences University (TANUVAS).

Rescue and Rehabilitation

A Rescue and Rehabilitation Centre was raised at the Chennai zoo in 2000 to accommodate 40 lions and 20 tigers. This was in the wake of the ban imposed on the exhibition of animals in the circus. Apart from these animals, rescued animals from regions around the zoo were also brought to the zoo veterinary hospital for emergency treatment. In addition, wild animals confiscated by the Wildlife Crime Control Bureau (WCCB), and the Customs Department are received and maintained in the hospital transit animal facilities till the time they are ready to be released back into the wild.

During my tenure at the AAZP, the zoo officials' joint endeavour with animal rescue and rehabilitation to curb the illegal wildlife trade was carried out with the Directorate of Revenue Intelligence, WCCB, and the Advanced Institute for Wildlife Conservation. Many indigenous and exotic animals, victims of the illegal wildlife trade, were seized and rehabilitated at the AAZP. This unit of animal rescue and rehabilitation remains isolated from the core zone of the zoo to ensure that these animals do not come in contact with the zoo animals. It was also ensured that the staff dealing with the rescued animals did not interact with the zoo animals.

One day, I got a call from the customs office informing me about the seizure of a leopard cub from the baggage of a passenger who had landed in Chennai from one of the Southeast Asian countries. A veterinary doctor along with zoo staff rushed to the airport in a wildlife ambulance. The cub was in a dehydrated state and was stressed. After first aid, the doctor felt the cub needed more medical attention and so it was brought to the zoo veterinary hospital. Following standard operating protocol, the cub was stabilized and essential supplements were given. The cub was determined to be around four months old; therefore, it was shifted to the neonatal care unit and closely monitored. It recovered well in a few days and continued to be housed in an isolated room at the zoo veterinary unit, pending legal proceedings in the court of law.

We did not stop just at the recovery of animals in our charge at the rescue centre but took action to rehabilitate the indigenous animals in the wild with the permission of the Chief Wildlife Warden (CWLW). These have included about 2,000 star tortoises, many spotted deer, reticulated pythons, night herons, painted storks, pond herons and a few other birds.

Education and Awareness

Zoo education is an important aspect of zoo management and my personal favourite. When I joined the zoo, I was informed that the AAZP had started a 'Zoo School' in 1998, with a mission to educate the public about the importance of living in harmony with nature and to promote wildlife conservation. Unfortunately, the activities of the zoo school had remained confined within the zoo premises and hence had not received much visibility amongst the people at large. Realizing the huge potential of the concept of 'Zoo School', we began to explore multiple ventures like lecture series, field-based education sessions, online sessions, awareness and educational events and contests to be conducted throughout the year.

Zoo outreach programmes were also conducted in rural, suburban and distant areas. Subject matter experts were involved, and about 2,000 government schools in rural areas were covered.

Zoo Ambassador

A new programme called Zoo Ambassador was started in April 2018. It soon became popular amongst the children in Chennai city. It was conducted as summer (April and May) and winter (December) camps. During these, the experts would lead children on walks around the zoo and speak on topics related to wildlife conservation, zoo, mammals, reptiles, birds and butterflies.

This four-day programme was divided into a day each for mammals, reptiles, birds and butterflies. The students were provided with a kit that included a bag, an activity book, a descriptive book, a notepad, a pen and a cap. Each of these sessions was handled by zoo biologists, veterinary doctors and subject experts from various reputed institutions and organizations, such as TANUVAS, Salim Ali Centre for Ornithology and Natural History (SACON) (Coimbatore), Snake Park, MCBT, and the like. On successfully completing the programme, the participating children received a certificate and the title of 'Zoo Ambassadors of Vandalur Zoo.' They also got a zoo passport for 10 free visits a year, and a free subscription to the zoo newsletter and a separate column in the newsletter for them to contribute either an article or a painting.

It was envisioned that the Zoo Ambassadors would share their knowledge and spread the message of conservation with family and friends. This programme became so successful that what initially started as a summer camp was repeated as a winter camp and later was also extended as a virtual camp for children from other states. During the Covid-19 lockdown, the virtual camp received many registrations—some even from different corners of the globe. Since 2018, we at the zoo have given away some 10,000 Zoo Ambassador certificates. My association with this programme has given me great satisfaction and happiness.

Soon our outreach expectations were exceeded, and we began to receive requests from parents and other adults. This led us to the idea of conducting special themed workshops run by professional field experts. Well-attended workshops on birds and bird identification, wildlife photography, butterflies, reptiles, etc., have since been conducted at the Zoo School.

Zoo Club

Another activity started under the Zoo School initiative is the Zoo Club. This encourages voluntary service during weekends and holidays by schoolchildren and college students or corporate and other professionals in zoo activities like cleaning the campus, assisting zoo visitors, etc.

Live Streaming of the Exhibits

The AAZP houses more than 2,400 animals of nearly 180 species. The zoo has an annual visitor footfall of about 20 lakh, of which more than 90 per cent are from Chennai and nearby places. So, to encourage anyone with an internet connection to view exhibits at the zoo, live streaming of the most popular animals through the zoo website (www.aazp.in) was planned. To make this facility operational, preparatory activities like a feasibility study, identification of popular exhibits, laying of optical fibre cable from the exhibit to the central server connected to the zoo website and placing of high definition cameras at the identified animal yards were carried out.

Presently, 15 animal exhibits are being live-streamed. These include gaur, lion-tailed macaque, white and Bengal tigers, lion, leopard, sloth bear, crocodile, hornbill, elephant, hippopotamus, chimpanzee and the Nilgiri langur.

Live streaming through cameras helps in showcasing the animal collection and the animal exhibits. It also helps in promoting zoo activities to people across the world. The animals can be watched at close quarters, and people become more appreciative of their behaviour. Social media has helped spread the message of live streaming of animals at the AAZP, and many people have started to watch the zoo animals remotely. Since its inception in 2018, there have been around five crore (50 million) page views on the zoo website till 2021.

Animal Adoption

Many zoos have animal 'adoption' programmes. But few people are aware of this and only a few people approach the zoo management to get details. We knew that animal adoption has a huge potential to raise funds for animals and also to spread the message of conservation. By adopting zoo animals, the contributors gain a feeling of participating in the conservation of that animal species and also help to spread a message to others about this. Knowing this, we made the whole process of animal adoption online. Anyone from any part of the world can choose the animal of their interest and contribute to that particular animal's welfare. We also added this feature to the AAZP mobile application. All the contributions go directly towards the cost of caring for the adopted animals. The publicity and awareness made for this helped the zoo receive a good response from people, including famous Tamil movie actors like Sivakarthikeyan and Vijay Sethupathi.

Visitor Management and Services

The AAZP gets some 20 lakh visitors every year, and on holidays and special occasions, such as Pongal festival, the footfall is much higher than the daily average. Records show that more than one lakh people visit the zoo over three days during Pongal.[2] So, the zoo management start preparing for the increase in the volume of visitors well in advance. These preparations include both the management of visitor numbers and the provision of essential facilities for them.

The challenge is enormous, and Zoo e-Eye has effectively assisted the management in handling a footfall of 50,000 in a single day. Zoo e-Eye is not just to keep an eye on the visitors through CCTV cameras but it also has a centralized public address system attached to it. This has been found useful in managing large footfalls and also dealing with any sort of emergency.

During occasions like Pongal, special arrangements are made for visitors, including additional parking facilities, free shuttle service, 300 special buses to the zoo, extra ticket counters, frisking of visitors to check for liquor, sugarcane, weapons or single-use plastics; hand tagging of children under five years; wheelchair services for senior citizens and differently abled; additional purified drinking water and toilet facilities; extra stalls for eateries; flying squad for rescue and special help desks and medical aid desk to attend to any emergency care provided by the zoo management. A large number of police officers and uniformed forest staff are deputed along with National Cadet Corps (NCC) and National Service Scheme (NSS) volunteers.

We introduced a digital payment facility for visitors through online ticketing, point of sale machines and mobile application. The innovative *Vandalur Zoo* mobile application has become very popular with visitors. It allows the user to book a ticket for a zoo visit and provides a zoo map for navigation, and animal information section with text and voice; 4-D animations of animals; an animal live streaming facility; animal adoption and a section on zoo events and games.

Conservation Breeding

Conservation breeding programme in zoos involves ex situ breeding and husbandry of species threatened in the wild due to habitat loss, fragmentation, poaching, illegal trade, climate change, etc. This is to conserve species' genetic diversity and restock or reintroduce them as self-sustaining populations in their natural habitat.

The CZA has identified the AAZP as a 'coordinating zoo' for the conservation breeding of lion-tailed macaque and Nilgiri langur. For this purpose, the zoo has created dry-moated enclosures for them away from the visitor area, with customized enrichments similar to their natural habitat. The successful lion-tailed macaque conservation breeding programme at the AAZP began in 2002, with 12 (seven females and five males) animals as the founder population. Similarly, Nilgiri langur breeding has also been successful at the AAZP.

Disaster Management

Chennai, a coastal city on the nation's eastern coast, experiences tropical cyclones from time to time. In 2016, the zoo lost close to 50 per cent of its tree cover due to the Vardah cyclone. Fortunately, there was no animal death, as the zoo management had planned well in advance to secure the animals soon after the meteorological alert. The following year, the city faced severe drought and there was an acute water shortage all over. The zoo management, too, faced serious difficulties in meeting the zoo's water needs.

Restoration of Otteri Lake

The AAZP has a rain-fed 18-acre-large lake called Otteri. Every winter, it used to attract thousands of migratory birds, but over time, it had silted and almost dried during the summer drought of 2017. The lake had not received enough rain in the past two to three years. So, we decided to do something about it. Bunds and weirs were strengthened, existing percolation ponds were desilted and new ones were created. Efforts were made to maximize the collection and storage of rainwater in the lake and recharge the park's groundwater. After restoration, the lake's storage capacity has increased, and the zoo's water problem has been resolved.

The AAZP Becomes an Institutional Member of the World Association of Zoos and Aquariums (WAZA)

WAZA is a global organization of the world zoos and aquarium community, and becoming a member of this association is an honour and a dream come true for many zoos. The AAZP, thanks to its track record in animal management and allied zoo activities, was accepted as an institutional member of WAZA on 8 September 2019. A proud moment for us all at the AAZP!

Notes

1. The author is grateful to the Tamil Nadu Forest Department and the AAZP Zoo Directors over the period 2017 to 2020—Thiru. S. Yuvaraj, Indian Forest Service (IFS); Thiru. Yogesh Singh, IFS; Thiru. Debasia Jana, IFS for their support and guidance to the

author. She owes thanks to the team of the Assistant Director, forest range officers, veterinarians, biologists, forest staff and animal keepers who continue to keep up the good work at the zoo.

2. 'Zoo, Children's Park See Record Number of Visitors', *The Hindu*, 18 January 2020, https://bit.ly/3yhEInC. Accessed on 4 July 2022.

UNRAVELLING THE UNKNOWN: RESEARCHING CHAUSINGHA IN THE WILD

KOUSTUBH SHARMA

'You won't even get to see it, how do you think you will do a PhD on it?' asked a senior officer when I enthusiastically told him about joining the Bombay Natural History Society (BNHS) for a project to study the ecology of the four-horned antelope or as it is better known in India, the chausingha—the only wild species in the world with two distinct pair of horns. He wasn't entirely wrong, for despite their uniqueness, little work had ever been done on the chausingha, making it one of the least studied antelopes of India, listed as data deficient by International Union for Conservation of Nature (IUCN) in their Red List.

It started years ago when I visited Churna village in the Bori Wildlife Sanctuary of Madhya Pradesh at the impressionable age of 15. Little did I know then that the three days spent in the pristine forest would change the course of my life. I was among the lucky few who attended a nature camp organized by a bunch of enthusiastic forest officers. It must have taken some commitment and effort on the part of forest officers, such as Giridhar Kinhal and Manoj Misra, to come together and part with their knowledge and privilege of spending time in the remotest parts of the forests of India with school kids. They probably didn't fathom, at that moment, the longevity of the impact they were going to have on several impressionable students; for at least three of us, who attended these nature camps made a career in ecology later.

Birding in Bhopal

Bhopal, the capital of Madhya Pradesh, has always been a green city. It offers immense opportunities to nurture one's interest in observing wildlife, especially birds. Subsequently, I got involved in a small study commissioned by the Bhoj Wetland Project, which was overhauling the lake systems of the city with support from the Japan Bank for International Cooperation (JBIC). The study aimed to develop a bird checklist and estimate their seasonal abundance, especially around Bhopal's upper lake. The small honorarium I received was the best-earned pocket money I could get while doing my master's in physics. Well, why physics, you ask? Since I enjoyed the whys and hows of things, and based on my limited exposure to options, I had hoped that training in at least one subject could possibly help me get through competitive exams that could subsequently allow me to work in India's forests. The study of birds required year-round observations in certain parts of the upper lake of Bhopal. With the help of two friends, I managed to build a formidable checklist and observed counts. The study helped the upper lake of Bhopal to be declared a Ramsar site and an Important Bird Area (IBA) by International Bird Conservation Network.

The reports I prepared from this study needed to be vetted by experts in the field, which is when I was introduced to India's oldest conservation organization, the BNHS. My background in physics was only as good as making good observations in this new role. It took several inputs and multiple rounds of edits from the then director of BNHS, Dr Asad Rahmani, to derive ecological meaning from our observations. One of the by-products of this work was a small software that I wrote in

Visual Basic (the popular object-oriented programming language back then) to identify birds. It was before smartphones were even invented and the internet was a luxury, where dial-up connections via phone lines were the only means to connect to the World Wide Web. I used to find it extremely frustrating to identify birds when I started birdwatching because most books arranged them taxonomically, and a starter would rarely know how to differentiate an egret from a crane. This egged me to develop something that could help people identify birds based on observed features. The software had a graphical user interface, allowing users to enter details about a bird they might have just seen using sketches I drew on paper and scanned to be displayed on drop-down menus. One could use the software to search for the bird, based on any number of known characteristics. The database had about 250 birds seen in Bhopal. Additionally, it showed the species' known distribution in Bhopal through a database of hand-drawn maps of the city.

These two years not only taught me the basic nuances of ecology but also improved my skills in writing scientific reports. This was also the first time I encountered incidences of poaching of birds and the difference it meant for the wildlife to be inside and outside protected areas (PAs). Fortunately, the Wild Life (Protection) Act, (WLPA), 1972, provides protection to all wildlife irrespective of whether they are inside or outside designated PAs, but the level of protection wildlife enjoys outside is often dismal. Regular write-ups in local newspapers, interactions with students from other schools in Bhopal and a few workshops in partnership with the forest department and BNHS widened the constituency of the birds of Bhopal. A few sightings of more than 100 sarus cranes on the banks of the upper lake put it on the global birding map and made for catchy news articles.

The BNHS Beckons

A few months after the completion of the bird study, I received an interview call from BNHS to study the chausingha, an animal I had barely even heard about, let alone seeing it. The Department of Science and Technology (DST), Government of India (GoI), had funded a project to the BNHS to study the ecology and distribution of chausingha, a species found only in India and Nepal. I had to pinch myself a few times for the possibility of working with BNHS—to observe wildlife for a living—was like a dream come true. Among the three who interviewed me, one had some idea about my work on the birds of Bhopal and was hopeful that I might be able to get the desired results. One was too thrilled about my changing gears from physics, and one dismissed me for being too naïve to conduct field research, let alone pursue a PhD. Fortunately, the rules had it clear that as long as I had a master's degree in science, it was my guide's headache to see if I was worth investing a few years in for a PhD. For reasons best known to him, Dr Rahmani thought I was probably worth the headache, but not before he tested my skills and abilities for one full year in the field. As luck would have it, I got offered the position of a research analyst and off I was on an uncharted path to try and decode the mysteries of the chausingha. Not often does one get so lucky to be offered the opportunity to earn from a hobby, and here I was, possibly looking at a few years in the forest, doing just that.

Travails and Pleasures

It started with several hours in one of India's finest libraries at the BNHS, with precious books from as early as the nineteenth century, to get a basic idea about what I was up against. A small animal that weighs approximately 20 kg, it preferred forested habitats, unlike other antelopes in India, and was often recorded close to water. But it was so difficult to see and observe in the natural setting that there was virtually no study on it other than a few anecdotal observations and generic taxonomic details. It was surprising that a species so intriguing, which the taxonomists had given it the scientific name *Tetracerus quadricornis* (four horns in Greek and Latin, respectively) had invoked little interest in field biologists. Or was it that it was so elusive that it could never be studied? Which means I had signed up for a project destined for failure. Clearly, the animal was rare enough for the GoI to have listed it in Schedule I of the WLPA, putting it in the same league as the tiger, snow leopard and rhinoceros.

Literature provided no information whatsoever about what it ate, other than that it was a herbivore. There was little information about whether it was diurnal or nocturnal. I reached out to scientists working in other parts of the country in landscapes that had reported the chausingha, but they were too protective of their data to share even the most generic details, such as whether it is seen during the day or night. There were few zoos that had the chausingha, and Bhopal's Van Vihar was one of them. Through proper permissions taken from the forest department, I was able to set up cafeteria experiments to figure out what the chausingha ate when given equal access to food items and if they spent more time active during the day or the night in a zoo setting. Despite all the criticism they receive, zoos do serve an important function in education, awareness and scientific investigation as long as animals are appropriately kept with sufficient environmental enrichment.

After the necessary literature review and preparing a tentative workplan (tentative because we were headed into unknown territory, given nobody had ever studied this animal before), Dr Rahmani and I decided that among all places we knew of, Panna Tiger Reserve in Madhya Pradesh offered the best possible opportunity to study the chausingha. It was a tropical dry deciduous forest, and an initial review through a snail-mail survey indicated that the chausingha seemed to be predominantly seen in such forest types. What I was embarking upon was more like a shift of my base from the cosy comfort of home in urban Bhopal to the rural setting of Panna's outskirts, where my workplace for the next several years would be the wilderness of a tiger reserve rather than an institutional building. My work timings would be from sunrise to sunset, and weekends would mean little. Where entertainment would mean sitting around a bonfire with forest guards and neighbours from the village; and any long-distance communication contingent on the functionality of the local public call office (PCO). I was planning on a life with nature as my classroom, forest guards and village folk as my teachers and trunkloads of printouts, books and photocopies as my reading material. To say the least, I was super excited, but for a glitch that I did not have a permit yet; a permit to live and work in a tiger reserve and national park, enjoying the strictest of the protection among all forest habitats in India. This is where my familiarity with the system and officials, and my experience of working in Bhopal proved helpful. With a detailed proposal in hand, I made a presentation to the then CWLW, Madhya Pradesh, A.P. Dwivedi, who seemed thrilled about the idea of someone wanting to study the chausingha but was also worried for me. He asked the Field Director (FD), Panna Tiger Reserve, to help me with my research work. In return, I was to provide periodic updates and support to the administration.

Among many, one of the primary methods proposed in the project document was to study the animal using radio telemetry, a method that requires physical capture followed by deploying a collar on the animal and systematic tracking over several months thereafter. Although many consider radio telemetry an invasive method, it is far less intrusive, as once collared, the animal's location and activities can be estimated from several kilometres away without causing any disturbance. While the presentation, the goodwill from previous work and the support of a reputed principal investigator got me the permit to live and start my study in Panna Tiger Reserve, the permit to put a collar on the animal (chausingha) was still not available. In the absence of clear guidelines separating handling animals for research from hunting, the process for physically restraining animals to deploy them with radio tags required the same level of paperwork and procedural hoops to jump through as it would have required to hunt it. Any attempt to physically handle a Schedule I species required a clearance from both the central and state governments. With chausingha in Schedule I, our proposal had to go through several rounds of review before one could get the permit to collar it. Given the uncertainties involved, we decided to start fieldwork and use telemetry as and when permission came through.

I Reach Panna

In November 2002, equipped with a laptop with a total of 4GB of hard drive space, a new pair of binoculars, a plant press, a ton of reading material, my own camera and a 4x4 vehicle, I was on my way to Panna Tiger Reserve. The drive for Mumbai to Panna took three days. While I had been instructed to avoid driving at night for safety reasons, even during the day, the crater-filled roads in Madhya Pradesh made driving a nightmare.

One of the best things about my spending the next few years in Panna Tiger Reserve was the opportunity to learn ecology from a stellar scientist, Dr Raghu Chundawat, who was studying tigers there. As part of his work, Dr Chundawat was collaring tigers and their primary prey (sambar and chital) to understand why tigers were declining at a fast rate from the tropical dry deciduous forests, which constituted 40 per cent of the available tiger habitat in the country. Soon after I arrived in Panna, I visited Dr Chundawat and his partner Joanna Van Gruisen, who is a renowned photographer and natural historian. Even though my physics background and its potential value to the science of studying wildlife intrigued Dr Chundawat, it didn't take long for him to realize that I lacked a formal education in biological sciences; for the next several months, I would spend most of my mornings and evenings trying to understand the forest and its wildlife, and to observe the chausingha wherever I would get to see one. I would spend hours reading about specific aspects of ecology before that one-hour meeting with Dr Chundawat, only to be dismissed in half an hour with notes on what else I needed to study. As gruelling as those meetings seemed then, it was most generous of Raghu and Joanna to open their excellent library of some of the finest books on field research and ecology for me to borrow and read. I still remember being red-faced when, in my enthusiasm for reading them cover to cover, I ended up damaging the edges of some of those expensive books, only to be graciously forgiven by the duo. In due course of time, I, too, was able to show off my skills in data management, statistics and mathematical modelling to them. Although valuable, mathematics can be hard work for a field biologist; however it came naturally to me, given my physics background. This ultimately led to a fascinating collaboration and useful synergy between the two ecological projects, one on tigers and the other on chausingha.

My very first chausingha sighting was a female that was tiptoeing on the forest road across a bend, walking away as we were driving in. She looked at us over her shoulder as we stopped about 40 metres away and hopped into the thick grass before disappearing. Little did I know that this would be the first of 705 sightings and more than 3,000 minutes of observations of my subject, the chausingha, that would accumulate over the next five years. A dainty-looking animal with a golden coat, it has big black eyes and a curved silhouette. Adult males have two distinct pair of horns; in some, the front pair grows almost as long as the rear one. Females don't sport horns and often give birth to two fawns.

Genetically, the chausingha is a close relative of the nilgai, and both belong to the Boselaphini tribe of antelopes, considered the ancestor of modern ungulates and livestock. They have small stomachs, which is why, unlike many larger ungulates, they depend more on quality than quantity of feed. It makes them finicky eaters and is most likely why they are typically solitary. They forage on a high-protein diet such as fruits, flowers and fresh leaves, but such a diet is always on a premium in a forest to be shared with herd members, and moreover, a tree can only provide these for short durations. That explains why the chausingha was more likely to be seen in areas with high tree diversity. It was these different species of trees that together provided a constant supply of preferred food to the chausingha by fruiting and flowering at different times of the year. So much so that we were able to almost predict which tree to look under when out in the field looking for a chausingha. Tendu, achar, semal, harsingar, mahua, palash, bhidara and so on, would often cue the possibility of sighting a chausingha for observation, depending on which one of them was blooming at that point in time.

The chausingha would often repeatedly defecate at the same spot, thus making heaps of dung known as middens. These middens were not exclusive to chausingha, but several of them were shared by nilgai and chinkara, the other two antelopes found in Panna Tiger Reserve. When foraging or moving about at ease, they would often bend their head and press it against a twig or grass blade, letting it poke through their periorbital glands situated right in front of their eyes. Such markings, along with the middens, seemed to be how this otherwise solitary and quiet species would communicate with others of its kin. On rare occasions, we would hear the chausingha making an alarm call, but that was only when one was in direct line of sight of a predator. These calls were distinctly different from those of other ungulates, such as the chital, nilgai or sambar, that one often hears in the forests. They could, at best, be defined as a husky, nasal cough or a 'pronk'.

Nothing is more educating than learning while walking in the forest. On one such walk through the thickets in the heart of Panna, I heard a distinct sound that was like the chausingha's alarm call but distinct in an inexplicable way. It was somewhat like the sound you would hear if a goat herd walked past you. I froze, trying to locate the direction from which I heard the call, and a few seconds later, I spotted a female chausingha trotting perpendicular to us. We waited a few seconds longer and heard the call again. It was confusing because never before had a chausingha made an alarm call on spotting us humans. Either there was a predator she was seeing and we weren't or something else was going on. We moved carefully without making much sound and suddenly noticed something hidden amidst the grasses. A tiny baby chausingha was curled up in the thick understorey. We realized that the mother was probably trying to draw our attention towards her or communicating with her fawn, but in either case, she was clearly distressed, as we had accidentally walked too close to her fawn. We carefully retreated without making any hasty moves to avoid startling the little fawn. Once at a safe distance, we watched the fawn tiptoe clumsily to her mother, and both vanished into the thickets. It is not uncommon for local people to bring a chausingha fawn to the forest department, claiming that it had followed the herd of goats on their way back from some forest patch where the goats went grazing. The frequency with which this happens suggests that the chausingha fawns probably get confused by the call of goats and end up following them to the settlements by mistake. Presumably, that's an entirely different level of threat that unregulated livestock grazing in forests cause to already vulnerable species.

Findings and Learnings

As a solitary animal, the chausingha predominantly relies on stealth to survive predators. During one of the road transects, I rolled my eyes at my field assistant for calling 'chausingha' in a hushed voice when all I could see was a leopard walking on the road. It was only when he pointed towards a bush about 6 metres from the road that I noticed a chausingha frozen like a statue while a full-grown leopard walked by. The chausingha remained frozen until the leopard was about 50 metres away. Then, it took a few prominent bounds away from the path, followed by a few metres of stealthy trotting in the grass to vanish out of sight. This strategy of preferring stealth over fleeing requires the chausingha to be inconspicuous. On the other hand, animals need means to display their sexual fitness in order to avoid avoidable fights and find mates. Unlike other ungulates that use charismatic horns, prominent colours and other visible tactics to show off their fitness, the chausingha seems to have evolved to use its additional pair of horns for the same. The two distinct pairs of horns seemingly allow the male chausingha to show off their fitness without compromising its ability to evade predators. The fact that on most occasions, when in a pair, a female was more likely to be with a male with a longer second pair of horns made us hypothesize the purpose of four horns.

Over the years spent in Panna Tiger Reserve, I was able to decipher much of the chausingha's ecology and behaviour despite being unable to track them with radio telemetry. I did receive the permit to collar the chausingha but only in the third year of my research work. The delay in getting permission to collar the chausingha led to some frustration, but we were pleased that we did not depend on it solely. With limited funds left by then, we could only make a single failed effort at capturing the animal. Our inability to capture a single animal on the maiden expedition led us to drop the idea of trying to collar the animal altogether. It restricted what we could have learnt about the animal. We still do not have many answers to several questions such as how big their home ranges are, how often they interact with each other, how often they give birth, if they are territorial, and if they are polygamous, polyandrous or monogamous. Answers to such questions can help improve the management practices for the conservation of lesser-known yet important species such as the chausingha. It is noteworthy that many forest habitats in India are managed for tigers under the assumption that conservation of tigers can lead to the conservation of all other species lower down the order. However, in the absence of comprehensive data about poorly studied species, tiger conservation is often limited to practices that aim to improve water availability, create grassland-forest ecotones, provide inviolate spaces by translocating human populations and enhance single prey populations such as chital.

The five years I spent in Majhgawan, a small village situated at the edge of the Panna Tiger Reserve, not only helped me learn ecology, it opened my eyes to the challenges our less-provided-for fellow humans face. I can never forget how my neighbour, Mangu, lost his two sons in quick succession to diarrhoea; how Purshottam, a young boy who came to play board games with me, died of appendicitis; and how Uttam, my field assistant, passed away of something as curable as tuberculosis. I saw young girls being married off at the tender age of 13, eyebrows raised at my enjoying sumptuous meals with someone who belonged to a certain caste or religion and folks losing their entire year's livelihood to wildlife, sometimes in the form of livestock depredation, sometimes with crops razed overnight by herbivores.

Several long walks in the forests with folks who lived in the village introduced me to the myths and practices from the remote parts of Bundelkhand; resulted in some of the most peaceful encounters with tigers and bears and an occasional spine-chilling greeting from dacoits on the run. I saw uncanny similarities in folks planning their future, but they did so in entirely different currencies from those who lived and grew up in urban areas. I saw an old woman bring her small crop of beans to the weekly market to make enough money to last a week, and I also saw local village lenders charge exorbitant interest rates from the hapless poor. I saw people from different religions and socio-economic statuses come together for those in need. I experienced the love and affection each villager in Majhgawan gave me, an outsider living among them. If anything, the five years in a remote village taught me to never judge people for following certain practices. Each person with whom I interacted taught me humility, compassion and empathy—lessons that I could have never learnt in a class, but ones that have helped me over the years.

While tiger populations flourished in Panna around the early 2000s, it didn't take much for their populations to plummet, primarily due to poaching. Such is the influence of the tiger as a keystone species that with the decimation of their populations, a rapid change was observed in other wildlife too. For instance, we noticed a surge in smaller predators such as the jackal. Tiger population decline also coincided with a sudden decline in chausingha populations, though it was not before I had wound up my research and returned to Mumbai to write up my thesis. Today, several years after the successful reintroduction and subsequent proliferation of tigers in Panna, tourist guides and foresters report a marginally higher number of chausingha sightings. However, other changes, such as the proliferation of generalist herbivores like chital, conversion of savannah into grasslands and management priorities solely focused on increasing tiger numbers seem to have taken a toll on the chausingha. While these are anecdotal observations, only systematic research can help understand what happened in the past two decades to the chausingha population in the park and why.

When I saw a four-foot-long cobra slide by our neighbour's courtyard while he and his two-year-old grandson sat on a cot, watching it slip out of sight without a strain of worry, it was a lesson for me in acceptance and coexistence. If there is one reason India is still rich in biodiversity, it is the acceptance of its people of the wildlife around them. It is time that we celebrate this acceptance and let people who share their spaces with wildlife be active partners in conservation.

Panna Tiger Reserve had 13 villages inside and at least thrice the number at its periphery when I started my field research. Humans have been a part of this landscape and have influenced it in multiple ways for millennia. There is no dearth of knowledge based on reliable and replicable science and social science that can be applied to improve the legal frameworks, and make them more effective and productive without compromising on the inviolability of natural spaces. The five years of research on chausingha in Panna resulted in five scientific papers and book chapters, four reports and a PhD thesis. As much as one would hope for such research to prove useful for management planning, little do they contribute to it in reality. The fact that scientific and social research is seen through the same lens as destructive activities such as mining, infrastructure development and poaching militate against knowledge generation and evolution of appropriate and effective management practices.

The premise that economic development can only occur at the cost of environmental protection and environmental protection can only be done by blocking economic development has led to a dichotomist approach that puts the remaining wild spaces under tremendous stress. If India's biodiversity has to survive, it is time for us to diffuse the dichotomy between the well-being of humans and wildlife that pit one against the other. Threats faced by biodiversity are often dynamic, and their drivers vary vastly. Developing flexibility to allow for adapting the best practices to conserve wildlife is the way the legal frameworks must develop so that they facilitate research, informed decision-making and a greater stake of the local communities in biodiversity conservation.

Species such as the chausingha play an important role in tropical dry deciduous forests. From dispersing seeds to becoming prey for the predators, this ancient antelope is also an evolutionary marvel in being the only living wild animal with four distinct horns. They also serve as an indicator of high floral diversity within tropical dry deciduous forests. Using species as an indicator of the health of ecosystems is not a new practice but is insufficient when limited to charismatic predators such as the tiger and leopard. Knowledge about species ecology can help the management of forest habitats avoid practices that might support certain generalist species at the cost of specialists such as the chausingha. There is hope that with better science and policy interface, future amendments to the WLPA will allow for the flexibility that science-based conservation requires, wherein knowledge generated through research can be utilized, and species- and site-specific conservation approaches take us towards holistic ecosystem conservation rather than remain fixated at species-specific conservation programmes.

A LIFE IN THE JUNGLES: WILDLIFE DOCUMENTATION TO TOURISM

JOANNA VAN GRUISEN

Margaret Thatcher became the prime minister in the United Kingdom (UK), in late 1979. Around the same time, I moved to the Indian subcontinent in South Asia. The two events were not entirely unconnected! I was not a supporter and vowed only to return after she had been ousted. But she remained in the seat of power for over a decade, by which time, my heart and home had become firmly established in India. My move to India occurred in 1981, when another Iron Lady was in power here, back after the debacle of the Emergency. Whatever else she did, Mrs Indira Gandhi is remembered as a stalwart of conservation in India, so with her in power and a near decade-old WLPA, I arrived at a nascent yet burgeoning time for conservation.

I came from several years living in the jungles of Sri Lanka as a member of a team headed by a Götz Dieter Plage, filming wildlife documentaries for the TV series *Survival* (1961–2001), created by Anglia Television. I arrived with another team member, Ashish Chandola. Ashish had been a naturalist at the pioneering wildlife tourism lodge Tiger Tops, in the Chitwan National Park of Nepal, when Dieter Plage went to film there. One summer, when Dieter had to be back in Europe and Tiger Tops was closed, he had given Ashish a camera and a crash course in 16mm filming. He requested that Ashish stay with 'Billy' Arjan Singh throughout the monsoon to cover his relationship over that time with Harriet, the leopard, and Tara, the tigress. The film clips that Ashish produced so impressed Dieter and *Survival* that he was taken on as Dieter's assistant when the crew (Dieter and his new wife, Mary Grant) moved to Sri Lanka. My entry was more lateral. I had met Ashish on a visit to my sister in Nepal in the late 1970s and been enchanted by the diversity of the wilderness in Asia and his reflective knowledge of it. I came from a sociopolitical community work background; and until I landed in Asia, I had seen a legal career in my future. There was not much I had to offer a film team, but I was an experienced driver and had used a still camera and video equipment, albeit only on human subjects until then. Dieter was the most wonderful guru one could have wished for—unremittingly good-humoured, single-mindedly into wildlife filmmaking and unusually munificent in his desire to share his knowledge and talents. We spent exciting and enjoyable years there with them both. When they moved east, Ashish and I moved to India to continue making wildlife documentaries for *Survival*. Although not known to many of the present generation, *Survival* was one of the longest-running, most successful nature documentary series. The company was set up by naturalist Aubrey Buxton, founder-director of Anglia TV. It first broadcast as early as 1961 and made over 1,000 shows in its 40-year existence. *Survival* was a pioneer, alongside David Attenborough and the BBC Natural History Unit, whose *Life on Earth* series and subsequent wonderful wildlife bounties were first shown in 1979. Baron (as he later became) Buxton brought in Colin Willock from a current affairs programme, *This Week*, to head the creative team. Colin was also a keen naturalist, and his background was in magazine journalism. He produced and wrote more than half of *Survival*'s documentaries. He had a great sense of humour and brought a light touch to the serious science that was a *Survival* hallmark.

Another distinctive feature of the *Survival* documentary was that it would present a story 'womb to tomb'. For us camera people, this would mean we needed to follow a species throughout its life—in those times, we could live and film in an area for a year or more to cover all the seasons and life history. It was a wonderful way to have time to observe and learn and be able to delve deeply into the subjects' lives; the slow pace seems almost unimaginable in today's fast-paced world. Ashish and I moved to Kashmir in 1981 and settled into a small green hut belonging to the wildlife department in the forests of Dachigam. Our main film target was the hangul or Kashmir stag, at that time believed to be a subspecies of the red deer (*Cervus elaphus*). More recently, as a result of mitochondrial DNA studies, it has been recognized as the nominate species, *Cervus hanglu hanglu* of a central Asian red deer group that includes the Bactrian and Yarkand deer.[1] But whatever its classification, the hangul is endemic to Kashmir, although earlier, a small number were reported in the Gamgul Siahbehi Wildlife Sanctuary in the Chamba district of Himachal Pradesh. The department in Kashmir was very supportive of our film project, and the chief wildlife warden (CWLW), Mir Inayat Ullah, became a friend and was most helpful: he assigned some of his best wildlife guards to work with us. One of them was Mohammed Qasim Wani, an elderly gentleman with a keen eye for spotting hangul on distant hillslopes and whose memory went back to the Maharaja's time (1910–1947). He regaled us with stories from those days, including that there were so many hanguls that in the rutting season, so many males calling that one could not sleep. E.P. Gee, a tea planter and renowned naturalist, estimated that the population then was in many thousands but believed that there were maybe around 2,000 by 1947, when the hunting preserve area was handed over to the government forest department. In the early years following Independence, uncontrolled poaching and encroachment took their toll on the hangul. Dachigam was declared a sanctuary in 1951 and became a national park 30 years later in 1981. In spite of the protection of this 141 sq. km area, the hangul numbers had dropped rapidly, and in 1970, International Union for Conservation of Nature (IUCN) ecologist Dr Colin Holloway reported a census figure of only 140–170 animals in the park, which, by then, was known to be the only existing truly viable population. This early huge decline was thought to have resulted from poaching, habitat loss, fragmentation and disturbance. But with attention and protection, the population had begun to grow, and when we were filming in the 1980s, it was estimated that there were around 600 deer. The subsequent years have shown those numbers to be a high point. The latest census figure for 2021 estimates a population of 261—worryingly low but at least a small increase on the extreme lows of 1994 and 2015, when the population had again dropped below 200.

Dachigam is an excellent example of where environmental preservation is essential both for wildlife and humans, as it is an important catchment area for the Kashmir Valley. The fresh water that flows through the park is a crucial source of sustenance for the people of Srinagar. It was recognition of this that led Maharaja Hari Singh to preserve the area of Dachigam in 1910.

I revisited the park in the summer of 2021. So many changes have occurred in the intervening decades, but Dachigam was still as beautiful as ever, the Dagwan waters flowing clear and clean. With reduced numbers, the hangul are not easy to spot, but Himalayan black bears are regularly sighted and seem to have become more used to human visitors. We had a few run-ins with these potentially dangerous animals, who, even without provocation, in earlier days, tended to charge the strange two-legged creatures roaming their forest. Indeed, I believe I owe my life or certainly escape from serious injury to the other guard who was assigned to work with us in Dachigam, Abdul Rahman Mir. I had returned in the late 1990s and was out in the Dachigam forests with him scouting for a New Zealand natural history unit production. Out of the blue, one large female bear charged at us: I was in the direct line of fire, but choosing valour over escape, Abdul Rahman stepped back towards me into her path and so he took the brunt of her attack. Fortunately, the bite and claw-raking narrowly missed all vital parts and he was able to walk out unaided to reach a hospital. And apart from a slightly torn sweater, I was totally unscathed, thanks to him.

Arriving from the West in the early 1980s, India was thrilling for me. Here was a country still with so much wilderness area, with agriculture for the most part, unindustrialized, therefore, rich in biodiversity and a people who had an inherent connection with and cultural respect for nature. People themselves were equally diverse and, to a newcomer, appeared to be bursting with abundant creative ideas and a strong sense of 'Indianness'—nationalistic without being jingoistic. India was, in many ways, independent of the global economy and proudly going its own path. Eighty per cent of the population still lived in rural areas, and I felt that the potential of India forging a new development path based on ecological economics could be an example to the world and steer others into new directions. The crucial role the environment plays in human well-being and the effect the industrial world was having on the climate were beginning to be known and discussed. But much of the West still plodded along its capitalist path, with its eye and targets on increasing growth. It took a couple of decades more for them to collectively even begin to realize the incredible dangers this entails. Sadly, as the West was waking up to this, India began its emulation march. Many of the power elite had been educated in western economic institutions, so these were the strongest voices—those on the ground in the rural areas were overshadowed. The 20 per cent of urban classes, especially the aspiring middle class, wanted what their western counterparts enjoyed, and their voices were more easily heard than those in the hinterlands. Of course, this is still the case—or was until the farmers of 2020 forced some hearing. Although the rural population has almost doubled in numbers since the 1970s–1980s, its percentage vis-à-vis the urban population has dropped from 80 per cent to 65 per cent. One hears successive finance ministers of various parties express a desire to tilt this even further towards the urban. I've never quite understood this, especially when urban area facilities are already stressed. Surely, more productive and healthier for the country and its people would be to improve livelihoods in the rural areas and reduce the migrant worker rush. My years working with wildlife and the environment see the possibilities for this. But we do need to step away from the conventional view of 'development'. In 2022, one would need to be willfully ignorant not to appreciate the self-destructive damage traditional development models are causing all of us on the planet.

My filming and photography work has taken me to some of the most stunning areas of India and, even more blessedly, allowed me to actually live there for months at a time. Apart from Kashmir, I have spent time in the sub-Himalayan Bhabar-Terai region of Assam (Manas National Park), trans-Himalayan high-altitude areas of Ladakh, the deserts of Rajasthan and the grasslands and dry forests of Madhya Pradesh as well as travelling more briefly to several other wild areas. Outside India and Sri Lanka, I have spent time in Nepal and, briefly, Tibet. In 40 years, one cannot help but notice changes, and, of course, not always for the better. When I came, India had next to no plastic—no packaging, no plastic bags—which has now become so ubiquitous and such a mega problem worldwide, but in India especially, as our garbage disposal systems are still catching up with the change in refuse. Earlier, when all was paper, it could happily be discarded to biodegrade and disappear with one monsoon. The same behaviour now blots the landscape with piles of plastic and other non-biodegradable waste, seen outside every town and village in India. On morning walks in central India, I pass an open patch that occasionally attracts car-borne picnickers. Whenever it does, the ground is left strewn with litter—plastic plates and mugs, biscuit and namkeen packets, plastic bags and other non-degradable detritus. In the mid-1980s, when we were filming in Manas, on winter days, nigh on 100 busloads of people would drive into the core of the park to picnic on the banks of the Manas River, facing Bhutan. There had been controversy over this, many feeling it was inappropriate and too much disturbance in the centre of a national park. However, Manas was then presided over by one of India's top forest officers, Sanjay Deb Roy. He was a man of deep integrity, with a gentle outlook and independent thinking. On the face of it, the easiest option of dealing with this management issue would have been to ban the buses' entry. Sadly, especially in the forest department, I've noticed this is the way many management issues are dealt with—banned rather than resolved. Mr Deb Roy was of a different calibre: he recognized that if and when any threat arose to Manas, these picnickers would be a major supporting constituency and that it was unlikely that these members of the local population would be able to enter and enjoy the wilderness area in any other way. So, he allowed it to continue, merely banning the loudspeakers and music that created the cacophony that used to be a part of the outings. But my point here is with regard to what was left behind. One carload of four to six people now creates well more rubbish than 400–600 people did then. This was still the pre-plastic-packaging era. Meals were cooked there and eaten on leaf plates, water drunk from the river or in steel glasses, snacks brought wrapped in recycled paper. Once departed, there was some leftover food for the peacocks but nothing to be an eyesore or danger for the park, nothing that would not return harmlessly to nature. This is hard to imagine now. India has, however, had an enviable history of recycling, even though much of it has rested upon an incredible army of ragpickers whose working conditions are worse than Dickensian. But now, so much is single-use or recyclable only minimal times. Another more recent issue is that the recycling systems have been hit by the Goods and Services Tax (GST), so, at least in our rural areas, this private recycling system has broken down.

But for all the eyesores and negative stories that emanate from India on the environment, it must be noted that there are an incredible number of success stories too. In spite of extraordinary population growth (India, in 2022, is home to nearly 2.5 times the number of people that lived here in 1972.), India still has some of the richest biodiversity of any Asian country. Although several species are now being pushed to the brink—the great Indian bustard (GIB) and vultures—others have been saved in the nick of time: the gharial, rhinoceros, tiger, pigmy hog and Ladakh urial are iconic species that come to mind amongst others. We may not have many more tigers than we did in the 1970s, when Project Tiger was inaugurated on a war footing, but at least we do have representative areas of all their various habitats intact and preserved; the foundation is there to build back. The nine tiger reserves that were the base of Project Tiger's protection have been increased to 52. Around 5 per cent of India is protected with over 900 parks, sanctuaries, and conservation and community reserves. But this does still fall well short of the global average of 15–17 per cent, and, sadly, even these areas, especially recognized for their ecological importance, are under threat and discarded in the name of 'development'. Roads, mines, dams and other infrastructure projects eat into India's wilderness every year, and the number of projects cleared even within her protected areas has doubled in the last few years—around 130 every year. Even large projects are being pushed through, like the ill-advised and socially and ecologically disastrous Ken–Betwa river interlinking one that would doom the newly restored and thriving tiger reserve of Panna and—contrary to the popular claims—would exacerbate the water stresses of Bundelkhand.

No doubt India has much to contend with: 2022 is a very different world both here and globally than it was in 1972. I feel so blessed to have enjoyed so much of the subcontinent's wild areas in those years of solitude. There were perhaps only three film teams shooting wildlife in India—it was virgin land, as Africa provided most of the subjects in the early years of wildlife documentaries on TV. This was long before digital imaging, and all were shot on heavy 16mm film cameras and sound recorded on tape recorders. It is hard for later generations to appreciate how different this was. There was no immediate check back; indeed, it could be several months before one saw or heard reports of the results. The raw film was sent to the UK for processing. In today's terms, one was shooting quite blind—even a minuscule hair in the gate of the camera could spell the loss of days of irreplaceable work. Detailed shot list records were written to keep us abreast of footage achieved and the shots still required. Film was expensive and limited, so we did not have the luxury of taking many shots from which to choose later; we needed to visualize what would work then and there, and shoot accordingly. Digital now gives unimaginable flexibility not only in the way it is shot but also when you can shoot. The near darkness in which it is now possible to film was impossible then. The highest ISO available for film (or ASA as we referred to it) was 500, but mostly we shot on 100; the best still film was 25 ASA/ISO, although 64 was my standard, sometimes 100 and maximum 400. Furthermore, we mostly had only a little over two minutes of shooting time per film roll; some cameras gave 11 minutes before having to change the roll in a black bag to prevent light leakage. So, if expecting action, one had to husband the shots so as to have enough to cover whatever might come. I remember one time in Manas when I wanted to take a slow-motion shot of the Bengal florican's display jump: I was using a hand-wound Bolex, which could run only for about 28 seconds for each wind-up. This was at the normal 24 frames per second. To slow the motion, one wanted a faster frame rate—the Bolex could go to 64—but this, of course, reduced the shooting time. If I remember correctly, I had around 11 seconds in which to capture the display, and this was pretty much the time it took the florican to complete. It took several attempts to accurately anticipate so as to cover the event from start to finish. In still photography, too, the 36 images per film had to be factored into the shooting, and although no black bag was required to change these, the seconds or minute it could take to rewind into the canister and reload a new one could be enough to make you miss the crucial moment. None of these are issues that today's digital camera people need to deal with. The limitations today are more in terms of how and where one can film—certainly, we had more freedom than is given now, and there were hardly any tourists sharing the wild spaces.

Wildlife or nature tourism has changed a good deal in the last 50 years. Indeed, when the Wild Life (Protection) Act (WLPA), 1972, came into existence, there was very little tourism. Travel was not simple, and accommodation was hardly available near the wilderness areas, apart from the forest rest houses. Tiger Tops in Nepal's Chitwan National Park, Kamrup Komplex, next to Kaziranga in Assam, and the Wright family's place in Palamau and, later, Kanha (Kipling Camp) were pioneers from the 1970s. Nevertheless, the first sprouts of tourism did exist—visitors came to see wildlife both from India and abroad. One unnamed 'wildlife lover' in an article in *The Indian Express* described the arduousness of train and bus travel then but noted that 'the overwhelming up-side was that one practically had the place to oneself.'[2] It was a very different experience then from today's drive or fly-in tourists who, for the most part, can only see wildlife from a vehicle; 'It was then mainly about a journey of discovery, often either walking the forest with the staff or swaying comfortably on elephant-back... enjoying the forest at an easy pace and listening to what the jungle was saying.' I would second those comments. They remind me of one long-ago visit to the Gir forest in Gujarat. I had gone out early with a wildlife researcher and the forest trackers, and we were following a pride of lions on foot down a forest track. After a while, we realized that our single-file walking was no longer lions in front and humans behind but had become lions followed by humans, followed by more lions and then more humans—happily, we seemed to have intermixed quite peaceably.

Unfortunately, though, such proximity between humans and wildlife, especially carnivores, is not always so benign, and as our population grows and there is more competition for space, conflicts increase. It might also be said that—though counter-intuitive—the exclusive conservation model path that was set by the WLPA may actually have exacerbated this. By separating wildlife from local communities, people have, to a large extent, lost the knowledge and ability to coexist. Furthermore, there has been a psychological shift with the government assuming ownership—from acceptance to hostility. Over the decades, I have observed a perceptible change in some communities: there was forbearance towards the animals and their predation on livestock and crops, as they were viewed as part of the environment in which they lived, and those afflicted found ways to maintain it at an acceptable level. Now the least amount is regarded as a menace for which the government is responsible and for which they (the authorities) should find the solution and pay. The relationship between the two or rather, the three—wildlife, forest communities and the forest department—is hugely affected by this, and indeed, the way it plays out elicits more tensions and antagonism than harmony and cooperation. No one benefits. And, sadly, to date, collaboration in wildlife conservation is a relatively rare story. However, five decades on, there are signs of some rethinking and some different evolution of attitude and practice, though much of this is outside of the forest department, which seems the most inured to change. While some have reached these views from an ethical stance, others may have come from the pragmatism of seeing that the success of the protected area (PA)-system spills into outside areas where an inclusive, not exclusive, approach is required. Whichever the approach path, one hopes that the future may be walked together, and new models and systems of conservation developed that also benefit the communities that live in the wilderness areas and allow us all to live compatibly with the universal biodiversity of the worlds in which we live.

My path has taken me through wildlife documentary filmmaking and photography, to conservation research and advocacy and now to a small tourism venture. Our eight-room, mud-cottage accommodation was created as a more culturally and environmentally appropriate place to stay for visitors to the United Nations Educational, Scientific and Cultural Organisation (UNESCO) World Heritage site of Khajuraho. Situated in a rural area, it is also aimed at giving the visitor a more holistic experience of the locality, beyond the fly-in and fly-out one-day visit to the temples. We conceived it as a way to provide us with the means to return to continue research and conservation in the forests around the Panna Tiger Reserve, where my partner, Dr Raghu Chundawat, had studied tiger ecology for nearly 10 years. This, therefore, has led us to look closer at the relationship of tourism to conservation and its potential as a development and conservation tool.

Unlike in other parts of the world, tourism in India, especially in wilderness areas, has long been viewed with suspicion and distaste. On the one hand, it is criticized for elitism and, on the other, for oversaturation. Tourism is a double-edged sword, no doubt, and does, therefore, need to be managed well; it can easily destroy the very aspects that create its rise. But it is a huge industry—one in 10 jobs worldwide is connected to tourism, and this is likely even higher in India. In rural areas, it has the potential to bring a benign development that most other industries cannot, since rather than being resource extractive, it can even be a catalyst for protection. We began to see this with the Earthwatch groups that we ran in Ladakh in the 1990s. A USA organization, Earthwatch, was founded 51 years ago, in 1971; it had a truly pioneering vision, developing a unique citizen science model that paired volunteers with scientific researchers. In Ladakh, travellers from across the globe assisted in gathering data and monitoring the snow leopards' prey; under Dr Joe Fox and Dr Raghu Chundwat's guidance, they were following up and extending Raghu's snow leopard ecology research there. Through this, we realized how tourism could benefit the local community as to and provide an additional source of income. Since we could not continue with the Earthwatch groups indefinitely, we discussed with Chering Norbu, an incredibly dedicated and effective wildlife warden, and members of the local tourism community as to how this economic benefit could continue. Ranger Norbu—as he was known—was already using his position to encourage the communities towards conservation by establishing local plantations and assisting families to predator-proof their livestock corrals. These discussions were part of the foundation that led to Rinchen Wangchuk developing the homestay model that began in Rumbak and a few other villages. Importantly, these were based on benefit to the village as a community rather than to individual families. Rinchen became the co-founder, member, partner of Snow Leopard Conservancy-India, established in 2000, that pioneered and advanced the homestay movement in Ladakh. I am happy to say this continues to this day as one of the more successful, long-running community tourism projects in India, a legacy to Rinchen Wangchuk, who sadly passed away at an early age in 2011.

These experiences have remained with me into the present day. Along with our tourism concern, we run a small conservation trust working with some of the communities on the outskirts of the Panna Tiger Reserve; we have a long-term vision of using tourism as one pathway for extending conservation areas and enhancing livelihoods in remote agricultural areas. Although much debated, there has been little factual evidence, one way or another, as to whether wildlife/nature tourism benefitted the local communities or not and if so, how much.

In 2017, with the assistance of the UK trust Travel Operators For Tigers (TOFT) India, whose aim is to improve the ecological and economic sustainability of the wildlands and wildlife, our trust Baavan—Bagh Aap Aur Van (named after one of Panna's tigresses)—undertook a study to look at the economics of wildlife tourism in four of Madhya Pradesh's tiger reserves; a report, *The Value of Wildlife Tourism for Conservation & Communities*, was the outcome.[3] What we learned was surprising and encouraging. Even without planning and direction, wildlife tourism was indeed bringing significant funds to the tiger reserves while also having a remarkable impact on raising awareness and appreciation of nature, and reducing rural poverty and enhancing livelihoods in the communities immediately around the reserve entrance gates. The total revenue generated through tourism around the four reserves was an amazing $25.94 million (₹166 crore). This, compared to the total budget for the reserves (in 2016–2017), which was $6.25 million (a little over ₹40 crore). Revenue from entrance fees alone came to more than the state government's contribution. Eighty-five per cent of visitors to the reserves are budget travellers, somewhat putting paid to the argument of wildlife tourism being elitist. All levels of lodging were found to be operating at a very low occupancy (averaging around 35 per cent), laying to rest another argument that it is an industry where outsiders reap high profits from the PAs. There was 80 per cent local employment, and at least 45 per cent of the revenue was ploughed into the local economy (over and above the substantial entrance fee amount). We also calculated that the amount generated beyond this by small businesses benefiting from the tourism presence was over $1 million (over ₹7 crore). The turnover of businesses in 'tourism villages' was three times more than in the others, and there was four times more employment there.

This information clearly indicates the potential of tourism in wilderness areas. However, it is not to say that we presently have a working model. The benefits occur more by accident than design and, at present, affect only a small proportion of the communities that live around the PAs. Also, from the tourists' perspective, the model, in most places, is very limited in that it offers little choice in the way to experience a wild area and is slender in enhancing a visitor's understanding. To date, India's wildlife tourism has been little different from other forms of tourism—a hotel is chosen on budget, a fee is paid to enter and you see the Taj or the tiger and leave. We need to move beyond this and make wildlife/nature tourism a more interactive learning experience. I think these last couple of pandemic years have helped many to come to similar realizations. I do believe other ways are possible, and over the years since 1972, with the several amendments, even the wildlife laws are moving in a more inclusive direction, slow may these be to seep into the managers' consciousness.

Fifty years on, I hope that more of us are better educated as to the pitfalls of environmental destruction and the loss of wildlife and biodiversity. I also hope that we can move towards more inclusive models of conservation that benefit the wildlife and those who share those resources. Certainly, the next 50 years will be challenging, but they will be crucial for developing new and innovative ways of enhancing livelihoods without further destroying the environment and raising our carbon footprint. The disparities between rich and poor, urban and rural need to be addressed and reduced, and our well-being measured less in acquisitions, consumption and economic growth than in health, happiness, and social and environmental justice. This is the only path to our own and to wildlife's continuing survival on this planet.

Notes

1. Brook, Sarah, et al., 'IUCN Red List of Threatened Species: Cervus Hanglu Ssp. Hanglu', *IUCN Red List of Threatened Species,* December 2016, http://dx.doi.org/10.2305/IUCN.UK.2017-2.RLTS.T113259123A113281791.en. Accessed on 18 July 2022.
2. 'Of Highways and Byways: A Wildlife Lover Recalls the Hard Days' Travel and the Small Joys It Guaranteed', *The Indian Express*, 19 February 2017, https://bit.ly/3OZUgmH. Accessed on 4 July 2022.
3. Chundawat, R.S., et al., *The Value of Wildlife Tourism for Conservation & Communities: A Study around Four Tiger Reserves in Madhya Pradesh: Part I: Tourism Infrastructure and Revenue*, Bagh Aap Aur Van and TOFTigers, October 2017, https://bit.ly/3bNbOEt. Accessed on 4 July 2022.

FROM COMMERCE TO CONSERVATION: SAVING CROCODILES WHILE FERRYING AS A WILDLIFE RESEARCHER

LALA ASWINI KUMAR SINGH

Darwin introduced the idea that 'a microscope was not needed to make ground breaking discoveries, but that some of the most complex processes could, in fact, be seen with the naked eye.'[1]

The Turning Point: Stepping out of the Textbooks

Twenty minutes had already passed. The foreign expert on the interview board, Dr H. Robert Bustard, the Food and Agriculture Organisation (FAO) consultant and architect of the national Crocodile Conservation Project, asked me about the kind of work I would like to be doing when I reached 40.

I was hardly 22, holding an Utkal University MSc degree in zoology and aspiring for a research position under the Government of India (GoI)/Government of Odisha/United Nations Development Programme (UNDP)/FAO project for crocodile conservation. With 32 contenders waiting outside and the five-member selection committee looking at me, I stammered, 'I think—working with crocodiles.'

By the end of the day, I was preparing to leave for the Tikarpada forests (Odisha), located on the banks of river

Mahanadi within the famous gorge called Satkosia (7 kos or 14 miles). I was to report for a further field test for five days spread over the next week. Months after joining the project, in mid-July 1975, I realized that for successful conservation, research and action must go hand in hand. Odisha Forest Department was incidentally the first to implement it in letter and spirit.

Angul to Satkosia

I had known Satkosia from a picture in the primary school book showing the river Mahanadi emerging out of the cleft between two hills near Majhipada, where Pandit Nehru had laid the foundation stone for a barrage in 1964. The barrage was never constructed, and the Satkosia Gorge was subsequently available for continuing with the possibilities for gharial (*Gavialis gangeticus*) conservation. According to some old legal provisions, the conservator of forests (CF), Angul, B.C. Kanungo had declared Satkosia as a sanctuary, affording protection to the gharial. The CF and Divisional Forest Officer (DFO) Nitya Ranjan Bohidar had engaged local fishermen on boat as gharial guards.

In school books, Satkosia was also described as a place of countless crocodiles, the forest overlooking the riverbank, abounding in tigers, bears, elephants and bison roaming wild. Another introduction to Satkosia for me was my maternal grandfather, who served in Purunakote as a police officer during the pre-Independence period. He had negotiated the forests on horseback and used the pigeon service for communications. The pigeon messenger service continued till the 1970s.

For me, it was a thrilling first-time visit. The bus journey from Angul to Tikarpada for the field test and later experiences were defining and lasting. Around five in the afternoon, the bus turned left from the national highway at Badakera and was soon at the Purunagad forest check gate.

At Karatapata Chhak, we stopped briefly for tea, and from there, the road entered the dense sal forest. The bus travelled past the daylight. It moved noisily, splitting the water over narrow culverts wide enough to accommodate all four wheels, the headlights tearing the darkness over the morrum-topped road, lined on sides with tall teak plantations and, at places, drooping bamboo clumps that elephants had pulled down. I had taken a front seat on the side facing the driver, but visibility was quite narrow beyond the sides of the road. No light from huts or houses was visible until we entered Jagannathpur and Purunakote villages.

The bus stopped suddenly with a screech. A wind-fallen tree had blocked the road. The bus staff and a few passengers took half an hour to clear the road, and we were back on our journey. One of my co-passengers gave me hope of sighting elephants, tigers, sambar, nilgai or spotted deer and a few more broken bamboo clumps. He was so sure, and I can confirm his certitude from my later trips while travelling through Jagannathpur–Purunakote–Hatibari and Tikarpada. That was Satkosia in those days, much before it was declared a wildlife sanctuary. Wild animals, including tigers and leopards, were often seen from the bus.

The Field Test

The field tests were conducted for five days from 5 July 1975, by Dr H.R. Bustard, Dr M.V.S. Rao and Saroj Raj Choudhury. Choudhury was the famous forest officer of pugmark tracking and 'Khairi' tigress fame. Dr Rao was a reader in ecology at the Utkal University. His PhD thesis was examined some years back by Dr Bustard. The field test was quite challenging and a new learning experience for all five of us who were vying for three possible research positions available under the project.

The first-ever hatching of gharial in captive conditions had taken place on 18 June 1975, creating a history of sorts for crocodile conservation in the country. A total of 42 gharials had hatched from eggs brought from the river Gandak in Bihar and were housed in five hatchling pools. They demanded steady attention as I sat inside the pen to make observations and take notes on their behaviour. Choudhury conducted the test inside the forest. The field test also comprised boat journeys, observation of large gharials and their bodies' spoor on sand besides those of the turtles. Raja Behera and Prafulla Behera, the boatmen from the Tikarpada fishing community, were knowledgeable. They could tell the sex of gharials from their size and ghada, but I wondered at that time if one could also determine the length from their spoor. I got that biometric relation within the next two years.

I was selected for research on the gharial at Tikarpada, Sudhakar Kar for the estuarine crocodile (*Crocodylus porosus*) in Bhitarkanika and B.C. Choudhury for the mugger crocodile (*Crocodylus palustris*).

During my first trip to Tikarpada by jeep with Dr Bustard I asked, 'What would my PhD research topic be?' That, to me, was a normal question asked by a student aspiring for research and higher studies.

'I am not the one doing this doctorate, *you* have to choose your topic,' was the sharp reply. Before joining research at Tikarpada, I had published five research papers from my work on aphid morphology and growth. That led me to look at gharial biometrics.

Basic and applied knowledge about a species is necessary to save it. I was lucky to have two good supervisors in Prof. Basanta Kumar Behura and Dr Bustard, who taught me how to organize my thoughts and present the findings. After testing my abilities to maintain and look after essential research tools, Dr Bustard handed me, with interval, a calculator, a Minolta camera, a thermo-hygrograph, a pair of binoculars and a portable

Olivetti typewriter. Before acquiring a table-top typewriter, Dr Bustard himself used to type out all the handwritten project communications and research papers I submitted on the portable Olivetti. Once, it fell off his cot and was damaged and wouldn't type. I spent the whole day diagnosing the defect and repairing it with makeshift tools accessed from the kitchen. The result was that the portable machine came into my possession, and it remained with me even after August 1978, by which time I had typed twice over, under lantern and Petromax lights, some 350 plus pages of my PhD thesis.

When I began the life of a researcher, Dr Bustard told me, 'You are working with facilities about a third of a British research scholar and about one-eighth or one-tenth of an American researcher.' I found it to be true during my later visits abroad and from interactions with fellow researchers there.

GRACU and the Research Base

After reaching Tikarpada, I was accommodated in a suite with an annexe in the old British-period thick-thatched forest rest house (FRH). Dr Bustard had settled in a suite adjacent the newly constructed reinforced cement concrete FRH that also became the headquarters of the FAO consultant. We named the captive husbandry unit down the hill slope from our dwelling as the Gharial Research and Conservation Unit (GRACU). Gradually, I learnt about various aspects of crocodilian biology and the history of its conservation project in India.

In 1971, the GoI initiated a proposal for crocodile farming for commercial utilization. After negotiations with the UNDP and FAO, a countrywide survey was undertaken in 1974.[2] In October of that year, Dr Bustard, then FAO consultant, submitted a report to GoI titled *India: A Preliminary Survey of the Prospects for Crocodile Farming* through the FAO. The objective of the survey was to indicate how best captive breeding could be carried out in the states of Uttar Pradesh, West Bengal, Orissa (now Odisha), Bihar, Tamil Nadu, Andhra Pradesh, Karnataka and Rajasthan to rebuild the crocodile populations and for deriving economic benefits from them. In 1972, the Wild Life (Protection) Act (WLPA) had already included the three crocodile species in Schedule I.

India is the natural home of three crocodilian species, namely the gharial, the mugger and the saltwater or estuarine crocodile, all of which also had natural abodes within the state of Odisha. The surveys led by Dr Bustard had found that the gharial was facing the threat of extinction, the mugger was depleting faster than it could reproduce and the estuarine crocodile was endangered along with its mangrove habitat.

So, it was commerce that initially became the cornerstone of the efforts in the 1970s to rebuild the crocodile populations in India. But much later, in January 1987, it became clear that commercial farming would not be taken up anytime in the near future. There was a stop or go-slow signal for the ongoing in situ rearing programme underway in about 30 rearing stations around the country by the Technical Committee on Crocodile Conservation Programme (TCCCP), of which I was the convenor by virtue of being the officer in charge of the erstwhile Central Crocodile Breeding and Management Training Institute (CCBMTI). The committee met for the last time that month. It was a high-profile committee. The members were V.B. Singh, advisor (Wildlife), government of Uttar Pradesh (Chairman); Pushp Kumar, chief wildlife warden (CWLW) of Andhra Pradesh; P. Padmanaban, CWLW, Tamil Nadu; R.N. Mohanty, CWLW, Orissa and J.B. Sale, FAO consultant at the Wildlife Institute of India (WII). M.K. Appaya, CWLW, Karnataka, hosted the meeting there, followed by field visits to sites in Tamil Nadu and Kerala.

Commercial harvest of crocodiles was also impossible because of their listing in Schedule I of the WLPA and the sentiments of people built around the captive-reared animals. Another argument was that if we allowed commercial farming of any kind, the protection of crocodiles and their numbers which had revived well, would become difficult.

Why Crocodiles Needed Human Assistance and Care

Early during field research, a question about crocodiles often intrigued me. A fully grown mother crocodile lays around 30–40, sometimes even over 50, eggs. The presence of just about 10 egg-laying mothers should result in thousands of crocodiles. But it doesn't happen. The success of the crocodile conservation programme in India is the result of the correct diagnosis of issues related to protection and hatchling survival; back then, it was often said that of about 10,000 eggs, hardly one reached adulthood to continue the race. The gharial and the mugger begin the breeding season in early winter and lay eggs in nest pits in March–April, while the estuarine crocodile lays eggs in May on a mound. Hatching starts after 60–80 days of incubation. The sex of the young is determined by the incubation temperature, perhaps during the first 21 days. Females are produced at 30 degrees Celsius while males are produced at higher temperatures.

A large number of eggs get lost to predation and adverse environmental conditions during the incubation period. Adults, while basking or guarding the nest, often become victims of poachers. Therefore, eggs were collected for hatchery incubation and captive husbandry of young ones till they reached 3–4 feet body length and were ready for release in the wild. This was done with the help of local people who worked for the hide hunters earlier or were themselves egg poachers. The entire operation from egg collection to release and protection in nature is termed the 'grow and release technique' for producing a large number of crocodiles in the shortest possible time.

Based on survival experiences in 1975 and 1976 from embryonic development and hatching, a recommendation emerged that the eggs that were to be shifted to the hatchery from the natural nest have to be collected within the first week or after 50–55 days of in situ incubation. Transportation shock may still be there. As a further precaution, in 1977, eggs in Nepal were collected and kept for incubation at Tiger Tops, Chitwan. Dr Bustard and I attended to the hatching and the post-incubation care as well as arranged the transport of hatchlings to India by air. A new facet of gharial biology, like the norms for egg translocation and a range of congenital defects, could be developed from research conducted this year onwards.

The Crocodile Institute, Hyderabad

I was associated for six and a half years (1981–1987) with the GoI, CCBMTI, Hyderabad (Andhra Pradesh), in the capacities of assistant instructor, instructor, research officer, assistant director and officer-in-charge. Within the country, around 30 rearing stations, 11 special crocodile sanctuaries and about 20 other wetlands for crocodile rehabilitation had developed by then. The CCBMTI imparted a 10-month diploma course to in-service officials from India, Nepal, Bhutan, Sri Lanka and Iran. It also functioned as the coordinating base for the crocodile project with the unit of UNDP/FAO. While leading the trainee officers to different parts of the country, it was enlightening to understand local intricacies and innovations in wildlife conservation. The syllabus and the expertise available at the CCBMTI with FAO inputs produced batches of wildlife managers trained in crocodiles, and other wildlife and sanctuary management.

After the first gharials were released in Mahanadi in 1977, I discussed with Dr Bustard about using radio tracking for monitoring purposes. He didn't favour it at that time, as even without such equipment, we had already collected good data on the movement of four adult gharials in Mahanadi. Our studies at the GRACU enabled us to identify individuals from the natural colour pattern on the tail. The trail of the tail along with the paw impressions distinguished the mugger from the gharial, and the tail spoor revealed the length of the gharial.

In 1982, I went on an FAO fellowship to the US to study wildlife management, particularly to look at the developments in crocodile research. At the end of the study, I attended the Crocodile Specialist Group (CSG) meeting at Victoria Falls and met crocodile experts from all over the world. Radio tracking of animals was one of the major items of my interest there.

Chambal Field Camp for Gharial Tracking

On return to India in 1983, I was obliged by a bond to work for the GoI for at least the next three years. So, at the behest of the GoI and support from J.J. Dutta, CWLW, Madhya Pradesh, a field camp of the CCBMTI was started on river Chambal at the Deori campus near Morena in Madhya Pradesh. My best experiences with the gharial and its ecological associates came here.

There are two sanctuaries on river Chambal for the conservation of the gharial. The Jawahar Sagar Sanctuary in Rajasthan was notified in October 1975, followed by the National Chambal Gharial Sanctuary (NCGS) by the states of Uttar Pradesh, Rajasthan and Madhya Pradesh, in three separate notifications (1979–1983). The gharial that frequented the Rana Pratap Sagar, a dam upstream of Kota in Rajasthan, had long adapted to mudbank nesting and were relatively safe.

Chambal opened up the multidimensional possibilities of research and conservation with the gharial at its focus.[3] I had taken a liking to Chambal from my very first visit made in 1978, to collect eggs for our work at the GRACU. Because of the untimely release of water from the Kota barrage on Chambal, sometimes the nests got inundated and spoiled. It was only after J.J. Dutta sent a communication to the barrage authorities that they started to release water in small volumes.

My second visit was in 1981 while leading the trainees of CCBMTI for field exercises involving nest location, egg collection, placing the eggs in wooden boxes with proper orientation, transport by rail and placing the eggs in the hatchery at the GRACU.

In 1983, the field camp and the project office at Deori, Morena, had very modest facilities and survey equipment. These included a high-keeled aluminum boat and a 20 hp outboard engine. A 5 hp engine was used when speed needed to be regulated. We also had radio-tracking equipment and a long-wheel Land Rover. S.K. Dixit, the project officer from the Madhya Pradesh Forest Department, was an alumnus of the CCBMTI. He was older than me and cautioned me often about taking precautions while working in the Chambal area. But I decided I would live with my family (wife and baby son) in the accommodation available at the Deori campus. Encouraged by this, a few other staff members also started residing on campus with us.

Locals Suspect the Radio-Tracking Equipment

The first batch of four gharials (246 cm to 279 cm in length) for radio-tracking experiments were brought from Kukrail to Lucknow and then by rail to Agra, and Deori by road. It was quite a journey, and transporting them by rail taught us to reserve a separate cabin in the future.

Techniques to attach transmitters to the animals were developed at the Deori Gharial Center. Two ordinary transmitters and two solar transmitters, all with activity notifiers, were attached over a synthetic collar on the animals, and they were taken for release beyond Basai Dang on 28 October 1983. Going was tough, since it was the first time we had tried to negotiate upstream of rapids with one country boat and another fitted with 20 hp outboard motor. Halfway, it became dark. Going to a village and leaving the gharials on the boat was not feasible. So, Jasram, the boatman, cooked chapattis and dal, and we slept on the sandy bank with the gharials safe in the boat.

We resumed our journey the following day after breakfast. After reaching a location around Sarsaini, upstream of Basai Dang, then releasing and watching the gharials for over an hour, it was late in the afternoon. As we then began preparations for a late lunch, we realized, to our dismay, that the matchbox had been lost while pushing the boat up the rapid in the river. Thankfully, I always carried raw groceries in a metal trunk, but that night we had to sleep on the riverbank on an empty stomach. The next morning, for breakfast, we partook raw wheat flour, pickle and water from the Chambal River and reached Rajghat in the afternoon, where our driver Yadgiri and my father (who was visiting) were waiting anxiously for us and the gharial release news.

The local people became suspicious about the radio-tracking equipment and our intentions behind it. After a few days, one transmitter was not traceable, another was recovered from a dead gharial, while yet another was found on a treetop in a village in Rajasthan, a few kilometres away from the river. Signals could be received only from the remaining tracker. It was very disheartening, but it prompted us to organize a few village meetings to inform them about the gharials, their conservation programme and that we were only research students studying their behaviour and movement patterns

In the last week of November 1983, the boats and

equipment were brought by road to Pali in Rajasthan, and we took to the river from Pali downstream. The Ranthambore Tiger Reserve adjoins the river Chambal on its left bank, and the local people advised us to avoid camping on the left bank, for tigers visited the river at times. After about three days on the boat, we reached a suitable location where we could attempt to capture a few gharials and attach transmitters on their tail. We camped on the left bank (Rajasthan) but, after dark, cleverly moved to the Madhya Pradesh side to escape getting noticed.

In the evening, we tried to catch gharials with a spotlight, using the noose I had brought from South Carolina. It was yet another lesson. A lot of practise was required for necessary coordination between the boatman, light-man and me, the noose-man, to happen. With disappointment writ large, we returned to the bank, had food and slept on the Madhya Pradesh side of the riverbank in a row of about seven to eight members.

'Gang of Nine' in the Wee Hours

The location is about 10 km upstream of Batesura, whose headman used to take pride in working as a watcher and boatman for the National Chambal Sanctuary. He and his son were with us. It seems that our changing of the camp from Rajasthan to Madhya Pradesh had not helped much. Sound of talk among people had woken me at around four o'clock. While pretending to be asleep on the ground, I had seen and counted nine persons, all clad in khaki, one with a gun and eight with lathis. They were standing on one side of the almost-dead fire, in talks with our people.

One of them, talking to our boatmen, turned to me and made me understand that they were Rajasthan Police and that they had come to enquire about us camping on the riverbank. He asked for my ID or any letter from the government about our ongoing work—we had not carried our IDs with us. He also wanted to know the possibilities of locating people with our radio equipment. In about 10 minutes, the boatmen invited them for tea. They left after tea with a message that if we were to come another time then we must come with an ID and prior intimation to the police. The next morning, we continued on the boat, and in the evening, camped in Batesura. As I sat on a rope-cot, the forest guard there came near me and whispered that the people who came in uniform were actually the members of the 'Gang of Nine'. So, every day in Chambal was a day of learning.

Wild Capture and Tracking Results

On 4 December 1983 at Pureini, which is at a distance of 230 km from Pali, we selected a place to set traditional drag nets and slept on the riverbank about a kilometre away on a bend. The next morning, we captured three wild-born gharials, measuring 183–222 cm and fitted the transmitter on the flat portion of their tail. Their radio tracking gave us an understanding of their initial exploration phase and movement in response to fluctuations in the water level. We realized that placing the radio transmitter on the flat portion of the tail instead of a neck collar worked better. Accordingly, we decided on the specifications for the next possible prototype transmitter for gharial monitoring. Our work at Chambal was encouraging and produced great results.

Why Did the Gharial Survive So Well in Chambal?

Difficult terrain and the presence of dacoits were blessings in disguise, enhancing the scope of survival of the gharial in the wild. One day, the District Magistrate (DM), Morena, with the Superintendent of Police, came to Deori. Thirty-seven years ago, the idea of producing results using radio transmitters were very novel and attracted their attention. They enquired about the scope of using our methods for search and tracking operations within the district. Before leaving, they advised me not to sleep on the riverbank in the future, 'Please move to the nearest dak bungalow before it is dark.' So, they knew what we had been doing!

Long-Term Ecological Monitoring (LTEM) and Local Conservation Beneficiaries

During the winter months of 1983–1984, I had planned a survey of the entire stretch of the National Chambal Sanctuary, and had, for the purpose, thoroughly studied the topo sheets newly obtained from the Survey of India. Upon discussion, V.B. Saharia, then acting director of the WII asked me to abandon the plan because it was risky. I told him that someone had to do it, so he should let me try it out. Now, after 39 years, I realize how productive that determination on my part proved then and later in my life.

I had planned to travel by boat the entire stretch of the National Chambal Sanctuary from Keshoraipatan to Pachhnada. On reaching Pali from Morena via Sabalgarh, we learnt that Pali to upstream Keshoraipatan is a narrow rocky stretch of 142 km, and were advised, 'Better not enter that stretch.'

So, much of the research work till today in the National Chambal Sanctuary has remained focused along the stretch of 430 km from Chambal–Parbati confluence at Palighat to Chambal–Yamuna confluence around Pachhnada. This covers the gharial, the mugger crocodile, the Gangetic dolphin, turtles, large raptor and non-raptor birds, and their population trends. Random mentions about raptors in our field notes have produced good comparisons with neighbouring Kuno–Palpur, Ranthambore and Sariska at some distance. Our team at Deori included Dr R.J. Rao (presently vice chancellor, Barkatullah University, Bhopal), Dr Rishikesh Sharma and the boatmen, such as Awadh. We also studied the otters around Dang Basei (Sarsaini), about 35 km upstream of the bridge at Rajghat. Suraj Gupta, a local boy from Morena who knew how to type, helped us maintain the camp office when the CCBMTI stenographer, Annathurai, was not in camp. Suraj has done quite well in life and is a fine example of the benefits to local people that wildlife conservation often brings.

It is a matter of satisfaction that the research and monitoring protocols developed by us in 1983 continue to be used to date at Chambal. These were simple, scanned topo sheets (1:50,000 scale) showing the study zone on a page with 5-km subdivisions of the river. Fortunately, a place in Morena could in those days scan copies using a photocharged glass plate and rolling ink granules.

Second Innings at the CCBMTI as Night Watchman

In the first week of February 1985, I was told by Mr. Saharia at Dehra Dun of my posting back in Hyderabad. It was a kind of the last hurrah for the CCBMTI. There were a lot of academic outputs, including participation in the preparation of the directory of Asian wetlands by Derek A. Scott, and *Wildlife Wealth of India: Resources & Management* (Tecpress Service, 1986), a book by Prof. T.C. Majupuria. One certificate course was conducted, research reports from Chambal were brought out, and three research fellows, Ainul Hussain, Vijay Kumar and Prahalad Kumar, joined in September 1986. In the same month, I was selected as a management faculty at the WII, Dehradun, with H.S. Panwar as the new director. Due to personal reasons, I declined the appointment and returned to Odisha.

Satkosia of Gharial Fame, Completing the Full Circle

In August 1987, I had a short spell at Satkosia-GRACU. 'Satkosia, it appears, is becoming more of a mugger sanctuary,' I told DFO Suresh Kumar Mishra. In 1991, with the gharial in Satkosia approaching local extinction, C.S. Dani, the CWLW, asked me to produce an analytical report on the reasons for the apparent disappearance of the gharial in Mahanadi. Bamboo rafting by Titaghur Paper Mills had stopped, but fishing nets had replaced the traditional baited hooks in many places. Sandbanks like Sunakhania, used for basking by gharials, now hosted fishing camps. Weekly market boats shuttled between Narasinghpur and Harabhanga-Boudh for four to five days a week. The ancient gharial, which I thought had reached evolutionary senescence, perhaps needed Chambal-like model conditions for survival.

Interestingly, the tranquility brought to Satkosia by Covid-19 lockdown in 2020 saw a return of gharials for breeding and nesting. Twenty-eight hatchlings discovered in May 2021 have raised hopes of a better future. After the Mahanadi high flood in 2021, naturally breeding adults were again seen in the gorge in December. While success stories of gharial breeding have also come in from other parts of India and Nepal, it is almost like completing a full circle in gharial conservation efforts that started at Satkosia in 1975.

Similipal-Ramatirtha MRACU

In November 1987, I joined as a research officer at the Similipal Tiger Reserve and spent eight of my 16 years at the Mugger Research and Conservation Unit (MRACU) at Ramatirtha. At Simlipal, I improved the pugmark-tracking system for tiger census and developed a 14-colour model, including the melanistic, to explain inbreeding depression in tigers. Here, I also wrote the first Project Elephant document for Odisha state. Ramatirtha became the research base for the Similipal Tiger Reserve and a training station for a range of students and professionals from all over the country and abroad.

For the mugger, their breeding performance was improved with supplements of vitamin-E and mineral salt, their territorial behaviour was better understood and methods were devised to recapture the adults when they escaped into river Khairi-Bhandan flowing down the campus. In 1979, I had come from GRACU for thorough survey of rivers and streams of Similipal, and found mugger crocodiles to be locally extinct. But today, after meticulous research, planning and human care, the mugger is back in the rivers of Similipal. Today, more than 80 muggers are seen, mostly in rivers West Deo, Khairi and Budhabalanga.

Conclusion

In the last quarter of the twentieth century, with just a pencil and a pocket book, I began my journey with crocodiles, tigers, elephants and their conservation needs. Then I entered the first quarter of the twenty-first century with a computer, a laptop, the internet, a search engine and the World Wide Web to store the writings on them for the next generation. There are many lessons and numerous experiences. We have built a knowledge base, and saved the crocodiles and other indicator species for the next generation. There is satisfaction in these professional accomplishments.

On separate occasions, I met crocodile experts in Nepal, Zimbabwe, Caracas (Venezuela), Darwin (Australia) and Sri Lanka. But my life experience was in Caracas in 1984, when the CSG chairman Prof. Harry Hessel called upon the entire house with 300 members to give a standing ovation for the success of the Indian crocodile conservation programme led by young field researchers. As I recall that day, I still get goosebumps!

Notes

1. Bahudodda, Sravya, 'Darwin & The Power of Observation–ST112 A Fall 2018', *The Colby College Community Web*, 5 October 2018, https://bit.ly/3agKcXJ. Accessed on 4 July 2022.
2. Bustard, H. R., 'Indian Crocodile Conservation Project', *Envis: Wildlife and Protected Areas: Indian Crocodiles*, Vol. 2, No. 9, June 1999, pp. 5–9, https://bit.ly/3RczG4K. Accessed on 4 July 2022; *A Preliminary Survey of the Prospects for Crocodile Farming (Based on the Work of H. R. Bustard, Consultant. United Nations Development Programme),* FAO, October 1974.
3. Singh, L.A.K., and R.K. Sharma, *Wetland Birds in National Chambal Sanctuary (Preliminary Report from Field Camp)*, Crocodile Research Centre of Wildlife Institute of India, Hyderabad, 30 April 1986, https://bit.ly/3aag00H. Accessed on 4 July 2022; Singh, L.A.K., and R. K. Sharma, 'Gangetic Dolphin, *Platanista Gangetica*: Observations of Habits and Distribution Pattern in National Chambal Sanctuary', *JBNHS*, Vol. 82, No. 3, 1985, pp. 648–53, https://bit.ly/3AlkVq8. Accessed on 4 July 2022; Singh, L.A.K., *Gharial Population Trend in National Chambal Sanctuary with Notes on Radio-Tracking*, Crocodile Research Centre, Wildlife Institute of India, 1985, https://bit.ly/3a8fwIt. Accessed on 4 July 2022; Singh, L. A. K., 'Significance and Achievement of the Indian Crocodile Project', *Envis: Wildlife and Protected Areas: Indian Crocodiles*, Vol. 2, No. 9, June 1999, pp. 10–16, https://bit.ly/3RczG4K. Accessed on 4 July 2022.

SAVING ENDANGERED WILD MAMMALS: REINTRODUCTION STORIES FROM MADHYA PRADESH

SUHAS KUMAR

In 2010, the wildlife wing of Madhya Pradesh had just begun experimenting with the technique of mass capture of herd-forming hooved herbivores. The purpose was to reintroduce them to suitable habitats in their original range of distribution from where they had gone extinct.

The first candidate for reintroduction was the gaur (*Bos gaurus*), also called the Indian bison. There were 30–35 individuals in Bandhavgarh Tiger Reserve till the early 1990s, but for reasons unknown, not a single gaur was sighted after 1996 (the population of 35 in 1992 dwindled to one by 1996 and became zero in 1998). There were several unverified theories about their disappearance.

After obtaining permission from the Government of India (GoI), in October 2010, the wildlife wing began preparations for the capture and relocation of the gaur. The then Chief Wildlife Warden (CWLW), H.S. Pabla, zealously spearheaded this task, overcoming all odds and opposition. He roped in experts from South Africa through &Beyond (called Conservation Corporation of Africa before 2008). Fifty individuals (14 males and 36 females) in all were translocated in two batches from the Kanha Tiger Reserve to Bandhavgarh. Nineteen of these, in January 2011, were captured with the technical support of

South African experts. This collaborative exercise built up the confidence of the field staff and the wildlife veterinarians. In March 2012, the second batch of 31 animals was captured and transported to Bandhavgarh without any external help.

Encouraged by the success of gaur relocation, the wildlife wing planned the reintroduction of blackbuck (*Antilope cervicapra*) into Kanha Tiger Reserve.

I was against the idea of reintroducing blackbuck into the Kanha Tiger Reserve, as I believed that it was not qualified to be brought back to a habitat from where it was extirpated owing to drastic ecological changes in the grasslands. The blackbuck is an animal that has evolved in open country comprised of grasslands with short grasses, cattle and cultivation. Several villages within the park had such a habitat.

The village Sonf was relocated between 1967–1969 to create suitable habitat for the barasingha, but after acquiring the status of a tiger reserve in 1973, 25 villages from the national park were relocated between 1974 and 1982; this action removed all cattle from the habitat. After its inclusion under Project Tiger in 1973, the tiger reserve came under strict protection against poaching, tree-felling and grazing by domestic cattle from surrounding villages.

Both actions resulted in the growth of tall grasses unsuitable for blackbuck but favourable for the hard-ground barasingha, which was on the verge of extinction. So, in my view, reintroducing a species that had gone locally extinct due to the transformation of its habitat was hardly desirable. Besides, the blackbuck, despite being included in Schedule I of the WLPA was not under threat of extinction. But, when these plans were being made, I was on sabbatical researching wildlife tourism in tiger reserves of the state, and I could not do much to convince my superiors to stop this unnecessary reintroduction.

The methodology for mass capture of blackbuck was borrowed from Andhra Pradesh. The process involved immobilizing a group of blackbuck in the night by playing high decibel sounds and flashing powerful searchlight into their eyes. The sound and strong light stunned the blackbuck into immobility, and then they were physically lifted and loaded onto trucks. This operation caused heavy mortality. The reason for mortality was the onset of capture myopathy that ensued as the captors physically handled the animals while they were fully conscious. This tragedy could have been averted had there been an attempt made by the officers of the wildlife wing to find out about the outcome of the mass capture already executed by their counterparts in Andhra Pradesh (I later learned that in Andhra Pradesh, no post-release monitoring or any mortality record had been kept).

We decided to train our staff in the African boma capture technique to avoid the recurrence of earlier mistakes. The boma capture does not involve any physical handling either before or after the capture of the animals. This technique had been partially deployed in the gaur capture exercise at Kanha in January 2011. But since it was not found useful in the wooded areas of Kanha, the gaurs were then captured by deploying a restraint drug—medetomidine.

Interestingly, the capture of gaur using a combination of muscle relaxant and sedative drugs was once attempted earlier in March 1980 but without success by S.M. Hasan and legendary J.J. Dutta in the Achanakmar Wildlife Sanctuary (now in Chhattisgarh). The purpose was to capture two calves to meet a demand from a German zoo. They had used darts to inject two calves with a Hellabrunn mixture (125 mg/ml xylazine and 100 mg/ml ketamine), but both animals died soon after darting. This failure led everyone to believe that the gaur was a hypersensitive species that could not be captured either physically or by chemical immobilization. So, no further attempts were made to capture and relocate the gaur till 2011. Fortunately, now several calming drugs (medium- and long-acting tranquillizers) are available for administering as soon as the animal is revived and also while transporting them. These drugs proved effective in stopping the onset of capture myopathy in the gaur transported to Bandhavgarh in 2011 and 2012.

Boma Technique

Besides re-establishing locally extinct species, we were also looking for a safe method for en masse capture of ungulates from areas of overabundance for restocking protected areas (PAs) deficient in deer and antelope. Therefore, it was decided to adopt the boma technique, used with success in Africa, and modify it to suit the central Indian conditions. The training of the staff began in earnest at Van Vihar National Park in Bhopal and at the Kanha Tiger Reserve. Around this time, we were facing an overabundance of chital in Van Vihar National Park, which is a 4.5 sq. km fenced area without any free-ranging carnivore except jackal. After obtaining the state government's permission, the CWLW ordered the capture of chital from Van Vihar for restocking some prey-deficient PAs.

After several trials and errors and innovations, by 2013, a team of staff at Van Vihar had become adept in capturing chital and safely transporting them to other PAs. By November 2014, 26 chital had been successfully captured and transported from Van Vihar to the Ralamandal Wildlife Sanctuary and Kamla Nehru Prani Sangrahalaya in Indore, and the Ratapani Wildlife Sanctuary (Bhopal). Thirty-one chital from Umaria were also relocated to the Sanjay Tiger Reserve (Rewa), using the newly acquired skills.

Story of the Capture and Relocation of Hard-Ground Barasingha from Kanha

The hard-ground barasingha (*Rucervus duvaucelii branderi*) is one of the three barasingha races with stiff hooves that have adapted to hard ground. The other one inhabits the western Terai grasslands, and the third one is found in the eastern Terai, restricted to the Kaziranga Tiger Reserve. Both species of Terai barasingha are adapted to wet, soft ground.

The march of agriculture into barasingha habitats as well as rampant poaching by both tribal people and gun-wielding shikaris, despite the hunting ban imposed by the government in 1954, took a heavy toll on the barasingha. Their number was estimated to be around 3,000 in 1938 in Banjar valley of Kanha National Park which declined to 66 in 1967.[1] The species was hanging precariously at the edge of extinction.

Alarmed by the fast-depleting barasingha population, the park managers implemented several ameliorative measures. Those efforts included the relocation of villages; protection, and management of grasslands; creation of ponds; erection of predator-proof captive breeding enclosures; stopping the practice of tying baits for tigers in the grasslands and also banning the age-old practice of annual burning of grasslands. These measures soon turned the tide in favour of the barasingha, and they began to increase in number and disperse to other grasslands created after the relocation of villages. But the extra cautious managers also decided to shift some of the animals to other habitats within Kanha and also to Bandhavgarh. The idea was to establish geographically separated populations to ensure the long-term continuity of the species in the event of an epidemic or natural calamity.

From the late 1970s to the early 1990s, the Kanha Tiger Reserve had attempted chemical restraint to capture and relocate hard-ground barasingha, but all those efforts were marred by heavy mortality. After those unsatisfactory trials to capture and translocate barasingha to Bandhavgarh and other available habitats within Kanha Tiger Reserve, the wildlife wing did not rethink their capture and relocation to other historical habitats for almost two decades. In 2010, with a focus on proactive management, the wildlife wing began pursuing its plan to reintroduce this critically endangered species from Kanha to Satpura Tiger Reserve, which had been part of its historical range of distribution.

The reintroduction of species had to proceed according to the reintroduction and translocation guidelines issued by the International Union for Conservation of Nature (IUCN) and the Central Zoo Authority (CZA). The habitat study was conducted by the scientists at the Madhya Pradesh State Forest Research Institute (MP SFRI), Jabalpur. Bori range in the Satpura Tiger Reserve was found most suitable to reintroduce the hard-ground barasingha, and a conservation breeding enclosure was built at Bori.

The population viability analysis (PVA) by the Wildlife Institute of India (WII) proposed establishing a founder stock of 20 individuals (with the male to the female sex ratio of 1:3) and to release them into the wild when the population reaches nearly 50. A predator-proof 27-ha enclosure was erected to keep the captive barasingha. The report suggested supplementing 12 animals with the same ratio of 1:3, every alternate year for the next five years. By the end of the fifth year, when the population in the enclosure would have reached 106, approximately 60 animals from the enclosure were recommended for release into the Bori meadow. A small breeding stock was to be retained in the enclosure to supplement the wild population from time to time. The released population was to be supplemented with 10 animals each year from the surpluses in the enclosure.

In May 2011, the GoI granted permission to capture 20 barasingha for reintroduction into the Satpura Tiger Reserve but withdrew it after seven months. Apparently, the heavy mortality reported in the blackbuck operation had prompted the GoI to take that drastic decision. Despite this setback, the wildlife wing relentlessly followed up with the National

Tiger Conservation Authority (NTCA) and the Ministry of Environment and Forests (MoEF) for over three years. Finally, on 3 January 2014, the concurrence from NTCA was received to capture and relocate barasingha from Kanha but with the following two conditions:

i. move two male and three female barasingha from Kanha to Van Vihar National Park to demonstrate the skills in hand; and
ii. use chemical restraint technique to capture the animals (barasingha).

Soon after receiving the go-ahead from the NTCA, preparations for the operation began. But I was not happy at all with the idea of transporting barasingha and 'introducing' them to Van Vihar to keep them in a display enclosure. Bhopal in the past was never a part of the barasingha habitat. As additional PCCF (Wildlife Management), I felt responsible for making use of the permission for a bigger purpose. Therefore, I convinced my boss to allow me to create a non-display conservation breeding enclosure in Van Vihar and build a facility from which we could provide barasingha for reintroduction to other suitable habitats in its historical range of distribution or for supplementing the reintroduced population at Bori. The CWLW, Narendra Kumar, readily accepted my proposal. Soon, I inspected Van Vihar and selected a suitable site for the enclosure. The CWLW endorsed the selected site, and a predator-proof enclosure was erected there.

Another condition imposed by the NTCA that mandated the use of drugs to capture the barasingha looked inappropriate to me, and the CWLW also ruled it out after listening to my arguments. I apprised him of the experiences of our seniors at Kanha Tiger Reserve with common immobilization drugs as well as with narcotics in the capture exercises carried out in 1977, 1981, 1982 and the early 1990s. Chemical immobilization did not bring about the desired results. Although the then managers were able to create a small population of barasingha at Supkhar in Kanha, all those attempts had involved heavy casualties. Only in the operation conducted in June 1981, where a ketamine and xylazine mixture had been used, the managers met with reasonable success when seven out of the eight captured animals survived. But the overall casualty figures had put a stop to further experimentation with chemical immobilization. Therefore, the boma technique—our newfound expertise in mass capture—offered us a safer option. Preparations were already afoot Kanha afoot and a boma was erected there within a 50-ha enclosure that then already held around 35 barasingha, some chital and few blackbucks.

The Capture and Relocation

Since 50 ha was a vast area for capturing barasingha using the boma technique, we, in a previous meeting held at Jabalpur, had decided to reduce it to a manageable size. At the headquarters at Bhopal, we awaited a signal from the Field Director (FD), Kanha Tiger Reserve, that his team was ready. This was received in the last week of December 2014. Informing the CWLW, I requested that before I proceed to Kanha, he should brief the Additional Chief Secretary (Forests) and the Forest Minister and apprise them of the risks involved. I thought it prudent that both the key decision-makers are aware and mentally prepared for casualties, if any that might result from the capture and translocation operation.

I proceeded to Kanha on 5 January 2015. When I reached Mandla the next morning, the FD dropped a bombshell, informing me that his staff could not habituate the barasingha herd to graze near the mouth of the loading chute. A loading chute is a funnel that connects to the loading ramp leading to the transportation truck. I was upset with this news, as this was a very important part of the technique we used in chital capture. We had introduced this modification to the South African boma capture technique.

In Africa, for mass capture, large herds of animals are driven across the open savannah either with the help of vehicles or the helicopters, but we in India neither have large herd-forming ungulates nor do we have extensive open grasslands; hence improvisation was called for. In the modified technique, a herd of target animals was habituated to graze at the mouth of the loading chute inside the boma by providing favourite grasses, dried mahua and salt for weeks, till the animals had dropped all their fears. On the day of operation, when the animals assemble to graze at the mouth of the chute, about half a dozen people hiding behind the camouflaged hides suddenly emerge. This startles the animals and they rush to escape and end up running into the loading chute. Once the animals get into the chute, the door is closed swiftly, and the animals finally run up the loading ramp and enter the truck.

When I reached the Kanha meadow around noon to assess our field preparedness, I found that the area of the boma, even after reduction, was a massive 26 ha. So, it was decided to reduce it further. By the evening of 6 January, the size of the boma had been reduced to around 3 ha by erecting a new chain-link fence. This had to be done to keep the animals in the smallest possible area. This ensured that once the animals entered the reduced boma, they could not return to the bigger enclosure.

A small portion at the far end was left open to steer some 15 barasingha into a smaller enclosure early the next morning. I asked Jodha Singh Baiga, in charge of the barasingha enclosure, whether he could drive 10–15 barasingha into the smaller enclosure through the small passage at one end. He readily agreed and boldly assured me that he would drive the animals in by 6.30 a.m. Keeping the animals localized in a small area would allow us easy manoeuvrability, and the animals would be confined and secure in a small area for repeated attempts, if necessary. After the field inspection, the team met at the upper cabin at Kanha to discuss the field operations and transportation details. It was a wide-ranging discussion that covered all the pros and cons of this delicate and important task. Team leaders were hand-picked for each important task related to the capture and transportation exercise.

Since the animals were not acclimatized to graze inside the boma, arrangements had to be made for hanka—a traditional shikar method used by the kings, jagirdars and British officers in the bygone era. In hanka, a wild animal is driven out of cover by a drum-beating crowd of people. The beaters drive the animal towards the shikari, who waits in ambush in a tree or a hide. In some African countries, helicopters or vehicles are used for similar drives. We decided on traditional hanka with the help of people. To ensure the safety of the people involved, they were instructed to wear helmets, and safety jackets, and carry protective shields.

Starting time of operation was fixed at 6.30 a.m., and such personnel that often frequented the barasingha enclosure and were well acquainted with their behaviour were directed to enter first and quietly steer the animals towards the boma.

The Capture Operation

The next morning, at 5.30, our team assembled in the meadow, enveloped in thick fog and a bone-piercing breeze numbing our limbs. But despite the odds, the team's spirit was high, and nothing mattered to us more than the task ahead. A team of six persons led by Jodha Singh Baiga entered the barasingha enclosure. This team gently steered a group of 10 barasingha into the smaller enclosure; three chital also came along with this herd. This area was now closed by a chain-link fence covered with green mesh. All animals were thus confined in this small area. The smaller enclosure consisted of woodland at the far end, followed by a stretch of grassland, and the truck was stationed connected to the loading ramp at the other end.

A break of two hours was announced to give enough time to the animals, now confined to the small enclosure, to calm down. After the break, a team of 30 persons gently ushered these animals towards the narrow end of the boma. After crossing the curtain, the animals slowly moved ahead and reached the wheel gate area. During this time, the sudden closure of the wheel gate and the drawing of the curtain produced noise; the animals, sensing danger, turned back and ran. They jumped over the curtain and dispersed into the woodland.

After this failed attempt, a second two-hour break was announced. And the team gathered for a quick debriefing. Soon we listed the reasons for our failure.

The smaller enclosure (3.01 ha) was still quite large and required more people to drive the animals into the boma loading chute gently. At least 30 more people were needed.

There had been a lack of synchronization among personnel deputed to close the gates of the boma. So, it was decided to depute some experienced members of the Van Vihar capture team to close the wheel gates in a synchronized manner.

It had also been noticed that the drawing of the curtain had produced a lot of rustling noise that startled the animals. It was also felt that the level of noise made by the hanka team was too high and the stick-wielding was unnecessary.

Lunch was announced and, in the meantime, Jasbir Singh Chauhan, FD, Kanha, arranged for another 31 staff members and watchers from Kanha and Kisli ranges for the hanka team. Soon we had a team of 61 people. Before the start of the operation, all the team members were briefed again about how the hanka should proceed. This time, it was decided not to draw the curtain, as it was not found useful, and its rustle had instead alarmed the animals during the previous effort.

The hanka began once again. A chain of 61 strong hanka team members gently pursued the animals towards the narrow end of the boma. This time, the animals moved up to the curtain area, but only one animal crossed the gate and ran through the loading ramp into the transportation truck. This animal was shifted and confined in the first compartment of the truck. The rest of the animals dispersed and returned to the woodland.

The direction team noticed that the hanka team was too slow and was over 50 metres behind when the animals reached the curtain area. This delay on the part of the hanka team gave enough time to the herd to turn back after sensing danger. Moreover, the team members were moving in a staggered fashion, leaving large open spaces for the animals to run back through them.

Before commencing the third attempt, the hanka team was instructed to form an impenetrable chain and walk together in a synchronized manner. They were also instructed to increase their pace and make a little noise as soon as the animals left the woodland and entered the grassland. This time the instructions were followed meticulously. As the animals crossed the wheel gate, it was quickly closed. The animals kept moving, and all the sliding gates were closed one by one. All these animals ultimately entered the transportation truck, and the truck's back door was closed. The solitary barasingha kept in the first compartment was freed by opening the compartment gate so that all the animals could be together during the transportation. The capture operation culminated at 12:30 p.m.

This way, the boma method was used to successfully capture seven barasingha (three males and four females) and three chital. We decided to keep the three chital, a sympatric species (different species that occupy the same geographical range without loss of identity from interbreeding) to give company to the barasingha at their new home in Van Vihar. With meticulous planning, this operation turned out to be extremely successful, with zero mortality. The wildlife veterinarians assessed the health status of all 10 animals. As all the animals were found to be in good health, and physically and emotionally fit, the transportation team began its long historic journey to Bhopal, some 530 km away. No sedative was ever used in the entire operation.

The Transportation

The transportation truck was piloted by a vehicle with a team of officers to ensure the safe and smooth passage of the captured animals. The truck was followed by two vehicles with wildlife veterinarians and support teams from Kanha Tiger Reserve and Van Vihar National Park. A wildlife veterinarian seated in the transportation truck monitored the animals through a CCTV screen. Every two hours, the animals were observed through the side windows by the entire team of veterinarians for any sign of indisposition.

Local forest officers of the respective forest circles piloted and guided the transportation truck through easier routes and by-passes to avoid traffic rush and prevent any untoward road mishap during the journey. The engine of the transportation truck was kept running even at brief stops to provide a feeling of continuous movement to keep the animals calm. The translocation team was provided with packed lunch and dinner by the local forest officers to avoid delays, if any, during the journey.

Throughout the journey, officers from the Kanha Tiger Reserve and Seoni, Chhindwara, Hoshangabad and Bhopal forest circles were in constant touch with the convoy leader on a cell phone. The transportation truck reached Van Vihar National Park at around 6.30 a.m. on 8 January 2015. The journey had taken around 17 hours. I was in constant touch with the transportation in-charge, Rajnish Singh, via cell phone from the train on which I was travelling. At one point, I felt that the transportation truck would reach the release site while it was still dark and well before the time of release. So, I instructed him to slow down the convoy so as to reach Van Vihar just before dawn, around 6.00 a.m.

As soon as my train reached Bhopal, I hopped into the waiting car and rushed to Van Vihar. The CWLW, Narendra Kumar, and other senior wildlife wing officers and Van Vihar national park officers were present to oversee the release operation. A well-camouflaged off-load ramp inside the conservation breeding enclosure was used to dock the truck to facilitate the safe release of the animals. The lights (placed behind the truck) were switched on to monitor the release of animals into the enclosure. The backdoor of the transportation truck was opened, and the sides of the truck were thumped to urge the animals to move. Just a few moments later, the animals ran out of the truck into the enclosure with agility and alertness, and vanished behind the tall grass. Visual barriers had been created with straw mats placed all along the wire mesh fence of the enclosure to prevent the animals from hurting themselves by dashing into the fence. Observation towers were erected along the fence to monitor the released animals. An elaborate monitoring protocol was prepared, and duties were assigned to the staff and the veterinarian.[2] Detailed planning and skilful implementation of it was the key to our success.

Barasingha Reintroduction at Bori in Satpura Tiger Reserve

Our success led the NTCA to allow the capture of 20 more barasingha for reintroduction into Bori in the Satpura valley. Three capture operations were conducted in Kanha meadow on 3 March 2015, 15 March 2015 and on 14 January 2016. These three operations resulted in the successful relocation of eight, eight and six barasingha, respectively. Later, between 2017 and 2020, another 46 individuals were brought from Kanha to supplement the population at Bori. By the beginning of 2020, the number of barasingha within the predator-proof enclosure at Bori had grown to 94.

Reintroduced barasingha, both at Van Vihar and at Bori, have bred successfully. At Bori, with the onset of winter, the resounding rutting calls of the majestic males resonate against the towering Bailkandhar hills to the delight of the onlookers. It gives one immense satisfaction to behold the cute, spotted fawns frolicking across the vast expanse of grassland where their ancestors once roamed.

A Mistake and Its Solution

Even after my superannuation in December 2015, I continued to keep track of the reintroductions and visited the Satpura Tiger Reserve in November 2020. There I learned that a release operation of 50 captive barasingha in the wild had been carried out in early 2020, following advice received from a committee of experts. I was certainly happy to learn that the managers have taken another step towards establishing a free-ranging population in Satpura Tiger Reserve. But I got worried on learning that the animals had been released at two different locations and not just at Bori as had been planned earlier based on the PVA. The cause of my worry was the news that out of the 25 animals released at Dhain, only seven survived, while of the 25 animals released at Bori, only 17 survived. This mortality rate in free-ranging reintroduced animals is unacceptably high. The PVA by the WII had considered just 15 per cent mortality to predict various extinction scenarios, while the current mortality rate was already around 28 per cent of the total population of 94 and 52 per cent of the released animals. I felt that the release of small groups of Barasingha at Bori and Dhain grasslands had been a mistake.

Perhaps the members of the expert committee failed to comprehend the risk aspect of releasing small populations in areas with a good number of predators, such as wild dogs, leopards and tigers. At the time of release, three packs of dholes (wild dogs) were operating in the Satpura Tiger Reserve, a good number of leopards were present in Bori and Dhain and the tiger population had also built up owing to two major interventions; large-scale relocation of villages leaving secured habitats for prey and predator both, and the release of some orphaned tiger cubs reared in wild conditions as well as capture and release of some dispersing tigers from hostile human-dominated areas into the Satpura Tiger Reserve.

Usually, in a predator-replete habitat, it would be wise to release a large number of target animals so that the population may withstand the predation pressure and grow over time. If the release of barasingha into the wild habitat was so urgent, another strategy, in this case, should have been to release a large number of buffer prey, like chital, in that habitat before releasing a small number of barasingha. The second significant error was splitting the populations into two very small populations and releasing them at two far apart places. I would have preferred releasing no less than 100–150 animals at one site along with a large number of buffer prey to cope with the predation pressure.

Another strategy that might work even now would be to select suitable release sites at different parts of the Satpura Tiger Reserve and replenish those habitats by supplementing them with missing habitat attributes—such as waterbodies, aquatic plants, grass species important for fawning and foraging, etc., and erect at each site predator-proof enclosures of at least 80 ha and release small populations in them in a ratio of 1 (male): 3 (females) and allow them to breed till the population is over 100. Once that threshold is crossed, release 100 chital as buffer prey in the habitat and then release 90 per cent of barasingha, keeping the remaining as insurance in the predator-proof conservation breeding enclosure.

I sent a note with these suggestions to the CWLW, and thankfully, the FD has taken steps to salvage the situation.

Notes

1. Panwar, H.S., 'Saving the Barasingha: A Conservation Saga', *Sanctuary Asia*, Vol. 2, No. 2, April 1982, pp. 150–57.
2. *Report on the Non-Invasive Capture & Translocation of Hard-ground barasingha (Cervus Duvauceli Branderi) from Kanha Tiger Reserve To Van Vihar National Park*, Technical Report-Madhya PradeshFD/WL/2015/01, Madhya Pradesh Forest Department, https://bityl.co/DBmg. Accessed on 26 June 2022.

BETRAYED LOCALS AND LIONS: THE STORY OF KUNO NATIONAL PARK

FAIYAZ AHMAD KHUDSAR

I first went to Kuno in 1999 at the invitation of the then divisional forest officer (DFO), J.S. Chauhan, now the principal chief conservator of forests (PCCF) and the chief wildlife warden (CWLW), Madhya Pradesh. In those days, only one bus plied between Vijaypur, the tehsil headquarters, and the Arrod village, and I then walked almost 7 km on a water-logged and muddy trail to the Agraa village to meet him. Today, as the roads are black-topped, many buses ply between Vijaypur and Agraa and even beyond. During a recent visit, I found it difficult to locate even the police station in Agraa, which at one time was the only visible building on a road, now having many such buildings on both sides of it.

I was in Kuno Wildlife Sanctuary to conduct ecological research and to assist the authorities in its habitat development activities in anticipation of the planned lion reintroduction.

I managed to get a pataur in Sahrana (a designated residential colony of the Saharia tribe) at Agraa. I stayed there for almost two years and learnt about their customs, requirements, lifestyle, food habits, etc. The village was picturesque, with the river Kunwari skirting it. Its catchment, a degraded reserved forest (RF), had been denotified and converted into agricultural and residential plots to rehabilitate villagers from within the sanctuary.

I remember going inside the sanctuary for the first time along with J.S. Chauhan and a team of scientists who had come from the Wildlife Institute of India (WII) for a site visit of villages already relocated and ones still inside the sanctuary.

Why a Second Home

Today, a single population of Asiatic lion (*Panthera leo persica*) exists in the world in Gujarat's Gir National Park. Conservation biology studies suggest that a small population restricted to a single site faces a variety of extinction threats. The real-life example of the Serengeti National Park, Tanzania, where a violent outbreak of canine distemper virus wiped out one-third of its lion population, despite both its population size and area of the protected area (PA) being large, points to threats that cannot be ignored. So, it was essential to realize the Asiatic lion's evolutionary potential and promote its genetic vigour to spread the single lion population in Gir National Park into several populations over its historical distribution range.

Historically, the Asiatic lion was distributed from Palestine in West Asia to Palamau in eastern India. According to available literature, in India itself, the Asiatic lion was widely distributed from Haryana (AD 1834), Abu (AD 1872), Ahmedabad (AD 1836), Baroda (AD 1832), Rewa (AD 1860), Gwalior (AD 1865), Guna (AD 1872) to Palamau (AD 1814) and many other places. A population and habitat viability analysis (PHVA) workshop for the Asiatic lion was held at Baroda (Gujarat) in 1993. The participants at the workshop, including those from the forest departments of Gujarat, Uttar Pradesh, Madhya Pradesh, Rajasthan and Haryana, were asked to suggest potentially suitable sites for the reintroduction of the Asiatic lion. Looking at the former historical distribution range, four wildlife sanctuaries, three in Rajasthan—namely Darrah, Jawahar Sagar and Sita Mata and Kuno in Madhya Pradesh—were shortlisted.

Kuno's conducive ecology and rich biodiversity, where an area of 344 sq. km had already been notified as Kuno Wildlife Sanctuary in 1981, and it being part of the lion's historical distribution range, stood out as an alternate home for the Asiatic lion. In 1994, a field survey conducted by the WII scientists reiterated the suitability of Kuno as the country's second home for the Asiatic lion. Subsequently, a separate Kuno Wildlife Division, spread over 1,269 sq. km, was created in 2002, with its office at Sheopur, the district headquarters. In 2018, the Kuno Wildlife Sanctuary was upgraded to a national park status, enhancing the area under protection to 748 sq. km and an additional peripheral forest area of 487 sq. km was brought under the unified control of the Kuno wildlife division.

Kuno National Park forms part of the Vindhyan Ranges and is located in the Sheopur district of northwest Madhya Pradesh. It derives its name from the river Kuno, a direct tributary of the river Chambal, which flows from south to north, vertically bisecting the area and remains the lifeline of the national park. Though the river Kuno does not flow throughout the year, it retains water in the form of pools (locally known as *deh*) throughout its length, including about 44 km within the core area of the national park. Some of the important water pools can be seen near Palpur, Paira, Basantpura, Khallai, Barrer and Nayagaon villages.

Kuno is popularly known as Kuno-Palpur owing to a seventeenth-century fort at Palpur, situated on the bank of the river Kuno. It was once the capital of the Palpur jagir under the Scindhia rulers of Gwalior. There exists an old forest rest house (FRH) in Palpur on the high right bank of the river Kuno, which has been a very important and popular destination in the past and even now.

My Entry and Studies

I had been working at the Kanha National Park with an organization called Tiger Trust (founded by Kailash Sankhla), where I met J.S. Chauhan sometime in 1997. He had just been transferred to Kuno as the DFO. With a master's degree in environmental biology from the University of Delhi under the guidance of legendary ecologist Prof. C.R. Babu, I could not resist an invitation from the new Kuno DFO, and I reached Agraa village for the first time in August–September 1999. My visit had been supported by a World Wide Fund for Nature-India (WWF-India)-funded project (courtesy my friend Arpan Sharma).

With limited resources, it was not easy to work in a remote area like Kuno; however, my meeting in the year 2000 with the noted wildlife biologist Raghu Chundawat not only helped me receive support from the UK-based Born Free Foundation but also taught me the intricacies of systematic ecological data collection. I have been privileged to receive unstinted support from the Madhya Pradesh forest department and the Kuno National Park management since I started working in Kuno.

Availability of fresh food items and water was a limiting factor at Palpur on account of its remote location. All of us, including the forest officers and staff, consumed the river water after letting it settle overnight. A dip in the river just down the FRH on one shore and a basking mugger crocodile on the other bank was quite common. Even today, a basking mugger crocodile can be seen from the Palpur FRH. Even the gharial is now found and seen in the river.

The Kuno landscape is a typical dry deciduous forest, described once as a 'dead' forest by my fiancée—Reshma—during her maiden visit made in extreme summer. Depending on the geomorphological characteristics of various sites, the forest communities here can be classified into kardhai (*Anogeissus pendula*), dhawa (*Anogeissus latifolia*), salai (*Boswellia serrata*), gunjan (*Lannea coromandelica*) and khair (*Acacia catechu*) found in different associations. Harron (*Soymida febrifuga*), with its highly palatable leaves, play an important role in some of the areas in Kuno, supporting the park's ungulate populations. I remember finding all the key ungulates, namely chital, nilgai, chinkara and the chausingha, together under a soymida tree along the river, feeding on leaves dropped by the langur monkeys up on the tree. The unique feature of water pools all along the river greatly supports the wildlife populations. Even in a severe drought in the year 2002, these water pools did not dry up.

Kuno National Park, at present, is one of the best-protected areas in India to have an excellent forest of kardhai and shows successful regeneration of salai. The bhimal (*Grewia*) forms thick understorey vegetation, almost climbing onto the kardhai. I recorded ambient temperatures in excess of 46 degrees Celsius in the month of May and less than 1 degrees Celsius in the month of December in the year 2004. The fallen dry leaves of kardhai along with sprouting bhimal species become major forage for the herbivores during extreme summer.

Resin derived from the salai tree, commonly called chir gond, is economically very useful, it is utilized for various purposes, including medicines. It was always an important part of livelihood support for the Saharia tribals. No wonder, in times past, live-standing salai trees were given away as dowry in the weddings of Saharia girls. I remember utilizing the resin, also known as Indian frankincense, in a campfire to relish its very sweet fragrance.

During my field studies, I found the presence of various insects, amphibians, reptiles, birds and mammalian species in Kuno National Park. Chital (*Axis axis*), chinkara (*Gazella bennettii*), sambar (*Rusa unicolor*), nilgai (*Boselaphus tragocamelus*), four-horned antelope (*Tetracerus quadricornis*), wild pig (*Sus scrofa*) and gray langur (*Semnopithecus entellus*) were commonly seen herbivores. Leopard (*Panthera pardus*), dhole (*Cuon alpinus*) and grey wolf (*Canis lupus*) were the main carnivores, and occasionally, a Bengal tiger (*Panthera tigris*) was also reported. I remember Claudio Sillero, a visiting professor from the Oxford University and chair of the Crocodile Specialist Group (CSG), who got very excited about seeing the Indian wolf in Kuno, probably his first sighting of the species in the wild.

I also saw caracal (*Caracal caracal*), a very shy cat, on several occasions. Kuno is a birdwatcher's paradise, with more than 175 species. I recorded many birds, such as the painted francolin (*Francolinus pictus*), painted sandgrouse (*Pterocles indicus*), painted spurfowl (*Galloperdix lunulata*), paradise flycatcher (*Terpsiphone* paradisi) and several migratory birds such as black-headed bunting (*Emberiza melanocephala*) during my study.

The forests and grasslands of Kuno support a variety of prey species, which, in turn, sustain many large and small-sized predators, including the leopard. During my initial study in 2004–2005, the chital population was estimated to be 6.61 animals per sq. km followed by chinkara at 3.62 per sq. km. Other studies also showed a substantial increase in the chital population at 18.83 per sq. km in 2008, 51.59 per sq. km in 2011 and 38.48 per sq. km in 2021, along with the population of wild pigs, sambar and nilgai. However, population of chinkara at 3.62 per sq. km in 2004, 1.98 per sq. km in 2008 and 0.99 per sq. km in 2011 has seen a decreasing trend over time, and two small populations of the blackbuck have already disappeared from within the core zone of Kuno. This indicates a marked change in habitat conditions in Kuno favouring large-sized prey animals at the expense of smaller ungulates like chinkara and blackbuck.

The previous agricultural fields of relocated villages have undergone many ecological changes. Initially, lot of weedy herbaceous species suddenly emerged in these fields followed by other species representing different successional stages, such as jhar beri (*Ziziphus nummularia*), which took over the entire field but slowly gave way to trees like reonjha (*Acacia leucophloea*) and small trees like birbira (*Dichrostachys cinerea*) along with some of the palatable grasses like *Dicanthium* and *Bothriochloa.* Aak *(Calotropis procera)*, often seen being eaten by chinkara also came up in these fields. Unfortunately for lack of proper ecological monitoring followed by suitable intervention, kusha (*Desmostachia bipinnata*) a fast-growing non-palatable grass species can now be seen at many places.

Relocation of Villages

When Kuno was selected as the second home of the Asiatic lion, the first task was to prepare the habitat, which involved relocation and rehabilitation of 24 villages from within the wildlife sanctuary. These villages mainly belonged to the Saharias, one of the primitive tribes of India. A cabinet subcommittee of the Madhya Pradesh government visited the sanctuary in January 1996 to take stock of the proposed village relocation and elicited the community views about their willingness or not to move out of the sanctuary. The cabinet subcommittee, in its report, recommended voluntary relocation and rehabilitation of the villages from the sanctuary at a suitable site. The Madhya Pradesh Cabinet approved the report in February 1996. A relocation plan was developed by the forest department as per the guidelines issued by the government of India (GoI) under the Centrally-Sponsored Beneficiary Oriented Scheme for Tribal Development. A preliminary list of beneficiaries was prepared, which was ratified by the competent authority after due diligence. For each beneficiary, a package of ₹1 lakh, 2 ha of agricultural land and 500 sq. metres land for house construction was earmarked. The funds were used for land development, building material, transportation of household goods, community facilities, creation of woodland and fuel wood development, pasture and fodder plantation, and cash incentive for shifting and miscellaneous activities. Almost all the villages were relocated and rehabilitated outside the sanctuary by 2021. The majority of villages were rehabilitated near the Agraa village in Vijaypur tehsil of Sheopur district, except two, which were rehabilitated in the Karahal tehsil of Sheopur district. Facilities such as road connectivity, fruit orchard, drinking water facilities, irrigation facilities, schools and hostels, electricity and other community facilities were provided at each settlement.

The entire process of Asiatic lion reintroduction in Kuno National Park has gone through many social, ecological, political and economic challenges. To begin with, relocating and rehabilitating villages from within the sanctuary was a Herculean task, and it is to the credit of the then DFO, J.S. Chauhan, and his staff that it could be accomplished without much problem. I remember how the two villages, Khallai and Barrer, came out the sanctuary much in advance of any plans on their relocation and how the DFO took pains to settle them with the resources available with him at that time and how his entire energy was channelized to provide respectable relief to them so that they could sustain themselves before systematic rehabilitation package was sanctioned for them.

A continuous hand-holding through discussion with the villagers at the eco-development centre at Agraa followed by a village visit to look after them was a routine exercise for many years. The initial major task was to educate and train the frontline forest staff for the very specialized assignment of village relocation and rehabilitation, which they had never been part of in the past. Most critical was identifying staff with appropriate leadership qualities and the willingness to take on new responsibilities. Range officers Rajeev Kaushal and the late R.L.S. Kushwaha were given the specialized task, and they became the driving force, under the supervision of the DFO, J.S. Chauhan. Several rounds of discussion were held to make them understand the enormity and sensitivities associated with the process of relocation and rehabilitation. Rajeev Kaushal was assigned the task of overseeing the entire rehabilitation programme with two self-motivated and intelligent forest guards, Gaya Lal Dhakar (popularly known as Dhakar Baba) and R.K. Narwariya. R.L.S. Kushwaha was given the task of monitoring the sanctuary along with staff like Babu Singh Tomar. Later on, both the tasks were ably taken over by another range officer M.M. Sharma, along with the already trained team of forest guards and foresters like Puronia ji, who is now a range officer at Kuno.

I recall how forest staff at Agraa village always kept a few bundles of bidi with them to facilitate easy dialogue with the villagers. The essence of successful relocation and rehabilitation was patient hearing given by the staff to the community members and solving their issues sympathetically and systematically.

In fact, relocation and rehabilitation were only possible because the villagers agreed on their relocation, seeking a better life for themselves and their children and a secure future for lions as a species.

It is a fact that for the Saharias, a change from a life of gatherer, cattle herder and partial agriculturist to solely practising agriculture wasn't smooth. It still isn't for the generation that collected and lived off non timber forest produce like salai, khair and dhawa resin, and many kinds of medicinal plants and honey collected from the forests. The next generation, though, has taken to better education, health, transportation and settled living in conditions not as hard as it previously was within the sanctuary. However, their access to the precious non timber forest products (NTFP) has declined drastically.

Improved and sustained management of habitat within the sanctuary has, over time, augmented the prey base for the intended carnivore, the Asiatic lion. So much so that mass capture techniques of crop-raiding nilgai from Chambal ravines were perfected in the Bhind district for further prey base supplementation once the lion had been introduced in the Kuno National Park.

Betrayal

It is a sad reflection on the state government of Madhya Pradesh and the central government that the planned reintroduction of the lion at Kuno has still not happened despite the restoration of its habitat in terms of vegetation and prey base, and its readiness since the early years of the new century to receive the lions. Reluctance on the part of the Gujarat state government to part with a few animals from its Gir National Park for reintroduction at Kuno is the main reason that a project endorsed and funded by the central government remains incomplete to date.

Ultimately, a Delhi-based organization approached the Supreme Court in 2006 with a prayer to direct Gujarat's state government to allow the Asiatic lion's reintroduction, suggesting, with scientific evidence, that Kuno was ready to become the second home for it. During the Supreme Court hearing, issues related to the presence of a tiger in Kuno were raised. In fact, Kuno is well connected with Madhav National Park on its east and the Ranthambore Tiger Reserve on its west. Therefore, the presence of migrating tigers in Kuno has always been a fact. However, no scientific evidence suggests that tigers and lions cannot coexist. In fact, some historical evidence suggests that both tiger and lions were together in central India and shared overlapping home ranges.

In the meantime, when there was an unprecedented delay in lion reintroduction, many other options were considered, including the introduction of the cheetah and even a proposal to bring zoo-bred lions for a captive conservation breeding programme at Kuno.

The Supreme Court, after hearing the petition for almost seven years, in April 2013, decided in favour of the reintroduction of Asiatic lions from Gir National Park, Gujarat, to the Kuno National Park, stating that the species is under extinction threat and urgently needs a second home. Further, the Supreme Court disallowed the proposal to introduce African cheetah in Kuno from Namibia, stating that the preservation of critically endangered native species should be given priority.

During the hearing in the Supreme Court, issues like whether lions from Gir could even be successfully reintroduced at Kuno were also raised. However, the fact remains that there have been several instances of successful reintroductions within the country—like the one-horned rhinoceros in Dudhwa National Park (Uttar Pradesh), gaur in Bandhavgarh Tiger Reserve and barasingha in Satpura Tiger Reserve (both in Madhya Pradesh). More recently, tigers have been successfully reintroduced in the Sariska Tiger Reserve in Rajasthan and in the Panna Tiger Reserve in Madhya Pradesh.

Therefore, the reintroduction of Asiatic lions to a large inviolate and suitably restored area of Kuno National Park as its second home cannot be doubted. It is a long-felt need and is necessary from a conservation biology point of view.

Inexplicably, the ghost of the cheetah has reappeared. Recently, the National Tiger Conservation Authority (NTCA) filed an affidavit in the Supreme Court stating that the African cheetah introduction in Kuno would not impact the lion reintroduction at a subsequent date. The Supreme Court has, thus, permitted the introduction of African cheetah in Kuno on an experimental basis under strict monitoring. A large high-tech enclosure is getting ready at Kuno to receive few African cheetahs.

It is my understanding that Kuno has been managed, from day one, to receive the Asiatic lion, and it was never seen as a site to introduce the African cheetah. Therefore, most of the open areas in the park have already been taken over by many woody species such as reonja and birbira. Grasslands have almost vanished, and with that has vanished the blackbuck, and the number of chinkara has greatly reduced—the two species that could have formed a prey base for the cheetah. The group size of other small prey species such as chital has gone down, too, due to the gradual loss of open areas available to them.

I have witnessed how the two small populations of blackbucks slowly disappeared from Poke Niviri and Manak Chawk in the Kuno core area, due to ecological succession and expansion of woodland and tall grasses such as *Themeda* and *Apluda* taking over some of the ecologically important sites. In the absence of any other large predator and availability of a breeding population of feral cattle along with chital and wild pigs, the leopard has grown in number and taken over the entire landscape. Under the circumstances, whether the introduced African cheetah can ever become free-ranging in Kuno is not too difficult to guess for an answer.

Today, many old-time forest staff and villagers are confused and demand an explanation from people like us who had convinced them that their relocation from the sanctuary would bring Asiatic lions into the areas vacated by them. The same has not happened even after more than 30 years of their relocation from the sanctuary—is this not a betrayal of their trust?

All said and done, what amazes me most is the fact that despite my staying more than a year in a Saharia pataur and being with them through thick and thin for over 20 years now, I am still locally known as '*Dilli ka patrakar* (the journalist from Delhi)'.

WILDLIFE LAW AND INSTITUTIONS IN FINE PRINT: VIGNETTES FROM MY DIARY

RITWICK DUTTA

India's principal law for the protection of wildlife, the Wild Life (Protection) Act (WLPA), 1972, was enacted during a fairly interesting phase in India's history. It was a time that saw increased centralization, nationalization and removal of the exalted status of the privileged classes through the abolition of the privy purse.[1] Prime Minister Indira Gandhi, with her deep interest in wildlife, felt the urgency of a comprehensive central law for the protection and conservation of wildlife. This was needed, given the fact that the subject of wildlife was in a 'State List' under the Constitution, which meant that only a state legislature could enact a law on the subject. However, using the constitutional provision[2] wherein, at the request of two or more states, Parliament could enact a law reserved for the state, the WLPA came into effect. Given the persona of Indira Gandhi, it is not difficult to fathom how 11 states passed resolutions to that effect so promptly. In many ways, the WLPA is a unique document. Unlike the Indian constitution, which was inspired by constitutional provisions of other countries, the WLPA was truly 'made in India'. However, this law, like any other law, has undergone a series of amendments since it was first enacted. Therefore, what one sees today is fundamentally different from the law that was enacted in 1972. For one, the law as originally enacted only provided for 'regulating' hunting; there were no Schedule I or Schedule II or others; all species were categorized in terms of their value for hunters. Thus, species were categorized as 'big game', 'small game' and 'medium game'.

For quite some time now, I have had the opportunity to focus on the WLPA as a lawyer, trainer and commentator. I must confess that despite working for more than two and a half decades on this law, one can, by no stretch, call oneself an expert on the subject. There are still many provisions of the Act that I never had a chance to deal with; there are provisions that have been so misinterpreted that the misinterpretations have replaced the actual understandings of the provisions, much like the doctrine of adverse possession, and the institutions created by this law that were meant as protector of wildlife have become the arbiter of their destiny, with power to exterminate species and their habitat. The exercise of authority has been replaced by the exercise of illegal power.

However, this is not about all that is wrong with the WLPA. This is about one's experience in the field and the court in trying to interpret and apply the law. A task that is not very easy, given the fact that despite after five decades of its existence, it continues to be seen as a 'new' law, with officers, judges and lawyers, all still trying to understand the 'wildlife law'—a process that may not always work in favour of wildlife. My experience tells me that the real understanding of the Act comes not from reading judgments or the law itself but rather from understanding how the law is interpreted and applied in the field. Of the many experiences, there are few that stand out, since they show how critical it is to have the correct understanding of the law and how misinterpretation can defeat its whole purpose.

Safed Bhalu

In early 2000, Achanakmar Wildlife Sanctuary in Chhattisgarh was still a relatively remote part in India. The journey from Bilaspur was rough and wild, and the Forest Rest House (FRH) had no electricity. This is where I learnt, in some detail, about the restriction on hunting and the powers of the chief wildlife warden (CWLW).

The ban on hunting is the first thing that comes to mind when one refers to the WLPA. There is a general belief that the Act bans the hunting of wild animals. The legal reality is that the Act only 'prohibits' the hunting of wild animals; there is no complete ban on hunting. All species listed in the Act can be hunted; only the situation and person who can authorize the hunting differs. The supreme decision-maker for the wild animals and birds is actually the CWLW—an office with no statutory qualification, experience or fixed tenure. There is no requirement under the law that the CWLW must have empathy, compassion or even a basic interest in wildlife. It is the state government's discretion as to who it appoints to the post. Yet, this is no innocuous post. The life and destiny of countless wild animals depend on the wisdom of the CWLW. They are judge, jury, prosecutor, along with being an administrator and manager. The reasons for this are not difficult to locate. As per the Act, the subjective satisfaction of the CWLW decides when an animal listed in Schedule I has become 'dangerous' to human life. The Act states as follows: 'the Chief Wild Life Warden may, if he is satisfied that any wild animal specified in Schedule I has become dangerous to human life or is so disabled or diseased as to be beyond recovery, by Order in writing and stating the reasons therefore, permit any person to hunt such animal or cause such animal to be hunted'.[3]

The emphasis here is on the use of the expression 'if he is satisfied'. All that the law requires is that the reason for the same has to be in writing. But what exactly is hunting? As it always happens, the legal definition is not always the same as what is commonly understood. Hunting in common parlance equals shikar. But 'hunting', as defined in the WLPA, has a much wider and more inclusive definition, and includes the acts of killing, capturing, coursing, snaring and trapping, and every attempt to do so. Even the act of baiting constitutes hunting, since the aim is to either capture or kill the animal.

The law states that once an animal has become dangerous to human life, the options available to the CWLW is to either get the problematic animal killed, capture it or release it back into the wild. It is purely discretionary. However, no administrative discretion is unfettered. The CWLW must follow the basic purport and objective of the Act as well as the applicable laws and principles.

Back to Achanakmar, I was told of an albino sloth bear that was caught near the forest a few months back and was now being kept in the state zoo. Being aware of the government's policy to not allow the capture of wild animals strictly for the purpose of keeping them in a zoo, I enquired further as to why the animal was captured at all. This is when the real story unfolded.

A local newspaper had reported that the villagers had regularly noticed a '*safed bhalu*'. This news item caught the fancy of the Chief Minister, who desired that such a 'unique' animal ought not to be in the forest but in the zoo for people to see. After all, what purpose is served if no one gets to see such an animal? However, his desire was met with a legal hurdle, since there were no legal provisions allowing such capture, and the sloth bear is protected under Schedule I of the WLPA. As it happens in most such cases, the officer who objected to the wishes of the Chief Minister was removed and replaced by a new CWLW, who promptly followed the dictates of his boss, and, within a few weeks, the unlucky animal landed in the zoo for public display, much to the joy of the viewers. The question that begs an answer is: how did this new CWLW achieve this feat? How did he cross the legal hurdle?

I had an opportunity to see the documents, and the revelations of this bureaucrat's mind could shame the legal minds of even the best lawyers. After the new CWLW assumed charge, it was reported by forest guards and FRH chowkidars that a strange white-coloured animal had started attacking them on a regular basis; so much so that they feared going out to patrol. The forest guards and watchers reported this fear to the higher authorities, who promptly responded to it. It is interesting that this white-coloured animal had a particular fascination only for the forest guards and staff of the forest department. No villagers or anyone from the local tribal community was reported to have been attacked. The new CWLW took this risk to human life very seriously, and orders were issued, under Section 11, stating that as the CWLW saw fit that the so-called white-coloured animal—namely the albino sloth bear—had become a danger to human life, and it, therefore, needed to be hunted down. However, he felt that there was no need to kill the animal, and trapping and sending the animal to a zoo would ensure the safety of both the animal and the people. This is how the bear 'legally' landed inside the prison called the state zoo.

I have cited this example to show how easy it is to misuse the discretion that is vested in the CWLW under pressure. The law requires the CWLW to be an independent, autonomous entity who is present to decide in the interest of wild animals. Unfortunately, today it seems to have become a post where decisions are often based on what is dictated from the 'above'. In law, this is called 'acting under dictation'. In simple terms, it means that though the law requires the authority to act in terms of its own wisdom; in reality, it acts primarily on the orders of its superiors.

The post of CWLW, at present, needs a thorough review. The wide discretion conferred on the position coupled with a lack of autonomy, basic minimum qualification and a fixed tenure means that, in its present form, the CWLW cannot be expected to decide in a free and fair manner on the fate of a wild animal. Rather, decisions concerning the life and liberty of wild animals should be the domain of the State Board of Wildlife (SBWL), just like the Juvenile Justice Board. Deciding whether a wild animal has become a threat to human life is not a simple administrative decision but requires adjudication. The Supreme Court had expressed its concern over excessive faith on certain posts and the dangers of discretionary powers:

> There is need to minimise the scope of the arbitrary use of power in all walks of life. It is inadvisable to depend on the good sense of the individuals, however high-placed they may be. It is all the more improper and undesirable to expose the precious rights like the rights of life, liberty and property to the vagaries of the individual whims and fancies. It is trite to say that individuals are not and do not become wise because they occupy high seats of power, and good sense, circumspection and fairness do not go with the posts, however high they may be. There is only a complacent presumption that those who occupy high posts have a high sense of responsibility. The presumption is neither legal nor rational. History does not support it and reality does not warrant it.[4]

Sarkari Hathi

This incident happened in the winter of 2004 while I was addressing a group of field-level forest officers in Jaldapara National Park (West Bengal). The forest officers had one major cause of worry—every time an elephant would raid a crop field, villagers would pelt stones at the nearest office of the range forest officer (RFO) or any other field office of the forest department. The reason was simple: since the elephant was the property of the government, it was the forest department's responsibility to ensure that the elephant did not indulge in crop-raiding. The senior forest officers accepted that it was their duty to ensure that the elephants remained within the confines of the forest. This made me think: are wild animals government property? If they are government property, it is imperative that it must be specifically mentioned in the statute itself. A reading of the WLPA showed the contrary. A myth has been perpetuated and followed by generations of foresters that wild animals are government property. Nothing could be farther from the truth. No legislation is perfectly drafted—the WLPA is no exception to this rule. The idea that all wild animals are government property is so deeply ingrained in the minds of forest bureaucracy that even forest officers serving as CWLW with decades of service are of the firm opinion that all wild animals are 'government property'. The reason for this misconception, too, is not difficult to locate. Section 39 of the Act begins by stating 'Wild Animals etc., to be Government Property'. This heading gives an impression that wild animals are indeed government property. However, if one reads the section as a whole, it is clear that contrary to general belief, wild animals are *not* the property of the government. Section 39 clearly states as follows:

> [W]ild animal, other than vermin, which is hunted under section 11 or sub-section (1) of section 29 or sub-section (6) of section 35 or kept or bred in captivity or hunted in contravention of any provision of this Act or any rule or order made thereunder or found dead, or killed by mistake.

From the above, it is clear that only a wild animal that is legally hunted on the grounds that it has become dangerous to human life or is so diseased or disabled so as to be beyond recovery is to be treated as government property. In addition, a live wild animal kept or bred in captivity in violation of the law is also to be treated as government property along with any animal that is found dead or killed even by mistake. Thus, it is clear that any wild animal in its natural state is not government property. Therefore, elephants moving in their habitat, whether in a forest or farms, are not the property of the government. Only when an offence takes place against the animal does it become the government's property. Thus, the forest department, or for that matter the government is not legally obligated to compensate for the loss caused due to damage by wild elephants for the simple reason that they are 'wild' and 'free' and not government or a 'sarkari' elephant. The Himachal Pradesh High Court clarified this issue by clearly stating:

> A bare reading of the above provision (Section 39) shows that the same would not apply to the wild animals roaming in the jungle. The mere fact that killing such wild animals is prohibited under the law and protection is provided to them would not mean that the state is the owner of such wild animals so as to make it liable for the damage caused by such wild animals.[5]

Many years later, while addressing a group of forest officers in Assam, the then CWLW was astonished when I told him that wild animals, unless hunted, are not government property. Convinced with my argument that they are not government property, he looked at me and said, 'The next time the ministers and the MLAs raise their voice and tell me to keep my elephants in control, I will tell them clearly that these are 'jungli hathi and not sarkari hathi!'

The Python That Was Not an Ajgar

In 2003, there was news about two magicians who were found guilty of possessing a python—a Schedule I species under the WLPA. The magistrate found the magicians guilty of illegal possession of the python and imposed a fine of ₹20,000, and set them free after the fine was paid. Officers of the forest department and the local representative of People for Animals, an NGO, wanted to challenge the magistrate's judgment at a higher court. A perusal of the judgment as well as the complaint filed by the concerned RFO revealed something very interesting. The WLPA clearly states that an offence against a Schedule I species is punishable with an imprisonment of at least three years (which may extend to seven years) and a fine not be less than ₹10,000. In simple terms, it means that once a court has concluded that a person has committed an offence against a Schedule I species, the court cannot set the offender free only on payment of a fine. In the judgment, the judge came to a peculiar finding to conclude that the offender need not be imprisoned. He concluded that what had been seized was an ajgar and not a python. The difference between an ajgar and a python, according to the court, is in terms of its age: it is only after an ajgar attains the age of maturity does it become a python. Since the snake that was seized was very young, it was concluded that it was only an ajgar and not a python; therefore, given the fact that the ajgar does not find mention in any of the schedules, no offence was committed by the magicians. After carefully looking at the legal provisions, it was decided to approach the high court. A petition was filed under Section 482 of the Criminal Procedure Code before the High Court of Punjab and Haryana on the grounds that the WLPA clearly states that the term 'wild animal' also includes their young and eggs. Therefore, offences against the young of any species are also covered under the provisions of the Act. It was also submitted that it is a scientific fact that there is no change in the species irrespective of age and that Homo sapiens will remain so regardless of whether one is young or old. The main contention before the high court was that species is not dependent on the age of an individual. After three years of hearings on multiple days, the high court concluded that the judicial magistrate had erred in not appreciating the fact that the WLPA makes no distinction between the young and the old, and that all wild animals, as long as they are listed in the Schedule are protected, and any offence against them invites the same level of punishment. However, the high court refused to intervene in the matter with respect to the sentence on the reasoning that what was seized was mentioned in the seizure memo as 'rock python' whereas what is mentioned in the WLPA is 'genus python'. The court concluded that 'genus python' is different from 'rock python' and is a distinct species; therefore, there had been no violation of the Act. An appeal was filed before the Supreme Court against the decision of the high court on the ground that 'genus python' includes 'rock python'; therefore, the high court decision was incorrect. The appeal became infructuous in view of the fact that the two magicians' who had illegal possession had died during the pendency of the litigation. The question of law as to whether 'genus python' includes 'rock python' was left open to be decided in another case.

The Himachal Pradesh High Court took a similar view when it held that a woman attacked by a bear is not entitled to any compensation, since she had mentioned in her request for compensation that a black bear attacked her. The high court reasoned that the state is not liable because there is nothing on record to show that the 'black bear' that attacked the plaintiff and caused injuries to her was of the species specified in the schedules of the Act, where only the sloth bear (*Melursus ursinus*) and Himalayan black bear (*Selenarctos thibetanus*) are mentioned.

Wildlife in the Stadium

The Jawahalal Nehru Stadium in New Delhi was the main venue of the 1982 Asian Games. Since then, it has served as the main sports stadium in the national capital and has hosted multiple national and international sporting events. However, from 2003 to around 2008, it was not uncommon to find lawyers in black coats, along with environmentalists, conservationists and tribal rights activists rubbing shoulders with athletes in the stadium. Again, the reason is not difficult to locate—Nehru Stadium also hosted the office and courtroom of the Central Empowered Committee (CEC), which was set up as an authority on the orders of the Supreme Court to assist the apex court in matters concerning forest and wildlife. Headed by P.V. Jayakrishnan, then secretary to Ministry of Environment and Forests (MoEF), with M.K. Jiwarajka as member secretary, it became a formidable body committed to forest and wildlife conservation. It was the CEC's report that became the basis of the Supreme Court's judgment that led to the closure of the Kudremukh iron mine; the CEC's report on the Niyamgiri mines in Odisha ultimately led to the cancellation of the forest clearance granted to Vedanta Limited and the Orissa Mining Corporation. The CEC emerged as the hope for wildlife and forests at a time when threats were increasing. The violators of forest and wildlife laws knew that once the CEC took notice, it was unlikely for them to escape unscathed. The CEC's report led to the first-ever instance of a Forest Minister and Additional Chief Secretary of a state (Maharashtra) going to jail for violating forest laws.[6] Those concerned about wildlife hailed the CEC as a shining example of what was possible if an institution was given power, authority and the autonomy to protect forests and wildlife.

Yet, if one carefully analyses the functioning of the CEC, it is clear that there are some serious problems in it, leading one to ask the fundamental question: is the continued existence of the CEC *actually* beneficial to wildlife and forest conservation?

One needs to dig deeper into the CEC constitution and its working to answer this question. The CEC is a multimember body headed by the chairperson, P.V. Jayakrishnan[7], who was appointed in his capacity as secretary, MoEF. He has been the chairperson for the last two decades: a record of the sort in government. Other members have also completed decades as members with no outer limit on their term in office. This in itself is a problem, given that decision-making cannot be monopolized by a group that has neither been chosen through an open process of selection nor elected. The other major problem is the opacity with which the institution functions—despite being a committee existing for two decades, it is yet to have a user-friendly website; its procedures for hearing and submitting reports are unclear. However, what is most problematic is its approach towards protection of national parks and sanctuaries. It has become a standard procedure for the Supreme Court to refer projects involving habitat destruction and diversion of lands in national parks and sanctuaries to the CEC for its opinion. In almost all instances, the CEC has followed a singular decision-making process: projects are allowed subject to payment of a certain percentage for conservation (usually limited to 5 per cent of the project cost) and other conditions as stipulated by the CWLW. The projects thus approved have included irrigation projects, highways, oil drilling, dams, power transmission lines and windmills, among others. What is deeply problematic here is that such a recommendation for the diversion of lands in national parks and sanctuaries for developmental projects is legally untenable as being against the letter and spirit of the WLPA. It is a trite law that if a law requires an act to be done in a particular manner, it must be done in that manner only or not at all. The WLPA states clearly in sections 29 and 35(6) that the destruction of wildlife and its habitat is permissible only if such activity is found 'necessary' for improving and managing wildlife and its habitat. Such diversion is allowed subject to approval from the National Board for Wildlife (NBWL). By no stretch of imagination can building roads and highways, oil and gas drilling, construction of dams, etc., be considered as an activity 'necessary' for improving and managing wildlife and its habitat. To state it bluntly, all such recommendations given by the CEC over the last few decades are clearly illegal, violating the law both in letter and spirit and defeating the purpose of having wildlife protected areas (PAs). Regrettably and contrary to general opinion, it is the CEC that has facilitated the opening up of India's PAs to destructive projects in violation of the provisions of the WLPA.

If the recommendations of the CEC have been contrary to the law, those of the SC of the NBWL have also been no different. Over the last two decades, the fact is that neither the NBWL nor its Standing Committee (SC) has acted in accordance with the law. The WLPA does not empower the SC to allow activities inside national parks and sanctuaries unless they are found necessary and are directly for the benefit of wildlife and its habitat. The only exception is tourism lodges in sanctuaries, which can be permitted with the approval of the NBWL. It is unfortunate that eminent conservationists, wildlife scientists and even seasoned administrators who have been members of the NBWL never bothered to check whether they were empowered by law to allow such diversion irrespective of the conservation bargains. In any case, if one examines the minutes of the SC, it is clear that since its inception, the NBWL has invariably declared that such diversions are only 'recommendations'. One may ask the question: to whom does the SC, which is headed by the Union environment minister, recommend? After all, there is no executive authority higher than the minister himself? Moreover, should not the findings of the SC become final only after their endorsement from the NBWL? The unfortunate fact is that the NBWL has failed to meet year after year, no matter who is in power. A similar situation exists with the SBWL also. The WLPA does not empower the board to decide whether the lands and the resources of sanctuaries and national parks should be diverted or not. Notwithstanding this, conservationists and conservation organizations across the country that are part of the state boards have been approving such decisions involving the diversion of lands in national parks and sanctuaries. This is nothing short of a breach of public trust.

The continued existence of the CEC has created other serious issues as well. As per orders of the Supreme Court, the CEC can examine the decision of the SC of the NBWL and present its recommendations to the Supreme Court, which then passes its orders based on them. On the face, it may seem to be a positive step. However, a closer look reveals how deeply problematic it is. Firstly, it usurps the power of citizens to question the decision of the SC of the NBWL before the high courts and even the Supreme Court and other judicial forums, since the Supreme Court has already taken a decision on the same. Secondly, the CEC is seen to follow a 'copy and paste' approach while recommending projects that legally could and should not have been permitted in the first place. It is common knowledge that the CEC rarely rejects any projects.

Today, if saving wildlife in the country is to become a priority, it is important to ensure that the NBWL and its SC functions in accordance with the law. It is also high time that the Supreme Court reviews the constitution and the functioning of the CEC, and takes steps to disband the committee as it stands because it has outlived its utility. The CEC had relevance in the absence of a statutory body, but now, with the NGT in place, there is no reason why the CEC should be the first appellate authority on the recommendations of the NBWL or its SC. The National Green Tribunal (NGT)

Act, 2010, could be suitably amended to include the WLPA within its jurisdiction.

Looking Ahead

Among all the laws concerning the environment, the WLPA stands apart due to one unique aspect: it is the only environmental law that has only been made stronger by every new amendment. Irrespective of the political party in power, efforts have been made to ensure that the provisions become stronger and stricter with time. Yet, one cannot close one's eyes to the fact that the WLPA, as it exists today, is largely out of tune with the challenges of present-day conservation. It was drafted at a time when the belief was that good faith, wisdom and empathy exist only in government officials and occupants of statutory boards and committees. It continues to treat communities that live along with wildlife with suspicion and disdain. It fails to recognize the inherent right of animals to live a life of dignity and freedom. Disturbingly, it classifies animals who, in nature, are all born equal in different schedules with varying levels of protection. Much like the caste system, to be born as a Schedule I species ensures, to some extent, a life of dignity, while being a vermin means nothing short of being assumed to be criminal and dispensable from birth. With the life and liberty of wild animals and their habitat at the mercy of the CWLW and the CEC, the future of India's wildlife is far from being secure. As the instances cited above show, even the best law is capable of wrong interpretation and misuse, defeating its very purpose. It is not to be forgotten that the WLPA is only a tool for conservation and protection; its efficacy ultimately depends on the wisdom, creativity, honesty and commitment of those who wield the tool and engage with it. The wielders of this legal tool have not covered themselves with glory for the last 50 years. One can only hope that the next 50 years see human ingenuity and creativity being used in a way that the albino sloth bear does not fall victim to a chief minister's fancy and that an ajgar is not required to prove that it is, indeed, the python.

Notes

1. Under Article 291 of the Indian constitution a privy purse was a fixed, tax-free sum guaranteed to the former princely rulers and their successors. This was abolished by a constitutional amendment in 1971.
2. Article 252 of the Indian constitution empowered Parliament to legislate on a subject in the State List if two or more State Legislatures passed a resolution authorizing Parliament to enact a law.
3. *The Wild Life (Protection) Act, 1972*, Parliament of India, https://bit.ly/3mPOtnO, Accessed on 15 June 2022.
4. 'Delhi Transport Corporation vs D.T.C. Mazdoor Congress', iKanoon, 4 September 1990, https://bit.ly/3RuhuDv. Accessed on 11 July 2022.
5. 'State Of Himachal Pradesh And Ors. vs Smt. Halli Devi', iKanoon, 4 May 2000, https://bit.ly/3z1wbaf. Accessed on 11 July 2022.
6. 'Maha Minister, Officer Sent to Jail', *Hindustan Times*, 11 May 2006, https://bit.ly/3Pj7xXO. Accessed on 11 July 2022.
7. P.V. Jayakrishnan retired as secretary to the government of India in 2002, however, the Supreme Court made it clear that he is holding the office in his personal capacity. It is interesting to note that the chairperson has been appointed by the Court till further order. Mahender Vyas, Advocate has also been member since its inception, while retired IFS officers M.K. Muthoo and S.K. Patnaik have completed more than a decade and a half.

NBWL: NATIONAL BOARD FOR(?) WILDLIFE

PRERNA SINGH BINDRA[1]

Happy to inform that in its 60th meeting NBWL has recommended the proposal for Tinaighat-Castlerock-Caranzol Railway doubling of Southwestern Railways, Karnataka with certain mitigation measures. #conservation#wildlife

—Prakash Javadekar, former minister of environment, forest and climate change, 6 January 2021[2]

Contained in this 37-word tweet is a powerful statement of the collapse of the National Board for Wildlife (NBWL), a key institution that governs India's wildlife and its degeneration from a force for conservation to one used to legitimize destructive projects within the sanctum sanctorum of the country's natural heritage—national parks and sanctuaries.

Here, the then Minister was referring to the permission granted by the NBWL, specifically its Standing Committee (SC), a core working group drawn from the larger body of the board, for the expansion of a railway line that cuts through the Kali Tiger Reserve (Karnataka), Bhagwan Mahaveer Wildlife Sanctuary and Mollem National Park (Goa). This region ranks among one of the world's eight 'hottest hotspots' of biological diversity[3], harbours myriad endemic, endangered species and is part of a critical tiger landscape that connects habitats across three states. The SC, NBWL, allowed the diversion of forests from these protected areas (PA) to enhance the capacity to transport minerals like iron ore and coal to the Mormugao Port Trust in Goa. The questions that need to be asked are: whose interests was the committee serving: mining or wildlife? What is the NBWL's mandate? And why is the Minster who served as the chairperson of the SC, NBWL, 'happy' about a clearance for a project that will 'damage the integrity of the last remaining wilderness of the Western Ghats'[4], as per a report by his own ministry's National Tiger Conservation Authority (NTCA)? And how does the diversion and destruction of this biodiversity hotspot translate to '#conservation #wildlife'?

To answer these questions and appreciate the import of the Minister's statement, it is important to first understand the history and evolution of the NBWL and its mandate.

The NBWL: A Historical Perspective

The NBWL's predecessor was the Central Board for Wildlife, created post Independence in response to the precarious status of wild animals: the cheetah was extinct, the great Indian bustard (GIB) had vanished from its earlier strongholds, and swathes of forests were being razed for agriculture, industry and dams. In its inaugural session held between 24 November–1 December 1952 in Bangalore, the board stated that 'the preservation of India's fauna and the prevention of extinction of species is of great national importance'.[5] Under the chairmanship of Jayachamaraja Wadiyar, the Maharaja of Mysore, it listed various tasks, some of which included the setting up of national parks and sanctuaries, declaration of certain species as protected and prevention of indiscriminate killing—legal at the time, with some wild animals considered vermin or trophies. The Central Board had as regional secretaries' stalwarts like E.P. Gee[6], Y.R. Ghorpade[7], K.S. Dharmakumarsinhji[8], who critically assessed existing legislature, wrote incisive reports on the status of wildlife in their region and drew up recommendations for its conservation. A significant recommendation was the setting up of wildlife boards in each state. A reading of regional reports[9] indicates that state boards were active as well. On the advice of its Wildlife Advisory Board, Saurashtra—a separate state then—amended its Wild Birds And Animals Protection Act, 1912, to make it one of the best preservation laws in the country. In its first meeting, the Central Board also renamed itself the Indian Board of Wildlife (IBWL).

Over the next few years, the IBWL made various recommendations such as affording special protection to highly endangered species, protecting urban wildlife and passing legislation to create and manage national parks. Though it did its work with due judiciousness, it lacked statutory backing. Conserving nature was not a priority of the government, especially as the country faced pressing challenges of food security and economic independence in the immediate aftermath of freedom.

Another constraint was that forests and wildlife were state subjects. As a national-level advisory body, it lacked the teeth to get state governments to 'to adopt and enforce its legislations'[10]. And those entrusted with carrying out the board's resolutions were 'utterly callous and indifferent to their enforcement when attention is drawn to them'[11], as pointed out by the late Humayun Abdulali, naturalist and former vice president of the Bombay Natural History Society (BNHS).

The Indira Gandhi Era: The IBWL Becomes a Powerful Force

This status quo would change when Mrs Indira Gandhi took over as prime minister in 1966. During her tenure, the IBWL became a force to be reckoned with. In 1968, she appointed Karan Singh, the then minister for civil aviation and tourism, as the board's chairman, though she herself took over as chair in 1980.[12] Over the years, it had as members legends such as Dr Salim Ali, M. Krishnan and Anne Wright. Speaking to the newly constituted board, Indira Gandhi expressed her hope that 'this board will be ever vigilant in the cause of our beautiful and free-moving fellow citizens, namely our wild animals and birds'[13].

In the same year, the IBWL banned the export of big cat skins, and two years later—at Indira Gandhi's suggestion—placed a five-year moratorium on the shooting of tigers despite immense opposition from the shikar lobby. The moratorium was to become a permanent ban as the board endorsed the passing of the Wild Life (Protection) Act (WLPA) in 1972; and, in 1973, the initiation of Project Tiger.

Though the state advisory boards were scripted in the WLPA in 1972, a deliberate decision was to leave the IBWL out. Dr M.K. Ranjitsinh[14], the key architect of the Act, explains that it was keeping in view the sensitivity of the issue, to not impose a statutory body on a state subject. It was only in 1976 that forests and wildlife became a concurrent subject.

Indira Gandhi's passion for nature and her immense political clout helped catalyse a fundamental paradigm shift in the practice of forestry from a commercial objective to a conservation focus. The PA network expanded and there were concerted efforts to revive the populations of endangered, lesser-known species such as the GIB, crocodiles, olive ridley turtles, etc.

There were some significant developments in the IBWL as well. Conservationist and author Valmik Thapar notes that it was a February 1981 meeting that laid the foundations for eco-development and involvement of local communities in conservation.[15] In its meeting in 1982, the chair of the IBWL drew up a visionary strategy for conservation. This included establishing a network of PAs representative of all ecosystems, restoration of degraded habitats, protection of wildlife in multiple-use forests and corridors for genetic robustness, and need for participation in international conventions, among others.

Unfortunately, these did not come to pass. With Mrs Gandhi's assassination in 1984, political will for wildlife conservation collapsed, and the IBWL was on a steady, steep decline.

The Decline

The next meeting of the IBWL was in 1997, after a gap of eight years. But it was a far cry from the invigorating, focused and successful meetings held earlier. The chair, the then prime minister, Deve Gowda, apparently dozed through the meeting—a feat repeated in 1998 by the next prime minister, I.K. Gujral, who also used the time to catch up on his sleep![16]

That two consecutive prime ministers snoozed through the meetings was indicative of the sheer political disinterest in wildlife. The 1990s was a critical time. There was an escalating demand for wildlife derivatives, such as tiger bones, used in traditional Chinese medicines. Poaching spiked and painfully revived tiger populations collapsed, including in star reserves such as Ranthambore and Sariska. This was also the decade that ushered in India's economic liberalization, which had unintended and devastating consequences on wildlife and forests. Economic growth was prioritized; safeguarding the environment was considered a luxury that could be taken care of later. Environmental safeguards built over the previous two decades were disregarded to promote investment and industry. The regulatory framework that protected forests and wildlife was eased as forests and natural habitats were razed for industry and infrastructure.

The IBWL remained a mute spectator to the decimation of wild habitats. In a letter written in 1997, conservationist and member of the board Bittu Sahgal drew the attention of then Prime Minister I.K. Gujral to the horrific 'dismemberment of contiguous forests by industrial and commercial projects that have the Government of India's tacit approval'.[17] He asked that as chairman of the IBWL, the Prime Minister, call for 'a White Paper to be prepared on the true State of India's Environment, particularly its impending loss of wildlife species and habitats'.

The appeal went unheeded

Be that as it may, the IBWL had a final hurrah in its twenty-first meeting in 2002 before it was dissolved. In a far-reaching decision, it advised the states to declare eco-sensitive zones (ESZ) of 10 km around PAs.[18] A comprehensive road map for securing wildlife and its habitat outlined in the National Wildlife Action Plan (NWAP) (2002–2016) was also released in the same meeting.

Constitution of the NBWL

The year 2002 was a landmark one. In an amendment of the WLPA, the IBWL was reconstituted as the NBWL. It was now a statutory body; its composition was changed and powers were clearly articulated.

The NBWL has 47 members, with the prime minister as its chair and the environment minister as the vice-chairperson. It has 27 public servants drawn from various government departments, the chief of army staff, and secretaries of defence, tourism, tribal welfare and expenditure, among others. It also has on board 15 non-official civil society representatives and non-governmental organization (NGO) with expertise in wildlife conservation.

Holding full board meetings may have seemed impractical. So, the 2002 amendment of the WLPA provided that the NBWL may constitute an SC 'for the purpose of exercising such powers and performing such duties as may be delegated to the Committee by the National Board'. It would have a member secretary and a vice-chairperson, who would nominate no more than 10 members from the NBWL to the committee.

The NBWL's mandate, as defined by Section 5C of the WLPA, is primarily the conservation of wildlife and forests. In its advisory role, the board counsels the central and state governments on policies related to strengthening wildlife conservation, such as setting up PAs, and preventing and controlling poaching and illegal wildlife trade. It is required to periodically assess what progress (or lack thereof) the country has made in conservation and brings out status reports on the country's wildlife. Another task is to assess the impacts of projects and activities on wildlife and its habitat.

The NBWL is also a decision-making body. Any alteration of PA boundaries or permitting any commercial tourist resorts, hotels, zoos and safari park in PAs requires the prior approval of the NBWL. Additionally, a 2006 Supreme Court order directed that all activities within the ESZs of PAs that have environmental clearances be referred to the SC, NBWL.[19]

India's 990 PAs are critical to conserve its increasingly endangered wildlife and cover about 5 per cent of its terrestrial surface, far below the world average of 9.3 per cent. Even our neighbouring countries fare better—Bhutan protects half of its geographical landscape, while PAs cover roughly 17 per cent of Nepal.

The last refuges of wildlife are bountiful with minerals, water, timber, land, and are threatened by various anthropogenic pressures, infrastructure and other development projects. In this context, a PA status helps conserve these habitats that otherwise would have been wiped off by the plough, the axe and industry.

The NBWL is the only independent, empowered body to safeguard PAs against the onslaught of development. This mandate is further strengthened by various court judgments. For instance, the Supreme Court in its 2013 order emphasized the board's role to 'promote conservation and development of wildlife and frame policies and advise the Central Government and the State Governments on the ways and importance of promoting wildlife conservation'[20]. It pointed out that the 'legislation in its wisdom has conferred a duty on NBWL to provide conservation and development of wildlife and forests'.

However, what the SC, NBWL has been working for instead—since its inception—is the development of highways, mines, dams, transmission lines, and other infrastructure inside and on the fringes of PAs.

Flawed Functioning of the SC, NBWL

In its fourth meeting in April 2005, SC member Dilnavaz Variava urged that they 'must dedicate at least 50 per cent of the time to proactive conservation issues and not merely on developmental (de-reservation) proposals'[21]. Ministry officials themselves pointed out the overemphasis on diversion proposals. In the following meeting held in October 2005, S.C. Sharma, who represented the environment ministry, reiterated that the committee must 'devote more time on various issues concerning wildlife conservation'[22].

This was to be a continuing battle, as I was to witness during my three-year tenure between 2010–2013 as a member of the NBWL and the SC. I will draw your attention to the infamous twenty-second meeting of the SC, NBWL, widely covered by the media for the unseemly haste in which developmental proposals were cleared.

Just two days before the meeting (22 April 2011, nearing midnight), we were mailed about 30 additional proposals, even though MoEF rules stipulate that the agenda must be circulated at least 15 days prior. This gave us no time to review and assess the projects for an informed decision-making process. We objected but were brushed off, and the meeting started on a sour note. In less than three hours, then environment minister,

Jairam Ramesh[23], cursorily dealt with about 60 proposals, clearing most of them, including a road through Kanha Tiger Reserve and the Desert National Park, the last refuge of the critically endangered GIB; a dam on Parwan River, a Chambal tributary that would submerge 82 sq. km of Shergarh Wildlife Sanctuary and the denotification of Trikuta Wildlife Sanctuary in Jammu.

Appalled at the conduct of the meeting, I expressed my anguish in an email to a fellow conservationist, 'The decisions are supposed to be collective, but I didn't see any of us getting a word in edgeways. We were hushed. I am now a party to decisions I do not agree with. If this situation continues, the NBWL will end up as a rubber stamp to the destruction of wildlife.'

The chair cannot go against the majority decision of the committee, though as the environment minister, in this case, Ramesh could overrule the committee's decision. This was clarified in a 2017 order[24] of the National Green Tribunal (NGT), where it determined that the then Environment Minister, Jayanti Natarajan had no power to overrule the majority opinion of the SC members who had unilaterally opposed the Lower Demwe Hydro Electric Project, Arunachal Pradesh.[25]

The decisions of the NBWL are subject to legal scrutiny, but the process was flawed, as we pointed out in a letter to then minister Jayanthi Natarajan.[26] Proposals were shoved through at the eleventh hour. Accompanying information was incomplete and shoddy. Even environmental impact assessment (EIA) reports and maps were usually not provided.

For us members, all of this seriously hindered informed decision-making. How could we possibly make just decisions on projects sitting in the corridors of power in Delhi, when the information provided did not remotely represent ground reality?

How would we grasp, say, the consequences of a proposed

road in Corbett Tiger Reserve, without knowing which areas it would run through? Did it cut through the heart or skirt the park or impinge on a frequented elephant corridor? Did it bisect, and thus, restrict wildlife access to a waterhole? Such information is critical to weigh in on a decision, but proposals rarely, if ever, contained such vital details. Important wildlife species in the area were missed out. Some projects would not bother to mention the number of trees to be cut; others underplayed it.

The information furnished was misleading and attuned to fast-track clearances. The extent of deception was shocking. In a proposal for the construction of a cement plant on the edge of the Kaimur Wildlife Sanctuary (Uttar Pradesh), the state failed to mention that this project was sub judice in the Supreme Court; the environment clearance granted to the project was on false grounds.

Such omissions and misinformation were the norm and, more often than not, deliberate. Officers involved with the process revealed they were asked to omit information 'that would show the project in negative ways'[27]. This was corroborated later by the deputy inspector general (DIG) (Wildlife) in the environment ministry, Prakriti Srivastava. For much of her tenure (2009 to early 2012), the SC was part of her portfolio. In a statement to the Central Bureau of Investigation (CBI), Ms Srivastava wrote that she was 'instructed (by her seniors) before every SC, NBWL, meeting not to include information in the agenda that would be detrimental to getting clearance'[28]. She further wrote that 'the agenda for meetings sent by the wildlife division with comments in favour of conservation was inevitably diluted and modified so as to benefit project proponents, rather than wildlife'.

We were fed convenient untruths while the inconvenient truths were avoided.

There were other concerns with the functioning of the committee. We found a lacklustre attitude to consider viable alternative sites and options for projects in PAs. Frequently, the projects came for clearance when they were already halfway through. It was a clever ruse, this fait accompli. Money, invariably running into thousands of crores, had already been sunk in the project and was used to apply undue pressure on concerned committees. When the 800 MW Kol Dam was tabled before us, half of it was already constructed with over ₹2,100 crore spent. The dam would submerge 125 hectare of Majathal Wildlife Sanctuary (Himachal Pradesh), taking the endangered cheer pheasant with it. It was rejected. We fought hard for this, but our 'no' hardly made a difference. We were shocked to learn—through a media report—that the proponents, the public-sector company National Thermal Power Corporation (NTPC) Limited, had continued to build with 80 per cent of the work done.

Minutes of the SC meetings were also sometimes manipulated, failing to give an accurate record of the proceedings. In its tenth meeting in February 2008, non-official members rejected a proposed road through the Srivilliputhur Wildlife Sanctuary in the Western Ghats. The road would also cut an elephant corridor. Their dissent was recorded in a letter to the MoEF, but the 'minutes of the meeting, published later on the MoEF website, falsely claimed that the Standing Committee had decided to recommend the proposal!'[29]

Personally and collectively, as members, we raised these issues repeatedly with the concerned environment minister. The SC, NBWL, we wrote, was failing in its core objective of promoting wildlife conservation, and 'its role has been merely limited to that of a clearing-house'.[30]

Hard to imagine, but things took a steep downturn. Clearances peaked, and what's more, the high rate of approval (650 projects in 7 months) was projected as an achievement of the environment ministry—thereby shedding the illusion of its conservation mandate.

Present Status: The NBWL, a Threat to India's Wildlife

In May 2014, India ushered in the BJP-led National Democratic Alliance (NDA) government with a thumping majority. While the earlier United Progressive Alliance (UPA) government had been steadily weakening environment safeguards, the NDA carried forward this agenda in a more aggressive and systematic manner.

In its first meeting in August 2014, the reconstituted SC, NBWL, cleared 133 projects and rejected only one. The then environment minister, Prakash Javadekar, reportedly said projects could not be held up due to 'frivolous reasons'[31]. One of the projects cleared was the construction of the Gaduli–Santalpur road in Gujarat's Kutch Desert Wildlife Sanctuary, which the earlier SC had advised against. It is the *only* known mass nesting site of flamingos in India, possibly Asia. Flamingos that you might see across the country, be it Chilika Lake in Odisha, Najafgarh in Delhi, Sewri in Mumbai or Pulicat Lake in Tamil Nadu, wing their way here from their nesting grounds in Kutch. The construction of the road would upset the fragile aquatic ecosystem, leading flamingos to abandon the site and their possible extinction in the subcontinent.

Frivolous? I think not.

This meeting set the trend.

Between June 2014 and May 2018, the rejection rate of projects was an abysmal 0.01 per cent, a sharp drop from the 11.9 per cent under the UPA-II rule between 2009–2013, as per an analysis by the Delhi-based think tank Centre for Science and Environment (CSE).[32] The overall loss of wildlife habitat was 24,329 ha (2014–2018) or an area twice that of Chandigarh.

Between 2019 and 2021 (till June), Delhi-based NGO Legal Initiative for Forests and Environment (LIFE) analysed that at least 3,067 ha were diverted from PAs and their ESZs.[33] It must be noted that this represents only the actual land diverted.

The influence area of such projects is far greater due to the disturbance caused by construction, the influx of labour and ancillary development such as roads, settlements, etc. A bulk of the projects granted clearances were roads, transmission lines, railway lines and other such linear infrastructure. These are especially damaging, as they fragment habitats, lead to degradation of forests around, cause fatal accidents of wildlife and hinder wildlife movement. And for all our chest-thumping on increasing tiger numbers—the fact of the matter is India is severely endangering its future—over 1,700 ha of tiger habitat[34] has been cleared for highways, railway lines, mines, nuclear facility and dams, among others. The SC, NBWL, has even given approval[35] to highly destructive projects such as the Ken–Betwa river interlinking that would destroy about a third of Panna Tiger Reserve's core area, drowning breeding sites of critically endangered vultures and tigers.

The projects are superficially assessed, virtually none rejected. What's also trending is the trick of doing a site inspection *after* granting clearance, which reduces it to a farce. Site visits provide for detailed and thorough scrutiny of project impacts. When conducted after the approval has been granted, it takes away the possibility of turning down the proposal if ground surveys indicate detrimental wildlife impacts.

The Covid-19 pandemic signalled a new low. During the lockdown, as the country grappled with the pandemic, the NBWL briskly conducted its business. Meetings were held virtually, leaving little room for debate, detailed scrutiny, and opinions of experts and other stakeholders. Projects approved included a railway line through a crucial tiger corridor that connects Telangana's Kawal Tiger Reserve and Tadoba Andhari Tiger Reserve, Maharashtra, a highway expansion through the Mollem Wildlife Sanctuary in Goa, and a diversion of 768 ha of forest land for a power project close to the Benog Wildlife Sanctuary, Uttarakhand.

Entire sanctuaries were denotified and erased off the map of India. One among these is the Galathea National Park, an iconic nesting site of leatherback sea turtles, the world's largest turtles. This 'coincided' with NITI Aayog's 'development' plans for Great Nicobar. Leatherbacks are migratory, swimming over 10,000 miles a year between foraging and nesting grounds. With their nesting beach soon to be annihilated for a shipping project, where would the leatherbacks go? Turtle populations are on a steep decline, their nesting sites shrinking. One would imagine the NBWL's lookout would be the turtles' precarious future, not cater to NITI Aayog's development agenda that would wipe off the nesting habitat of the endangered turtles.

The above is a tiny representation of the litany of destruction that the NBWL has unleashed in a blatant abuse of its power. The minutes of the SC, NBWL, meetings make for depressing reading. They are an inexhaustible list of decisions that recommend either deleting parts of PAs or diverting land for roads, railway lines, power projects, and so on. India's apex body for wildlife protection has become an active agent in its destruction, a one-point clearing desk for damaging projects in fragile wildlife habitats.

Shockingly, the approvals granted by the SC, NBWL, are ipso facto illegal. The law (Section 29 and Section 35(6) of the WLPA) is unambiguous in that no destruction of wildlife and their habitat in a national park or sanctuary is permissible unless the same is for the benefit of wildlife.[36] If there is some way in which annihilating a sanctuary or drowning it, or blasting and cutting through habitats where animals live, mate and nurture their young, helps wildlife, it escapes me. In my three years on the board, and an exhaustive reading of minutes of various meetings[37], I am yet to come across a decision to divert PAs that is backed by credible reasons as to how it benefits wildlife.

The constitution of the present committee itself is flawed. The SC has no independent NGO. Of its three 'independent' members, one is a retired government official, another is a serving forest officer—the director of the Gujarat Ecological Education and Research (GEER) Foundation[38], an autonomous body set up by the government of Gujarat. The only apparently independent member is R. Sukumar, a professor at the Indian Institute of Science, Bengaluru.

The NBWL's three-year term got over in July 2017. But the incumbent government ensured the continuity of this conveniently plaint committee through an arbitrary amendment made to the NBWL rules. Now, the term of the members can be extended till such a period as the government deems fit. Additionally, the SC has failed to function as stipulated under the full board's 'superintendence, direction and control'. It exercises full powers of the NBWL but fails to consult or even ratify its decision with the board, and as such, its decisions are without authority.

NBWL: A Force for Good?

As a member, I can say with certainty that the NBWL can affect change. Being a member of the SC presents an unparalleled opportunity to speak up, to take a stand where it counts.

We were able to stop a few destructive projects. One was a missile-firing testing system in the Tillanchong Wildlife Sanctuary, a narrow strip of island in Nicobar. The firing would have been particularly damaging to the endemic Nicobar megapode, which is a ground-nesting bird.

Following up with the ministry ensured that minutes were diligently recorded in detail. We put on record our dissent articulating reasons why the approvals that were given were unwise—and this counted. I put in a dissent note on the decision to drill through—for a ropeway—the nesting site of critically endangered vultures in Girnar Wildlife Sanctuary. The Supreme Court's Central Empowered Committee took note and ruled that the ropeway should not be allowed in the sanctuary. We were also able to help steer the creation of a few new PAs, one example being the Nandhaur Wildlife Sanctuary (Uttarakhand), and expand the area of existing wildlife sanctuaries.

The point I am trying to make here is that the NBWL was meant as a force for good, and undermining it—as has been happening with successive governments—simply must stop.

National Board for Wildlife 'Destruction'

The 'Great Indian Clearance Sale' of our natural heritage by the NBWL continues.[39] With its rapacious attitude, the SC, NBWL, destroys not just wildlife but ecosystems—forests, grasslands, rivers, and mangroves—that shield our people from floods, cyclones, droughts and climate crisis impacts. These are ecosystems on which millions of people depend.

We are at a time when the NBWL has not bothered to meet even once since September 2012.[40] Its constitution is questionable, and its SC is exercising authority without accountability, signing away wildlife habitats without any application of mind and in gross violation of its statute. If this continues, the last refugia of our magnificent flora and fauna will be wiped off, the loss irrevocable.

Fifty years after its inception, the NBWL's glorious legacy stands tattered. A vibrant, critical and committed board has turned tame and servile to the government's destructive development agenda. Should we say then, the NBWL can now be appropriately named the 'National Board for Wildlife "Destruction"'.

Notes

1. I owe thanks to Prakriti Srivastava and Ritwick Dutta for helping me understand the functioning of the NBWL and its SC, related legal aspects and other matters. Our conversations have

informed this article. Ritwick's article in *Economic & Political Weekly* 'National Board for Wildlife and the Illusion of Wildlife Protection,' was particularly useful. I relied also on Valmik Thapar's *Battling for Survival* and Jairam Ramesh's *A Life in Nature* for a historical perspective. Thanks are due to Mridhu Tandon for her work on analysing some of the SC, NBWL, minutes.

2. Prakash Javadekar [@prakashjavdekar], *Twitter*, 6 January 2021, https://bit.ly/3uCarz5. Accessed on 29 June 2022.
3. 'Western Ghats', UNESCO World Heritage Centre, https://bit.ly/3OVHBl3. Accessed on 11 July 2022.
4. Site Appraisal Report Pertaining to Diversion of 10.45 Ha (9.57 Ha in Dandeli Wildlife Sanctuary and 0.88 Ha in Haliyal Division) of Forest Land for Non-Forestry Purpose for Doubling the Railway Track between Tinaighat, NTCA, Regional Office, Bengaluru, 20 July 2020.
5. Ramesh, Jairam, 'Lecture: Jayachamaraja Wadiyar and the Indian Board of Wild Life', The Hindu Centre for Politics and Public Policy, 20 February 2020, https://bit.ly/3c8LAws. Accessed on 29 June 2022.
6. Tea planter-conservationist and author of the seminal *The Wildlife of India* (HarperCollins, 1964).
7. The last raja of Sandur, a princely state in Karnataka. He was a well-known wildlife conservationist and a member of the BNHS.
8. Naturalist, writer, painter, and author of *Birds of Saurashtra* (1955) and *Reminiscences of Indian Wildlife* (1993).
9. Text of the reports also available in Thapar, Valmik, *Battling for Survival: India's Wilderness Over Two Centuries*, Oxford University Press, 2003.
10. Khan, M. A., 'Letter: Wild Life Problems', *JBNHS*, Vol. 57, No. 1, November 1959, pp. 218–19, https://bit.ly/3ynrTbm. Accessed on 29 June 2022.
11. Abdulali, Humayun, 'Some Sorry Notes on Wild Life in NW. Madhya Pradesh', *JBNHS*, Vol. 56, No. 2, 1959, pp. 319–12, https://bit.ly/3aqQiVQ. Accessed on 29 June 2022.

12. Ramesh, Jairam, *Indira Gandhi: A Life in Nature*, Simon & Schuster, 2018.
13. Thapar, Valmik, *Battling for Survival: India's Wilderness Over Two Centuries*, Oxford University Press, 2003, p. 267.
14. Former bureaucrat and many times member of the NBWL and various state wildlife advisory boards.
15. Thapar, Valmik, *Battling for Survival: India's Wilderness Over Two Centuries*, Oxford University Press, 2003, pp. 288–89.
16. Ibid. 351–352.
17. 'India's Dismembered Network of Sanctuaries and National Parks', Yogesh Wadadekar, Tata Institute of Fundamental Research, https://bit.ly/3OZO7Yj. Accessed on 11 July 2022.
18. 'Guidelines for Eco-Sensitive Zones around National Parks and Wildlife Sanctuaries', Ministry of Environment and Forests, 2 September 2011, https://bit.ly/3bS2ajM. Accessed on 29 June 2022.
19. According to a Supreme Court order in 2006, all projects granted environment clearances within a 10-km boundary of national parks and sanctuaries would have to be approved by the SC of the NBWL, unless a site-specific ESZ has been notified by the state, after which activities will be regulated as per the notification. This was in pursuance of a decision of the Indian Board of Wildlife in its 21st meeting.
20. Radhakrishnan, K.S., 'Centre for Environmental Law v. Union of India', 15 April 2013, https://bit.ly/3yv4Rj1. Accessed on 11 July 2022.
21. Standing Committee of National Board for Wildlife, *Minutes of the Fourth Meeting of Standing Committee of National Board for Wild Life,* MoEFCC, 6 April 2005, https://bit.ly/3ap5zXb. Accessed on 11 July 2022.
22. Standing Committee of National Board for Wildlife, *Minutes of the Fifth Meeting of the Standing Committee of National Board for Wildlife*, MoEFCC, 4 October 2005, https://bit.ly/3NQ8upq. Accessed on 11 July 2022.

Otteri Lake in the Arignar Anna Zoological Park (AAZP), Tamil Nadu, after rejuvenation.
Photo by Sudha Ramen.

The AAZP's Zoo Ambassadors smiling wide.
Photo by Sudha Ramen.

A lone and curious chausingha in Panna National Park, Madhya Pradesh.
Photo by Koustubh Sharma.

Koustubh Sharma (extreme right) in the field.
Photo by Koustubh Sharma.

Author Joanna Van Gruisen rests on a ridge behind Rumbak village, Ladakh, with a magnificent view of the Ladakh range.
Photo by Joanna Van Gruisen.

Majestic hangul in the snow in Dachigam National Park, Jammu and Kashmir.
Photo by Joanna Van Gruisen.

Buses full of tourists by the Manas River. In the 1980s, hundreds of visitors would come in buses to the heart of Manas National Park and leave not an iota of non-biodegradable waste.
Photo by Joanna Van Gruisen.

Mother gharial safeguarding her hatchlings the Chambal River, Madhya Pradesh.
Photo by R.K. Sharma.

Gharial hatchlings in the Chambal River, Madhya Pradesh.
Photo by R.K. Sharma.

Translocated gaur in the Bandhavgarh Tiger Reserve, Madhya Pradesh.
Photo by Suhas Kumar.

Boma enclosure at the Kanha Tiger Reserve, Madhya Pradesh.
Photo Courtesy: Kanha Tiger Reserve.

Barasingha released one early morning at the Satpura Tiger Reserve, Madhya Pradesh.
Photo by Subhranjan Sen.

River Kuno, a lifeline of Kuno National Park, Madhya Pradesh.
Photo by Faiyaz A. Khudsar.

Palpur Fort stands resolute by Kuno River on a misty day, Kuno National Park, Madhya Pradesh.
Photo by Faiyaz A. Khudsar.

A baby elephant plays with Usha Rai in Corbett National Park, Uttarakhand.
Photo by R.K. Dayal.

Honorary Zoo Wardens hold a quick briefing meeting, New Delhi.
Photo by Sharad Gaur.

Assisting in the confiscation of a large illegal consignment of skins. *Photo by Sharad Gaur.*

The first issue of the *Nature Clubs of India* newsletter, October 1976. *Photo by Sharad Gaur.*

Mr. Billy Arjan Singh speaking to the campers at Dudhwa National Park.
Pic. Sharad Gaur

Soft mud in a clearing in the elephant grass bore marks of passage of a couple of male tigers and a tigress with a cub who had visited the place to quench their thirst. Mr. R. L. Singh showed the participants how the pugmarks revealed the sex of tigers. As we approached the core area, fresh excreta of a big cat lay in the path. The park director explained how undigested hair can reveal the identity of the prey species.

Suddenly the forest opened out and a vast, shallow lake stretched for a kilometer. The far shore was bordered by elephant grass which spread in an unending expanse to the foot of dim hills on the horizon. Cormorants, spoonbills, teals and storks dotted the lake. Binoculars changed hands impatiently, and very young members sat on the shoulders of the seniors to get a

the birds in the thick foliage. A large green barbet, a racket tailed drongo and the small scaly-bellied wood-pecker were the chief rewards of the session.

We started taking turns on elephant and jeep trips to try our luck in spotting a tiger. One Delhi group had the luck that very evening in spotting one big cat near a kill made the day before. Everybody wanted to go to the same area in a jeep with the same driver. Tiger, however, did not oblige again. We had a great campfire that night. Mr. R. L. Singh read his poetry, told us of human population pressures that drove the big cats to become man-eaters. He also related his experiments to wean a way a man-eater from his habit.

Mr. Billy Arjan Singh visited the camp the next day. Among many questions he answered some

From the pages of history: a World Wide Fund for Nature (WWF) Nature Camp.
Photo by Sharad Gaur.

Team Panna in the field (Nayakheda), tracking tiger T3.
Photo by Pooran Singh Kushwaha.

Tigers playing in the water on a hot summer day in the Panna Tiger Reserve, Madhya Pradesh.
Photo by Rajiv Sharma.

Fisherpeople in Mannar repairing their nets after the morning auction. *Photo by Bhuvana Balaji.*

Fisherpeople of the Gulf of Mannar working together to pull their catch of the day.
Photo by Bhuvana Balaji.

Adult male great Indian bustard (*Ardeotis nigriceps*) with a full gular pouch on display in Desert National Park (Rajasthan).
Photo by Radheshyam Pemani Bishnoi.

A flock of great Indian bustards in non-breeding season in Desert National Park (Rajasthan).
Photo by Radheshyam Pemani Bishnoi.

Great Indian bustards in Desert National Park near Jaisalmer, Rajasthan.
Photo by Joanna Van Gruisen.

Badlav Conservancy: an oasis near Ranthambore Tiger Reserve, Rajasthan.
Photo by Aditya 'Dicky' Singh.

A tiger lounges about in Badlav Conservancy, Ranthambore Tiger Reserve, Rajasthan.
Photo by Aditya 'Dicky' Singh.

23. Minister of State (independent charge) at the Ministry of Environment and Forests from May 2009 to July 2011.
24. Jyothimani, P., Dr, 'Demwe Lower Hydro Electric Project Forest Clearance', Appeal No. 30 of 2015, 24 October 2017, https://bit.ly/3NUFmNB. Accessed on 11 July 2022.
25. Dutta, Ritwick, 'National Board for Wildlife and the Illusion of Wildlife Protection', *Economic & Political Weekly*, Vol. 56, No. 3, 16 January 2021, https://bit.ly/3AVw4hR. Accessed on 11 July 2022.
26. Standing Committee-NBWL, 'Letter from the SC, NBWL Members to Smt. Jayanthi Natarajan, Minister of State for Environment and Forests (Independent Charge, from 12 July 2011 to 20 December 2013', 25 September 2011.
27. Personal interview with the author.
28. Written statement by Prakriti Srivastava to the CBI in the matter relating to grant of mining lease for iron ore and manganese ore to M/s JSW Steel Ltd on receipt of the summons as per letter No.1383 PE220/2014/E/0003. The probe (preliminary enquires) was for environment clearances given during Environment Minister Jayanthi Natarajan's regime.
29. Bhargav, Praveen, and Shekar Dattatri, 'Betraying India's Wildlife', *Conservation India*, https://bit.ly/3uF5JQZ. Accessed on 29 June 2022; also revealed in an email exchange between the author and Praveen Bhargav.
30. Standing Committee-NBWL, 'Letter from SC, NBWL Members to Smt. Jayanthi Natarajan, Minister of State for Environment and Forests (independent charge, from 12 July 2011 to 20 December 2013)', 25 September 2011.
31. Goswami, Urmi A., 'Standing Committee of the National Board of Wildlife Clears 140 Wildlife Projects', *The Economic Times*, 14 August 2014, https://bit.ly/3yywcAG. Accessed on 11 July 2022.
32. Bindra, Prerna Singh, 'India's Fast-Tracked Wildlife Clearances Threaten Last Wild Areas, Water Sources And Hasten Climate Change', *IndiaSpend*, 22 September 2018, https://bit.ly/3PmtvJD. Accessed on 11 July 2022.

33. Sharma, Tanvi, *Analysis of Forest Clearances in India, 2020 (January-December)*, Legal Initiative for Forest and Environment, July 2021, https://bit.ly/3uD3xJX. Accessed on 29 June 2022.
34. Ibid.
35. Standing Committee of National Board for Wildlife, *Minutes of 39th Meeting of the Standing Committee of National Board for Wildlife Held on 23rd August 2016*, MoEFCC, 23 August 2016, https://bit.ly/3uEL3bL. Accessed on 29 June 2022.
36. Dutta, Ritwick, 'National Board for Wildlife and the Illusion of Wildlife Protection', *Economic & Political Weekly*, Vol. 56, No. 2, 16 January 2021, https://bit.ly/3AVw4hR. Accessed on 29 June 2022.
37. Most of the minutes of the meetings of the SC-National Board for Wildlife from the second meeting onwards are available on the MoEFCC website here https://bit.ly/3uDz12u. Accessed on 11 July 2022.
38. Gujarat Ecological Education and Research Foundation is the nominated NGO member, and is represented by its director, a serving forest official. It is an autonomous body, set up in 1982 by the forest and environment department, Government of Gujarat, and is governed by a board of governors chaired by the state's chief minister.
39. Bindra, Prerna Singh, 'Great Indian Sale of Its Wilderness', *The Telegraph*, 23 September 2021, https://bit.ly/3uF4Qb7. Accessed on 11 July 2022.
40. Kukreti, Ishan, 'National Board for Wildlife Hasn't Met Even Once since 2014', *DownToEarth*, 10 April 2020, https://bit.ly/3yX17bG. Accessed on 29 June 2022.

PART TWO

THE INCREDIBLE SALIM ALI

ASAD R. RAHMANI

It isn't easy to write about a man who has been written about so much already and who himself left behind a stupendous body of splendid writings, particularly books and research papers. But I will attempt and hope to do justice to this great man.

When I was asked to write on Dr Salim Ali for this book, I was flabbergasted. My first reaction was: can I do justice to the man who has been a conservation icon for almost 60 years in India, the legendary 'Bird Man' of India, and an internationally recognized and celebrated ornithologist? The invitation said, 'Salim Ali as seen and experienced through your eyes; it is your own story which is the key.'

First, a few facts. Salim Ali was born on 12 November 1896 in a Bohra family in Bombay and died on 20 June 1987 in Mumbai. So much changed in India in 91 years of his life that it will take a couple of books to chronicle the details. His father died when he was a year old, and he was raised by his benign maternal uncle, Amiruddin Tyabji, and his childless aunt, Hamida Begum. In a large Suleimani Bohra Muslim joint family, no one was left uncared of. He studied up to matriculation (dropped out due to health issues). Like youngsters at that time, he was interested in hunting. When he shot a 'sparrow' with a yellow throat, he took it to his uncle for identification, who told him that it was a common house sparrow. When the curious 11-year-old boy pointed out the yellow patch on the throat, his foresighted uncle saw genuine inquisitiveness in little Salim. He took him to the Bombay Natural History Society before (BNHS), where Honorary Secretary W.S. Millard, much used to meeting British officials and maharajahs to exchange natural history and hunting notes, found a dark Indian boy with a carcass of a yellow-throated sparrow asking for identification. That serendipitous visit to the BNHS changed Dr Salim Ali's life. As cliché goes, the rest is history. I recommend Dr Ali's eminently readable biography, *The Fall of a Sparrow* (Oxford University Press, 1985), to interested readers. The BNHS and Dr Ali were so interlinked for the next 70 years that many people think he established the organization. This great organization was established in 1883, 13 years before Dr Ali was even born, but the contribution of Dr Salim Ali, his cousin, Humayun Abdulali, and J.C. Daniel in nurturing the BNHS after India's Independence should not be underestimated. They were the pillars of the BNHS all their respective lives.

My own association with Dr Ali and the BNHS goes for almost five decades or more. I must have been about 13 years old when I first saw *The Book of Indian Birds* (BNHS, 1941) and drew in watercolour the magpie robin based on this book. It took me another 10 years to get my own copy of this wonderful book. Once I got the address of the BNHS, I started writing to Dr Salim Ali and J.C. Daniel, sometime in 1971–1972. For an MSc student of 21 years, getting replies from great men like Dr Ali and Daniel, was a great achievement. It was the age of 'slow' mail, but both the gentlemen were very fast with their replies. No reply took more than a week to arrive. Soon, '46, Pali Hill, Bandra, Bombay', and 'Bombay Natural History Society, Hornbill House, Fort, Bombay' were a part of my memory.

I first met Dr Ali in 1974–1975 in Sapanmori, the Bharatpur Bird Sanctuary (now Keoladeo National Park). I went there with Dr Hameeda Sayeduzzaffar, head of the Department of

Ophthalmology at the Jawahar Lal Medical College of Aligarh Muslim University. She was known as a strict disciplinarian, a sort of martinet, but she was kind and motherly with me. Surrounded by thousands of birds, Dr Ali was in his element, despite his frail body and advancing age. I had been to Bharatpur earlier, but meeting Dr Ali in his favourite sanctuary was the icing on the cake. I was amazed to see hundreds of thousands of birds, but Dr Ali was worried about the decline in bird numbers, as he had seen many more birds in 1940–1960. In 2018, when I went to Keoladeo, I was horrified to see an enormous decline in bird numbers, but the young birdwatchers there were thrilled to see 'many' birds. I now realize that every generation has its own definition of common and rare. What had been millions of birds in 1940–1960 became a few hundreds of thousands in the 1970s and 1980s, and today, their numbers have reduced to a few thousand, while some only remain in a few hundreds.

Dr Ali was not a 'qualified scientist' in the classical sense, as he did not have a science degree. His early education was at St Xavier's College, Mumbai. He joined studies as a private student but could not complete it again due to health issues; instead, he went to Burma (now Myanmar) to look after the family business of mining and timber. This gave him ample opportunities to live in close contact with nature, further increasing his interest in ornithology. But he could not stay for long in Burma and returned to India to look for a job. He applied for an ornithologist's position in the famous Zoological Survey of India (ZSI) but was not selected, as he did not possess a formal degree. Instead, he landed a job in the newly opened Prince of Wales Museum (now the Chhatrapati Shivaji Maharaj Vastu Sangrahalaya) as a 'nature guide' of its highly popular natural history section. After two years, he got an opportunity to study scientific ornithology under Professor Erwin Stresemann at the Natural History Museum, Berlin, Germany. In Germany, he learnt taxonomy, taxidermy and other aspects of ornithology. In 1958, Aligarh Muslim University honoured him with an honorary doctorate, which he always cherished. Later he received two more honorary degrees—Delhi University (1973) and Andhra University (1978). His awards list is too long to mention.

Besides his own contribution to ornithology, I think Dr Ali's biggest contribution is helping the BNHS survive after Independence, when the exodus of British managers left it leaderless and homeless. For almost 70 years, the BNHS had been hosted in the office of the Phipson and Company (6, Apollo Street, Fort, Bombay), but when the company wound up its Bombay office in the early 1950s, the BNHS became homeless. The Ali brothers, Salim and Abdulali, took on the responsibility of looking after it. By then (the 1950s), Dr Ali was already famous, thanks to his popular book *The Book of Indian Birds*, first published in 1941. It was a standard book for the putative birdwatching community of the newly independent nation. Even Pandit Jawaharlal Nehru had a copy that he gave to his daughter, Indira Gandhi. Mrs Gandhi was one of the six founders of the erstwhile Delhi Bird Watching Society. The Government of India (GoI) came to the rescue of the BNHS and approved funds to build the famous 'Hornbill House' to accommodate the BNHS office, its valuable specimen collection and its large library containing treasured books and original manuscripts.

Spearheaded by the Ali brothers, fieldwork has been the forte of BNHS. Dr Ali was famous for his long field surveys in Kutch, Hyderabad, Gwalior, Kerala, Sikkim, etc., sometimes sponsored by the then rulers of the state. The results of the surveys and bird collection trips were published in great detail in the *Journal of the Bombay Natural History Society (JBNHS)* and later in book forms (e.g., *Birds of Katch* [Oxford University Press, 1945], *Birds of Kerala* [Oxford University Press, 1969], *The Birds of Sikkim* [Oxford University

Press, 1962]). In the 1950s and 1960s, Dr Ali and BNHS undertook many bird-ringing activities all over India, joined by enthusiastic youngsters. Results of bird ringing published in the *JBNHS* and in the form of popular articles created more birdwatchers in the 1960s and 1970s, resulting in the heightened popularity of BNHS and Dr Ali. The landmark publication of the 10-volume *Handbook of the Birds of India and Pakistan* (Oxford University Press, 1969 [1st edn.]) by Dr Salim Ali and Dillon Ripley from 1968 to 1974 created an aura around Dr Ali's persona. His erudition of Indian ornithology was recognized all over India and the world. By the 1970s, Dr Ali had become a celebrity, a recognizable face on the streets and a much-loved doyen of the Indian science community. I have personal experience of this. In the 1980s, I had the privilege of driving him from the BNHS to his residence in Pali Hill on a few occasions. People would look at him admiringly at every red signal our car stopped. In 1986, when he was sick and staying in the Royal Bombay Yacht Club near the Taj Mahal hotel, I would take him for his evening walks on the seafront near the Gateway of India. Many times, old and young people would hesitantly come and ask for his autograph, which he would smilingly oblige.

As a person, Dr Ali was kind, gentle and considerate, but up to a certain extent. He would not tolerate obsequious people and fools, and would soon express his annoyance through gestures and expression. Mr Daniel, his lifelong colleague in the BNHS, told me in his own waggish style, 'It was my job to take away such people before the Old Man explodes.' In the BNHS and to close friends and admirers, Dr Ali was known as 'Old Man' more with affection and admiration for his grit despite his advancing age. I do not know whether he was amused or not. Dr Ali was known for his short temper, but by the time I started working under him on a project in the 1980s, I was told that he had calmed down. I experienced one sample of his temper in Sailana when I was a bit late. That is a long story that I will carry in my autobiography.

Like most non-governmental organizations (NGOs), the BNHS has always lived a hand-to-mouth existence despite a grandiose Hornbill House (donation from the government) in the prime locality of Bombay (now Mumbai) and a long history of exemplary work. It used to get small grants for field surveys and bird ringing. Dr Ali was extremely particular about the proper utilization of funds. For him, every rupee allocated for a project should be spent carefully and accounted for. So was the case with Mr Abdulali, Mr Daniel and others. I would say the BNHS has been surviving for 140 long years mainly because it had some of the finest and most committed human beings at the helm of affairs. This old organization has great ethics—honesty and sincerity to work are much more important than earning money. All activities are related to conservation. There is no place for dishonesty, either in money matters or in science. I enjoyed working in this great organization for almost 38 years, first as a senior scientist and then as a director (with six years in between spent as a teacher in the Department of Wildlife Sciences, Aligarh Muslim University). Hard work and sincerity have percolated down to the junior-most staff. When I joined the BNHS in 1980, Uma Pratap was the guard at Hornbill House, and Mr J.C. Daniel was the chief executive officer (CEO) (the post was called 'curator' at that time due to museum collection). Uma used to live in the office, so he was on duty 24 hours a day. Mr Daniel would come exactly at 10.00 a.m., many times much before, and work till late evening. Every day he would make an 'unexpected' round of the whole office, talking to every member of the staff. His affable behaviour would quickly remove the tension, if any, from a new staff member like me. He was more like a father or an elderly brother than a boss. However, he was also tough and would not tolerate any laxity. I admired him more than I feared him. He had the true leadership qualities that are taught these days in MBA courses. Another person feared and admired in equal measure was Humayun Abdulali. From Abdul Rahman Street, where his business office was located, he would come to the BNHS after lunch and would work on bird specimens for three to four hours. I was told that Mr Abdulali came to the BNHS for almost 60 years, worked on museum specimens or papers but never took a single rupee from the BNHS. Even the chai he would drink and offer guests was bought from his pocket. How many people would devote so much time and energy as a volunteer? People like Mr Abdulali made the BNHS what it is now.

Dr Ali would come once a week, more often when there was a meeting. His presence at Hornbill House would activate, energize and motivate everyone in the building. His presence would attract hordes of admirers, some with appointment and some without. No one was denied audience, but considering the tight schedule of Dr Ali, Mr Daniel would use his well-known skills to deftly tell the overstaying guest that their allocated time was over. We scientists were allowed to meet Dr Ali if we had to discuss something with him.

Dr Ali was fond of fast bikes and cars, and would drive down to the BNHS in his own car till the advanced age of nearly 80 years. When he was not allowed to drive on the doctor's advice, sometimes Mr Daniel would ask me to drive him back to Pali Hill. The first time when I drove him, I was nervous and drove slowly, even on the clear road of Marine Drive. He kept looking at me, which made me more nervous. When he got down from the car at his home, he said in his inimitable style, 'Asad, you have taken twice the time that I would take to cover this distance of 20 km. I hope you learn to drive better than this.' I got the hint, and the next time I drove him home, he was at his destination within 40 minutes. Of course, on the crowded streets of Mumbai, that's a short amount of time.

Both Dr Ali and Mr Abdulali, were fond of bikes. While travelling with me to Solapur to see the GIB, Abdulali told me that once (probably in the late 1930s), he and his friends decided late at night to have coffee in a famous restaurant in Pune, about 177 km away. They quietly left home at 11.00 p.m., drove to Pune, drank coffee and returned home before daybreak. Dr Ali's fondness became legendary when, in 1950, he reached the International Ornithological Congress, Uppsala, Sweden, in his Sunbeam motorcycle just as the conference opened. People came out to see Dr Ali sitting on his bike loaded with luggage. Most people thought he had come all the way from India on his motorbike! Actually, he had shipped his bike to Europe a few months ago and went around the continent on it, arriving at the right time to attend the conference where the world's famous ornithologists had gathered.

Dr Ali was a light eater. At Hornbill House, his lunch would be two hot idlis and one banana, along with coffee or tea. I remember, when he visited Point Calimere Bird Sanctuary, Tamil Nadu, in 1980 to see our ringing work, he enjoyed hot idlis from Poonarswamy Illum. Point Calimere introduced me to healthy South Indian food, which I now miss in Lucknow.

To comment on Dr Salim Ali's ornithology work is like *suraj ko diya dikhana*. His incredible observational skills, impeccable command of the English language, long time spent in the field, meticulous note taking and tremendous ability to assimilate existing information—all are reflected in his numerous books, research papers, speeches and articles.

Till the 1970s, the BNHS was a small organization with three or four senior scientists (Dr Robert Grubh, Mr S.A. Hussain, Mr Naresh Chaturvedi), a dozen research scholars and museum staff, and few office staff. Once the GoI deployed the PL 480 funds United States Agency for International Development (USAID) that were lying underutilized in India, they were used for funding projects, including wildlife. At that time, BNHS was perhaps the only wildlife research organization, so a kind of bonanza came the BNHS way in 1980 in the form of four major projects. They were 'Bird Ringing Project', 'Ecology of Keoladeo National Park', 'Endangered Species Projects of Great Indian Bustard' and 'Asiatic Elephant'. The BNHS, which, till then, had done small field projects with its limited staff and with the help of members, was suddenly asked by the U.S. Fish and Wildlife Service to recruit scientific staff. The inflow of 30–35 young scientists, some with fresh MSc degrees, changed the character of the BNHS, creating some tension between the members and the newly recruited staff. Dr Ali and Mr Daniel spearheaded this changeover deftly. I witnessed all this as I joined in 1980 after completing my PhD.

The real challenge came in 1983, when the BNHS celebrated 100 years of its existence. I must say that Mr Daniel played a key role in bringing members and staff together to make the centenary functions successful. One of the landmark functions was the three-day wildlife conference—perhaps the first-ever gathering in India of field biologists, decision-makers, forest department officials and the general public with interest in wildlife. It was held at the Indian Institute of Technology, Mumbai, and I was put in charge of the audio-visual presentations. It was the age of slide and overhead projectors, so I had a tough task, approaching the speakers, collecting their slides, maps/tables, etc., and projecting them deftly. I remember Dr Ali came for the conference on all three days and attended the majority of the lectures. Having gone hard of hearing, he would sit silently on one side of the dais, listening to the speakers with a hearing aid in his ear. Finding a speaker going on and on, Dr Ali would wordlessly switch off his hearing device and smile at the verbose speaker.

By 1986–1987, Dr Ali had become increasingly frail from cancer and age-related issues. But his mind was alert. Dr A.N.D. Nanavati, the honorary secretary of the BNHS and one of the finest human beings that I have met, would regularly update the BNHS on the old man's health. He had been shifted to his relatives' place in Bandra and was looked after well. I visited him a few times. One day, Mr Daniel told me that Dr Ali wanted to see my pictures of the great Indian bustard (GIB) once again. I took a hand-held slide project and spent an evening on 18 June 1987 with him. He was very weak, sitting in an armed chair, but his eyes twinkled every time I changed the slides as if he was seeing them for the first time. He asked me to stay back for dinner, which was an elaborate affair for me. Two days later, he was no more.

People like Dr Salim Ali, Mr J.C. Daniel, Mr Humayun Abdulali, Dr A.N.D. Nanavati, Dr C.V. Kulkarni, Prof. P.V. Bole, Dr Rachel Rueben, and later, Mr B.G. Deshmukh and other stalwarts created a strong BNHS—one that carries forth the legacies of these legendary experts nearly 140 years since its founding. The onus is now on the younger generation to keep the legacy shining. The problems and challenges in wildlife conservation have multiplied, and so have our responsibilities.

IN THE WILDS: REPORTER AT LARGE[1]

USHA RAI

In the early 1960s, straight out of college, I worked as a trainee journalist with *The Indian Express* in Bombay. I learnt on the job, accompanying my seniors into the field as they and I reported on the same subject and compared notes on where I had missed out and how to make a copy newsy, readable and crisp. My first big assignment, very much like a sniffer dog out with his master, was covering the Panshet Dam disaster near Pune. It was my first experience of a man-made environmental disaster and a front-page story for *The Indian Express*. It was an important story done by one of the seasoned senior reporters, but I could travel with him to see the disaster first-hand and learn who and how to interview to ferret out information.

Two years later, I joined *The Times of India* in Delhi as their first female reporter and was assigned the beat, which included wildlife, animals and nature. With greater experience and interaction with activists and change-makers in the field, such as Kailash S. Sankhala, the director of the Delhi Zoo in 1965 and, later, director of Project Tiger; Sunderlal Bahuguna, environmental activist and Chipko Andolan leader; Dr Nalini Jayal, director of Indian National Trust for Art and Cultural Heritage's (INTACH) natural heritage cell; and Vandana Shiva, environment activist, reporting on wildlife and environment issues became a passion and also my mission. It is not that I wanted to become an environmental journalist. I was pushed in that direction. The all-male reporting team at *The Times of India* had cornered all the 'important' beats, whether it was covering the local administration, the political parties, the civic bodies of New Delhi and Delhi and even the University. Not to dampen my enthusiasm, I was asked to report on talks and lectures, attend flower and fashion shows, cover the annual Shankar's On-the-Spot Painting Competition and sundry other routine stories like price rise resistance and the still-nascent women's movement.

Being a female reporter in the 1960s had many disadvantages. No one took you seriously. They thought that journalism was a fleeting interest and that I would marry and leave. I had to wear saris to be taken seriously and prove I was no butterfly. Also, male journalists were entertained with drinks and the story, but there was hesitancy in engaging in this manner with women. I, too, was not open to late nights at the Press Club or other places. However, once you prove you are a serious professional, doors open up, regardless of your gender. In any case, not many male journalists were interested in the areas in which I chose to specialize.

Getting to Know the Animals in the Delhi Zoo

I lived close to National Zoological Park, which was then known as the Delhi Zoo, so I was advised to visit it regularly and see if I could pick up a good story. I fell in love with the place. It was picturesquely laid out against the backdrop of the Purana Quila, and large waterbodies and moats added to its allure. There were hoolock gibbons, orangutans and chimpanzees with their antics, the elephants doing odd jobs around the zoo and even giving rides to children. I was privileged to see abandoned baby tigers being hand-reared at the Zoo Director's home, otters swimming up to pool sides, standing in neat rows, hoping to get a tasty morsel from visitors.

I soon got to know not just the Director, but the Curator, the veterinary doctor and even the keepers. I learnt from all of them about animals and birds, and their behaviour. I also learnt about human frailties and how cruel we could be. There were visitors, mercifully just a minuscule number, who irritated the monkeys and chimpanzees, wanting them to perform like circus animals. Some people threw burning cigarette butts and even blades at monkeys, injuring them; they gave lit cigarettes to chimpanzees because they had seen movies in which chimps, dressed as humans, smoked.

There were some visitors with suicidal tendencies who jumped into the lion's enclosure or swam a moat to get a look at the hideout of the black and brown bears. There was excitement galore and a rush of visitors when giraffes came to Delhi Zoo for the first time. Some single animals were leading lonely lives, and I campaigned vigorously for mates for them, whether it was a hippo or a rhinoceros.

Many years later, in 1986, when Zoo Director, Kamal Naidu rescued tiger cubs from a poisonous snake that got into their enclosure, he got bitten. The cubs were saved, but Naidu almost died. It was my exclusive story and on the front page of the leading national daily of the country. In another case, a young child lost his hand when he stuck it in a tiger's enclosure from an area where the bar was missing in the chain-linked fence. The parents were looking elsewhere when the incident happened. Though the zoo authorities blamed the parents for it, the courts awarded compensation to the child.

With a ringside seat, I was able to dash off story after story. The Delhi Zoo became a popular destination for children and adults from far and near. In fact, Mr Sankhala, who became a good friend, even offered me a night in a zoo enclosure as a wedding gift when I was getting married! Alas, my biggest regret is that I did not convert all my zoo articles into a children's storybook on animals.

My friendship with Mr Sankhala, who went on to become the first director of Project Tiger, enhanced my appetite for wildlife and nature stories. My first vision of a leopard in the wild was when I was with Mr Sankhala. We were exiting Corbett National Park, and sprawled out on the branch of a tall tree was a majestic leopard. Mr Sankhala's camera was packed in the boot of the car, so the car was reversed quietly, and the camera pulled out before the car sneaked up again for a great photograph.

Moving On: The Bigger Picture

It was Mr Sankhala, again, who introduced me to the graceful pink flamingos of the Rann of Kutch, Gujarat, through a film show at the India International Centre in Delhi. The Rann of Kutch is one of the biggest nesting sites of flamingos. Hundreds, thousands of these beautiful creatures that look like ballerinas in pink-and-white costumes, land from all over to build nests, breed during the winter months and fly out with their young ones before summer sets in.

As Mr Sankhala became the first director of Project Tiger, my canvas too widened, and I began looking at national parks and sanctuaries, and the importance of the tiger in the ecosystem of the country.

The Importance of Newspaper Reports

A good journalist with reliable contacts in the field and access to the ministry, the Forest Department and the powers in the government acts as a link in the environment ecosystem and can sound the alarm, somewhat like monkeys sounding the alarm call when tigers are on the prowl. I, too, was able to sound the alarm and bring attention to important parks and sanctuaries. In the mid-1980s, the young environment group

Kalpvriksha, based out of Sardar Patel School, was very active, and some members would cycle down to my office to invite me for birdwatching or tell me about their forays into nature. With their help, I was able to alert the public about the threats to the richly forested Delhi Ridge with proposals to set up schools, construct roads, etc.

The Ranthambore Tiger Reserve in Rajasthan was an extremely popular destination for the sighting of tigers. So, when the young environmentalists heard of an industrial group wanting to set up a plant on the outskirts of Ranthambore, they alerted me to the possibility of a story. I used my contacts in the ministry to find out the rules on such projects coming so close to a reserve and did the story. It was used as a front-page anchor in *The Times of India,* and soon, the alarm bells rang. Kalpvriksha followed up with several letters to the editor as well as one to Prime Minister Rajiv Gandhi, who loved national parks and wildlife. The project was shelved!

Soon after, there was a move to denotify a wildlife sanctuary in Himachal Pradesh to facilitate the setting up of a cement plant. The sanctuary did not have any big animals, but it had abundant bird life and some rare ones like the western tragopan, called the monarch among birds, the monal, the chestnut crowned laughing thrush and many others. For the first time, I realized the power of the pen, when the owner of the plant or its PR brethren visited my home to see if I could be persuaded to change my mind. The wooing of journalists for favourable press is an old practice that sullies the image of newspapers. A timely write-up stalled the project and saved my reputation!

National Parks as Militant Hideouts

Corbett National Park has been quite a favourite destination both for pleasure as well as work. The Khalistan movement was in disarray in the late 1980s and early 1990s, and many of the pro-Khalistan elements moved into Corbett, using it as a hideout. Many farmers from Punjab had settled in the Terai region adjoining the park. There were several incidents of kidnapping and killing of farmers and innocent people by the disgruntled people of the movement. They also poached and killed wildlife, so the park was closed to tourists.

The park's director, Mr A.S. Negi, was a known contact, and I went from *The Indian Express* to do the story on the impact of militancy on the park. It was a long and arduous mission to catch and expel them from the Paterpani area of the park. Eight of them were arrested. The huge coverage the story received not only pressured the central government to act but also boosted the morale of the park Director and its staff.

Earlier, from the *The Times of India,* I had gone on a similar mission to the Manas National Park, which had been taken over by the Bodos demanding a separate Bodoland. It was one of the most beautiful parks I had ever seen, nestling on the foothills of the Himalayas with the Manas River flowing through it. It was a United Nations Educational, Scientific and Cultural Organization (UNESCO) Natural World Heritage site, a tiger reserve with a wealth of elephants and the famous one-horned rhinoceros. It was ravaged and pillaged and some 100 rhinoceros were killed. It was a political as well as an ecological story, and it was only because of my deep interest in wildlife and nature that I was given the opportunity to do the story.

Most journalists, however, are not subject specialists. They learn on the job by contacting those with knowledge and information and, like the chital and the barasingha, keep their antennas up. I was assisted in the coverage by Mr Deb Roy, one of the most well-respected foresters from the Northeast, who became a good friend when he moved to Delhi and the Ministry of Environment and Forests (MoEF).

It took a long time to restore peace and tranquillity in Manas and rehabilitate it with the reintroduction of the rhinoceros. Today there are close to 40 rhinoceros in Manas.

Poaching in Protected Areas (PAs) by the Rich and Powerful

Should national parks be closed to tourists so that the wild animals can breed in peace without honking cars, jeeps and noisy visitors disturbing them? There have been heated debates on this issue. Parks need visitors to bring in the money. They are also a great source of education and research for people to understand our natural habitats and respect the myriad creatures that make them into a paradise. Very often, the rich and influential politicians break the golden rules that ensure the safety of humans and wildlife in a PA. Poaching frequently happens around wildlife areas for food and livelihood by chopping trees in the PAs and smuggling animal skins, rhinoceros horns and tiger parts. But in Corbett, during the tenure of Mr Negi in the early 1990s, there was a new form of poaching that shocked wildlife lovers. It is believed that the rich and well-connected Thapar brothers (of JCT Mills, Phagwara), who had their own resort close to the park, would fly in helicopters and shoot at wildlife from the air. They would organize big parties and entertain visitors by taking them on a shoot around New Year.[2]

It required courage for the park Director to take action against such powerful people. So, I got a call late one evening asking if I could help. For me, this was a big story, and it had to be done carefully without revealing the source of information. There was pressure on the newspaper as well from the forest department not to pursue it. But the cat was out of the bag. It was a crime that could not be forgiven or forgotten. If action was not taken, there could be more such poaching by the rich and powerful. It took time, but justice was done! Sameer Thapar was arrested by the forest department late in 2016, and arms and prohibited items were recovered.[3]

Heroes of the Jungle: Skirmishes with Tigers and Crocodiles

In addition to writing about what was going wrong in our forest ecosystem, I loved writing about the heroes of the lantana jungle. At any given time, for some years now, Corbett has had over 100 tigers lurking in its tall grass and thick lantana undergrowth. Elephant herds can get belligerent when they find jeeps overflowing with tourists disturbing the serenity of their abode. Visitors are, therefore, forbidden from walking in the jungles.

Those who survive a tiger attack, an angry charge by a lone male tusker or the toothy jaws of a crocodile are lucky to get a second lease of life. They become legends in their lifetime and add to the mystique of the jungles. Subedar Ali (35), Sher Bahadur (37), Shafi Khan (32) and Saira Khatoon were four tiger- and crocodile-scarred legends that I met in Corbett. Ironically enough, three of them were looking after elephants as mahouts and chara cutters, and the woman was a mahout's wife. All of them had spent long years in the jungles and recognized the telltale signs of danger. They could pick up the alarm calls of the langurs, the barking deer and myriad other signs of birds and beasts when the tiger was on the prowl. Even the elephants they rode indicated danger by raising their trunks and sniffing the air or agitatedly swaying and hitting the ground with their trunks.

Early one morning, Subedar Ali on elephant Gomti and his friend, Qutb riding Mauli set out from Dhikala, where the forest office and guest houses are, to collect fodder from Chuha Sot. Qutb was a kilometre behind Subedar Ali. Subedar Ali had collected a substantial amount of chara when Gomti, who was tethered to a tree, trumpeted. He untied Gomti and was ready to return to Dhikala when he saw he had left behind some chara. So he tied Gomti again to the tree and went to retrieve the chara. He was several feet up the tree when Gomti called out again, but Subedar Ali ignored her warning. Suddenly a tiger, later identified as Sheroo, who had killed a person two years earlier, jumped up and pulled Subedar Ali down. In the struggle that ensued, the tiger ripped off Subedar Ali's scalp, and it hung over his eyes. Though conscious, he lost his voice. The tiger began to drag him off when courage returned and he caught hold of a tree and tried to fight it. It caught him by his legs, threw him a few feet away and jumped on him. Suddenly, Subedar Ali found his voice and he screamed out to Qutb. Simultaneously Gomti started trumpeting in fear. Qutb then came on Mauli and forced the tiger to retreat. Subedar Ali dragged himself to Gomti and untied her. She gently lifted him onto her back and raced off with him to Dhikala. The angry and frustrated tiger followed the elephants for some distance!

Subedar Ali had 35 wounds all over his body and face, and his scalp had to be stitched back. The hospital in Kashipur could not cope with his wounds, so, with the help of the honorary warden, Brijender Singh, and his wife, Don, Subedar Ali was shifted to AIIMS. He was there for nine months and underwent nine operations. Returning to the jungles was not easy. An unknown fear seized him, and he could not sleep at night for several weeks. The award from the International Union for Conservation of Nature (IUCN) and kudos from far and near sustained him. The man-eating Sheroo was trapped and sent to the Kanpur Zoo.

Sher Bahadur and Shafi Khan, too, were attacked by a tigress in their home near Dhikala after midnight in May 1988. Sher Bahadur had kept the door of his hut open for some air when the tigress attacked. It was pitch dark, and Sher Bahadur initially thought it was a wild boar foraging for a meal. It was only when the sharp claws and teeth ripped his face and neck that he realized it was a tiger. When chased away, among others, by Shafi Khan, it returned a little later and pounced on Shafi, sitting at the door of his house close to Bahadur's house. While Bahadur had 25 stitches on his face, head, neck and inside his mouth, Shafi lost his teeth and his ear was disfigured with his hearing impaired. The tigress that turned man-eater was being baited, allegedly for research work at Khinnanauli in Corbett. Though baiting was forbidden, it was done for VIPs to get a better look at the king of the jungle as well as for photography. Fortunately, this horrible practice has stopped.

Saira Khatoon was attacked by a crocodile in October 1993 when she and her neighbour in Dhikala, Rehana, and their children went to fetch water from the Ramganga. While the children played in a shallow part of the river, Saira sat on a stone, washed a few clothes, and then decided to have a bath. The water was barely 2–3 feet high, but it was muddy. She had barely put her foot in when she felt something sharp cut it. Thinking it was a stick, she put her hand in the water, and a 3-foot-long crocodile attacked her thigh. She fell back on the stone with her legs still in the water, and her legs and hands were attacked. Rehana, who was close by, shooed the crocodile with sticks and stones, and Saira Khatoon, who had fainted, was rescued. The women and children had broken an important rule of the forest. They had no business stepping in the Ramganga or other streams inside Corbett, which, in those days, were estimated to have 150 crocodiles and gharials.

There was group insurance only in case of death. There was no disability insurance or medical aid. Media taking up cudgels on behalf of the forest dwellers definitely helps. A few years later, the government agreed to give compensation of ₹50,000 and ₹1 lakh to staff and foresters, respectively, killed in Project Tiger areas. It was poor compensation for human life, and I hope it has been further raised!

When Tigers Breed in Sugarcane Fields

Between 1987 and 1988, the sugarcane fields of Lakhimpur Kheri, Pilibhit district of Uttar Pradesh, close to the Dudhwa Tiger Reserve, became the breeding ground for tigers. It was an unusual story, and I had to meet many experts from Project Tiger, farmers and people in the field to understand what was happening. There was growing resentment against the tigers attacking people who came into their fields to water or cut the sugarcane. In addition to tigers, there were plenty of wild boars in the sugarcane fields, and the tigers were probably lurking around for them. After some farmers and their family members were killed, the farmers retaliated by poisoning the tigers. The poison would be kept in the remains of the tiger-kill, like a boar or a buffalo.

Project Tiger was still nascent when 10 tigers were poisoned at Lakhimpur Keri. Alarm bells started ringing. Having the sugarcane fields so close to a tiger reserve was asking for trouble, but it was not easy to get farmers to change their cultivation practices. Compensation was also offered for every human attacked, injured or killed by tigers. The media focus helped speed up the remedial steps by the Uttar Pradesh government and Project Tiger. Poisoning of tigers by disgruntled herders and farmers continues to be a problem wherever there is a sizeable population of tigers and shrinking prey species.

Wolves Preying on Children in Uttar Pradesh

Like the tigers in the tall sugarcane fields of Lakhimpur Kheri, in the latter half of the 1980s, wolves would come through agricultural fields to Bandipur village near Rae Bareli, Uttar Pradesh, to pick up weak toddlers wandering around on their own. Terrified villagers would keep their children close to them and retire early. I was part of an investigative team formed by the MoEF and led by forester Kishore Rao to visit the area and report to the government. In the combing operations by the forest department, 10 wolves were killed. I had an opportunity to visit the wolf burrows close to the village's agricultural fields and see first-hand how precarious life was for those living on the margins.

The Gaja of Our Scriptures and the State of Our Elephants

The gaja, or the elephant of Indian scriptures, was and still is undoubtedly my favourite creature of the jungles. The swaying walk of the gaja could well be that of a dancer. These huge animals are extremely intelligent and can be both gentle as well as unforgiving when angry. They develop a great bond with the mahouts who ride them and the chara cutters who provide fodder for them, as demonstrated in the story of Subedar Ali. But with forests shrinking, and roads and railways cutting through what has been their terrain for centuries, elephant numbers are declining in India. Mining and other 'development' projects also add to the elephants' woes. It was heartbreaking to see and write about elephants dying on railway tracks, of elephant herds and mama elephants refusing to leave their babies who had died on the tracks. So, there were trips to the ministry to meet officers in charge of Project Elephant and do stories on the need to stop railways running through PAs. All of these were memorable stories that enlarged my vision and love for wild animals and nature.

But not all stories were of gloom and doom. There were enchanting stories of elephant herds stopping trucks carrying sugarcane and demanding a share of the juicy cane before allowing them to move. Some of the finest stories were shared by Mr Deb Roy. There was the story of a foreign tourist on an elephant safari who dropped his purse in the jungles and didn't realize it till he dismounted from the elephant and looked for his wallet. The wallet had a lot of money and other important cards. As the tourist cursed his luck and gave up all hope of finding it in the jungles, the elephant raised its trunk and dangled the wallet in front of the tourist. The mahout who saw the elephant pick up the wallet said the elephant was demanding baksheesh so the two could share a bottle of the local brew! I have also heard of angry elephants razing the huts of villagers who drove them out of their favourite forest areas because of *jhum* operations. In one such attack, the elephants destroyed every hut but left untouched a little child who the fleeing villagers had left behind. There was undoubtedly a message. Unlike humans, the elephants would not harm a baby—their own or that of a human!

Olive Ridley Turtles on Odisha's Beaches

I would like to believe that the media has had a role to play, however small, in the survival of the olive ridley turtles. Along with researchers, activists, wildlife lovers and foresters, the media continued to watch over the journey of these turtles to India every year for nesting. We wrote front-page stories and editorials when the mechanized trawlers began dredging ocean floors of their wealth of fish and sea life; when dead olive ridley landed up in the fish markets of Kolkata as a delicacy; when dogs and humans scavenged the Odisha coastline; and when bright lights and destructive development work on Odisha's beaches impacted their nesting at the Gahirmatha beach and Rushikulya rookery. This was not my exclusive alone. It was a chorus of alarm calls raised by journalists!

In March 2020, when the coronavirus pandemic restrained human movement, nature was in full flow, and an estimated 8 lakh olive ridley turtles came to nest in Odisha, of which 4.75 lakh are said to have nested at Rushikulya.

One of my biggest regrets is that I did not meet the great Dr Salim Ali, ornithologist par excellence, who, to me, looked like a tiny bird himself. I did, however, keep a copy of his book on Indian birds and, as a novice, flipped through the pages to identify birds that I saw around my home and in national parks. I also got to know Asad Rahmani and other scientists of the Bombay Natural History Society (BNHS). I was briefly on the Indian Board of Wildlife (IBWL) and the Rajasthan State Board of Wildlife (SBWL). I accepted these positions not because I was an expert in anything but in the hope that they would give me contacts, story ideas and more insights. However, there was much disappointment because the boards did not meet often enough nor bring about real changes on the ground.

Rivalry Dampens the NGO Spirit for Wildlife

Having worked 33 years with three mainline newspapers from Delhi—*The Times of India*, *The Indian Express* and *Hindustan Times*—I felt I needed a change—to see the world from the vantage point of non-governmental organization (NGO). I knew both Mr Samar Singh and Dr M.K. Ranjitsinh, IAS officers from Madhya Pradesh, belonging to erstwhile royal families and related. Dr Ranjitsinh was the prime architect of the Wild Life (Protection) Act (WLPA), 1972, and played a great role in India's wildlife conservation history. He had helped save the Central Indian barasingha from extinction, and, being a contact from the MoEF, as well as my neighbour when I lived in Kaka Nagar, he had helped put blood and sinew to my innumerable stories on the dancing deer or the sangai of Loktak Lake, Manipur, the disappearing great Indian bustard (GIB), and others. He was passionate about bringing back the cheetah to India and finding a second home for the lions in Madhya Pradesh. With Mr Samar Singh, I had done stories on aerial seeding of the Chambal ravines, and he was a great source of information when I was covering the Earth Summit at Rio and he was there from the MoEF. Both were polite and extremely knowledgeable about nature as well as government functioning.

In mid-1998, when Dr Ranjitsinh asked if I would like to work with him in the WWF-India on a special project of the WWF-International on the tiger, I thought it was an excellent opportunity for me to help conserve the habitat of the king of the jungle, wearing a new hat. There was concern about the dwindling Indian tiger population, and the WWF-International empowered this initiative under Dr Ranjitsinh. Having never stepped out of journalism, I accepted the offer with some intrepidity. While Dr Ranjitsinh headed an independent tiger cell, Samar Singh was head of WWF's India office. It was a great learning experience for me as head of the communications cell. I took teams of journalists to protected areas to understand the challenges in saving the tiger, the man/animal conflict, poaching and trade in wildlife parts. We brought out a magazine as well as some videos on the work being done and the status of the tiger. We also lobbied for better compensation for villagers and cattle herders whose buffaloes or goats had been picked up by tigers and tried to win their sympathy for the big cat.

However, my rose-tinted outlook on the NGO world was soon blurred. The two powerful Indian Administrative Service (IAS) officers, each with a commitment to wildlife and nature, flexed their seniority and authority. In the games of one-upmanship, members of the tiger team were seared. Even if it was just a turf war, it damaged the cause of saving the tiger. Sixteen months after joining WWF, I walked out!

The other inspirational person totally committed to wildlife was Billy Arjan Singh, a hunter turned conservationist who became a legend in his lifetime. I met him only a few times; a small feisty man, muscled and outspoken, he could take on the world as he fought for space in the Himalayan foothills for tigers, leopards and the barasingha. He built his home, Tiger Haven, on a plot of farmland close to the Nepal border in 1959. He appealed to the IUCN to ban tiger hunting and subsequently, in 1988, got the Dudhwa Tiger Reserve notified. I met him in Tiger Haven twice while doing a story on the tigers breeding in the sugarcane fields of Lakhimpur Kheri and when a second home was found for the rhinoceros in Dudhwa. Billy was the first person to reintroduce a leopard and a tiger, Prince and Tara, respectively, from captivity into the wild—and get flak from the forest department that Tara had turned man-eater. Billy, however, was confident that Tara's progeny, over a dozen of them, had enriched Dudhwa's tiger population.

Prince and Tara were brought up like pedigreed dogs. The bonding between the animals and their foster parent was clearly evident. Once, C.Y. Gopinath and photographer Raghu Rai were doing a story on Billy for *Junior Statesman*. Rai recalls how he and his colleague were sleeping on the terrace of Tiger Haven on a breezy August night when Prince came and sat on Gopinath's chest. A terrified Gopinath nudged and whispered to Raghu to help him. Earlier in the day, Prince had greeted the two journalists by knocking them down. Raghu got up gingerly to find Billy, but the big cat scampered off. He was just like any large pet dog, but clearly, his size was intimidating.

Having spent 50 years in journalism and environment reporting, there is a sense of disillusionment. There are still a few highs now and then, but they are like shooting stars! Our forests and wildlife continue to shrink. There is a crazy rush for development, even if it is not sustainable! There is lip-service to conserve nature. The earth is warming up, and glaciers are shrinking. Climate change has become a reality. Torrential rains, floods and landslides are the order of the day. As Billy Arjan Singh said, 'The air we breathe and the water we drink stem from the biodiversity of the universal environment and its economics. The tiger is at the centre of this truth. If it goes, we go!'

Notes

1. All names, designations and facts carried here are based on first-hand information and personal memory of the author as a journalist of long standing.
2. Sharma, Seema, 'Thapar Booked Earlier Too for Landing Chopper inside Corbett', *The Times of India*, 3 January 2017, https://bit.ly/3abP1BP. Accessed on 29 June 2022.
3. Talvar, Gaurav, 'Court Issues Summons to Samir Thapar and 15 Other Accused in Kolhu Chaur Forest Trespass Case', *The Times of India*, 1 May 2017, https://bit.ly/3yfai5t. Accessed on 29 June 2022.

MORE THAN BRICKS AND MORTAR: MAKING OF THE WILDLIFE INSTITUTE OF INDIA, DEHRADUN

VISHWAS B. SAWARKAR[1]

After India's independence, there were desultory efforts to set up national parks and sanctuaries; quite a number of those were by default. The laws protecting wild animals across the states of the Indian Union depended on what the states thought were the important species. These laws were also not connected across the regions on an ecological basis.

Building the Capacity to Manage Wildlife

All this changed, some directly and some obliquely. The Tenth General Assembly of the International Union for Conservation of Nature (IUCN) held in New Delhi in 1969 was unanimous about the threatened status of tigers in India.[2] During the same year, a separate course dedicated to wildlife management with a term of six months each for field practitioners—foresters and wildlife managers—was established in Dehradun as an adjunct to the Indian Forest College (IFC), rechristened the Indira Gandhi National Forest Academy (IGNFA) in 1987. The course duration was later enhanced to 10.5 months. A brilliant forest officer from Odisha, Saroj Raj Choudhury, was placed in charge of the training. The direction Choudhury provided to the training set the tone for the future. Choudhury was an erudite trainer, teacher and martinet. He had his own library and collection of scientific papers that represented modern science and practice. It is to be remembered that there was no internet at that time, and coming across appropriate literature took some effort. As a trainer, he expected discipline and dedication like an instructor on a military drill square, nothing less. When he got annoyed with someone, his favourite term to express that was 'Idiot!'—a very mild word indeed, considering the crass epithets on common TV programmes today. His diction and brilliance were effective enough to enthral the listeners even as he laid great emphasis on fieldwork. He used the Rajaji National Park in proximity to Dehradun and the Gir National Park in Gujarat as his training backyards. While he was in charge of the training, all licenced hunting had legally come to an end in India by 1970, and the Wild Life (Protection) Act (WLPA), 1972, had been promulgated in 1972 to give teeth to wildlife conservation across the country. I had heard of the great man for the first time in 1969, when I was undergoing my probation in the West Nasik Forest Division in Maharashtra as a greenhorn trying to find my ropes in the profession. The introduction to Choudhury had come through a circular that had stated—'Let Us Count Our Tigers'. It was the protocol for the first real attempt at estimating the population of tigers on the basis of tiger pugmarks. The missive had piqued my interest. Over the years, the method has been heavily criticized for its unsuitability by some. There was a Byzantine struggle over this in the emerging science. The field had buckled under the weight of criticism, but in 2005, the Wildlife Institute of India (WII), with some modification in the technique, proved the merit of the fundamentals—the pugmarks indeed could discriminate identities and gender of individual adult tigers.[3] But that is a different story worth a book.

A Step Forward

It was time for the training to take on a larger shape. In 1976, the training was upgraded to one of the directorates of the Forest Research Institute (FRI)—the Directorate of Wildlife Research and Education (DWRE). The whole length of the west wing on the first floor of the FRI building was assigned to the DWRE to set up its training facilities. Another brilliant officer with a scientific bent of mind, N.R. Nair, from the Kerala cadre of the Indian Forest Service (IFS), was posted as the first director of the DWRE. He, like his predecessors, had been blooded in wildlife management in the field. On his joining his assignment at Dehradun, Nair had set about creating a group of external resource persons—from the forest department and scientists from relevant disciplines to design a training curriculum. He had access to the forest botany and zoology laboratories of the FRI. A very short-sighted scientist was lent from the division of entomology within the FRI to the DWRE. He had problems distinguishing a dung beetle from a magpie robin and had a rich and unprintable vocabulary that, fortunately, the wild animals could not understand.

During this time, I was posted as assistant director in the Melghat Tiger Reserve, Maharashtra, which was among the first nine tiger reserves to be notified in the country. In April 1977, my boss, the Field Director (FD), informed me of the government's decision to relieve me to join the wildlife management course at the DWRE, Dehradun.

The training course at the DWRE involved spending 50 per cent of its term field training in various protected areas in the country. When I reported for training at Dehradun, we were all together 11 officers. DWRE was assigned hostel accommodation for officers under training in a barrack within the campus of the then Northern Forest Ranger's College (NFRC). A new forward control minibus was assigned to DWRE to be used for study tours. The driver, Sadhu, was unlike the qualities associated with his name and was frequently inebriated. On tour, our camp clerk, Khushal Chand, matched Sadhu glass for glass of the country liquor. In fact, he had a nose for sourcing the libations. We had rechristened him Daru Chand.

We visited Rajaji National Park frequently for various field exercises. The first extended tour was a month-long learning of various aspects of veterinary science. We were provided accommodation for the duration in the student's hostel within the campus of the Indian Veterinary Research Institute (IVRI) at Izatnagar. To understand the management of different habitats and species, we visited selected protected areas (PAs) in the Kashmir Valley; the Similipal Tiger Reserve in Odisha, which was mandatory as the great teacher Saroj Raj Choudhury was the FD there; and the Palamau Tiger Reserve, Bihar (now in Jharkhand). For the tours in South India, the first visit was to the Bandipur Tiger Reserve.

Tragedy Strikes

That day, 6 December 1977, dawned like any other in the field, or so we thought. I was the duty officer, and my task was to prepare to strike camp. Our next destination was the Periyar Tiger Reserve. N.R. Nair wished to photograph dholes that were sighted in the forests nearby. With that intention, he left the camp at daybreak, stating that he would be back in time. He did come back but not alive. Nair was exploring a forest road about 2 km away from the camp. A.J.T. Johnsingh, then a researcher studying dholes, had accompanied him. It transpired that Nair had not come across dholes that were frequently seen in that portion but instead had sighted a young tusker quietly standing some distance away. Nair, in trying to get at a better distance and angle to photograph the elephant, had moved closer, and the elephant had charged, coming straight at him.

Nair, in order to escape, had entered a lantana thicket with the elephant close at heels. There was a shout and then all was quiet. This we learned from a highly distraught Johnsingh, who had come back to the camp in the vehicle that had been used for the trip. Accompanied by Surendranath Asari, my fellow course-mate from Kerala, I had gone to the site indicated to us by the forest guard on that ill-fated trip. We had found the lifeless body of Director Nair inside the thicket.

Becoming a Part of the Future Institution

After having completed the training, I returned to rejoin my posting in Melghat Tiger Reserve in the middle of March 1978. In mid-1979, I received a letter from Vinod Behari Saharia, the new director, DWRE, asking me whether I would be willing to join DWRE as a senior research officer (SRO) with the responsibility for training officers in wildlife management. My posting in Melghat and my training strongly drew me to wildlife management. In response, I had expressed my interest. I finally landed in Dehradun on 18 December 1979 to join my new posting at a time when the second PG diploma course was underway. Besides me, there were two other SROs at the DWRE—forest officers Vinod Rishi from West Bengal and V.K. Sood from Tripura. I had known both of them. There was a research officer, the same inimitable short-sighted entomologist with the penchant for profanity. I had also made a renewed acquaintance with Sadhu, the driver, and his sidekick Daru Chand.

The WII: Early Years

In May 1982, the journey that had started in 1969 under the watch of Choudhury from the IFC to the DWRE had arrived at another milepost with the DWRE becoming the WII, established as the subordinate office of the Ministry of Agriculture, a step closer to the ultimate autonomy that would be attained after four more years. The change had triggered the merger of the Central Crocodile Breeding, Management and Training Institute (CCBMTI), based in Hyderabad, with the WII. The CCBMTI at that time was technically assisted through a project of the FAO. The personnel working on that project, the movable assets, faculty members and staff in CCBMTI were all transferred to the WII. The Food and Agriculture Organisation (FAO). project was redesigned to assist the WII, with J.B. Sale, a British ecologist who had earlier worked in Africa, becoming the project's chief technical advisor (CTA). L.A.K. Singh and B.C. Chaudhary, both scientists who were involved in pioneering work at CCBMTI, and their junior colleague K.G.M. Pillay became our first set of new colleagues. By this time, the space that WII had in the FRI's west wing began to get crowded. The two end rooms—north and south—housed the offices of the director, WII, and the CTA, respectively. Besides a large classroom, another room was partitioned to accommodate the office staff. There was a deep veranda—a lobby, if you like—running the entire inner length of the west wing, which was suitably partitioned to accommodate the new faculty members. The FAO project soon had another addition. W.A. Rodgers, who had extensive field experience in Kenya and Uganda as a wildlife warden, had arrived as a management specialist. During his tenure at the WII, he was destined to make a significant contribution.

In January 1984, another training course in wildlife management, the first certificate course for range forest officers and equivalent ranks spread over 12 weeks, was established. Like the postgraduate diploma course, half of its duration was assigned for field exposure.

At this time, a political tussle began for the relocation of the WII. The two candidates were Jabalpur in Madhya Pradesh and Dehradun in Uttar Pradesh. There were strong lobbies at work, and both locations had their pros and cons.

Acquiring an Independent Identity

Cometh the hour, cometh the man—Rajiv Gandhi was a Member of Parliament (MP) from the Amethi constituency in Uttar Pradesh. All the advantages that Dehradun otherwise had over Jabalpur were bolstered by his support. Fate had decreed that the WII would be established as a separate institution in Dehradun. Narayan Dutt Tiwari was the then chief minister of Uttar Pradesh. Suitable land for the prospective campus of the WII was made available in Chandrabani Arcadia, 6 km from the FRI off the Dehradun–Saharanpur road. The approach road was earthen—a dirt road with ruts. The government of Uttar Pradesh promised water and power supply, and to convert the dirt road to a black-topped one. It was decided that Rajiv Gandhi would lay the foundation stone for the campus on 15 October 1984.

The foundation stone-laying ceremony proceeded without a hitch. Rajiv Gandhi made a short but effective speech that focused on forests and wildlife conservation, and the significant role expected from the WII to serve the nation in its capacity. Fifteen days later, Prime Minister Indira Gandhi was assassinated, throwing the country into turmoil.

The post of the director, WII, had been advertised. H.S. Panwar became the new director. He came with the reputation of being an outstanding forest and wildlife manager, with a rare combination of professional vision and leadership qualities. He was the director, Project Tiger, in New Delhi, even as he accepted his new assignment at Dehradun. The WII became an autonomous institution of the Ministry of Environment and Forests on 25 March 1986. It was registered as a society under the Societies Registration Act, 1960. With this change in its status, the WII had an apex decision-making body—the governing body chaired by the secretary, MoEF, with members selected on a fixed tenure. The WII's society, on the higher plane, was presided over by the minister of MoEF, with members elected on rotation as per its constitution.

Building of an Institution: More than Bricks and Mortar

The new Director had taken on a great responsibility on his shoulders for leading the institute on its journey to fulfil the promise to nature and the nation. The WLPA had been in place for the past 14 years. Besides being a legal instrument, it had expectations that the Director could read between the lines—the demands on the ecology of the listed species, the diversity of habitats and the responsibility for their conservation. The interface between the wild lands and those dominated by the human population represented many potential conflicts. These needed to be addressed with great sensitivity. The development agenda of the country represented a separate steep challenge. The Director's first intuition was to define the scope of wildlife science, which integrated wildlife biology, landscape ecology, insular biogeography and socio-economics. The former three were merged much later as science progressed—the science of conservation biology. The Director was aware that other branches of science, such as captive breeding and management, veterinary science and practice, would intersect at some point. To translate this complex into a fresh agenda for the WII, in addition to training professionals in the field, it was considered necessary to have an academic degree programme at the postgraduate level and research programme in wildlife science for building capacity and capabilities for understanding development projects—their objectives, impacts on wildlife, ecosystems, on the local and other communities at large, which would later develop into advisory functions of the WII. None of these components was considered to be stand-alone. These considerations had given birth to three interacting faculties—Wildlife Management, Wildlife Biology and Wildlife Extension, to be staffed by scientists and wildlife managers from the field. The scientists from various disciplines and field managers tested for their merit had to be recruited.

The Director had laid out the WII's vision and mission. The former was for the institute to become a centre of excellence for wildlife conservation—nationally and internationally. The mission was stated in terms of aims and objectives.[4] The Director, accordingly, had made a proposal to the MoEF, wording it with all the skill at his command—which was in plenty.

Fate had conspired to provide the strongest support for shaping the institute's future, which was garnered from the clear vision and experience of two personalities. One was the Director, WII, and the other was the formidable T.N. Seshan, secretary, MoEF, Government of India (GoI). Seshan was brusque, hard to please, called a spade a spade, prefixed by suitable adjectives, and even his gentler pronouncements, if you could say that, would sound like an admonishment. He was upstanding, fair and just, all at the same time. He had appreciated the proposal for the future of the institute that had landed on his desk. Unlike most other secretaries, with the exception of Pradipto Ghosh, who came much later in the life of the institute from 2004 to 2007, if an idea did not sit well with Seshan, he would provide a new direction about how best to hit the bullseye. Thus, a partnership based on mutual trust and respect was forged with a clear understanding of not to be bothered about the state of the wicket. The work agenda was in place, and the proposed recruitment of prospective scientists and managers had received the green signal.

The Bricks, Mortar and Much More

Having touched the heart and soul of the dream, it was the turn of bricks and mortar—to plan the edifice that bespoke the sacred mission it represented.

The Director was clear on the concept of the structures. These, while pleasing to the eye in appearance and serving the specific needs and facilities, could not dominate the natural environment—the verdant area. Such a concept would represent what the institute was all about. Further, there were to be no more than two storeys. In his thoughts, he had an architectural design that was different from typical government buildings. The buildings, besides their aesthetics, needed to serve safety, security and a beneficial ambiance for the occupiers. Government buildings pay scant attention to the combination of these factors. Not surprisingly, many government functionaries are considered serious of countenance and irate.

An advertisement was placed to attract architectural firms of national reputation and likewise to create a logo for the institute. While the Secretary was the approving authority, he had granted full freedom to the Director to have his say. The logo was duly designed, and the Delhi-based architectural firm Kothari Associates was awarded the work to plan and build the WII's edifice. The main building would have offices, a boardroom, classrooms, a spacious library and laboratories, all connected with covered passages. There would be 10 faculty bungalows, including the residence for the director; a guest house and a hostel block for those arriving for training, the students and researchers. The site, when taken possession of, had degraded sal forest with thickets of lantana. Cutting of trees to make way for construction was kept to a minimum. The natural drainage was to be kept intact. Effective access roads with culverts, and small bridges as necessary were planned. The stream between the two large plots out of the three granted to the WII was trained without any obvious signs of artificiality. It ultimately drained into the river Asan that flowed north and northwest of the campus later to meet the Yamuna.

All structures were to have a matching design and colour scheme to match the sky, and the exterior had stone cladding.

The Director had a detailed discussion with the architects to express what was on his mind to ensure that the architects were on the same page.

Orientation of Faculty Members

On weekends, the Director led the faculty members to the WII's site in Chandrabani. There he led the task of removal of lantana mechanically. Besides the lesson in the dignity of labour, it was about forging unity, discipline and team spirit. He also used to set out time for discussion of a work plan for the institute. At intervals, the Director arranged field tours to orient the new faculty members to promote confidence, field learning and hands-on experience. Forest officers who were inducted as faculty on deputation helped significantly to cement the relationship between research, academics and field management.

The WII on Its New Campus

By the year 1991, the new campus at Chandrabani was on its way to completion. Some buildings had been put to use even before that. An avenue plantation was established along the approach road in consultation with the local residents. The black-topped access road to the WII was extended to the habitations along the WII perimeter. A small bridge was built for the people to negotiate the stream, and a local city bus route was added to facilitate transport, especially for schoolgoing children. The WII had thus earned the unstinted support of the local community. This was living up to what the WII had set itself to profess.

The building that housed the faculty and staff was ready by 1992. The offices—the administrative sections and those of the faculty—had personal computers (PCs) on their desks.

The library had become rich and functional. A computer centre was established, and the laboratories started progressing under the supervisory responsibilities of faculty and accredited technicians.

Expansion of Programmes

While the postgraduate diploma and certificate courses were on track, the preparation for a master's degree course in wildlife science had been taken up. The objective was to train young minds and prepare them for careers in wildlife research and management. A symposium jointly held by the WII and the Aligarh Muslim University in 1986 about teaching wildlife conservation in universities encouraged further efforts in this direction. It shaped the syllabus for the master's degree course in Wildlife Science by FAO-WII in 1988. It was vetted by the Saurashtra University, Rajkot. Thus, the first MSc course in Wildlife Science at WII began in 1989–1991 and was affiliated with the Saurashtra University. The course has been conducted every alternate year since then.

Research, surveys and monitoring capabilities already considered critically important had proceeded on course. An Research Advisory Committee (RAC), made up of eminent individuals comprising scientists from various disciplines representing different organizations, academicians and state wildlife organizations, including chief wild life wardens (CWLWs) of states and Union Territories in rotation, was established. Later this was expanded to include academics and training; thus, the Research Advisory Committee (RAC) metamorphosed into the Training, Research Advisory Committee (TRAC) to ensure relevance, maintenance of standards and delivery of future programmes. Since 1987, the WII has been holding an Annual Research Seminar (ARS), inviting participation from various disciplines of science, non-governmental organization

(NGOs) and field personnel. Presentations at the ARS generate scientific papers that get published in national and international peer-reviewed journals.

Researchers continue to be recruited for the WII's projects via an all-India advertisement and competition to recognize merit. Researchers receive fellowships on scales prescribed by the government. They are thoroughly trained in all aspects of science before settling in the field. They are provided with all facilities for their stay in field camps, expenditure and mobility. They are supervised and mentored with a strong tie-up with the jurisdictional departments. Each researcher is encouraged to enrol for a doctoral degree.

Organizing the PA Network for the Country and Much More

In 1983, the government of India had desired a comprehensive network of PAs to serve as a keystone of the National Wildlife Action Plan (NWAP). In 1984, the WII was appointed to formulate such a plan. The WII enlisted the help of large numbers of consultants, with the WII faculty members chipping in. In 1988, this resulted in a report titled *Planning a Wildlife Protected Area Network in India* crafted by the FAO specialist W.A. Rodgers and the director, H.S. Panwar. The report of national importance runs in two volumes. It has established a biogeographic classification of the country, a hierarchical system that allows from the vast biogeographic regions, in all 10 in number, to the identification of a specific PA in the given portion of the country. Important biological parameters for practical application were selected; the existing PA network was reviewed, and the creation of new PAs was recommended so as to cover the full range of the country's biological diversity. Today, with minor modifications, the time-tested report continues to be used as a guide for the country.

Over the years, the WII has added a string of guides—one for field techniques, a manual for conducting wildlife census or population estimation, and a manual for planning wildlife management in the PAs during 1995 that, in 2005, was enlarged to include forest areas managed for production of timber and non timber forest products (NTFP)—an integration of forest working plans with wildlife management principles and needs. There is a guide for eco-development and another for addressing the environment impact assessment (EIA). All these are based on tenets of modern science, existing laws, regulations, field realities and the working style of various implementing agencies.

Another very important initiative concerned the science and practice of wildlife health. This was new and had not been attempted before in the country. For this purpose, the WII took on board PA managers, state wildlife agencies, state departments of animal husbandry, veterinary colleges and institutions such as the IVRI and Indian Council of Agricultural Research (ICAR). In association with National Wildlife Health Centre (NWHC) of the United States Geological Survey (USGS) a nationwide programme titled 'Development of Indian Wildlife Health Cooperative' was initiated in 1994.

Resurgence of Forest on the WII Campus

The natural area within the campus at Chandrabani had fully regenerated in response to protection. The Director's decision in 1986 to set aside as much of the degraded area possible for the purpose was thus vindicated. The northern portion of the institutional block now has a dense growth of sal (*Shorea robusta*) plus some miscellaneous species. A masonry bund was constructed south of this patch on the small seasonal stream. This created a nice little wetland that attracted several species of waterfowl. An excellent paved network of walking trails was built. What was a highly degraded forest with lantana in 1982, today is a small natural forest with predominantly wild plants and animals. This small but rich wilderness has become an excellent outdoor training and research laboratory. In acknowledgement, a leopard or two regularly visit the campus every winter. Once, even a wild elephant broke through the campus wall and deposited an impressive pile of droppings almost at the doorstep of the bungalow occupied by the faculty member specializing in wildlife damage control!

Overcoming a Roadblock

Having guided the institute on the path of excellence the director, H.S. Panwar, opted for voluntary retirement in early 1995. S.K. Mukherjee, the senior-most faculty member, was selected as the new director. Over the years, there have been other officers who have succeeded him. It was a smooth transition with the future work agenda well in place. Since the very beginning, the WII has maintained complete transparency in all its tasks. Management of personnel, and the welfare of students, researchers and the officers under training had maintained the desired standards. With research, training, academics and field practice backed by modern science and field realities, the institute continued to be called upon to prove its credentials. However, some of those attempts were not to the liking of some members of the governing body, and questions began to be raised.

By 1998, a committee was established under the chairmanship of Biplab Das Gupta, a member of the Rajya Sabha and of the WII's Society, to probe the institute's credibility. The committee had carried on its task for several months. A large number of scientists, former students and researchers, forest officers, other field practitioners, NGOs and well-informed amateurs interested in nature were contacted to seek their opinion. Armed with information, the committee had held several meetings. The entire process had finally ended with the WII receiving a clean bill of health.

The Tiger Crisis

By the end of 2004, the prestigious Project Tiger received the biggest blow when tigers went locally extinct in the Sariska Tiger Reserve, Rajasthan. The WII worked hard to find the causes and presented a report to the National Board for Wildlife (NBWL) on 5 March 2005. Under the steerage of the secretary, MoEF, Pradipto Ghosh, the matters had gone the right way. The report had resulted in setting up the Tiger Task Force (TTF), which, besides discussing the status of the tiger in the country, suggested various conservation measures.[5] Pradipto Ghosh, during his tenure, had recognized the worth of the WII's work. A minor storm raised in the governing body earlier over consultancy fees paid to faculty was smoothly resolved. Under his leadership, the WII continued to prosper.

One of the TTF's recommendations had resulted in establishing the National Tiger Conservation Authority (NTCA) in New Delhi in 2005. The WII joined the NTCA to develop a detailed, sophisticated scientific protocol for countrywide assessment of the tiger population, co-predators and prey species. The first report was tabled in 2006. Thereafter, the operation was repeated at an interval of 4 years. The last or the fourth report pertains to the year 2018.

Establishment of the Centre on World Natural Heritage Management and Training for the Asia-Pacific Region

The WII Category 2 Centre on World Natural Heritage Management and Training was established in 2015. A separate matching facility was constructed for the purpose. It has conducted many thematic capacity-building and outreach programmes on world heritage conservation. A two-year residential interdisciplinary master's degree course in Heritage Conservation and Management affiliated with the Saurashtra University, Rajkot, was established. The first course was timed to start during July 2019 but could not make that target for reasons that I will discuss later.

Towards the Capstone of Excellence

On 14 November 2018, *Business Standard* carried the most important news for the 36-year-young WII. The Union Minister for Ministry of Environment, Forest and Climate Change (MoEFCC). Harsh Vardhan, had stated that inter-ministerial consultations on the draft cabinet note for conferring the status of an Institute of National Importance (INI) on WII had successfully taken place. Drafting the INI Bill had been completed and the proposal was ready to be carried further for the approval of the Union Cabinet and then Parliament. It meant that the WII would be among 92 INIs in the country, such as All India Institute of Medical Sciences (AIIMS), Indian Institute of Technology (IITs) and National Institute of Technology (NITs). The status would grant WII autonomous power to design special courses, hire more people, grant degrees and get fixed and enhanced funding from the central government. It was an honour well earned.[6]

Unbeknownst to the nation and the institute's well-wishers, fate was holding a different deck of cards for the institute.

A Gathering Storm

The Department of Expenditure (DoE), within the Ministry of Finance, Government of India, in 2020, reviewed 194 autonomous institutes across 18 ministries. It recommended 109 of those for merger into 26 of those existing and the government had to disengage from 23 autonomous institutions. The WII was named among the five of those under MoEFCC recommended for disengagement.[7] Among all the institutes reviewed by the DoE, there was not a single one that was anywhere near the WII's enormous reach of science in its agenda for training, research, academics, and complex field practices involving terrestrial, freshwater, estuarine and marine ecosystems, and equally so for its valuable advisory services rendered to several ministries of the central and state governments. Further, the WII's work agenda was strongly aligned with and served the intents and purpose of several international conventions, treaties and agreements to which India is a signatory. What is more, some two years ago, the WII was about to be cleared for the status of an INI.

The journal of the Centre of Science and Environment, New Delhi—*Down to Earth*—reported that the Director, WII, on 15 October 2020, had written to the government that the functioning of the WII would not be viable without the financial backing of the MoEFCC.[8] The WII had no revenue from course fees; the courses that fulfil the nation's needs and the savings from research projects from other sources were limited. The institute had 112 serving employees and 65 pensioners. The MoEFCC, on 28 October 2020, wrote to the Prime Minister's Office (PMO) that the WII could best serve its mandate for wildlife science and conservation by remaining within the ministry and proposed reconsidering the disengagement on the anvil.

A coup de grace followed. In its annual audit of the WII conducted by the Comptroller and Auditor General (CAG), in 2019, the WII's tie-up with the Saurashtra University, Rajkot, since 1987, for its MSc and PhD programmes in wildlife science and research was objected to, citing the University Grants Commission's (UGC) circular of 2015 that laid down that state universities could not establish off-campus centres beyond the territorial jurisdiction of the concerned state. Thus, the MSc and PhD programmes and also the master's degree course in Heritage Conservation and Management of the WII were held in abeyance, with the future of students and researchers in balance.[9]

There was a glimmer of hope as the media announced on 19 December 2021 that the WII had signed an MoU with the Doon University located in the same city to enable the researchers in WII to pursue their PhD programme.[10] Dialogue concerning the WII's MSc programme was treading a positive path with the Delhi-based Academy of Scientific and Innovative Research (AcSIR), an INI. Since then, both these academic programmes of WII are recognized by the AcSIR for awarding degrees as a result of an MoU signed between the two institutions.[11]

The internationally acclaimed WII is in great distress at the moment. The institute's astounding freefall neither stands to reason nor appears to be insurmountable if the right forces get realigned on the basis of facts and value. How and why the DoE arrived at its decision would enter into the annals of unsolved puzzles. One can only hope that in time and soon, the storm will lose its power and blow away with the descent of 2021 into 2022, marking the fiftieth anniversary of WLPA. Although there are some better signs, there still is a way to go.

Notes

1. The author is grateful to Dr Bitapi Sinha for contributing the origin of research at WII and its framework; his colleagues at WII, past and present, for their knowledge, wisdom, friendship and support; Saroj Raj Choudhury, who introduced him to the enchanting world of nature; V.B. Saharia, for opening the doors to WII for him; and H.S. Panwar, for shaping the author's vocation, inspiring his thoughts, words and deeds, and the happiness that came along with those in his life.

2. *Tenth General Assembly: Volume II Proceedings and Summary of Business*, IUCN and UNESCO, 1970, https://bit.ly/3ImGRDb. Accessed on 7 July 2022; Task Force: Project Tiger, *Project Tiger: A Planning Proposal for Preservation of Tiger (Panthera Tigris Tigris Linn) in India*, Ministry of Agriculture, 1972.
3. Sharma, Sandeep, et al., 'Identification of Individual Tigers (Panthera Tigris) from Their Pugmarks', *Journal of Zoology*, Vol. 267, No. 1, 2006, pp. 9–18, https://doi.org/10.1017/S0952836905007119. Accessed on 7 July 2022.
4. Panwar, H.S., 'WII 1991: The Making of an Institution, Down the Memory Lane', *WII Newsletter*, Special Commemorative Issue, 1982–1991, October 1992.
5. *Joining the Dots: The Report of The Tiger Task Force:* Union Ministry of Environment and Forests (Project Tiger), 2005, p. 206, https://bit.ly/3uwVj5P. Accessed on 22 June 2022.
6. 'Talks on Granting Institute of National Importance Status to WII Completed: Harsh Vardhan', *Business Standard*, 14 November 2018, https://bit.ly/3RiOUVR. Accessed on 7 July 2022.
7. Das, Kalyan, 'Govt Plans to Cut Funds to 5 Autonomous Bodies', *Hindustan Times*, 19 October 2020, https://bit.ly/3OIZALD. Accessed on 7 July 2022; Mishra, Ishita, 'Government Plans "Disengagement" from Five Premier Environment-Related Institutions by Withdrawing Funding', *The Times of India*, 18 October 2020, https://bit.ly/3uve9ua. Accessed on 7 July 2022.
8. Kukreti, Ishan, 'Disengaging with WII Should Be given Rethink, MoEF&CC Tells PMO: RTI', *Down to Earth*, 4 December 2020, https://bit.ly/3yN7KwX. Accessed on 7 July 2022.
9. Rajpurohit, Shivnarayan, 'Over 2 Years after CAG Red Flags: WII Director Takes Unilateral Decision to Keep MSc & PhD Courses "in Abeyance"', *The Indian Express*, 29 September 2021, https://bit.ly/3yllEF6. Accessed on 7 July 2022.
10. Azad, Shivani, 'WII and Doon University Sign MoU, to Offer PhD Courses', *The Times of India*, 19 December 2021, https://bit.ly/3NQC3qG. Accessed on 7 July 2022.

11. 'WII and Academy of Scientific and Innovative Research (AcSIR) Signs Academic Agreement', Wildlife Institute of India 7 March 2022, https://bit.ly/3IiR5of. Accessed on 7 July 2022; *Agreement between Academy of Scientific & Innovative Research, Ghaziabad and Wildlife Institute of India, Dehradun*, Government of Uttar Pradesh, 7 March 2022, https://bit.ly/3REDw6J. Accessed on 7 July 2022.

SPAWNING A GENERATION OF CONSERVATIONISTS: REMINISCENCES OF WWF-INDIA

SHARAD GAUR

I often wander down the memory lane, reminiscing about the experiences that shaped the early lives and careers of so many of us who chose to work in nature conservation and found our professional alma mater in WWF-India. Those experiences are unforgettable and worth sharing. Several young environmentalists grew up here, and many of these people remained in professions connected somehow with nature conservation.

I also remember with wonder how, in that pre-digital and largely manual era, we were able to maintain countrywide communications; develop linkages with members including thousands of youth; run awareness campaigns and field projects across the country; maintain and update fairly sizeable databases; and so on. Especially for those who may have seen and interacted with World Wide Fund for Nature-India (WWF-India) only after it moved into the plush and fully computerized secretariat building and a rather corporate setup, it will be difficult if not impossible to comprehend the earlier years of the organization. We were supposed to be a volunteerism-based organization. How could we run professional projects in conservation? In an age when wildlife and field ecology were not taught in many places, how did WWF-India get, train and retain professional staff?

In the very first month of my MSc Zoology course at the Delhi University, we were set working by our professor to organize a series of do-it-yourself student seminars in biology. I offered to do one on wildlife conservation. Unknown to me, he had invited as observer the honorary education officer of WWF-India, Mahendra Vyas, someone who was to become my mentor, guide and lifelong friend. Although I had been a member since my undergraduate days, the names World Wide Fund for Nature (WWF) and International Union for Nature Conservation (IUCN) were really big for us students. Some of our teachers used to speak about them in lectures as 'the United Nations of conservation'! After the seminar, when we were introduced, I mentioned to him my deep interest in conservation. Within a few days, he took me to the WWF office to meet with the trustee, Duleep Matthai, and honorary secretary, Dr Amrita Patel. And in another week's time, I joined WWF-India as a part-time stipendiary in October 1978. I was a student, and I was working, and it was *the WWF*!

It was early years after the promulgation of the Wild Life (Protection) Act (WLPA), 1972. Project Tiger had been launched, but India's wildlife was perhaps in its most vulnerable phase. Tiger numbers had touched their lowest; hunting was on despite the law; and illegal trade in poached wildlife parts was rampant. The boundaries of many protected areas were still unclearly defined. Enforcement in the new PA was in its nascent stage. Matters related to the conservation of species and habitats were supposed to be of concern to either the professional foresters or the select few naturalists, and only an occasional news item would catch the larger public attention. From the point of view of involvement in wildlife conservation and related careers, those were challenging but exciting times.

WWF-India was then the World Wildlife Fund-India, an autonomous member of the 28-nation family whose declared objective since inception in 1969 was the preservation of endangered species and habitats. Indeed, for a good two decades, the main focus remained on a few charismatic species. Only in 1987 did the name change to World Wide Fund for Nature-India to reflect its enlarging focus, which today spans the whole gamut of environmental concerns—species, habitats, sustainable development, pollution, energy, climate change and urban environment, and so on.

My involvement started as a member, then a stipend holder, and eventually as a full-time staffer on completing my master's degree. As an assistant education officer for the northern region, I devised and conducted programmes for public awareness on conservation, expanded membership and organized members' events, conducted the Nature Clubs programme with youth groups in colleges and schools, and organized nature camping for the members. I was also supposed to provide administrative backup to the office, which serviced Delhi and northern states and was also the organization's main hub for coordination with the central government.

Campaign against Bustard Hunting

One of my earliest experiences as well as informal training in wildlife protection activism was to assist and join a protest in January 1979 organized by the Delhi office. It was targeted against bustard hunting by some princes from Saudi Arabia. In the mid-1970s, oil supply from Iran had stopped, and under pressure to ensure that oil from Saudi did not stop, the Indian government was forced to relax the ban under the WLPA and issue permits to the visiting sheikhs for hunting bustards in the Thar Desert, Rajasthan. These were most likely houbara bustards, whose meat is fancied as a supposed aphrodisiac. However, the area also had great Indian butard (GIB), chinkara and blackbuck, all endangered species and favourites of hunters, besides several other rare species, including wolf, fox and caracal. There was no way of checking what was being hunted by the diplomatic royals in that remote area. The expedition was operating with trained falcons, long-range rifles, binoculars, radio transmitters and freezer vans. Worse still, they had entered by road from Pakistan and were in an extremely sensitive area close to our international border. The news of this surreptitious 'oil diplomacy' reached WWF-India through supporters, and while other conservation groups were still mulling over how to react, our Delhi office quickly decided to organize an awareness and pressure campaign. The news was conveyed among the youth volunteers on bicycles and scooters, planning meetings were held, campaign material was hand-prepared, and a band of dedicated volunteers held a sustained protest outside the embassy of Saudi Arabia. It soon sparked some press coverage and led to public outcry. We even handed over a memorandum to the Ministry of External Affairs, who were playing host to the foreign guests. By this time, many more groups had got involved—the Bishnoi community in Rajasthan was up in arms—and media coverage was growing. The campaign had its effect; the permits were cancelled, and the entire entourage was quickly withdrawn.

Later in the same year, about 300 Delhi citizens took out a march, where several of us from WWF also joined, against the Delhi administration's plans for a series of construction projects in Delhi that were ecologically disastrous for the city. The Ridge forest was being fragmented by a number of developments. The Ring Road—being built as a fast route encircling the urban limits of Delhi—was not yet a complete ring; some connecting portions were going to eat through good forest patches in outlying areas. There were other areas as well where tree felling was underway, or forests were being turned into parks or garbage dumps. Several natural forest areas of Delhi were falling prey to encroachment also, but there was general administrative apathy towards the protection of these wilderness pockets and their ecological values.

There were a plethora of other environmental issues in Delhi, and small protests by local citizen groups had started right from the mid-1970s. A group of young volunteers founded Kalpavriksh in 1979, an action group to make activism stronger and faster. Over the next several years, this non-governmental organization (NGO), fledged from the WWF nest, was to spearhead a number of environmental actions—notable among them being the Narmada campaign, as also an information network on PAs, and more serious-level work on the Delhi Ridge, including the cementing together of a joint NGO forum and representation on ridge management bodies set up by the Delhi government. The result of all such combined initiatives was that, finally, the Delhi administration, in 1996, declared large parts of the Delhi Ridge as a reserved forest (RF) under the Indian Forest Act (IFA), 1927.

In Tandem with the Government Authorities

Authorities at the Delhi Zoo had been discussing with WWF-India how they could collaborate to enhance public awareness beyond the existing signboards and also orient visitor behaviour. Working together, we launched an Honorary Zoo Wardens scheme in which WWF-India members, from seniors to youth, worked at the zoo for a few hours each week, assisting with public information, awareness and a kind of social watch to check vandalism in the 250-acre sprawling landscape. Wearing printed armbands for identity, they offered their free time and worked in team shifts of up to 30 people each day. This scheme ran fairly well for about two years. Then the portfolio of Wildlife, including zoos, changed from the Ministry of Agriculture to the new Ministry of Environment and Forests (MoEF). The dealing officials changed, the zoo directors changed, and in this maze of administrative changes, the scheme fell between stools. It was, after all, something voluntary offered by WWF-India, with no budget lines in government files. But while it was functional, it provided a good learning in multi-agency coordination, teamwork, leadership and public awareness.

Busting Wildlife Trade

WWF-India offices, led by some of the more proactive trustees, especially Duleep Matthai in the north and Anne Wright in the east, used to carry out tasks such as gathering intelligence about illegal wildlife trade, providing alerts to enforcement authorities, and frequently assisting in raids and confiscations. A lot of this work was happening much before the international Trade Record Analysis of Flora and Fauna in Commerce (TRAFFIC) network arrived in India and became a programme division of WWF-India. I, too, assisted our trustee Duleep Matthai in a few such operations. As a trained zoologist and a keen wildlifer, I was supposed to have an eye for identifying skins or specimens. So, I went out on several assignments—covert observation of the illegal partridge fights, and trade in falcons and other wild birds taking place in Old Delhi; joining raids as a witness and helping in confiscation and stock checking; gathering intel on poaching and other wildlife crimes through 'listening' during field journeys. Some of this silent work helped the Wildlife Inspectorate of the then Delhi administration in making sizeable hauls of skins and nabbing poachers. It also led to an honorary wildlife warden's position for me in the Delhi region, which I served for a number of years. Similar work by our teams in the eastern region led to the wildlife authorities and the Calcutta Port Trust making a few large hauls of consignments of furskins, snakeskins and live turtles.

Education and Awareness Building

In those days, access to authentic and good-quality resource material on Indian wildlife was quite a challenge. The visual material, in particular, used to be either in the form of published photographs in books and magazines, or people's personal slides and prints. WWF-India had a newsletter for members and also *Nature Clubs of India*, the independent newsletter of the Nature Clubs movement. However, both these publications were quarterlies and had a long waiting period between issues. Many times, the news or issue would lose its impact if people were reading about it after three months. Both these magazines carried news on conservation issues, articles and features, book reviews, activity reportage from across the regions by staff and nature club members or teachers, and quizzes and small action ideas. There was also a pen pals column helping to connect interested people far and near. The accompanying pictures and illustrations were in black-and-white in those days, but members eagerly read them end to end and even kept them as collectors' items, for there wasn't much more. I still hold on to my crumbling copy of the very first issue of the *Nature Clubs of India* newsletter published in October 1976, which I received during my college days.

Motion footage of wildlife was available in the form of documentaries that came on reel film. There were, of course, private holdings with a few, but those were mostly unedited raw footage of motion cameras. Just a few institutions—natural history museums and some embassies—had lending libraries of documentary films on nature and wildlife, and one felt very lucky to be watching such a movie. Many WWF-India offices across the country had made arrangements for borrowing such films. Each office used to have a members' event once a month, where a nature film would be screened, or there would be a talk with a slide show on some conservation topic, frequently knitted into a travelogue of someone's recent wild trip. There was also a small collection of films at the Bombay office, from where these were lent to regional offices via parcels.

Today, it might have faded from most people's memories, and to the digital generation with 24/7 availability of video content, it might sound like a useless narration, but in the yesteryears, when such screenings and members' meetings were organized, they became great platforms for wildlifers and conservationists to discuss and learn about issues. People came forward and offered their time and energy to volunteer for the cause in whatever capacity they could—from opening a nature club in their school to promoting the wildlife greeting cards and calendars, which were important fundraisers; from offering their vehicles for carting bundles of newsletters to various post offices to licking and pasting a few hundred postage stamps month after month. It did not matter how big or small the task; the cause was important. There were parents offering to deposit their kids at the WWF offices to work as volunteers after school or college hours.

Quite apart from the social bonhomie and the warmth for the cause it created, this whole phenomenon was also leading to a latent kind of talent hunt and filtration, which often resulted in the induction of people into WWF-India. Trustees, senior staffers from branches and other honorary office-bearers interacted with hundreds of people each month during events, meetings, nature trails and other outings. These were informal opportunities to help identify the more serious ones and gauge their commitment and aptitude, and vice versa, for the serious volunteers to express their interest in working more closely. Till the mid-1970s, only the secretariat in Bombay had a core team of staff, for coordination with regions; administration of the education and nature clubs programmes; finance and accounts; design, production and countrywide supply of resource material, including the newsletters and fundraising products. The existing four or five regional offices were working on the strength of just one or two staffers (the organizer or coordinator), supported by a band of committed volunteers. Many of them were raised to a 'semi-staff' level through honoraria or stipends.

WWF-India and the Bombay Natural History Society (BNHS) were the only large conservation organizations that could be called national in stature. The BNHS was the older of the two and had a wider public support base, but it did not build a countrywide presence through offices. The education and youth action programme of WWF-India that contributed a great deal to the growth of conservation activism was the Nature Clubs of India (NCI) movement established in 1976. The secretariat provided the administrative backup to the four regional and 18–20 branch offices spread across the country. We were a memorable education team running this flagship programme, and many of us doubled up as field personnel for several conservation projects as well.

The NCI operated through nature clubs—organized groups of youth, led by staff advisers and serviced by the WWF education team. These clubs were in schools, colleges, neighbourhoods, and in some army units too. Regular activities were organized, local conservation issues were studied and action ideas evolved. Youngsters learnt to manage their projects, from background research to keeping accounts, from fundraising to lobbying and coordinating with local authorities. It was like an informal cadre training from which several young professionals emerged in conservation.

Camping was the most popular part of the activities. There was a year-round calendar of camps, held in selected wilderness areas, including sanctuaries and national parks. We had three levels of camping. Nature orientation camps were meant for first-timers to provide exposure to the basics of nature study, ecological principles and conservation issues in a non-technical, informal manner. Nature leadership camps trained selected Nature Club members, advisers and volunteers to take on the tasks of leading and conducting environmental education, small conservation projects and activism. These were usually one week long, slightly more regimented and technical compared with orientation camps. For many years, the forested training ranges of the National Defence Academy, Khadakwasla, Pune, provided us the venue for these camps. The carefully tailored training schedule and participatory activities enabled the participants to become leaders and organizers. Over the years, these camps helped spawn a corps of dedicated volunteers and organizers who lent vital support to WWF-India's programmes. Many of them matured into serious environmentalists in their own right. Many indeed became staffers of WWF-India and other conservation organizations. Even those who did not take up directly environment-related jobs continued to support conservation work and apply their learnings in whatever professions they chose.

Environment education workshops (EEWs) were the third-level camps of the NCI movement. These were primarily aimed at identifying and training potential conservation professionals, including educators. The first of the EEWs were started with initial support from the U.S. Fish and Wildlife Service and the U.S. National Parks Service. These workshops attempted to achieve a multiplier effect so that part of WWF-India's limited financial and manpower resources were utilized in training those who could further spread the conservation work to a much larger target group than we could ever reach out to.

The emotional connection of this entire network was strong, as evidenced by several experiences. During one camp, a child was injured, and we were desperately trying to locate medical assistance. The park director passed on wireless messages to the headquarters in the town more than 10 km away, while we tried to attend to the child with whatever basic camp supplies we had carried. But there was a continuing bleed, which could soon pose an emergency. The area had had several man-eating episodes, and the park authorities were in a dilemma whether it would be safe to let us drive to town in a forest department jeep. Just then, a young doctor drove up in the middle of the forest at night and provided professional first aid and medication. Once the situation was under control and the tension had eased, he mentioned that he had been a WWF supporter in his student days. So, when he heard about the accident from the range office in the city, there was no way he could stay away. On other occasions, we had railway officials go out of their way to extend group reservation assistance or concessional fares, since their children had been our nature club members or campers. Thus, even when people were not professionally related to the WWF, they assisted in whatever capacity they could. In later years, even though the organization grew into a more corporate structure with much better finances and vastly improved facilities, perhaps this spirit of volunteerism slowly died out.

National Network

WWF-India started with just a handful of regional offices, but within a decade, it was expanding to state-level offices. Gujarat and Maharashtra even had some city-level offices. In addition, many upcoming projects opened their own field offices. At one stage, there were more than 20 offices across the country. When this expansion and addition of offices was happening during the late 1970s and early 1980s, we saw a concomitant growth in staff strength. Apart from the administration and support staff, many of those who joined education or project posts had academic backgrounds in life sciences, earth sciences, social sciences, communications or management. A few had had some prior experience with other organizations in conservation or social sectors. But it is interesting to know that till several years into this growth, there was no practice in WWF-India of advertising for vacancies. Talent was scouted; it was not a job market. Prior to the 1990s, I have no recollection of any newspaper ads or campus notices announcing vacancies.

When the MoEF took shape in 1984–1985, we were entrusted with a number of key programmes. By this time, many of the science and technical persons had been drawn into the newly created Environment Support Group (ESG), the research and consultancy arm of WWF-India. Here, from an education officer, I became the resident life scientist. I was part of the core team that conceptualized and wrote up the National Environmental Awareness Campaign. For the first few years, we were also the central executing agency for this scheme, in which hundreds of NGOs were financially and programmatically supported to carry out intensified awareness activities around environmental issues. We also produced several editions of the directory of environmental NGOs in India, which honed our skills in information management, maintaining large databases and networking with organizations, much before the advent of computer technologies and mobile communications. From sorting and cataloguing thousands of handwritten cards in cardex cabinets to manually typing on stencil sheets, cyclostyling the required print quantities, set-making, bookbinding and even bulk postal despatch, everyone learnt and did everything by rotation. Those were truly the days of learning by doing. There were many other firsts we did during this phase—the first journal of environmental abstracts, the first compendium on environment-related proceedings in Indian parliament and another compendium on the coverage of the environment by the Indian print media. Many of these went into multiple editions and were adopted under the ministry's growing ENVIS, a countrywide distributed network of information services. We also set up a query handling service, an early version of the helplines of today! All such projects built up our partnerships with the government and enmeshed WWF-India with the nucleus team of MoEF that worked on implementing the policies regarding environmental awareness, information networking and NGO support. Along with each such initiative, the professional growth of each one of us was expanding.

Short-term exposure programmes leading to the professional development of young environmentalists were constantly explored and tapped. I remember quite a few colleagues being sent on scholarships to the Smithsonian, the Jersey Wildlife Trust or other leading institutions, or on study tours to various WWF national organizations. When the opportunity arose for someone to take up higher studies or even an assignment in another place, it was facilitated without giving rise to any souring of ties. I experienced the extreme degree of this encouragement when, one day in early 1989, our most lovable secretary-general and director, ESG, Thomas Mathew, came back from some meeting and told me, 'Listen, the Wildlife Institute is announcing some faculty positions, and Panwar Saheb (then director WII) feels you should be there. Let me know if you wish to apply.' It left me choked and speechless.

I applied, went through the due selection interview and recruitment processes, and thus started another memorable part of the professional journey as Scientist-B (associate professor) in the extension faculty of Wildlife Institute of India (WII) Dehradun. Due to the quirks of destiny, it lasted only a year, as I was forced to return to Delhi on account of a series of mishaps in the family. But the professional and personal associations formed during this short tenure have been amazing and long-lasting.

Back in WWF-India, where I served for 10 more years, I rejoined the team that was taking the organization through its continuing phase of professional growth. The secretariat had, by now, moved from Bombay to the new building in New Delhi. The organization was abuzz with growth. To address the broadened scope of work following the change of name and expansion of the mission, well-defined functional divisions were being established and staffed with young as well as senior professionals. The traditional core areas were education; conservation (comprising wetlands, rivers, species and PA subdivisions); communications and media; programme coordination; membership and networking; sales and fundraising; and administration and finance.

New divisions and cells were established to take up work in several additional areas and also to give a more formal impetus to some previously existing work areas—pollution control, climate change, tiger cell (with support from WWF US and UK) and an army conservation cell. The TRAFFIC India cell worked against the illegal wildlife trade. The Centre for Environmental Law was set up as Asia's first diploma-level enviro-legal education unit and also to provide much-needed legal support to the organization's emerging legal activism. The Indira Gandhi Conservation Monitoring Centre (IGCMC) came up as a data centre and information repository on natural resources, PAs and conservation issues. With initial support from the MoEF and the British Official Development Assistance (ODA) (the future Department for International Development [DFID]), the IGCMC developed a mapping and GIS facility and also took over Environmental Information System (ENVIS) tasks, such as the making of the directories and the state biodiversity profiles. The directorship of the IGCMC happened to be my last two-year stint in WWF-India (1998–2000).

A couple of programmes deserve special mention since these were specifically aimed at the capacity-building of youth and small NGOs in professional environmental work. The Conservation Corps Volunteers (CCV) programme identified young aspirants who were desirous of working in conservation projects in field situations. They were given stipends and placed as apprentices in various host NGOs or with WWF-India field projects for up to

24 months. Here, they developed their skills in fieldwork, data gathering and analysis, report writing, visual documentation and coordination with official agencies. Some used this placement opportunity for writing up their own student dissertations or project reports, leading to their personal advancement. Some had been sent from their parent NGOs for skill building. There were a few who got inducted into WWF-India through this route also and built their careers further up.

Another such initiative was Conservation Action Support Programme (CASP), a small-grants-based scheme to enable NGOs or individual conservationists to take up focused action projects. Similarly, the Community Biodiversity Conservation Programme (CBCP) identified, and financially and technically supported several initiatives by local community groups for the protection of biodiversity resources, or securing community-conserved areas, or documenting local biodiversity through area profiles or other reports. Both of these schemes, too, led to a number of good projects getting developed and implemented in the field, with capacity-building and professional growth of the respective executants. As manager (Education) and, later, manager (Conservation), I had the good fortune of contributing to the growth of these programmes.

It is important to note that nearly the entire professional capacity built up by WWF-India till the early 1990s came either through its internal growth or recruitment of people experienced from other conservation or development-sector NGOs or research and academic organizations. Starting sometime in the 1990s, we saw certain deep-rooted changes in the governance, staffing and functioning of our alma mater. Understandably, these developments must have been deliberated upon and instituted by the apex decision-making body, the board of trustees, and were ostensibly aimed at betterment. However, many of these had impacts that completely took away the character of this organization.

In the past, we had seen personnel being drawn into WWF-India from government, industry or commerce sectors, and a few defence personnel too. But they had all crossed over from their previous jobs or had retired and sought re-employment. Now, for the first time, we started seeing the phenomenon of deputation of serving government officials. This was a veritable can of worms. How does an NGO remain 'non-government' any longer when it takes in government officials? And if such deputation was acceptable, how could the converse not be acceptable? Why could not a single person ever be deputed from WWF-India into any government assignment? There had been cases where the expertise of WWF-India persons was recognized and their services requested by government agencies, but those were denied. Had the board of trustees convinced themselves that there was no conservation expertise in-house and was only needed from outside? Also, the deputationists remained in the WWF for short durations; they would go back as soon as promotions or better prospects arose in their parent departments. So, in reality, this action did not lead to any professional development of the organization. On the contrary, it limited the growth of many WWF people. It also created immense disparities of emoluments between the WWF-India staff, who subsisted on typical NGO-level salaries despite giving 10–20 years to the organization, and the government deputees who brought in their protected pay and allowances and increment scales. This new, improved WWF did not have the money to give decent increments or allowances to its dedicated staff, but was coughing up two to three times the amount for the deputees.

Slowly but unmistakably, more changes were brought to the organization. The chain of command was broken from one to many; parallel administrative, financial and reporting structures were set up, giving it the feel of rival companies operating from one building; distances and secrecy increased between teams that were working in close cooperation till yesterday. A few key programmes faced closure—either they were no longer considered good enough or their finances failed. In their next attempt to 'fix' the situation, the board brought in non-conservation persons with commercial management styles. A two-year phase around the turn of the century saw the exodus of over 150 people countrywide. All these and more were the traumatic events through which this organization passed.

Many of us became outsiders and heard about the travails that were faced by the later teams. Over the past few years, the organization has improved its position programmatically and financially, and one wishes that the good efforts will continue in the right direction. I, for one, would love to see a greater degree of reconnection with its half-century-long history and institutional memory, and a much stronger return of the spirit of volunteerism for which WWF-India has been so well known. Please, our work with volunteers did not start in 2016, and no, our 53-year institutional history does not deserve four paragraphs in a half-page, as the beautiful WWF-India website would make you believe!

PARADISE REGAINED: STORY OF THE PANNA REVIVAL

R. SREENIVASA MURTHY

Taking Charge at Panna

In October 2008, I was posted as chief conservator of forests (CCF) (Projects) to head the Ecosystem Services Cell at the principal chief conservator of forests (PCCF) office, Bhopal. With formal training in wildlife management at the WII, I had been closely following events at the Panna Tiger Reserve. On one occasion in 2007, I had learnt from a Panna friend that only five tigers were left in the reserve. This was while all along the local managers had been maintaining that all was well with the tigers there. When I went to meet Chief Wildlife Warden (CWLW) Dr H.S. Pabla, after two tigers (T1 and T2) had been translocated to Panna in March 2009 from Bandhavgarh and Kanha tiger reserves, respectively, his demeanour expressed anxiety about translocation in particular, and Panna in general. T1 and T2 were both female tigers that had been brought to Panna to augment the female numbers in the park, as the sex ratio in the park had become skewed in favour of males.

Unconfirmed news about Panna having lost all its tigers began to make rounds. On 21 May 2009, a news article in *The Times of India* (Bhopal Edition) seemed to confirm the rumour.[1] After reading the said news item, I told my wife Komali, 'Get ready for field posting.' The next day, orders for my posting as the new field director (FD), Panna Tiger Reserve, were received. My wife decided to stay back in Bhopal to take care of my younger son's education. Soon, feelers started coming my way that 'if you are not interested, the order can be revoked'. Posting as the FD of a tiger reserve that had 'lost' its tigers had turned it into a hot seat. To dispel rumours and to put an end to any ambiguity, I joined Panna on 29 May 2009.

Finding the Truth

It was my firm belief that unless we got to the bottom of the tiger debacle at Panna Tiger Reserve, revival could not be properly planned. Three reports, one by the WII, another by a Special Investigation Team (SIT) set up by the National Tiger Conservation Authority (NTCA) and the third by an expert committee headed by the legendry forester J.J. Dutta (instituted by the government of Madhya Pradesh) had gone into the likely causes of the disappearance of the tiger at Panna. Poaching had been identified as the key reason, although P.K. Sen, a former director of Project Tiger and a member of the NTCA, SIT, had cautioned me regarding the suspect loyalties of the park's frontline staff.

As the new FD, I decided to carry out my own investigation into the matter. So, soon after joining, I started my search for answers to how the tigers were lost by meeting and asking the same question to all the relevant people. These included the ministers, all the higher officials and members of the Panna Tiger Reserve staff, local politicians and the general public. A small study was also commissioned to Shodh, a Nagpur-based non-government organization (NGO), to help me unravel the mystery. Soon the picture started to become clear. The malaise had been deep-rooted.

Panna is a region with a long history of feudal social structure, where shikar by the elite had been a way of life.

So, even if caught, they managed to get the better of the law through influences of different kinds. Whistle-blowers were ignored. Lower subordinates, many local and already under the influence of feudal social order, had little confidence in the higher management providing them support and security in case they caught and initiated action against an influential wrongdoer. There had been no upgrades in the protection paraphernalia available to the park staff; security issues were complicated due to illegal farming practised inside the park; Pardhis (a hunter-gatherer tribe) and fish poachers in the river Ken were having a field day; and the ingress of dacoits into the park every harvest season to levy tax on the villagers was rampant. Above everything, the local people in and around the Panna town had no love lost for the park, its managers or its tigers. In short, it was a recipe for disaster.

I decided to address each of the said causes, but how was I to begin without any clues? I knew I had to lead from the front, and providence was kind to provide me with a perfect opportunity for the same.

Blessing in Disguise: The Escape and Return of T3

Two female tigers, T1 (from Bandhavgarh Tiger Reserve) and T2 (from Kanha Tiger Reserve), were already in Panna when I joined there in May 2009. By September, a tiger revival plan for the park had been prepared, with scientific inputs from the WII and guidance received from the new team of higher officials at Bhopal. It provided for the introduction of a male tiger as part of the founder population for the new batch of tigers at Panna. In fact, the plan envisaged a total of six tigers, four female and two males, as the founder stock. Since we already had two females, a male was urgently needed.

A male tiger (T3) was then brought from the Pench Tiger Reserve in south Madhya Pradesh. For genetic enrichment and avoidance of sibling pairings, males from Bandhavgarh and Kanha were avoided, for the females (T1 and T2) with us had come from there.

T3 reached Panna on 6 November 2009 without the mandatory radio collar. He was kept in an enclosure at Badagadi for a week before he was sedated and radio-collared on 13 November and released in the open the next day. It was our expectation that in due course, T3 would make friends with T1 or T2, and tiger revival in Panna shall begin in right earnest. But T3 had other ideas. In about 10 days, on 25 November, he left the park and moved southwards, presumably led by a homing instinct.

Over the next 30 days, he travelled more than 200 km, with 70-strong park staff, including me, following to keep him safe from threats like shooting, poisoning or electrocution—the perfect entourage for a king.

Another dilemma facing us was whether T3 would survive chemical immobilization for the third time in less than a month? I sent a report voicing this concern and started preparations for him only after receiving a go-ahead from the higher-ups. Four elephants joined the caravan at this point in time.

I accompanied the team throughout and roughed it out in the open, travelling through forests and open country till we managed to capture T3 from the Tejgarh forests of the Damoh district and bring him back to Panna on 25 December. All through this chase, the sane counsel and the brief presence of Jasbir Singh Chauhan, a colleague, added greatly to my confidence.

Those 30 days proved momentous like never before. It transformed not just the atmosphere and work culture in the Panna Tiger Reserve but also helped invigorate everybody concerned, including the state's political leadership, higher officials and, most importantly, the staff at Panna Tiger Reserve and the local people in and around it. The story of the escape and capture of T3, as reported daily by the media, helped transform the despondent atmosphere regarding the tigers in the state into one of hope, and left us with some important learnings and lessons for the future.

Of the learnings, the first was the inept manner in which the park's staff handled the radio telemetry equipment to keep track of T3. Even the sedation and capture of the animal could have been done more professionally. Clearly, the staff needed to be well-trained in restraint and monitoring techniques of wild animals.

Learning number two was the electrifying change in staff morale and team building that happened when I led from the front as the park's top manager. Those 30 days determined the entire future of tiger revival in Panna, for, now, the park staff was convinced that they had a leader who would stand by them through thick and thin. I cannot ever thank T3 enough for helping me realize my own potential as an effective leader.

T3, on return, was released in the early hours of the next day into the open at Khamani talaab area of the park. We were advised but found it inappropriate to place him inside an enclosure. But, to prevent him from leaving the park again, we successfully used female tiger urine as bait, a technique suggested by Dr Shekhar Kolipaka, a wildlife biosocial researcher in Panna. Incidentally, on the fourth day of his second release in the park, T3 met tigress T1 and made friends.

The Panna Model of Tiger Conservation

Emboldened by the return of T3 to Panna Tiger Reserve and his making friends with T1, I was more than convinced that the tide had turned, and now nothing could stop us from ensuring the revival of Panna Tiger Reserve as the abode of tigers, yet again.

The road map I followed included raising the morale of my staff; equipping and training them in all essential technical needs of animal and park management; endearing local villagers and people in the landscape to the park, and implementing the land law without any favour or fear.

During the golden 30 days of the T3 saga, I was able to build a core team, to whom I said, 'Today the world is blaming you and me, but if we move carefully and cautiously in unison and withstand external pressures of poaching or otherwise, and thereby secure our tigers, the time is not far off when the same world shall start praising us. To reach that goal, 700+ members of "Team Panna" need to come together. We need to work unafraid of any adversaries. If there is any issue, please let me know, I will be between you and the adversary.'

Slowly and surely, Team Panna began to gel into a formidable unit. We followed a communication strategy devised by Dharmendra Shukla, my senior colleague at the headquarters in Bhopal and the designated mission leader of the Panna revival effort. He was my single line of communication with Bhopal, which eased my work greatly. R.S. Negi, then CWLW, Madhya Pradesh, deserves all kudos for making this happen.

With a focus on tiger revival, review meetings were held fortnightly with the tiger monitoring units, while once every two months, an open house was held with the entire park staff. These meetings were in addition to day-to-day, one-to-one telephonic or on-the-field in-person communication that I had with my officers and field staff.

We converted every celebratory occasion, big or small, into a park-level affair, where everybody, including the higher-ups, participated. For example, when T3 was brought back to the park after 30 days of jaywalking, Principal Secretary (PS) (Forests) Malay K. Roy, CWLW R.S. Negi and Mission Leader Dharmendra Shukla came personally to congratulate Team Panna for 'making the impossible, possible'. Similarly, when T3 and T1 became friends, it was duly celebrated, as was the first litter of T1 and T2. We had succeeded in capturing a semi-wild elephant, Ganesh, when he entered the Panna Tiger Reserve, and the event was an occasion to celebrate. Such instances are many.

Soon, with more success in hand, as a key morale booster, I went out of my way to get Team Panna recognized, appreciated and rewarded. Dr Pabla, who was back in the saddle as CWLW, greatly aided my work with his quality of quick decision-making.

When Dr Rajesh Gopal, member secretary, NTCA, took me to Union Minister of Environment and Forest, Jairam Ramesh, I elicited a promise from him to join us in Panna on 16 April 2011, the first anniversary of tiger birth in the revived Panna Tiger Reserve. True to his word, he not only came but signed and handed out a letter of appreciation to 100 officers and staff of Team Panna. In 2012, on my insistence, 12 of my team members were given the state-level wildlife conservation award, and the NTCA recognized Team Panna in 2012 and 2014 with the Award of Excellence in the Active Management category. In 2010, I was given a civic felicitation by the people of Panna city and, in 2011, WWF-India conferred on me the Bagh Mitra Award.

The Panna model of tiger recovery came to be recognized far and wide. Members of the World Bank-hosted Global Tiger Initiative (GTI), an alliance for tiger conservation, visited Panna in 2012. So did the Russian and Cambodian teams in 2013 and 2015. Panna Tiger Reserve became a learning laboratory for forest officers from the rank of forest guards to Indian Forest Service (IFS) officers from all over the country.

Obviously, all this greatly impacted the staff morale and team spirit in Panna Tiger Reserve. Within less than three years, the same dispirited, unworthy and suspect Panna staff had delivered what is now called the 'Panna model of tiger conservation', celebrated all over.

Skill Development

As per the International Union for Conservation of Nature (IUCN) guidelines of reintroduction, monitoring the reintroduced animal/s is a mandatory protocol to ensure success at their place of introduction.[2]

Our problem was that there were neither any precedence of large-scale successful tiger translocation nor any post-release monitoring protocols to follow in pursuance of the IUCN guidelines. One thing was certain: we had to monitor our tigers round the clock and round the year with a technique that wasn't too intrusive. For that, radio telemetry is perhaps the best available scientific tool. So, we devised our own radio telemetry-based monitoring protocols.

By August 2012, Panna tigers had delivered five litters and 17 cubs. They all needed to be tracked on a regular basis. They also needed to be physically restrained when in need of help or otherwise. So, two skills were key to success here. One was animal tracking using radio telemetry, and the other was animal restraint through chemical immobilization and subsequent revival. Ravi Parmar, a research assistant from the Wildlife Institute of India (WII), Dehradun, at Panna Tiger Reserve, taught us the skills required to effectively use radio telemetry when T3 was out of the park. In due course, most of our staff members became expert handlers of radio telemetry equipment and tiger monitoring.

Previously, animal immobilization works in the state were research-related, and authorities remained dependent on external experts, mostly veterinarians from the WII, for any management-related sedation of an animal, and if, for some reason, these experts were not available, then the operation had to wait. Such a wait could prove costly in case the animal was hurt and in need of urgent help, more so in a pioneering effort involving tiger reintroduction. So, I requested my in-house veterinarian, Dr Sanjeev Kumar Gupta, to not only acquire the skill but to develop an in-house tranquilization team, which he did in no time. I took all the responsibility for any failures and causalities during such operations, and gave full operational freedom to the team. I learnt these skills and was present in person during all initial sedation operations. In one such operation led by my deputy, Vikram Singh Parihar, just a seven-member team completed the exercise successfully in less than 30 minutes in one of the toughest terrains in the park. During my tenure at Panna, 34 tiger tranquilizations were carried out without a single casualty. Dr Sanjeev Gupta's successful tranquilization count today stands at a whopping 69.

Starting from three tigers in the beginning, we monitored 13 radio-collared tigers in 2013, which was a stupendous task. Besides, we also learnt to follow different vocalizations that the tiger makes in different situations. We were initiated in this interesting but very useful skill by Sanjay Thakur, a freelance naturalist helping us plan nature camps in the park for schoolchildren. Our monitoring teams observed and recorded tiger movement, behaviour, pairing, advanced pregnancy, exact birth dates, cubs weaning from mothers, subadult dispersals and territorial interactions within the tiger population. In short, it was a crash course in tiger ecology for Team Panna. Creditably, most of these observations were recorded by largely illiterate casual labourers on an hourly basis for more than six years. These critical insights helped us to anticipate and plan in advance as the tiger population in Panna Tiger Reserve began to grow. This also helped us pre-empt T3 trying to jaywalk out of the park. (That is another story for another time.) Subsequently, this 24/7 monitoring was given the name of 'managerial monitoring' to distinguish it from academic monitoring, often carried out for research purposes. This Panna model of monitoring protocols now forms a part of the NTCA tiger reintroduction standard operating procedure (SOP).

Managerial Monitoring

I was clear and told my team that no tiger should die in the park due to a managerial lapse of any kind. Even if a tiger were to die of natural causes, we would know about it within six hours as per the fitted radio-collar software programme.

What started initially as a preventive measure to keep T3 confined within the park through 24/7 monitoring became the park's monitoring SOP for all the tigers over time. Each tiger had a field monitoring unit of three people with assured vehicle help, and they worked in three shifts over the day. For security purposes, it was decided that any tiger event, like pregnancy, birth, etc., shall not be transmitted using the park's wireless system. Hourly tiger monitoring information was recorded by the field units in a register, information from which was transmitted fortnightly for further analysis to the Tiger Research and Monitoring Cell at the park headquarters. A senior range officer inspected all monitoring units during the nights once in 24 hours. A daily telephonic reporting system on each tiger was established. The monitoring unit head reported at 8.00 a.m. to a designated sub divisional officer (SDO), who reported further to the park's deputy director, who, in turn, provided a synthesized report to the FD. These reports were utilized to give necessary instructions to the field units immediately. In addition, each tiger under monitoring was to be observed ocularly once a month by a senior officer to report on its health status. Compiled data and monthly reports were sent to the mission leader at CWLW office, Bhopal, and NTCA, Delhi, through email.

Intelligence and Legal cell

I had been informed, during my initial interactions with the staff, that, sometimes, the elite and well-connected offenders got away scot-free, while those from weaker sections of the society received severe punishments. I told my staff in no uncertain terms that such things should not happen in the future, and they must work without any fear or favour. I also told them that any slackness or connivance on the part of any park staff would not be tolerated.

I kept my word, which helped in trust-building between the foot soldiers and senior park management. After research and investigation for more than a year, I came out with my own 'Panna Debacle' report and submitted it to the government. I traced the poaching history of Panna in that document and found that over two and a half decades (till 2010), not a single conviction had taken place in the court of law in any tiger or leopard poaching case. In the first place, very few tiger and leopard poaching cases were registered. Then, whatever cases were registered, in all of them, the documentation was very poor. Most importantly, witnesses, including government officials, had turned 'hostile' while deposing before the court of law. Acquittal resulted in all cases. This emboldened the accused and made them lose any fear of the law. That Pardhis, a traditional hunting community native to Panna, made matters worse.

An Intelligence and Legal Cell was established in 2010, and Mrs Manjula Shrivastava, a wildlife advocate from Katni (Madhya Pradesh) and a crusader who had won more than 100 wildlife poaching cases in the courts, was taken on as a legal advisor for Panna Tiger Reserve, a first for the state. She had graciously volunteered to help the cause in a pro bono manner. An intelligence network was developed in and around the park for advance information about any possible misdemeanour, and this improved manifold the protection aspects in the park.

River Ken had been identified as a porous point from where offenders, in the garb of fishermen, entered the park. More than 15 security posts were established all along the river. A river patrol was made operational with assistance in the form of boats received from the Mumbai-based Wildlife Conservation Trust (WCT).

Zero tolerance towards poaching of any kind, including that of herbivores, was part of park's work culture. Four of our uniformed staff were sent behind bars for their omissions and commissions in poaching cases.

Special training sessions on wildlife crime prevention were held for forest staff of the park and the adjoining forest divisions in the area. Regular coordination meetings were held with the judiciary. A leopard poaching case in the north, Panna division was successfully prosecuted within 11 months and all 13 accused received jail terms ranging from three months to three years and a fine. In an attempted poaching case inside the park, two locally influential people were put behind bars for more than four months before they could get bail from the high court at Jabalpur.

The Pardhis couldn't enter the park, and cases were registered against those who still attempted to enter with criminal intent. These measures resulted in an atmosphere of tranquillity within the park.

The menace of dacoits was tackled with the help of intelligence gathering about their movement and active help received from the police department, which sanctioned 10+2 team of the Special Armed Force (SAF) for the purpose. It wasn't an easy challenge, but we prevailed nonetheless.

Taking People Along

When I joined in 2009, park–people relations was at a low ebb and marked by antipathy. So much so that many people thought that Panna losing its tigers was a boon in disguise, for, now, the local developmental activities that were halted or held back due to the park's presence in the area would perhaps begin. Perplexed, I tried to discuss and analyse this antagonistic state of affairs with Shekhar Kolipaka and Shyamender Singh, a local park enthusiast. Finally, we concluded that there was no other way but to involve the people in our efforts to revive the tiger presence in the park. Shekhar gave the idea of taking people's support for the park by convincing them about its importance to the area.

This was a tough task, but I wanted to give it a fair try. I met and requested Mr Nagendra Singh, an erstwhile royal, a local politician and the state's Public Works Department (PWD) minister, to provide local-level political leadership in the matter. He had his own misgivings about the bureaucracy, and hence, it required a lot of explaining before he agreed. Once he was on board, the state's Forest Minister endorsed the idea. All the political outreach by us throughout the tiger revival period was apolitical in nature; hence, local politicians of all hues helped us get popular support.

A consultative meeting where more than 250 local people participated was held on 5 November 2009 at Madla on the banks of the river Ken. This included the entire district-level government officials of Panna and Chattarpur districts, and all local politicians. A day-long free and frank discussion took place on Panna losing its tigers and how the situation could be reversed. All opined that poaching was the main cause, and many blamed the forest department for the security lapses and later efforts to cover up the lapses, and the loss of tigers in the park. At the end of the meeting, everyone was urged to join hands with the park management to make the tiger revival programme a success. The loss of tigers at Panna Tiger Reserve had dented Bundelkhand's pride, and its revival could help regain it too. This made sense to most and became the basis of widespread ownership in the region of the programme *Jan Samarthan se Bagh Samrakshan* (Tiger conservation with the people's support), to revive tiger presence at Panna Tiger

Reserve. Friends of Panna, a public-private platform, was created at the end of the meet.

The next day, on 6 November, T3, the male tiger, came to Panna from Pench and moved out of the park on his release. The rest as they say, is history! T3's sojourn over the next 30 days and his return helped galvanize support for and the ownership of the programme. Of course, the consultation process continued all throughout, and valuable inputs continued to be received from time to time from the members of the public, politicians and officials on various matters, including tiger management and resolution of park–people issues.

Panna Nature Camps were started with the help of WWF-India in 2010 to make the people, especially children, understand the park, its values and its importance for the region. These have continued ever since till the Covid-19 pandemic put a halt to it in 2020. Panna Nature Camps got national recognition in 2017 when the Sanctuary Nature Foundation awarded their Green Teacher Award to the teachers who ran it. Panna's annual vulture estimation started in 2011, and became another interesting and useful means to involve the people in park affairs at the pan-India level. From 2015 onwards, tiger births and birthdays began to be celebrated in the park not just as an in-house event but a public event where locals participated.

Tigers from Panna began to disperse into the larger landscape from 2012 onwards, following an increase in their numbers, and stories of these dispersals circulated and began to interest people from all over.

Word-of-mouth and media stories about the Panna tiger revival gave a huge fillip to tourism in and around the park, and local people began to benefit from the same. Bundelkhand restored its pride, and the state of Madhya Pradesh regained its lost 'Tiger State' status with the Panna success story in 2018.

When the government of Cambodia declared, in 2015,

its preference for the Panna model of tiger conservation for bringing tiger back into the country, it gave international glory to the Panna effort.

Tiger Numbers

When I left Panna in 2015, the tiger numbers had risen to 34. All the founder tigers at Panna were given individual identification (IDs) as T1 to T7, following the sequence of their arrival. T1, T2, T4, T5 and T6 were females, while T3 and T7 were males. T2, T4 and T5 were brought from Kanha, while T1 was from Bandhavgarh, and T3 and T6 were from Pench. T7 came from the Bhopal forest division. All Panna-born tigers were given the prefix 'P' to enhance their sense of ownership and pride by the local people.

The mascot of Panna tiger revival, namely T3, made friends with T1 and T2 soon after returning from his 30-day-long adventure outside the park. This resulted in the first breeding success of the reintroduction effort when T1 delivered four cubs on 16 April 2010 in the Dhundhwaseha (gorge). Thereafter, in the month of October 2010, T2 delivered another litter of four cubs.

Rewilding of Hand-Reared Tigers

T4 and T5 were orphaned female siblings brought from Kanha. They had been hand-reared, and hence, their rewilding required special care. They were not only successfully released in the wild but achieved breeding success, becoming perhaps the first-ever such successfully documented case of rewilding of hand-reared tigers. (The breeding success of Tara, the hand-reared tigress, by legendry Billy Arjan Singh in the Dudhwa in Uttar Pradesh during the late 1970s has remained controversial and was never irrefutably proven.)

T6 was another female brought from Pench, while T7 was a male that had to be captured and brought to Panna, since it had entered the precincts of Bhopal city in October 2015.

T4 and T5 died in 2014 and 2016, respectively, and T1 and T2 have gone past their breeding age for the last two to three years. As per the official projections of the forest department, Panna will ultimately have 21 breeding tigers within its core area, with a total tiger population of 70–80 tigers in 2022.

Panna tigers have enriched the Sanjay Tiger Reserve in the Sidhi district in 2014 (P212), Sarbangha forests in the Satna district in 2016 and the Bandhavgarh Tiger Reserve in 2017 (P213-21 now called T71 there). Dr Suhas Kumar, a senior colleague, deserves credit for training the forest staff around Panna Tiger Reserve and the frequent morale-boosting of Team Panna for facilitating the smooth and safe dispersal of Panna tigers.

The span from 2009 to 2022 resulted in a vastly different picture of conservation history at Panna. From 'Panna Lost' to 'Panna Regained' was not a simple story. It was and remains a story full of challenges, which were and continue to be met with full dedication, and Team Panna has delivered it with élan. It is basically a story of people and tigers, and Panna is today standing tall with 70 plus tigers against zero in 2009. All is well that ends well.

But is it, really?

A planned high dam at Daudhan on the river Ken right in the heart of Panna Tiger Reserve's core zone threatens to bifurcate the park and drown its key tiger natal zones like the *seha* and the unique vulture habitats in the form of cliffs. The bifurcation shall also close the opportunities for the westward dispersal of animals along the river Shyamri, which itself shall get submerged if the dam becomes a reality.

I would like to believe that the above scenario is no more

than a bad dream, and tigers in Panna shall continue to flourish after the Supreme Court has disallowed the dam based on the findings of the court-mandated Central Empowered Committee.

Notes

1. 'Madhya Pradesh CM Orders Transfers of Three National Park Directors', *The Times of India*, 21 May 2009, https://bityl.co/D79z. Accessed on 7 July 2022.
2. *IUCN Guidelines For Re-Introductions,* IUCN/SSC Reintroduction Specialist Group, 1998, https://bityl.co/DDMV. Accessed on 13 July 2022.

JOURNEYS IN ARUNACHAL PRADESH

APARAJITA DATTA

I was fascinated with animals and wild places from an early age. I loved to read, and my parents and grandparents always gifted me books on nature. I read James Herriot, Gerald Durrell and David Attenborough. I spent part of my childhood in Zambia, and had a wonderful biology teacher in school. When I was 13, I moved back to Kolkata to study. I lived with my grandparents, returning on my holidays to visit my parents in Zambia. Since my teenage years, I knew I wanted to study ecology. But I had not spent much time outdoors or in nature in India. I studied botany in Presidency College, but these years were mostly spent in addas and having fun with friends. The way botany was taught was not interesting. I pursued my interest by talking to the late Kushal Mookherjee, a naturalist who was a mentor to many people, and Devika Kar, World Wide Fund for Nature-India's (WWF-India) education officer in Kolkata.

My plans to study ecology became a reality when I joined the Wildlife Institute of India (WII) for a master's degree in wildlife ecology. Those years were a wonderful time of real learning. I truly loved what I was doing. Everything was new and exciting, and there were many people around to learn from—my peers, senior researchers and faculty.

For my master's dissertation in 1992, I spent six wonderful months in the Bori Wildlife Sanctury (now the Satpura Tiger Reserve) in Madhya Pradesh. It was my initiation into the joys and trials of field research. I studied the space use and foraging patterns of the Indian giant squirrel.

The Early Times in Arunachal: Pakke Tiger Reserve

I first went to Arunachal Pradesh in 1995 as a research fellow at the WII to conduct a study to assess the responses of primates and squirrels to logging.

I remember the day I arrived in Seijosa in November 1995—the headquarters of Pakke Tiger Reserve, then known as Pakhui Wildlife Sanctuary—on a bus from Itanagar. It was getting dark, and I trudged on to meet the divisional forest officer (DFO), D.N. Singh, in his bungalow. He introduced me to Japang Pansa, who was asked to accompany me in the forest and work as my assistant. Japang was a Wancho tribal from the Tirap district in eastern Arunachal. Japang would become a friend, confidante, guide and teacher over the next 10 years.

I was excited by the novelty and wonder of everything around me and of being in Arunachal for the first time. We began fieldwork and walked 13 km to reach Khari, as there was no road in those days. I was fortunate to have Japang accompany me in this completely new place, as it seemed from the very first meeting that he knew the forest well—from the trees to the animals.

Japang's knowledge of plants was remarkable. I had to do vegetation plots in that study, and in every plot, we would find unknown species. Japang knew the Assamese names for them. For the ones that he did not know, he would tell me something interesting about them, like when they fruited, what colour the flower or fruit was or who ate them. It was a difficult exercise, as in one plot, we would find many trees, most of which were new; in the next, we would find more new ones plus some of the unidentified ones in the previous plot. Japang was so well-versed with the wildlife that he would remember the many unidentified species between plots and cross-reference them in his own way. I have no idea how he distinguished and remembered. We often had disputes during this data collection. I recall once we had a heated argument in the forest about the possible identification of some trees. In the end, he turned out to be right.

I was a hard taskmaster, as after the morning transects walks to count squirrels, primates and hornbills, we would do the vegetation plots and return to the base camp only around 3.00 p.m., having been out since 5.00 a.m.

It was only after Charudutt Mishra, my husband and friend, visited us in the field that I realized I was overdoing it—and that we should probably have eaten or carried some food. It had been drilled into us by Dr A.J.T. Johnsingh that we needed to be out in the forests by dawn. I also realized that Japang would have a quick breakfast of leftovers in the morning before we left to cope with the long hours. I was still a rookie in Arunachal and not used to eating so early, but I soon learnt to eat globs of rice at 5.00 a.m.

After that glimpse of Arunachal, I was hooked and decided I would go back and work there. During the logging study in Pakke, hornbills had caught my eye—they were conspicuous, loud and fascinating. I had always been more interested in mammals and never been much of a bird person, but hornbills were large and unmistakable. I decided to study hornbills for my PhD—their basic biology (foraging, roosting, nesting and diet), and I also wanted to examine their role as seed dispersers of forest trees. During my three-year fieldwork, I also got to learn much more about the history, culture and lifestyle of the people of Arunachal and fell more in love with Arunachal.

When I began my PhD study on hornbills in Pakke, little was known—apart from Dr Salim Ali's notes, a few studies in South India and a few by foreign academics. So, we had been at a loss regarding how and where to find hornbill nest trees, their roosting sites or their food trees. Japang showed me my first two hornbill nests in 1997—one of these nests was still active last I heard about it in 2019. And together, we found several more. Pakke is home to three hornbill species in the lower elevation forests—the great, wreathed and the oriental pied.

Apart from academic learning, the shared moments in the forest were equally valuable and enriching. One day, fed up with the daily routine, we decided to explore newer parts of the forest. We spent the day wandering, and by late afternoon, we were lost—we finally managed to find our way back, tired and hungry but exhilarated after a lovely day.

Another day in Pakke, we were looking for fruiting trees and hornbills. We noticed a fruiting fig tree a little inside the thickets, away from the path. I asked Japang to get a leafy branch for our herbarium collection. I wandered ahead, looking at some birds. At one point, I turned around and saw a makhna right on the path just 15 metres from me; his trunk was curled upwards as if he was smelling me. I did not scream or run but quietly tiptoed into the undergrowth and hid under a small tree. I was worried about Japang—I did not want to shout as I did not think that would be prudent. I tried whistling ineffectually. After a while, I saw Japang running very fast, with the elephant charging right behind him. Fortunately, the elephant took a left turn and crashed away into the forest. Japang was angry with me once he saw me coming sheepishly out of the undergrowth, asking me why I had not warned him. That encounter taught me to be always careful in any forest with elephants. We had many more encounters, but Japang knew what to do, and we never panicked.

Japang is a remarkably skilled naturalist. His contribution to my research has been tremendous. His jungle skills and observation powers are unparalleled. He never went to school, yet his intelligence, careful reasoning and keen observation is remarkable and better than many educated people. He told me he had run away from school when he was young and always regretted doing so. Now, he has taught himself and can read in basic English and vernacular. His transformation from a hunter to someone who cares for the fate of wildlife and forests is remarkable.

Learning from the People

Many of the experiences in the forests over the last two decades would have been much poorer had it not been for some special people who knew the forest and shared their knowledge of the wild, and showed and taught me things with utmost generosity.

People from indigenous communities[1] in Arunachal Pradesh have been a crucial part of my journeys and of some of the big and small discoveries we made together. We often refer to them as field assistants, but they are the backbone of our research and conservation work. Their contribution remains largely unappreciated, except for the cursory thanks we give to our 'field assistants' in the acknowledgements of peer-reviewed papers and reports. They have taught me natural history and how to observe nature, which I would never have known as a city-dwelling person.

One such man was Taya Tayem—a Nyishi, the *gaon burra* from one of the villages near Pakke. He was a renowned hunter and knew the forests well. He had shown me some hornbill nests during my PhD fieldwork. In 2004, he started working with us to help us find hornbill nests, and he found 14 nests in one year. One day, he told me that he had found an injured great hornbill and walked 10 km to take it to a vet, hoping it could be helped. Another time, he saved a drowning elephant calf literally roping in his entire family and risking his own life in a fast-flowing river in spate. Tayem, who had once told me that he had killed at least 30 great hornbills, became a protector of Pakke's wildlife. Sadly, he passed away in a car accident in 2006. Six years later, his eldest son, Ohey, became a nest protector and is now Pakke's first nature guide. In 2014, Ohey received a Sanctuary Asia Award in Mumbai on behalf of the nest protectors.

In Pakke, our long-term monitoring of hornbill nesting and roosting relies on our field staff. Khem Thapa is observant, reliable, makes meticulous field notes and is always quick to learn new skills—such as climbing 40-metre-tall trees to repair hornbill nest trees and install artificial nest boxes. Khem also does unbelievably funny impressions and never fails to get a laugh. Kumar Thapa, who sadly passed away in 2021, was a happy-go-lucky person and would always have goodies to share in the forest.

Most of us would have taken much longer to learn about the forests and the hornbills but for the knowledge and guidance of such people. The transfer of that knowledge is so seamless and organic that we are often unaware of how much is being shared. We take it for granted, but we would know much less if there were no forest people with close connections to nature.

In the last 25 years, apart from Japang, Tayem, Khem and Kumar, there have been many others—Narayan Mogar, Pradeep Adhikari, Rasham Brah, Akhi Nathany, Duchaye Yobin, Ngwa-akhi Yobin, Budhiram Tai, Tajek Wage and Tajik Tachang.

Some younger people came later, with whom I have spent less time in the forests—such as Tali Nabam, Turuk Brah, Sagar Kino, Sitaram Mahato and Kezacho Dukpa. They too have wonderful skills which they have shared, and I have learnt from them.

Journeys in Arunachal

In 2001, after finishing my PhD, I moved to Mysore and started working with the Nature Conservation Foundation (NCF) and the Wildlife Conservation Society (WCS) India programme. I established a conservation and research programme in NCF with a geographical focus on northeast India.

In April 2002, I conducted a survey to assess the status of hornbills and hunting practices among tribal communities in eastern Arunachal.

Travelling in northeast India can be an amusing, exhilarating experience or nerve-wracking and frustrating, depending on your frame of mind. In the 1990s, the road network connecting places within Arunachal from west to east was non-existent, leading to difficulties and long circuitous road journeys. It has improved considerably in the last five years. I have had many mishaps and adventures. Earlier, as a researcher on a low budget, I travelled alone, lugging my backpack on buses and other public transport. Later, during my PhD fieldwork, I had a rickety old jeep whose radiator would often leak, splutter and stop on some highways.

It's safe to hop onto trucks or hitch rides in Arunachal. I have had the most fun travelling on buses, trucks and ferries, meeting curious amused people who were invariably helpful. It is possibly the only region in India where it is safe for a woman to travel alone in the public transport system.

However, periodic spurts in militant activities, bandhs in the neighbouring Assam and increased vigilance by the army sometimes made it difficult to move around. The dreaded Armed Forces Special Powers Act (AFSPA) also meant that there were frequent checks on many routes. Sometimes, when I was travelling in a hired vehicle, they would 'requisition' the car. I remember being stranded alone in the middle of the night in towns during curfews, with no place to go and no transport. But once I reached the villages, all was fine, as I stayed in peoples' homes in comfort, and was very grateful for the wonderful hospitality, warmth and the delicious local food.

In those early years till 2003, I remember wonderful journeys travelling through the mountain roads, mostly on the rickety Arunachal State Transport buses, to reach small towns and then walking to remote villages and forests—places like Palin, Ziro and Tale valley in Lower Subansiri, Pakke Kessang in East Kameng, Roing and Mayodia Pass in Dibang Valley, Nampong, Rima, Changlang near the Myanmar border, Deomali, Khonsa and Pongchau in Tirap. I enjoyed meeting and conversing with strangers and getting to know Arunachal and its people.

Exploring Eastern and Western Arunachal

In the winter of 2002, I undertook an exploration survey with help from knowledgeable tribal people to search for the leaf deer (*Muntiacus putaoensis)* in eastern Arunachal. In 1997, it was described as a new species by the late Dr Alan Rabinowitz in neighbouring Myanmar. I suspected that it also occurred in adjoining forests in eastern Arunachal. This was also corroborated by conversations with Tangsa and Lisu (Yobin) villagers during my earlier survey. I set out on this expedition with Japang, who was now working as a mahout in Namdapha. Together, we surveyed forests and villages covering 300 km on foot in Changlang district, conducted interviews with hunters, sat at salt licks at night to try to catch a glimpse of the elusive leaf deer, which the Tangsa called the *lingpun* and the Lisu called the *lugiche*.

We went on fruitless walks with hunters hoping to catch a glimpse. We searched in tribal households among the animal trophies they displayed. The leaf deer is only 10–12 kg but morphologically looks like the barking deer, which is twice its size. One key difference is that the males have short unbranched antlers and the female have equally long canines as the males.

In Mossang Putok, a Tangsa village near Myanmar, Japang first noticed an unusual skull among some old dusty ones, and it turned out to be the first leaf deer skull we got—a female with canines. Later, I found more skulls in Lisu villages beyond the Namdapha National Park. We published a paper describing the find, with Japang as the co-author.

We made another discovery in a Lisu village, thanks again to Japang. A deer skin was spread out on the bamboo wall of the house. It was very dark with a longer tail and quite different from the barking deer. It turned out that the Lisu also considered it a different species, calling it *che-mey*, which means black deer. It would turn out to be the Gongshan muntjac *(Muntiacus gongshanensis)*, described in the 1990s as a species from Yunnan in China.

Thus, we found evidence for two new muntjac species, the leaf deer and the Gongshan muntjac in eastern Arunachal, previously unreported from India.

In July 2003, we set out on another expedition in western Arunachal's high-altitudes in Tawang and West Kameng districts. This one was led by Charudutt and friend and NCF colleague Dr M.D. Madhusudan. I have mostly worked in the lower altitude areas of Arunachal, but on that survey, we covered the high altitudes (areas above 3,000 metres). I was thrilled that we went up to 5,200 metres, the highest I have ever been in Arunachal.

We traversed around 200 km on foot and covered around 800 km by road in two months. We did a 16-day trek with our Monpa guides and horses through parts of West Kameng and the Tawang district, from Thembang to Jang. I recall we did not have a bath the entire time. We stayed in herder camps and slept on cold stone slabs huddling by the smoky fire. For most of the trek, it was grey, misty and raining. We walked through some spectacular landscapes without realizing it, as often, we could barely see a few metres ahead.

During the later part of the trek, the weather was better, and we saw some magnificent high-altitude lakes, Gorichen and many of the snow-covered peaks. In the alpine meadows, many species were flowering, and we made a small herbarium to get them identified by Dr K. Haridasan, an expert plant taxonomist in Arunachal who was then with the State Forest Research Institute (SFRI). Some species we figured out by referring to the book *Flowers of the Himalaya* (Oleg Polunin, Adam Stainton, Oxford University Press, 1984).

On the walk from Mago to Jang, I got bitten by several wasps (which I am highly allergic to) and had to walk with a swollen head for two days, much to everyone else's amusement.

We saw pikas, Himalayan marmots, blue sheep, a leopard cat and several primate species. But we recorded evidence of many other mammals only through skulls, skins, horns and/or tracks and droppings.

We also saw troops of a macaque species that looked different from the Assamese macaque known from the area. After studying it thoroughly with our primatologist friend Anindya Sinha (Rana), we described it as a primate species—the Arunachal macaque (*Macaca munzala*), new to science. *Munzala* was the name given to this species by the Monpa people who already knew it to be different from the Assamese macaque, which they called the *pangzala*.

Charu and I had an exciting sighting of what used to be known as the long-tailed Chinese goral (*Nemorhaedus caudatus*) on the walk between Mago and Thingbu. The classification of gorals has changed subsequently, creating some confusion.

The Namdapha Years

After several years of wildlife research and surveys in Arunachal, I felt the need to 'do something' to address some of the conservation problems (such as hunting) in Arunachal Pradesh. I believed that local support was essential for long-term conservation success, and that it was imperative that short-term costs borne by local communities around PAs be addressed and offset by conservation practitioners. I believed this could happen through engaging with the local people and informing them of their socio-economic needs and attitudes to wildlife conservation. Reconciliation of people and wildlife is difficult in many places where wildlife conservation goals come in conflict with people's immediate needs and wants but is absolutely necessary to move forward.

Arunachal is magnificent, but to me, among the most magical is the Namdapha National Park. I had visited Namdapha in 1996 and 1997, and had only been on the Deban–Hornbill–Firmbase route. It was only after I first undertook the walk from Miao to Vijaynagar in November 1998 with the forest department staff that I realized the vastness and beauty of Namdapha. After the leaf deer survey in 2002–2003, I decided that I must work there.

This 1,985 sq. km park lies in the easternmost corner of India, in insurgency-affected Changlang district in Arunachal. It is among the last large tracts of wilderness areas in Asia and flanked on the south and east by the Patkai Hills and to the north by high mountain passes and the Himalaya—with the last remaining large tracts of lowland dipterocarp forests in India, the world's northernmost rainforests, contiguous with primary forests to the north, south and east in neighbouring Myanmar. Its altitudinal range (150–4,500 metres) has resulted in a diversity of habitats, from lowland rainforests and river valleys to temperate forests and snow-capped peaks. Its biogeographic location and heavy rainfall also add to its diversity with over 1,000 plant species, over 100 mammals, including at least 15 globally threatened, 400 plus bird species and much more. Much of this area remains unexplored due to the steep terrain, high rainfall and no roads.

We established a research and conservation programme that tried to address some of the socio-economic needs of the Lisu, engage in dialogue and to win their support for conservation through various community welfare and livelihood interventions. The goal was to reduce hunting and encourage recovery of wildlife populations, so part of our research work there included determining the status of important mammal groups, such as the primates, small carnivores and ungulates. Several Lisu worked with us on the wildlife monitoring programme. We did intensive field surveys using remotely triggered camera traps and other field survey methods. We obtained photographic evidence of rare and threatened mammals for the first time from these areas. Fieldwork was exciting with our Lisu team—Akhi Nathany, Duchaye Yobin and Ngwa-akhi Yobin, and others. They were skilled in the forests. During the wildlife surveys, we would carry our rations and camping gear and set up camp at each location for a few days before moving on to the next one.

The main Lisu villages of Gandhigram (Shidi), Sidikhu, Hazulu and Vijaynagar lie beyond the south-eastern boundary of the park. A 157-km road once ran from Miao to Vijaynagar (M–V road) through the park. This road was an overgrown forest path broken up by numerous landslides. From Miao, Gandhigram is a walk of three to seven days through the park. The road from Miao is motorable up to Deban (26 km). The time and route you take each time varies depending on the weather. You have to walk through knee-deep sinking mud, negotiate landslides, and cross rivers and streams. The Lisus have to do this trip several times a year for supplies, work, access to healthcare and better schools. They even carry tin sheets, rice mill machines, dismantled cycles or 29-inch TV sets from Miao.

There are a few air sorties from Mohanbari in Assam to Vijaynagar—but waiting for them is a frustrating experience. Walking is faster and less stressful than the uncertainty of a sortie. I have walked between Miao and Vijaynagar about 13 times, sometimes both ways. The return journey is usually by the air sortie on the Russian AN-32 planes or the helicopter.

I remember I used to get nervous about crossing the fast-flowing Namdapha River. Sometimes the water was chest-high, and it was hard to fight the strong currents while trying to cross it upright. Once I was almost swept away by the current and fell into the water. Akhi pulled me out, laughing as if nothing had happened. He was more concerned about not getting my rucksack and binoculars wet. I told him that he should worry less about all that stuff and more about me!

I have many memories of those walks along the M–V road and the river valley. By the last day, some stretches would be endless slush and we would be yearning to reach the village. We would feel a sense of homecoming and relief when we got that first glimpse of the Shidi valley.

Even after having spent so much time in Namdapha, we know that many of the exciting mammals exist only from the camera trap pictures we obtained from 2004 to 2007. The only relatively common mammal is the barking deer. Apart from the hoolock gibbons, Assamese macaques and several tree squirrels, mammal sightings are rare. Our fieldwork showed that the populations of many species are low, even compared to other rainforest areas. I often complained about not seeing anything despite miles of walking. But fortunately, the forests are not quite empty yet. The diversity of species is much more than anywhere else. It is just that they are rare and elusive. Many species are nocturnal, and in a dense rainforest, sighting mammals is not easy. Though rare now, tigers as a species can return and flourish, given the large forest area. This is, of course, contingent on the state and the people taking protective measures.

Namdapha has much to offer in terms of birds. The rare white-bellied heron and ibisbill are seen in a few locations along the rivers. The white-winged wood ducks can be seen in some forest pools. The wonder of watching the diverse mixed-species flocks, the endemic snowy-throated babbler and the beautiful nuthatch. The many kinds of parrotbills, yuhinas, babblers and shrike-babblers that are often difficult to see in the dense undergrowth. The four species of hornbills—the great hornbill seen only up to 1,000 metres, the wreathed hornbill flying high like raptors, seen in large roosting flocks in the evenings at Firm base by the Namdapha river or along the Noa-Dihing River. Rohit Naniwadekar, my first PhD student, started his study on hornbills in 2008 and established that they are very abundant in Namdapha during the non-breeding season. Wreathed hornbill densities could reach a whopping 160 birds per sq. km on the Hornbill Plateau. The beautiful rufous-necked hornbill is resident in the mid-elevation forests flying in the mid-canopy, usually seen in pairs. The less colourful brown hornbill is a cooperatively breeding bird, usually seen in flocks of 10 to 15 birds.

We worked with the community members to set up kindergarten schools with support from Katha, a non-governmental organization (NGO) in Delhi, as there were few teachers in the area. We transported books and other educational material bought in Tinsukia to Gandhigram with porters carrying them on foot from Deban. We provided medical support, healthcare training, and medicines that we had bought in Bangalore or Guwahati, which were then brought to Miao and carried all the way on foot. We addressed rural energy needs in one village, tried out various livelihood options and helped the community protect their agricultural fields against erosion.

This work initially resulted in the community taking a stand against hunting and some reduction of hunting; however, given the people–park conflict over land and the proposed relocation of people from the park, it did not have the desired conservation outcome of reconciliation between people and wildlife.

I was also appointed a member of the National Tiger Conservation Authority (NTCA) from 2010 to 2012 and was on the State Board of Wildlife (SBWL) of Arunachal for two terms. I also helped draft and provided technical inputs for the management plans of some tiger reserves and PAs. I critiqued the environmental impact assessment (EIA) reports of several proposed hydropower projects.

During that period in Namdapha, we also continued monitoring hornbill populations, nests and roost sites and other wildlife in Pakke. We noted an alarming loss of forests in areas near Pakke. We began a Hornbill Nest Adoption Programme in partnership with the Nyishi people and the forest department, with support from citizens to protect hornbill nests outside the reserve. We started a forest restoration project in 2014 to assist in the recovery of degraded forests. I have also been interested in nature education and have written books for children on hornbills and rainforests. In 2017, friend and colleague Pranav Trivedi helped us start a nature education programme for children around Pakke, which is led by Saniya Chaplod.

While a primary focus of my research has been on hornbills and seed dispersal, a large part of my work has been on conservation action, some of which failed in terms of its outcomes. After 25 years, I believe that achieving conservation outcomes is difficult and complex. One needs resilience, persistence and patience to engage with people at many levels. Reconciliation between wildlife and people is not always possible with the rigid stances that mainstream wildlife conservationists often adopt.

Prof. Bill Adams, a scholar of environmental development and conservation, once said: 'The challenge is not only to preserve "the wild" but also peoples' relationships with the wild'. I concur wholeheartedly.

Notes

1. Arunachal Pradesh is culturally and linguistically rich, with 26 tribes and 110 subtribes with diverse beliefs, customs and religious practices. Some of the main tribes are Monpa, Sherdukpen, Miji in the western part, who are mainly Buddhist. In the central part

are the Nyishi, Apatani, Adi/Galo, while a little further east in the Mishmi Hills are the Mishmi group (the Idu Mishmi, Digaru Mishmi, Miju Mishmi) and the Khampti. Towards the south, in areas bordering Myanmar and Nagaland, are the Wancho, Nocte, Tutsa and Tangsa tribes. There are also several other tribes such as the Bugun in the west, Singpho, Yobin (Lisu) in the eastern part and others in the northern areas of Arunachal. The populations of these tribes are smaller. The Nyishi and the Adi tribes are the most dominant tribes.

SHIFTING SANDS: DIARIES FROM THE GULF OF MANNAR NATIONAL PARK, TAMIL NADU[1]

STELLA JAMES, NAYANA UDAYASHANKAR AND BHUVANA BALAJI[2]

Reflections on 'Flow'

Keelamunthal
5 September 2019

I am living with the famous Selvi *akka*, known to her entire fishing community in Ramanathapuram district as a woman with unmatched wisdom about people, land and waters. I start my mornings at the ocean as the sun rises across the horizon, witnessing the *elam*. The fishermen draw their boats onto the shore just in time for the elam, their wives waiting in anticipation for the catch of the day. They then pull out the fish and segregate them by species to be set up at the *elakkadai*. The next two hours are spent at the auction. Later, the families sit on the shore, untangling the nets and stitching up torn edges so they can have them ready for the next morning's journey back into the ocean. The weather is warm, the waves rushing to my feet, gently inviting me into the waters.

This may sound still—as if life never shifts, but this is far from the truth. I am learning here that the marine system is a system of flow. Everything is in constant movement. Ocean currents, rain and the moon determine where fish go. The winds guide the birds hunting them. Marine organisms change habitats, diets and even their sex as they go through life. Even corals, stoic and steady in the ever-shifting oceans, send their offspring far into the ocean currents to find new places to settle and grow.

The lives of the people that are part of the gulf are also in constant flux. The fishermen follow the wind, the birds and the current, playing tag every day as they try to keep up. The tides tell the women when crabs and clams will be available to collect for their meals. In the Gulf of Mannar, neither the water nor the land is stationary. Islands that form part of the gulf have gone underwater[3], and in the southern part, between Kanniyakumari and Thoothukudi district, the land erodes faster than anywhere else in the country.[4]

It is unsettling to be living here. I can feel the firmness of land giving way under me to the rise and fall of the sea.

Reflections on 'Wind'

Dhanuskodi
8 September 2019

I went to the temple town of Rameswaram this morning, at the northern tip of the gulf. Ancient temples and swanky new buildings sit next to each other in Rameswaram, and tourists and fishers jostle side by side on the beaches. About 30 km from the town of Rameswaram is Dhanushkodi. Old legends say that this is where Lord Rama built a bridge across the Gulf of Mannar to reach Sri Lanka. Modern legends say that the British built a railway bridge across the Gulf of Mannar to reach Sri Lanka. Today, neither of them exist. But when I stood right at the edge of that long, thin stretch of land and stared really hard into the distance, I almost convinced myself that I could reach out and touch Sri Lanka.

Heavy winds whipped my face as I stood there, the flying sand stinging hard. A handful of tourists stood around, faces wrapped with shawls, determined to brave the winds to be in this holy place. This area, the very tip of Dhanuskodi, is known to the local people as Arichal Munai—the land of the shifting sands.

'There are 18 types of wind that blow here,' explained Prakash *anna*, one of the activists who work with traditional fish workers here. I had heard of types of flora and fauna, but this was the first time I heard of types of wind. 'The fishing is adapted to the kind of wind that blows,' he continued. I was told that every kind of wind has a name, and each type of wind influences the waters of the sea, the fish that live in the water and the time of the tides.

I watched as two fishermen carried a heavy-looking bucket to their boat parked on the sand. Their faces were uncovered, their bodies used to the merciless rush of the wind and sand. 'This is our food and water for five days,' one of them said, pausing to catch a breath. 'The wind is always rough here; we don't know when we can come back.' He pulled out the rosary from around his neck and was about to say more, but the other man looked at him impatiently. He shrugged, and they set off again across the sand to join the rest of their crew. I watched them pull their boat into the water, six rash men on a perilous but necessary journey. I watched them until their boat was just a speck in the water.

Standing at that absolute edge, completely surrounded by the water from almost all sides, I felt as if the wind would blow me off my feet and carry me into the ocean. I could hardly believe that anyone would brave the winds and venture out into the sea to fish.

Reflections on 'Rigidity'

Nallathanni Theevu
10 September 2019

Today, I took a boat 1 km towards Nallathannitheevu (island), about 3 km away from the village of Keelamunthal. Earlier, villages across the shore used these near-shore islands in the gulf as a refuge during the off-season for fishing. Fisherpeople here adapt to the fluidity of the ocean, and it was common for them to migrate to the *theevu*, construct temporary huts and stay there for short periods.

Selvi akka looked distantly at the theevu from our boat, 'We used to camp three months every year on the Nallathannitheevu when the ocean currents were rough near our village. The coral reefs prevent the sea from affecting the island and the resources around it. After 1989, the forest department, which is in charge of the island, currently told us the law prevents us from going to the island. They said we are destroying the corals. Our whole life and livelihood depend on the corals. Why would we harm them?'

Nallathannitheevu, I learned, is part of 21 islands that form the Gulf of Mannar National Park, notified in 1980. Nine years later, in 1989, these islands became the core area of the Gulf of Mannar Biosphere Reserve, an area of 10,000 sq. km.[5] After this notification, the villagers stopped being allowed inside.

The Gulf of Mannar National Park is one of 25 areas listed as a marine protected area (MPA) in peninsular India and 104 MPAs in the islands of India.[6] The Environmental Information System (ENVIS) network website of the Ministry of Environment, Forest and Climate Change (MoEFCC) announces boldly that an MPA is 'essentially a space in the ocean where human activities are more strictly regulated than the surrounding waters—*similar to parks we have on land* [emphasis added].'[7]

MPAs in India are not a specific category under law but simply extensions of the categories of national park, sanctuary and others within the Wild Life (Protection) Act (WLPA), 1972. *Similar to parks on land*, I thought. But the socioecological systems of terrestrial landscapes are very different from marine systems. The properties of water itself—fluidity, openness and connectivity, among others—have serious effects on the ecology of marine systems.[8] A protected area (PA) system borrowed from land just would not work. Protecting marine systems requires a legal system that is 'spatially and temporally dynamic'[9], one that matches the fluidity of the water that forms the basis for life in the oceans.

After some time, Selvi akka spoke up again, 'Earlier, the guards, who were from our own villages, could not let us in to visit our *kuladaivam*, Muniasami. We had to make multiple requests to the government to allow us to go and pray to our God. Since 2011, with permission from the forest department, which is not very easily given, we have been allowed to visit the island for religious purposes. Our kuladaivam is on the island. How can they stop us from visiting our God?'

I had nothing to say to her. I sat there on the boat, bobbing up and down on the waves, feeling Selvi akka's pain at not being able to go to her island freely and thought again of fluidity and rigidity. The oceans move constantly, and so must any legal system that attempts to work in the ocean.

I wondered about the dilemma the forest guard must face in such a situation. A forest guard is usually recruited from a local village, as they have familiarity and intuitive knowledge of the area, making them an asset to the forest department. The job is by no means an easy one. Forest guards are hired to implement the laws—laws that often put them in conflict with the people of their own community.

In the afternoon, I went to talk to the forest department. The courtyard of the office was filled with chains and buoys.

For a while, I stood staring. These were the devices being used to imprison the ocean and its people.

Reflections on 'Protection'

Pamban
20 September 2019

'My grandfather taught me to do this when I was 16,' one of the older women said.

The younger ones laughed, 'She is the one who taught us.'

I was sitting with the famous women seaweed collectors of Ramanathapuram district. Every day as dawn breaks, about 10 women get into a boat heading out towards a set of islands close to the shore. Here, they tuck their sarees into shorts, wrap a piece of cloth around their fingers, and with a basic mask and paddle but no breathing equipment, they free dive into the water to collect seaweed.[10] These women are truly remarkable, the only women in the whole world who do this work in this way.

However, despite their fame and the uniqueness of their skill, their work is fraught with uncertainties. The older woman said with frustration, 'The forest department doesn't like us doing this. They say that it's a national park, and we are not allowed. They say we will harm the corals.'

Another woman piped up angrily, 'It doesn't make sense. We only collect seaweed from the dead corals.' She told us about the precautions they take—12-day bans on collection every month, ban on metal scrapers and restriction on the areas that they collect from.

But for the forest department, it's not enough. The department's nervousness is understandable. The forest department here is responsible for the conservation of the unique and incredibly biodiverse ecosystems. The gulf teems with life, filled with more than 450 species of fish, 250 species of birds, four species of dolphins, all five species of turtles found in India and the elusive dugongs. One forest officer pointed out to me that 'there is no real buffer area in terms of the ecology in the gulf. The seaweed is too close to the islands and falls within the core area of the Gulf of Mannar National Park.'

Perhaps this is why MPAs are so controversial.[11] PAs, even on land, have come under severe criticism both globally[12] and in India[13]. These same questions of social justice arise with MPAs that replicate the exclusionary model of land-based conservation.[14] With marine systems, even the long-term sustainability and ecological efficacy of exclusionary MPAs are in question.[15]

The department is not in an easy position either. Their hands are tied. They have a job to do—implement the WLPA. Unless the law itself changes, right now, the implementation involves stopping the women from collecting seaweed in the park. Another officer pointed out to me that they have been trying to work with the community to involve them in 'alternative livelihoods'—ornamental fish culture, jasmine plantations, tourism, among others—but the fishers have not been responding positively.

The officer spoke earnestly about the tourism plan they've been trying to get the communities involved in and his disappointment at the people not responding well to his ideas. Despite what must be a frustrating conversation for him, he insisted gravely, 'Ecotourism requires community participation. We will not do this without their involvement. You explain to them when you meet them that this is for their benefit only.'

Later, when I asked a fisherman, he responded angrily, 'Why should we be drivers on their boats? We know how to run a business. Why can't they let us do the tourism ourselves?' Despite the earnestness of the officer, the conversations are simply happening at cross-purposes. I'm reminded again of what Selvi akka had said to me a few days ago—that because of the creation of the MPA, the communities lost a section of their livelihood and access to their kuladaivam. The pain runs deep, and trust for the forest department runs low.

Honestly, I am writing in exasperation today! For how long can we be stuck in this 'parks vs people' debate, this endless loop of 'nature protection' that denies rights and justice to people. So many ways in which marine systems can be protected work for both ecology and the people. But in the gulf, the relationship between the forest department and the people needs much healing and repair. We are headed into a climate crisis, where, more than ever, we need to strengthen the relationship between people and nature. How can this happen if the different people working to conserve our ecosystems are alienated from each other? How can we hope to do that if our conservation methods ignore and weaken the complex relationships that local communities have with their landscapes?

Reflections on 'Development'

Rameswaram
25 September 2019

I went around more of Rameswaram today, taking in the place. The landscape here has unparalleled natural beauty and uniqueness that captures the imagination. But it was a difficult day. The changing, degrading landscape of the gulf is keenly observed by those whose lives depend on it.

Pamban island is surrounded by the salt water of the ocean, but the groundwater is rather sweet. Little wells dot the island, some within 30 metres of the sea, and the water is still fresh. I marvelled at this. 'The ground naturally has corals and calcium rocks, which protect groundwater from getting saline,' said Mr Rajesh, a citizen activist we met. We were sitting outside his office, a small inconspicuous-looking house with three chairs. You wouldn't know from looking at it that this is the place from where Rajesh had launched a long battle against groundwater extraction by the powerful aquaculture industry.

He continued sadly, 'Shrimp farms extract a high volume of freshwater to sustain themselves. They also break the protective calcium layer in order to get easy access to underground water, affecting the salinity of our drinking water.' I remembered all the water tankers I had noticed passing me when I was walking around Rameswaram the other day. 'Yes, that is for the shrimp farms. Also, for the tourism industry! Rameswaram has more than 450 lodges, and only around 150 of them might have good water. The rest, they buy around two tankers a day.'

'How much water is in a tanker?' I asked apprehensively.

'1,500 litres,' he said.

I was appalled, 'That's 9,00,000 litres of water a day!' Rajesh merely shrugged.

I went near the Rameswaram temple for lunch. I couldn't stop thinking about what Rajesh had said in the morning. I saw a defunct sewage treatment plant and recalled clips from a documentary I had watched before leaving home. It showed how waste water and sewage from hotels and resorts were let directly into the sea[16]. So, pollution too! And pollution in one part of the ocean spreads everywhere because of water's fluidity. Doesn't the industry need better regulation?[17] I found out that this is true of the aquaculture industry as well.[18] As I walked around Rameswaram, watching the tourists throng the ghats and the temples, I didn't know what to think.

After lunch, I took a bus to meet one of the members of the fishing union, Peter anna. He greeted me with 'Sorry I couldn't meet earlier. I was dealing with the case against me'. I was alarmed. What case? 'Oh! for protesting. But the case is less important than what is happening. Do you know that they are planning a thermal power plant in Uppur? Our people live there.

They go fishing in that area. If a power plant comes, and they destroy the beach and the ocean resources, how will we live?'

Just before I sat down to write this, I looked it up. I found out that the Tamil Nadu Generation and Distribution Corporation (TANGEDCO) had initiated a project for a supercritical coal thermal power plant with a capacity of 1,600 MW near Uppur village.[19] The project was repeatedly questioned by fish workers and farmers for the impacts that it would have on the gulf and on their lives. Thankfully, the project is stalled while a case is pending before the Supreme Court and the National Green Tribunal (NGT).[20]

I'm sitting here now thinking about the whole day and all the long, difficult conversations I had today. They said that the Gulf of Mannar National Park was created with the explicit objective of conserving and protecting marine ecology. Yet, it appears that very little is being done to look at and stop the industrial activities along the gulf coast. How is it that there is so much effort taken to stop the fishers and the seaweed collectors from their livelihoods because of a national park tag, but the aquaculture, tourism, thermal power and other industries were allowed to wreak havoc on the same system with impunity? Wasn't it obvious that the land and sea were interconnected and interdependent?

What would development projects look like if we kept the natural flow of the wind, water and land in mind, I wonder?

Some final thoughts

Bangaluru, Karnataka
31 December 2021

I'm sitting here at my desk, attempting to write this piece, looking at the mango tree outside my window and the traffic flowing all around it. I'm supposed to be writing this piece about MPAs, but I don't know what to say any more. I keep coming back to the pain of the people I met in the gulf. I keep thinking about how I would feel if I were forcefully cut off from my traditions or what it would mean to lose my livelihood. I know that this is a global issue. Forums like the Convention on Biological Diversity (CBD) have discussed the importance of 'governance diversity' in PAs, an acknowledgment of local ecological knowledge and recognition of the rights of local communities to govern PAs, including MPAs.[21] But it appears that India's legal framework is yet to catch up with this. Caught between the two seas—the Bay of Bengal and the Arabian Sea—the fisherpeople of the Gulf of Mannar have an intimate knowledge of the oceans and the islands, knowledge that has been passed on from one generation to another. Yet, this knowledge seems to have no place in the WLPA or other laws.

We all know that our marine ecosystems are in dire need of attention. We all talk about the urgency of the conservation measures we need. Even in the National Wildlife Action Plan (NWAP), 2017–2031, the Government of India (GoI) talks of protecting and conserving marine systems by proposing the creation of more MPAs. But the language of all these laws and policies continues to fail to recognize the fluidity of the oceans, the interconnectedness of the land and the seas or the rights of local communities. Of course, there are changes needed in the laws. But, more importantly, I feel changes are needed to how we see and perceive the oceans.

I admire how much the people of the sea know about the waters, the land, the winds and the fish, and the complexity of their relationship with nature. This is slowly but steadily slipping away from them like the sand from underneath our feet.

My own words are failing me, so I leave you with the words of people wiser than I am—'We are living through a moment of profound alienation from each other, the ocean, and nature... If we ignore marine justice, we risk losing something sacred as well. We believe that marine justice is not only an intellectual position worth defending but also one worth celebrating.'[22]

Notes

1. This chapter on MPAs has been written based on fieldwork done by the authors in the Ramanathapuram district across several months in 2014 and 2019, where we were able to meet several local community members and witness their everyday lives. Some of the accounts have been modified to suit the narration, but the descriptions of places and quotes are taken directly from our observations and conversations with the people of the Gulf of Mannar. Names have been changed to protect the identities of the people involved.
2. We owe a huge debt of gratitude to the people and organizations who've taken us on this journey, in particular, the Ramanathapuram Fisheries Trade Union, the seaweed collectors of Rameswaram, the people of Keelamunthal, especially Selvi akka, the kind officers of the forest and wildlife department of Ramanathapuram, Social Need Education and Human Awareness (SNEHA) and Equitable Tourism Options (EQUATIONS).
3. Asir, N. Gladwin Gnana, et al., 'Eroding Islands of Gulf of Mannar, Southeast India: A Consequence of Long-Term Impact of Coral Mining and Climate Change', *Natural Hazards*, Vol. 103, No. 1, August 2020, pp. 103–19, https://doi.org/10.1007/s11069-020-03961-6. Accessed on 7 July 2022.
4. Sheik, Mujabar and Chandrasekar, 'A Shoreline Change Analysis along the Coast between Kanyakumari and Tuticorin, India, Using Digital Shoreline Analysis System', *Geo-Spatial Information Science*, Vol. 14, No. 4, January 2011, pp. 282–93, https://doi.org/10.1007/s11806-011-0551-7. Accessed on 7 July 2022.
5. *Information Booklet on Gulf of Mannar Biosphere Reserve*, ENVIS Centre Department of Environment, Government of Tamil Nadu, 2015, https://bityl.co/D7Jc. Accessed on 7 July 2022.

6. Sivakumar, K., et al., *Coastal and Marine Protected Areas in India: Challenges and Way Forward*, WII, p. 12, https://bityl.co/D7JZ. Accessed on 7 July 2022.
7. 'Marine Protected Areas', ENVIS Centre on Wildlife & Protected Areas, https://bit.ly/3yGLIL0. Accessed on 7 July 2022.
8. Carr, Mark H., et al., 'Comparing Marine and Terrestrial Ecosystems: Implications for the Design of Coastal Marine Reserves', *Ecological Applications*, Vol. 13, No. sp1, 2003, pp. 90–107, https://doi.org/10.1890/1051-0761(2003)013[0090:CMATEI]2.0.CO;2. Accessed on 7 July 2022.
9. Sridhar, Aarthi, and Naveen Namboothri, 'Wildlife Action Plan: More Work Ahead from a Marine Conservation Perspective', *Hindustan Times*, 31 October 2017, https://bityl.co/D7Hw. Accessed on 7 July 2022.
10. International Collective in Support of Fishworkers (ICSF), *Shifting Undercurrents: Women Seaweed Collectors of Gulf of Mannar, India*, YouTube, 2022, https://ytube.io/3UEH. Accessed on 7 July 2022.
11. Agardy, Tundi, et al., 'Dangerous Targets? Unresolved Issues and Ideological Clashes around Marine Protected Areas', *Aquatic Conservation: Marine and Freshwater Ecosystems*, Vol. 13, No. 4, 2003, pp. 353–67, https://doi.org/10.1002/aqc.583. Accessed on 7 July 2022.
12. Brockington, Daniel, and David Wilkie, 'Protected Areas and Poverty', *The Royal Society*, Vol. 370, No. 1681, November 2015, https://doi.org/10.1098/rstb.2014.0271. Accessed on 7 July 2022.
13. Rangarajan, Mahesh, 'The Politics of Ecology: The Debate on Wildlife and People in India, 1970–95', *Economic & Political Weekly*, Vol. 31, No. 35/37, 1996, pp. 2391–409, https://bityl.co/D7I4. Accessed on 7 July 2022.
14. Rajagopalan, Ramya, *Marine Protected Areas in India*, ICSF, 2008, https://bityl.co/D7I9. Accessed on 7 July 2022.
15. De Santo, Elizabeth M., 'Missing Marine Protected Area (MPA) Targets: How the Push for Quantity over Quality Undermines

Sustainability and Social Justice', *Journal of Environmental Management*, Vol. 124, July 2013, pp. 137–46, https://doi.org/10.1016/j.jenvman.2013.01.033. Accessed on 7 July 2022.

16. PSBT India, *Coral Woman*, YouTube, 2021, https://ytube.io/3UEL. Accessed on 1 July 2022.
17. *Coastal Blues*, EQUATIONS, 30 March 2021, https://bityl.co/D7IV. Accessed on 7 July 2022.
18. A., Neelambaran, 'Shrimp Farms Cause Water, Soil Pollution on Rameswaram Island', *NewsClick*, 23 November 2021, https://bityl.co/D7IS. Accessed on 7 July 2022.
19. 'Madras HC Stays Construction of Uppur Thermal Plant Citing Defunct Land Laws', Land Conflict Watch, 17 March 2020, https://bityl.co/D7IX. Accessed on 7 July 2022.
20. Ibid.
21. Fischborn, Marie, and Zhanna Levitina (eds), *Solutions in Focus: Community-Led Successes in Marine Conservation*, IUCN, as part of Blue Solutions project, 2018, https://bityl.co/D7Ic. Accessed on 7 July 2022.
22. Martin, Jennifer A., et al., 'What Is Marine Justice?', *Journal of Environmental Studies and Sciences*, Vol. 9, No. 2, June 2019, pp. 234–43, https://doi.org/10.1007/s13412-019-00545-0. Accessed on 7 July 2022.

BOOMERANG: WHEN SUCCESS BEGINS TO BREED CONTESTATION

ISHAN KUKRETI

The killings took place on the night of 21 October 2020, and the bodies were strewn around Rajendra Babulal Bopche's house. That night, as the village slept, a temple near Bopche's house played devotional songs all night to mark the nine-day festival of Navratri. The songs and the darkness of the night provided the perfect cover for the killer—a pack of Indian peninsular wolves.

The next morning, around 5.00 a.m., his neighbour woke him up to tell him about two of his goats lying dismembered in the lane separating their houses. Three others were found dead in his goat shed, and one was missing.

'The door of my goat shed was made of logs; the wolves broke it and entered. They came like ghosts—no one heard anything. They only took one goat to feed on. The rest were killed for no reason,' Bopche told me when I visited Manegaon in early September 2021.

Bopche, who also sometimes works as a manual labourer in Gondia or Nagpur, gets a substantial amount of his income from goat-rearing, which he then sells for meat. That night, with those six goats, he also lost a fair part of this income.

I was in Gondia to understand and report on the human–wildlife conflict (HWC) there. What happened in Manegaon was unusual for a few reasons. Although depredation by wolves has been common in the fields and forest near the village, this was the first time a pack had entered the village and lifted goats from a shed—a possible sign of an increase in wolf numbers in the region.

This attack had got the villagers worried and also resentful, both towards the wolves and the forest department. But, through my conversations with the villagers, I realized that they also blamed themselves for the increasing depredation by wolves.

I was told that the villagers themselves conserved a nearby 140-ha patch of wooded grassland through their initiatives. Not only did they plant indigenous varieties of grasses there but they also stopped the forest department from raising a plantation there. And, to my surprise, they told me that they did it for wildlife—especially the blackbuck—present there.

I was surprised, and this might be a little reductionist in its outlook because in communities living inside and around the forested landscape, although the relationship with flora is highly valued, the same cannot be said about fauna. It is often pointed out from the slogans of rights-based movements in these landscapes, like '*Jal,* jungle *aur jameen*', how the mention of wildlife is conspicuous by its absence. This relationship, in most cases, is, at best, apathetic to wildlife.

However, in a way, it can be argued that the essence of any relationship lies in acts of exchange and revolves around give-and-take practices. If the same is extended to human interaction with the natural world, then this apathy towards wildlife can be seen as a result of the exclusionary forestry policies and practices of the Raj, which were then continued by the democratic Indian government post-Independence. The colonial game reserves or democratic India's reserved forests (RFs) or protected areas (PAs) are legally out of bounds for people living near these landscapes. How, then, can one forge a relation with something when interaction with that thing itself is illegal and attracts penalties? So, local species of trees like mahua or a tendu is valued—and therefore, conserved and even encouraged for its produce[1], establishing a mutually beneficial relationship between the natural and the human world. There is no such scope for a similar relationship, in whatever form, between humans and wildlife.

The people of Manegaon were telling me that not only did they have a healthy relationship with the wildlife in their backyard, so to speak, but they had also taken concrete steps to conserve it. But they were also telling me that, over time, this relationship had turned sour.

Livestock depredation is usually seen as a sign of low prey density in an area, making the carnivores supplement their diet with livestock. However, in Manegaon, although there is enough prey in the area, the wolves are still lifting goats. According to Dr M.D. Madhusudan, a conservation biologist, the population of carnivores in an ecosystem initially depends on the number of herbivores—the prey. The higher the number of prey, the more the carnivore population can sustain the ecosystem. This is called bottom-up control.

'However, once a carnivore population threshold is crossed, the control becomes top-down, and the hunting pattern of the carnivores begins to regulate the population of herbivores. The increased number of carnivores also means that some of them will kill the herbivores, but some will also lift livestock,' Dr Madhusudan said.

I must clarify that this positive relationship is in no way unique only to this village in the country. Such examples of positive relationships are documented and recognized phenomena, so much so that, apart from wildlife sanctuaries and national parks, the other two categories of PAs legally recognized since 2003 in India under the Wild Life (Protection) Act (WLPA), 1972, are 'community' and 'conservation' reserves. The administration of these two categories of PAs is indeed rooted in and encourages this idea of a positive human relationship with fauna. It is a shame that these two categories of more inclusionary conservation landscapes have failed to take off despite having statutory backing.

In Manegaon, this relationship, at least initially, was based on tourism or a hope for it.

Chunnilal Bhalave, who was the Manegaon sarpanch between 2004 and 2009, told me, 'People came to see blackbuck from all over. The Navegaon-Nagzira Tiger Reserve, which is a dense forest, does not have blackbucks; they are only found in some pockets like in our village. We thought if we could help increase their numbers, it would not only make our village famous but also bring tourism here.' Surely, for the people, it was the incentive in the form of tangible monetary gains from tourism that motivated them towards conservation. But there was another motive, too, that Bhalave was hinting at. This motive was much less tangible than money but equally, if not more, important from the perspective of ensuring long-term conservation goals. It was the village's pride in a wildlife species.

Sure enough, as any relationship based on the right incentives is bound to blossom, since 2006, when the conservation efforts first started in Manegaon, the herbivore population—blackbuck and spotted deer—has increased drastically. As a testimony to the health of the ecosystem, in 2011, a pack of wolves—the apex predator of a grassland ecosystem—moved into the area and, by 2021, as Bopche's loss shows, even into the village.

Manegaon presents an example of a community-led conservation effort resulting in better outcomes for conservation but not for the community. This is primarily due to government policies surrounding conservation. Manegaon is also indicative of what is unfolding across the country and, more importantly, of what may happen to the much-publicized 'tolerant' spirit, or even this sense of pride Bhalave talked about, towards wildlife in the future.

◆

In the last 50 years, the protection bestowed on wildlife, mainly through the creation of national parks and wildlife sanctuaries as a safe haven, has increased the population of some wildlife species in the country. However, a conservation model that created islands of inviolate landscapes, aiming to draw a sharp line between the natural and the human world at the gates of these national parks or wildlife sanctuaries, over the years, has, naturally, resulted in transgression of these artificially drawn boundaries. Now, half a century since, there is a situation where many animals like the tigers, leopards and elephants are outside park boundaries, and conflict is increasing.

Take the example of the national animal of India, the tiger. The first Tiger Task Force (TTF) of 1972, which led to the launch of Project Tiger, had recommended the creation of inviolate spaces to conserve the tiger.[2] The task force wanted an area of around 2,000 sq. km, plus adjoining areas, for every 300 tigers (a requirement that would mean to host the 2,967 tigers of India today an area of around 19,000 sq. km would be required, or an area equal to five times the state of Goa). Obviously, such huge tracts of inviolate land could not be found in a land-stressed country like India, and it settled for 'small units as model parks to preserve the tiger while continuing efforts to create more sanctuaries.'

A thing to note here is something that the report points to in its earliest parts. By the time the TTF sat down to draw up a plan to conserve tigers in 1972, their population had already dwindled from around 40,000 at the end of the nineteenth century to a mere 1,800. I wonder if the need for such huge tracts of inviolate spaces was felt because of the dangerously low numbers of tigers left in the wild and whether the TTF members could even imagine where their recommendation of creating inviolate spaces would lead to in the future when both tigers and humans would be vying for space?

Could they have ever thought of a situation like today's, where the population density of tigers in one of the oldest tiger reserves of the country, Corbett Tiger Reserve in Uttarakhand, is higher than the population density of humans in the Lahaul and Spiti district of Himachal Pradesh (Lahaul and Spiti has the lowest population density in the county with two people per sq. km, according to the 2011 census. The Corbett Tiger Reserve (521 sq. km) has the highest tiger density of any reserve in the county, at 14 tigers per 100 sq. km or around seven tigers per sq. km, according to the environment ministry's *Status of Tigers Co-Predators and Prey in India* released in 2019) and that many are outside PA boundaries?[3] And if they could, would they have recommended something else, something more nuanced and inclusionary?

What is true for tigers also holds true for elephants, lions and leopards. Moreover, wildlife species like wolves, which have always thrived and shared spaces with humans, find themselves not only in the fringes of the forests but also on the fringes of the policymakers' attention. The conflict with these species remains largely ignored, as the case of Manegaon shows. My conversations with the residents of Manegaon showed that a one-size-fits-all approach to mitigating HWCs falls flat on its face when dealing with species that have never had a spotlight shining on them.

A major component of this one-size-fits-all approach is the monetary compensation for the depredation of livestock to mitigate HWC. The amount—around 50 to 60 per cent of the market value of the animal—is seen as an ex gratia amount paid by the forest department. It prevents retaliatory killing by building tolerance towards predators and livestock lifting.

In the case of depredation, the owner has to collect the evidence of the kill—bodily remains, photographs—get a veterinarian on the spot who has to certify that it was indeed a wildlife species that made the kill, and then, the evidence and the veterinarian certificate has to be handed over to the forest department.

But depredation by wolves presents a unique problem. Unlike the kills made by a tiger, where the parts of the carcass can be found, the kills made by wolves are mostly never found.

'The preferred prey of wolves is fawns of blackbuck, deer and goats. Wolves hunt in packs, and unless the pack is disturbed and forced to abandon the kill, it is rare that even an earlobe of the livestock will be found,' Ankit Thakur of Self Employed Women's Association (SEWA), a Gondia-based conservation non-profit, who has been tracking the developments in Manegaon for some time now, told me.

There are other reasons too for the difference in wolves' hunting and feeding behaviour. Dr M.D. Madhusudan says that there is a difference in the way the species of the cat family, such as tigers or leopards, kill their prey and the way that members of the dog species, like wolves and dholes, hunt. 'The members of the cat family can kill bigger prey, and they usually hide their prey. So, a tiger will make a kill and drag and hide its prey, returning to feed on it. However, dog family doesn't hide or drag their prey. Whatever is killed has to be consumed or left behind. Usually, the killing and feeding happen in an open area, so even if the wolves leave the carcass behind, other scavengers like domestic dogs finish the kill,' he said.

This minute difference between the wolf and the tiger, on whose predatory behaviour the compensation approach is largely based, has made all the difference in the villagers' attitude. Although in Bopche's case, with the evidence strewn all around for everyone to find, compensation was paid, but there are many people in Manegaon who have not been so lucky. Almost always, there is nothing to show to prove livestock depredation.

With the policy stuck in inflexible gear, the forest department, too, cannot do anything. 'How can we compensate for livestock when there is no evidence of depredation? In cases where there is evidence, we act, as in the case of the six goats that were killed in Manegaon, but otherwise, we can't. There are a lot of false claims too,' said K.U. Kadambh, the forest beat guard of Manegaon.

The problem of Manegaon shows the need for a more targeted conflict mitigation approach. A one-size-fits-all approach is not working in a world where both humans and wildlife are vying for space.

And this space is shrinking.

◆

HWC is usually seen as damaging interactions between humans and wildlife species, mostly in landscapes outside PAs (although with around 300 million forest dwellers[4] living or subsisting on forested landscapes, including PAs, these interactions are not limited to only non-PA landscapes).

Between the 1970s and now, the population of India has increased from around 567 million to 1.3 billion. But the population increase figure on its own won't be accurate due to the varying levels of consumption and environmental footprint of people. However, a better sense of this shrinking space can be gauged when these population figures are seen with the land use and land-use change data over the years. So, while the total agriculture area stood at 1,204,000 sq. km in 1970[5], it went up to 1,999,880 sq. km in 2017–2018[6]. In the same period, the built-up area went up from 10,200 sq. km to 1,21,848 sq. km in 2016[7], and the total length of railways tracks increased from 98,546 km to 121,407 km[8]. In the same period, the number of PAs has also increased from six national parks and 59 wildlife sanctuaries in 1970[9] to 104 national parks and 566 wildlife sanctuaries in 2020[10].

These interactions can result in death, livestock depredation and damage to property. Images of people chasing leopards, cruelty towards elephants, and death, depredation and property loss for humans evoke strong emotions. Studies have found that the most damaging of these interactions are with elephants, followed by tigers and leopards. Around 69 per cent of all conflicts between 1976 and 2015 took place outside PAs.[11]

While these interactions and the reasons for it are mostly seen as resulting from the trespass of the humans into the wild habitats and vice versa, a border perspective would point to activities beyond these regional territorial transgressions. In a way, these transgressions, forcing these damaging interactions upon humans and animals, start far away from forested areas. They begin with the stroke of a pen in the Indira Paryavaran Bhawan, the seat of the Ministry of Environment and Forest and Climate Change (MoEFCC) in Delhi, in the meetings of the Forest Advisory Committee (FAC) or National Board for Wildlife (NBWL), which regulate forest land diversion in the county. Although lip service is paid to wildlife habitat and their corridors in these meetings, they remain just that. Mostly, diversion is based on political demands rather than the dictates of science. So, for instance, in 2014, the Madhya Pradesh Forest Department, despite recommending the diversion of 900 ha of forest land in Buxwaha forest in the Chhatarpur district for a diamond mine, noted the presence of wild animals using the area, including the tiger. However, things changed by 2020. In a span of six years (or of two companies), the Madhya Pradesh Forest Department turned the wildlife-rich area into one that had presence of 'no species of specific importance of any wildlife.'[12]

Interestingly, even if the science is robust, the legal procedures lag behind. So, in the same case, while the Madhya Pradesh State Biodiversity Board identified the patch of Buxwaha forest in question as a tiger corridor, they were never formally notified, completely lowering the stakes from a legal point of view.[13]

This gap between the legal and the actual ground realities, along with indiscriminate diversion of PA land, is a major contribution to the shrinking and vying for space. This is also at the centre of the most damaging of these interactions, the one between humans and elephants. Both elephants and humans continue to die in an invisible struggle raging across elephant habitats in the country. However, since both elephant reserves and corridors have no legal sanctity under the WLPA, anyone can walk in and start mining coal or set up a resort.

The history of elephant conservation in India gives an insight into what might explain this sad state of affairs. Seen from this perspective, it seems that, more than anything else, it's the monetary value of a wildlife species that determines its importance as a species of interest for conservation.

The elephant was the first wildlife species to be given legal protection during the sunny days of the British Raj in South Asia. The Madras Wild Elephant Preservation Act of 1873 criminalized the killing of elephants on government lands.[14] However, it was a decision based not on the role of the gentle giant as nature's gardener but because it was a draught animal used to lug timber from the depths of the forest and as a mode of transportation for general mobility and during hunts. Now, with that aspect of the elephant's utility sacrificed at the altar of modern machinery, the species finds its habitat virtually absent of any legal provision. But on the other hand, the monetary value of the tiger has increased. The species rakes in conservation and tourism money like a magnet. After all, the financial outlay of Project Tiger, as mentioned in the TTF report, stood at almost ₹7 crore (just for comparison, this was higher than the total outlay for centrally sponsored schemes for elementary education [₹5.56 crore] or almost 17 per cent of the total outlay for all the social welfare programmes [₹41.38 crore] in the Fourth Five-Year plan of 1969–1974). So, the tiger, which was once the vermin of forests, with designated offices of tiger slayers wiping it out from the countryside for payments during the Raj, now has a conservation budget that overshadows that of all the other species combined. In the Union Budget of 2021–2022, the outlay for the conservation of tiger at ₹250 crore was higher than the outlay for all other species, including elephant conservation at ₹33 crore or even the general outlay for wildlife habitat development at ₹116 crore.

On the other hand, while the fate of tigers and elephants has reversed, the apathy towards other species remains the same, if not worse. Take the wolf, for instance. The apex predator of the grassland ecosystem probably had a death toll higher than even the mighty tiger during the Raj, as historian Mahesh Rangarajan estimates.[15] Independence and the WLPA may have put the species on the list of conserved species, but not a single estimation process has been initiated to know its numbers in the wild. Apart from the stray reference in the tiger estimation reports and studies done here and there, there is no clarity on the pan-India number of these species. While the species remains neglected, its habitat is even more so. Grasslands are still seen as 'wastelands', a land categorization dating back to colonial times due to the inability of these ecosystems to turn into revenue-yielding agricultural fields. Today, this idea of grasslands as wastelands means that they are often sought out to undertake tree plantations or infrastructure development.[16] While the acrimony of the Raj at least had logic to it—settlement of villages and expansion of agriculture—today's apathy carries on for no rhyme or reason. To this list can also be added golden jackals, hyenas and even sloth bears, which can most easily (and with high stakes on one's well-being as both sloth and Himalayan, bears rank high in terms of attacks on humans) be sighted digging for food in the trash cans of Mount Abu.[17]

Today's conservation policy prescribes the same outfit for all species and then wonders why their clothes don't fit. Meanwhile, over the years, the number of species involved in the conflict has gone up from 38 during 1976–1995 to 76 during 1996–2015. This is partly because of the attention given only to the conservation of a few species. The umbrella is held over these few, while the others somehow try to find their place under it.[18] The diversion of forest land continues unabated, on most days, ignoring the legal procedure, forcing on both people and animals these mutually damaging interactions. To make matters worse, what remains of wildlife habitats is being burned to the ground due to an increase in the frequency of forest fires because of climate change.[19] There are also studies showing evidence of vegetative decaying and browning in PAs.[20]

All this points out how wildlife species are being pushed to the corner for survival, and in the absence of a housing-for-all type deal for *them*, chances are things aren't going to improve any time soon.

Notes

1. Shahabuddin, Ghazala, and K. Sivaramakrishnan, *Nature Conservation in the New Economy: People, Wildlife and the Law in India*, Orient BlackSwan, 2019.
2. Task Force: Project Tiger, *Project Tiger: A Planning Proposal for Preservation of Tiger (Panthera Tigris Tigris Linn.) in India*, Indian Board for Wild Life, 1972, https://bityl.co/D7WU. Accessed on 7 July 2022.
3. Roy, Esha, 'WWF-UNEP Report: 35% of Tiger Ranges Outside Protected Areas', *The Indian Express*, 10 July 2021, https://bityl.co/D7WL. Accessed on 1 July 2022.
4. *Status of Forests in India*, Parliamentary Standing Committee on Science and Technology, Environment and Forests, 12 February 2019, https://bit.ly/3Pt4fkC. Accessed on 7 July 2022.
5. Anand, Shaurabh, and Sindhu Radhakrishna, 'Investigating Trends in Human-Wildlife Conflict: Is Conflict Escalation Real

or Imagined?' *Journal of Asia-Pacific Biodiversity*, Vol. 10, No. 2, June 2017, pp. 154–61, https://doi.org/10.1016/j.japb.2017.02.003. Accessed on 1 July 2022.

6. *Land Use Statistics at a Glance 2008-09 to 2017-18*, Ministry of Agriculture and Farmers Welfare, July 2021, https://bit.ly/3oh8Wm1. Accessed on 7 July 2022.
7. Ibid; Anand, Shaurabh, and Sindhu Radhakrishna, 'Investigating Trends in Human-Wildlife Conflict: Is Conflict Escalation Real or Imagined?', *Journal of Asia-Pacific Biodiversity*, Vol. 10, No. 2, June 2017, pp. 154–61, https://doi.org/10.1016/j.japb.2017.02.003. Accessed on 1 July 2022.
8. 'About Us', Indian Railways Civil Engineering Portal, https://bityl.co/D7UW. Accessed on 7 July 2022.
9. Badola, Ruchi, 'People and Protected Areas in India', *Decentralization and Devolution in Forestry*, Vol. 50, No. 4, 1999, https://bityl.co/D7Ue. Accessed on 1 July 2022.
10. 'Protected Areas-Subject Area: Wildlife Institute of India, Ministry of Environment & Forests', ENVIS Centre on Wildlife & Protected Areas, https://bityl.co/D7Uk. Accessed on 1 July 2022.
11. Anand, Shaurabh, and Sindhu Radhakrishna, 'Investigating Trends in Human-Wildlife Conflict: Is Conflict Escalation Real or Imagined?', *Journal of Asia-Pacific Biodiversity*, Vol. 10, No. 2, June 2017, pp. 154–61, https://doi.org/10.1016/j.japb.2017.02.003. Accessed on 1 July 2022.
12. Kukreti, Ishan, 'The Contested Treasure inside Madhya Pradesh's Forests', *Scroll.in*, 18 August 2021, https://bityl.co/D7Uu. Accessed on 13 July 2022.
13. Ibid.
14. Mandala, Vijaya Ramadas, *Shooting a Tiger: Big-Game Hunting and Conservation in Colonial India*, Oxford University Press, 2018.
15. Rangarajan, Mahesh, and K. Sivaramakrishnan, *India's Environmental History: Colonialism, Modernity, and the Nation: A Reader*, Permanent Black, 2012.
16. Kukreti, Ishan, 'Why the Return of Wolves to an Indian Grassland

Is a Bittersweet Story', *Scroll.in*, 6 October 2021, https://bit.ly/3AuM8qj. Accessed on 7 July 2022.

17. Prajapati, Utkarsh, et al., 'Vulnerable Sloth Bears Are Attracted to Human Food Waste: A Novel Situation in Mount Abu Town, India', *Oryx*, Vol. 55, No. 5, September 2021, pp. 699–707, https://doi.org/10.1017/S0030605320000216. Accessed on 7 July 2022.
18. Kukreti, Ishan, 'In the Shadow of the Tiger, Its Co-Predators Are Suffering', *Down to Earth*, 29 July 2020, https://bityl.co/D7Vj. Accessed on 7 July 2022.
19. Ahmad, Firoz, and Laxmi Goparaju, 'Forest Fire Trend and Influence of Climate Variability in India: A Geospatial Analysis at National and Local Scale', *Ekológia (Bratislava)*, Vol. 38, No. 1, March 2019, pp. 49–68, https://doi.org/10.2478/eko-2019-0005. Accessed on 7 July 2022.
20. Koulgi, Pradeep S., et al., 'Extensive Vegetation Browning and Drying in Forests of India's Tiger Reserves', *Scientific Reports*, Vol. 9, No. 1, 18 October 2019, https://doi.org/10.1038/s41598-019-51118-8. Accessed on 7 July 2022.

ELEPHANT IN THE CITY

RABINDRA K. SINGH[1]

If anyone wants to know what elephants are like, they are like people only more so.

—Peter Corneille

It was a cold winter night on 6 December 2016. After a long, hectic day, I went to sleep at midnight. Around 5.00 a.m., my cell phone's screaming ringtone woke me from a deep sleep. As I quickly glanced at the display, wondering what would have prompted anyone to call me in the wee hours of the morning, the calling number on the screen got me worried. It was the Inspector General of Police (IGP), Surguja range, calling to inform me about a herd of elephants seen by the police patrolling team within the Ambikapur city.

'Where?' I asked, unable to mask my fear, realizing the high risk involved in the presence of elephants within a densely populated city.

'Can't tell you the exact location right now,' he responded with urgency and went on to inform that since the Superintendent of Police (SP), Surguja, was on leave, he would have to monitor the operation himself, though the SP of the adjoining district had been sounded to report with additional police force. We discussed for a while the possible strategies in such a situation and the role of police and civil administration, especially in crowd management. Immediately thereafter, I contacted the

Divisional Forest Officer (DFO), Ambikapur, who assured me an apprisal after ascertaining the facts.

After about an hour and half, the DFO called to inform me that a group of 11 elephants, identified as the Ashok Dal[2], had entered the Mission orchard in the city by breaking its masonry boundary wall. The orchard is located behind the Holy Cross School on Manendragarh road and is surrounded by many educational institutions. Sufficient food for the elephants is available within the 50-acre orchard, where bamboo, banana, potato, papaya, cabbage and potato have been grown by the Mission authorities. The orchard is also surrounded by paddy fields spread over an area of about 100 acres. It also has two ponds with sufficient water. The elephants appeared comfortable and not hungry, for they might have consumed enough food and water during the night. We discussed plans for the safe exit of elephants, crowd management and steps to prevent injury or loss of human life.

Ambikapur, the headquarters of the Surguja district, is one of the northern districts of Chhattisgarh state. It is an old city with an estimated human population of 1,14,575.[3] *Ain-I-Akbari*, written in the sixteenth century, mentions the presence of elephants in Bastar, the southern part of the state.[4] The northern region of Chhattisgarh, including the Surguja district, was also home to wild elephants.[5] It was a regular source of supply of elephants to the armies during the fifteenth century. The elephants were so numerous, and ravages by them so serious that several villages were abandoned till a large number of elephants had been captured. By 1909, the elephant population had become scarce.[6] The exact process of elephant disappearance from the state is not known, but it seems that years of trapping and crop protection measures eliminated them.[7]

The Central Indian elephant landscape witnessed major dispersal events during 1987–1988. Elephants from south Bihar (now Jharkhand) moved to the eastern region of Madhya Pradesh (now Chhattisgarh) and the southern part of West Bengal, which had not been a range state for the past several decades. The elephants from south Bihar reappeared in the Surguja district of Madhya Pradesh first in the year 1988. Subsequently, they also began to come from neighbouring Odisha.

Anthropogenic factors such as mining, industrial development, linear infrastructure intrusions into a natural habitat, expansion of agriculture and settlements, and change in land use have led to habitat loss and fragmentation of elephant range in these states.[8] Elephants require extensive land areas to meet their ecological needs.[9] They also require large quantities of water for drinking and wallowing. In 1986, the percentage departure of rainfall from normal in the Bihar plateau meteorological subdivision was minus 31 per cent. This was followed by the drought of 1987, one of the worst in this century. Although the Bihar plateau was in the normal category (+19 per cent to -19 per cent), rainfall had been erratic and there were long dry spells.[10] The climatic variability may, thus, have forced elephants to break out of the established home ranges and disperse in search of better habitat. Elephants might also have found the Surguja district, with about 58 per cent of its area under forests, relatively more suitable.[11]

This dispersal of elephants in 1988 into the eastern region of Madhya Pradesh led to serious human–elephant conflicts (HEC). These included crop-raiding, damage to property, injuries and even deaths of both humans and elephants. Unfortunately, the forest officials in the areas newly visited by elephants had no understanding of elephant behaviour and ecology, which could have effectively helped them manage these conflicts. The current generation of local people also lacked the astuteness to live in harmony with wild elephants, for the latter had been absent from their environs for many decades.

In this case, the Madhya Pradesh government followed an undeclared policy of 'driving back' elephants to the state they had come from—southern Bihar (now Jharkhand). But the elephants started to migrate every year, following almost the same route. They would stay for some days and then be driven back by the joint efforts of local people and the forest department staff. While in Madhya Pradesh, they continued to raid crops and break into houses to feed on stored grains, salt and mahua (local liquor). Sometimes this led to loss of human life. An 'elephant camp' was established in 1989 in the Lalmati village of south Surguja forest division to prevent these incidents. The camp was established to monitor elephants' movement and manage HEC situations. The local people in the affected areas were trained to mitigate in different ways, such as beating drums, burning chilly ropes, chilly grease fencing, and use of high beam lights, mashal, etc., to drive the elephants away. But by the time communities learnt to use these deterrents, the elephants learnt how to breach them. Therefore, these deterrents proved only partially effective. The forest department then used solar-powered electric fence to confine the elephants within select forest patches away from human settlements. But these remained effective only for a few months (January–August 1990), after which the elephants succeeded in breaching it. Thirty persons were reportedly killed and 10 injured in HEC incidents between 1988 and 1993. Unrest among the affected villagers continued to grow with each new incident.

Towards the end of 1992, the Government of Madhya Pradesh decided to capture and domesticate the migrant elephants with expert help from the Karnataka Forest Department. Eleven elephants were captured (one died during the capture operation) with the help of trained staff and six kumki elephants that came from Karnataka. The captured elephants were then domesticated and trained. After training, these elephants were sent to different national parks in Madhya Pradesh, where they have since been used for patrolling and anti-poaching surveillance. To everybody's relief, elephant herds from Bihar (now Jharkhand) stopped coming to Madhya Pradesh from 1993 till about 2000. Elephants have an amazing capacity to communicate with one another in the multilayered social network over a long distance.[12] But seismic vocalizations of elephants are potentially detectable up to only a distance of 32 km.[13] It is, thus, unlikely that elephants in Bihar could have received distress calls from the elephants captured and domesticated in Madhya Pradesh. So, what stopped their migration from south Bihar to Madhya Pradesh remains a mystery!

The present state of Chhattisgarh was carved out of Madhya Pradesh on 1 November 2000. It is an amazing coincidence that elephants began to visit the newly created state of Chhattisgarh from its year of inception. In September 2002, the forest department recorded the presence of 32 elephants in the Jashpur, Raigarh, Surguja and Korba districts in north Chhattisgarh. Their number has increased over the years. During the last two decades, some herds appear to be in the early phase of settlement, as they have begun to show a fixed pattern of movement and use of areas within the state for extended periods. From 122 elephants in 2007, their number increased to 247 in 2012. All-India synchronized elephant population estimation conducted during the year 2017 also reported the same number in the state, including 70 adult females and 30 calves.[14] According to the daily monitoring report of elephant groups, maintained by the forest department, the maximum number of elephants reported in the state during the year 2021 was 312.

The dispersing elephants are also expanding their range in search of a favourable habitat to 'settle down'. During the initial stage of migration, elephants migrated to only the state's northern districts, but now they have started to move into the central and southern parts of the state.

Movements into the neighbouring states of Madhya Pradesh, Uttar Pradesh and Maharashtra have also been noticed (Map 1). With the technical help of the WII, Dehradun, and

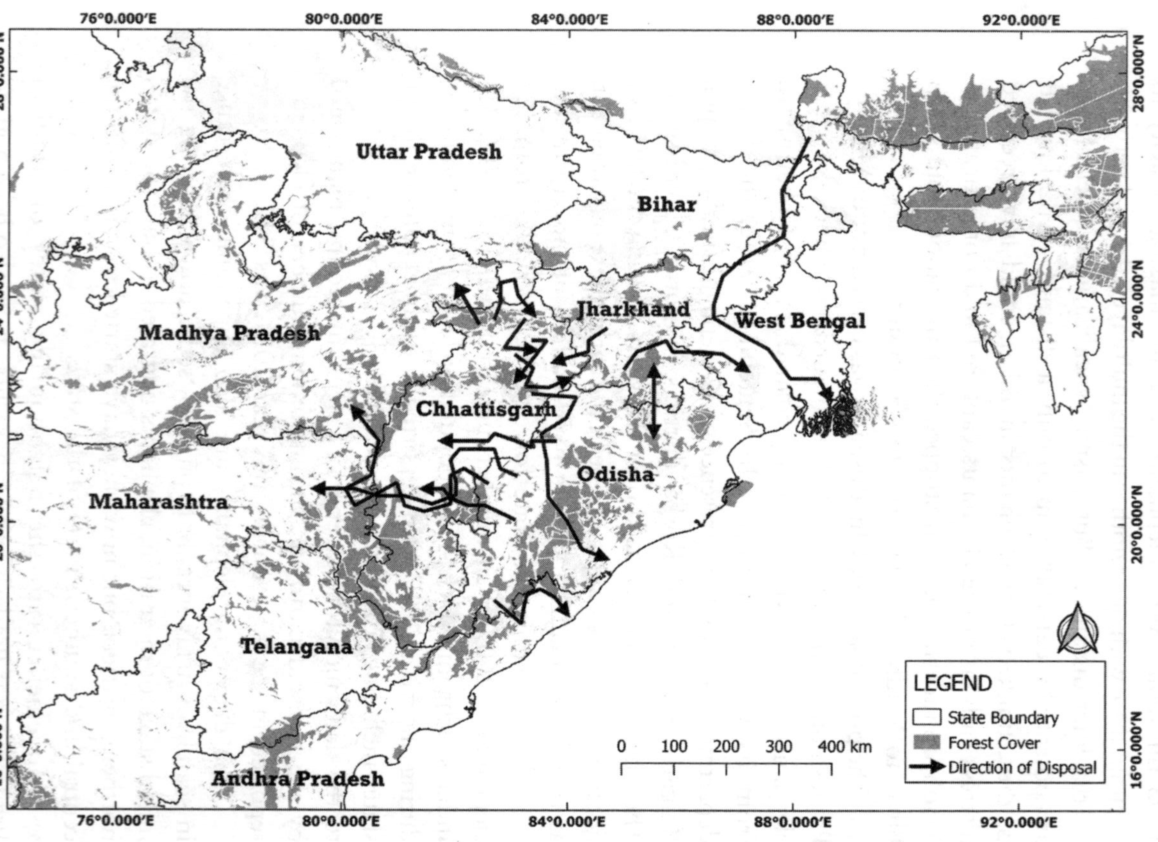

Map 1: Dispersal of central range elephants into neighbouring states.[15]

Wildlife SOS, New Delhi, the forest department has been radio-collaring a few elephants since May 2018 to understand their home range, dispersal, and movement patterns.

The estimated home ranges of elephants in the Rajaji National Park, Uttarakhand, have been reported from 188 sq. km to 400 sq. km.[16] The average home range in the Nilgiris landscape, Tamil Nadu, has been reported to be around 651 sq. km.[17] However, the estimated home range of radio-collared elephants in northern Chhattisgarh has varied from 1,200 sq. km to 2,500 sq. km, some of them moving at times into the neighbouring states of Odisha, Jharkhand, and Madhya Pradesh.[18] Large variation was observed in the home range size of one radio-collared adult female called Chanda in central Chhattisgarh. In the first year (September 2018 to September 2019), it was 612 sq. km, while in the second year (October 2019 to October 2020), it became 4,301 sq. km. Such a large variation could be explained by less traffic and human disturbance resulting from extended lockdown due to the Covid-19 pandemic in 2020, as well as many farmers beginning to use solar power fences to protect their crops.[19]

Elephants in Chhattisgarh operate in highly fragmented forests, which they use as a daytime refuge, and forage on the cultivated crops during the night. Therefore, home ranges tend to be large, as small patches of forests cannot hold elephants for longer durations. In a landscape where elephants have 'settled down', their home ranges are mostly within protected areas (PA) and forests with minimal overlap with human-use areas. However, the 'dispersing' elephants operating in northern Chhattisgarh are spending close to 40 per cent of their time in human-use areas for both movement and feeding on cultivated crops.[20] This results in farmers resorting to desperate measures to drive elephants away from their farmlands.

When elephants are driven from multiple sides by the surrounding villages, they tend to lose their orientation and digress from their intended path of movement. On 6 December 2016, Ashok Dal raided crops in the adjoining villages of Lakhanpur forest during the daytime. The forest staff monitoring the elephants had advised the villagers to stay away from the elephants. The forest staff monitored this group till the time elephants returned to the forests, and it was only around 11.00 p.m. that the forest staff returned to Ambikapur. Ashoka Dal then travelled around 25 km during the night to reach Ambikapur city via Torna, Salka, Singitana and Vishunpur villages of the Lakhanpur forest range. Presumably, this happened because villagers from multiple sides were driving them, although they denied having done so on later questioning. Whatever might have happened in this case, it has been observed that dispersing elephants are not averse to running off in any direction, including into human-use areas.[21]

Most of the people in Ambikapur were unaware of the presence of wild elephants in their city, for the elephants had entered under the cover of mist at early dawn. The forest team feared that information about the presence and location of elephants would spread fast, and a curious and noisy crowd would start gathering around the boundary wall of the orchard. This might make the elephants stressed, afraid and even offensive, endangering both humans and themselves.

The forest, police and civil administration quickly assembled at the site to prepare a safe exit plan for the elephants while ensuring no risk or damage to human life or property. Different government functionaries agreed on their roles and responsibilities. The civil administration and police took upon the responsibility of crowd management, maintaining law and order, and communication within the city. An order was issued at 7.30 a.m. by the District Collector, Surguja, to close all educational institutions within the city until further orders were given. News about the presence of elephants in the city was given to residents via social and electronic media. Police personnel was deployed near the orchard to prevent crowding by people. Public address systems mounted on vehicles along with hooters and sirens were used to make necessary announcements in and around a 4-km radius of the orchard. City residents were kept informed about the inherent danger in approaching the orchard and were advised to stay safe in their homes. The public representatives also made an appeal to people to cooperate with the administration in maintaining law and order. The main road leading to the orchard was barricaded.

After assessing the situation, it was decided to retain the elephants at the site till evening, with the hope that the elephants would, if adequately facilitated, move away on their own. A team led by the Sub Divisional Officer (SDO) (Forest) was assigned the responsibility of monitoring the elephants and taking appropriate action, if any, at the site, in addition to providing regular updates to all the officials involved in the operation.

All escape points from the orchard were closed using a barbed-wire fence. The route for the elephant herd's exit was identified by the Chief Conservator of Forests (CCF), Surguja, after carefully assessing various options. The finally selected exit route was cordoned off from both sides with trucks to prevent elephants from straying.

Around 100 trained members of Hathi Mitra Dal and Haka Dal (Anti-Depredation Squad) from the Jashpur and Surguja forest divisions arrived at the site around 11.00 a.m. They prepared around 300 mashals for use in driving the elephants. At about noon, sugarcane, peepal and bargad leaves and jaggery were kept close to the elephants. One tusker chased the workers while they were keeping the food items inside the orchard. Few elephants came and sniffed the food items but did not consume them. By 1.00 p.m., some 3,000 people assembled on the rooftops of the nearby buildings to watch the operation. The police immediately asked them to vacate, since their noisy presence was making the elephants restless. Soon, the crowd obliged and the elephants became normal and started to consume bananas, bamboos, potatos, cabbages, papayas and other vegetables available in the orchard. The calf started suckling, and a few elephants began playing in the dust.

At around 4.00 p.m., a drone camera was flown over the elephant herd. Hearing its sound, the elephants became restless, and so it was immediately withdrawn. Elephants have an excellent sense of smell.[22] Around 4.30 p.m., they started to sniff the breeze by lifting their trunks upwards. It appeared that the elephants were ready to move, as they were trying to get a sense of direction. The forest team informed all those concerned that the drive operation would begin in another 30 minutes. The team leader gave a final briefing to the team members. At 5.30 p.m., around 100 members of the Haka Dal carrying mashals, flashing lights and beating drums started moving slowly towards the elephants from three sides. Drones were once again flown over the elephants; they began to move and, by 6:30 p.m., vacated the orchard and proceeded on the same route they had taken to enter the city. Around 7.00 p.m., the herd reached the Gangapur ward of the city. Despite repeated requests, people kept crowding on the rooftop of buildings on the intended movement path of the elephants.

Suddenly, someone lit fireworks, and the elephants panicked. They left the designated route and moved in a different direction, damaging the boundary walls of two nearby houses. Fortunately, no other untoward incident took place, and soon, the elephants reached Saad Bahar on the outskirts of the city. The time was 10.30 p.m., and the trained Haka Dal had successfully driven the elephants out of the city. But providence had other ideas. A young local boy who had crept along with the Haka Dal in excitement to show the moving elephants to his family members, made a video call, not realizing in the poor light of the mashals how close he had moved to the herd. He was immediately crushed to death by a member of the herd. What should have been an occasion to celebrate turned into one of grief, sorrow and despair.

On the night of 12 November 2017, Padmavati—a female elephant of the same Ashok Dal—accidentally fell into a 20-feet-deep dry open well while the herd raided the Nawadhakki village in Surajpur district. The group had damaged a kutcha house on one side of the dry well. The houseowner on the other side of the dry well used a high-beam torch to drive the group. Padmavati fell into the dry well while trying to chase the houseowner. She was rescued 42 hours after the accident, on 14 November 2017, with the help of cranes and an excavator, and brought to the Elephant Rescue and Rehabilitation Centre (ERRC) at Pingla. She had fractured both her hind legs and injured her spinal cord. A team of three veterinarians attended to her but were unable to save her despite their best efforts. She passed away on 17 November 2017 from heavy internal haemorrhage. Barely two weeks later, on 30 November 2017, Ashok Dal moved back to Jharkhand state, and it hasn't returned since then to Chhattisgarh.

Deaths from HECs continue to be the most important concern of the forest department. According to government records, 395 persons have been killed and 186 persons injured in human–elephant encounters over five years (2015 to 2020), while more than 28,740 ha of agricultural crops have been damaged. The elephants have also damaged houses and other properties, and negatively affected the emotional well-being of the local people. Human deaths mostly occur in crop fields, around houses and inside the forests. Dispersing elephants may initially be obligate crop raiders, but gradually, they become habitual crop raiders. Many families still live in kutcha houses close to their farms in poorly lit villages. When elephants move into these villages, it becomes difficult for the villagers to move their elderly and children to safer places. Therefore, they resort to driving the elephants away, exposing themselves to the risk of injury and even death. A significant number of casualties happen during such unplanned drives. Often these drives force elephants into newer areas, causing more harm than good. A significant number of deaths also occur from accidental or surprise encounters with elephants in and around the houses of the victim or in the forests during the collection of non-timber forest products.[23] Eighty-six elephants have also died during the same period in the state from causes like electrocution, disease, accidents and infighting.

There has been a marked shift in the approach to preventing and mitigating HEC after the formation of the Chhattisgarh state. The focus has shifted from the earlier undeclared policy of driving the elephants back to the states they come from to multiple strategies that include efforts to provide suitable habitat to the migrant elephants. The forest department has made concerted efforts, largely driven by site-specific factors, to prevent, minimize and resolve HEC and protect human life. These efforts could be broadly classified into three categories: retaining elephants within forest areas, community-based mitigation measures in human-use areas and dealing with emergencies.

Secure Forest Habitats

Chhattisgarh government has, on 15 September 2011, declared Tamor Pingla (608.53 sq. km), Semarsot (430.36 sq. km) and Badalkhol (104.45 sq. km) wildlife sanctuaries as part of an elephant reserve intending to provide suitable habitat for wild elephants. Recently, on 22 October 2021, another 1,995.48 sq. km forest area was declared as the Lemru Elephant Reserve. Availability of water has been improved through various measures in the forest occupancy areas that had the potential to retain elephants. Invasive alien species have been removed, and seeds of grasses and wild leguminous plants have been broadcasted to improve the availability of native palatable grasses. Rehabilitation of degraded forests (RDF) and assisted natural regeneration (ANR) have been implemented to restore native vegetation. Solar electric fences and elephant-proof trenches (EPTs) around the shelter/habitat of the elephants have also been created to retain elephants inside forests.

Community-Based Mitigation Measures

These include regular village and school-level meetings, messages on village walls, distribution of posters, flyers, leaflets and daily radio broadcasts to spread and sustain awareness about the precautions to be taken by the villagers against dispersing elephants. Storytelling, and folk dances and songs in the local language have been used effectively by the frontline forest department staff. Hathi Mitra Dal have been constituted in many vulnerable and affected villages. They have been trained and provided resources for taking measures against crop-raiding elephants. The villagers have also been trained to use high-beam torches, blinking lights, chilly smoke, loud noises, etc., to protect their crops and to drive elephants back into the forest areas. Anti-depredation squads equipped with vehicles and tools have been placed in the affected areas. All elephant groups are regularly monitored, and information about their presence and possible direction of movement is broadcast every evening through the All India Radio (AIR) stations. Information sharing with the villagers on WhatsApp about the elephant movement has been found to be very useful. Portable solar/battery-operated fences have also been found effective in blocking the entry of elephants into the villages.[24] Some villagers have also started using solar fences to protect their crops, though it is not very successful. The forest department pays compensation for crop damage to people affected by HEC.[25] Many villagers, though, feel that the compensation amount paid for elephant damage to their crops by the forest department is inadequate.[26]

Emergency Response Measures

Three male and two female elephants with the potential to become kumki were brought from Karnataka in 2018. Subsequently, they were trained as kumki to deal with emergencies. Kumki, mahouts and kawadis have been trained to monitor, capture, tranquillize, translocate and train elephants-in-conflict. They are now being used for tranquillizing and capturing elephants for radio-collaring. Pingla EERC was also established in the year 2018 for housing kumki and elephants-in-conflict that have become dangerous to human life.

The unfortunate reality is that all these measures have helped only to some extent in containing the HEC in Chhattisgarh. Providing effective protection to villagers' life and property from dispersing elephants remains a huge challenge for the forest department. The root cause of the problem lies in the degradation and fragmentation of forests in the home ranges of these dispersing elephants. Between 1930 and 2013, around 29.41 per cent of forest cover was lost in the elephant range of Central India. Forests in the central range were also the most fragmented among the elephant ranges in India.[27] The degradation and fragmentation of forests in Jharkhand and Odisha have resulted in the dispersal of elephants into other states. Both goals of economic development and long-term conservation of elephants could be simultaneously pursued only when economic development plans take into account the ecological needs of elephants, and elephant conservation plans take into account the needs of local people.[28]

On 25 October 2021, at around 5.00 a.m., another herd of 29 elephants came up to Smriti Van, which is 4 km away from Ambikapur city. The forest staff had been closely monitoring this herd. A large crowd gathered from the nearby villages to watch the elephants. A police force was immediately dispatched to control the crowd, and the forest department staff, with the help of Hathi Mitra Dal and some local people, managed to block the movement of elephants towards the city and succeeded in driving them back into the forests.

Rapid urbanization and the spread of cities into erstwhile wilderness areas is a readymade recipe for an increase in human–animal conflicts (HAC). Not just wild elephants but instances of sloth bears, leopards, gaurs and hyenas entering cities are being reported. So, unless urgent steps are taken to protect wildlife habitats and corridors for wildlife movement, and prevent rapid land-use changes, future scenarios can only be grim.

Notes

1. The author thanks Prabhat K. Dubey, Chudamani Singh, Mohammad Shahid, Prem Kumar and Himanshu Gupta for sharing information about the operation to drive elephants away from the Ambikapur city.
2. Elephant groups in the state of Chhattisgarh are given names, like the 'Ashok Dal', for ease of recognition, tracking and communication about their movement in the state.
3. 'Top Metropolitan/Urban Regions of India by 2011 Population Census', Census 2011, https://bit.ly/2UwHH5M. Accessed on 4 July 2022.
4. Fazl, Abul, *The Ain-I-Akbari of Abul Fazl 'Allami*, Translated by H. Blochmann, Vol. 1, Gorgias Press, 2010.
5. Brandar, A.A. Dunbar, *Wild Animals in Central India*, Natraj Publishers, 2009.
6. Madhya Pradesh, Directorate Of Gazetteers, *Gazetteer of India: Madhya Pradesh State, Surguja District*, Director Gazetteers, 1989.
7. Olivier, Robert, 'Distribution and Status of the Asian Elephant',

Oryx, Vol. 14, No. 4, November 1978, pp. 379–424, https://doi.org/10.1017/S003060530001601X. Accessed on 4 July 2022.

8. Singh, R.K., *Elephants in Exile. A Rapid Assessment of the Human-Elephant Conflict in Chhattisgarh*, Occasional Report No. 5, Wildlife Trust of India, 2007, https://bit.ly/3Apr7gP. Accessed on 4 July 2022; Tiwari, Sandeep K., et al., 'Elephant Corridors of North-Western India', *Right of Passage: Elephant Corridors of India,* Sumanta Kundu et al. (eds.), 2nd edn., Wildlife Trust of India, 2017.
9. Sukumar, Raman, *The Living Elephants: Evolutionary Ecology, Behaviour, and Conservation*, Oxford University Press, 2003.
10. Mishra, D.C., *The Drought of 1987: Response and Management*, Department of Agriculture and Cooperation, Ministry of Agriculture, Government of India, New Delhi, 1990.
11. 'Physical Resources | LAND', Government of Chhattisgarh, https://bit.ly/3R5LLZf. Accessed on 1 July 2022.
12. Payne, Katharine B., et al., 'Infrasonic Calls of the Asian Elephant (Elephas Maximus)', *Behavioral Ecology and Sociobiology*, Vol. 18, No. 4, February 1986, pp. 297–301, https://doi.org/10.1007/BF00300007. Accessed on 4 July 2022.
13. O'Connell-Rodwell, C.E., et al., 'Seismic Properties of Asian Elephant *(Elephas Maximus)* Vocalizations and Locomotion', *The Journal of the Acoustical Society of America*, Vol. 108, No. 6, December 2000, pp. 3066–72, https://doi.org/10.1121/1.1323460. Accessed on 4 July 2022.
14. *Elephant Census 2017*, Chhattisgarh State, Forest and Climate Change Department, Government of Chhattisgarh, 2017.
15. Map 1 prepared by Swaminathan S., Wildlife SOS, New Delhi. This pictorial representation of some of the states of India is neither purported to be correct nor authentic as per the Survey of India directives.
16. William, Amrithraj Christie, et al., 'Ranging and Habitat Selection by Asian Elephants (Elephas Maximus) in Rajaji National Park, North-West India', *Journal of the Bombay Natural History Society*,

Vol. 105, No. 1, 2008, pp. 24–33, https://bit.ly/3Ob2DuN. Accessed on 4 July 2022.

17. N., Baskaran, et al., 'The Home Range of Elephants in the Nilgiri Biosphere Reserve, South India', *A Week with Elephants*, edited by H.S. Datye and J. C. Daniel, Bombay Natural History Society, 1995, pp. 296–313.
18. Nigam, P., et al., *Conservation Management of Elephants in Chhattisgarh: Capacity Building Initiative on the Dispersal and Ranging Patterns of Elephants for Effective Management of Human-Elephant Interactions*, Project Report 3 (2019–2020), Wildlife Institute of India and Chhattisgarh Forest Department, 2021, p. 67.
19. Swaminathan, S., et al., *Technical Report on Radio-Collaring and Early Warning Alert System of Human-Elephant Conflict Mitigation Project in Chhattisgarh State (2018–2021)*, Wildlife SOS, p. 129.
20. Nigam, P., et al., *Conservation Management of Elephants in Chhattisgarh: Capacity Building Initiative on the Dispersal and Ranging Patterns of Elephants for Effective Management of Human-Elephant Interactions*, Project Report 3 (2019–2020), Wildlife Institute of India and Chhattisgarh Forest Department, 2021, p. 67.
21. Personal communication with A. Desai on 25 May 2018.
22. Sanderson, George P., *Thirteen Years Among the Wild Beasts of India: Their Haunts and Habits from Personal Observations: With an Account of the Modes and Capturing and Taming Elephants*, W.H. Allen, 1879.
23. Pandav, B., et al., *Second Annual Report: Conservation Management of Elephants in Chhattisgarh: Capacity Building Initiative on the Dispersal and Ranging Patterns of Elephants for Effective Management of Human-Elephant Interactions*, Wildlife Institute of India, 2019.
24. *Proceedings of the Second Meeting and Field Visit of Central Project Elephant Monitoring Committee (CEPMC) Held at Surguja-Jashpur Elephant Reserve, Chhattisgarh on 29th-30th*

June 2019, MoEFCC, 7 August 2019, https://bit.ly/3uqEGZx. Accessed on 4 July 2022.

25. *Guidelines for Management of Human-Elephant Conflicts*, MoEF, 6 October 2017, https://bit.ly/3yDwuHN. Accessed on 4 July 2022.
26. Swaminathan, S., et al., *Technical Report on Radio-Collaring and Early Warning Alert System of Human-Elephant Conflict Mitigation Project in Chhattisgarh State (2018–2021)*, Wildlife SOS, p. 129.
27. Padalia, Hitendra, et al., 'Assessment of Historical Forest Cover Loss and Fragmentation in Asian Elephant Ranges in India', *Environmental Monitoring and Assessment*, Vol. 191, No. 3, January 2020, p. 802, https://doi.org/10.1007/s10661-019-7696-5. Accessed on 4 July 2022.
28. 'The Asian Elephant Conservation: A Global Strategy', *Gajah*, Vol. 18, pp. 21–39, https://bit.ly/3OJyQup. Accessed on 1 July 2022.

SURVIVAL: THE EXISTENTIAL THREAT FACING THE GREAT INDIAN BUSTARD

SUMIT DOOKIA

It is a stately bird with 'Indian' in its name. Once a strong candidate for becoming India's national bird, it lost the race to the peacock, according to some sources, as its name could be misread or mispronounced! A pity, actually, for without the status, it soon fell into relative oblivion and now struggles for survival.

Yes, I am talking about the great Indian bustard (GIB; *Ardeotis nigriceps*), which, at one time, was found in thousands all over the subcontinent, except the Northeast and the Himalayan belt.

But today, its fate hangs precariously in the balance.

Alarm

One winter morning in 2017, I received a call that a male GIB was lying dead below some power lines in a field near Khetolai village, Jaisalmer, Rajasthan. I alerted my volunteers to reach the spot quickly, take stock of the remains of the bird and inform forest officials about the death of yet another member of this fast-disappearing species. This was the third reported death of a GIB between May and December 2017 from three different locations in Jaisalmer. The death set alarm bells ringing in the GIB conservation fraternity. There were then just two high-power lines in the area, which also proved fatal for this unfortunate bird.

Four more GIB deaths were reported due to the power lines from Ramdeora in June 2018, Dholiya in November 2018, Rasla village in September 2020 and Parevar in May 2022. There may have been many more deaths of these tall birds that went unnoticed and unreported, but these seven verified deaths at different locations proved that the dwindling GIB population was facing the biggest threat to its existence from killer power lines in its home territory. With the desert areas of Rajasthan having the only viable breeding population of GIBs left in the world, so many deaths pointed to the urgent need to give the highest priority to saving the remaining birds.

My Initiation

Since childhood, I was fascinated by the natural world around me and started to learn about plants and animals in my vicinity from my zoologist father, who retired as the principal of a government college. My interest in wildlife grew, and I chose zoology over botany and chemistry for my master's degree from Jai Narain Vyas University, Jodhpur. There, I attended a talk by Dr A.R. Rahmani, then director of the Bombay Natural History Society (BNHS), on the wildlife of the Thar Desert, and the GIB and its status. I also received a large poster of the GIB from Dr Rahmani, as we chatted over tea. I pasted that poster in my hostel room wall and waited for an opportunity to see the bird in real life. Though it was the 'state bird' of Rajasthan and known locally as *godawan*, I had never seen it.

After completing my master's in zoology, I wrote to Dr Rahmani, expressing interest in joining any research project on the GIB. I was overjoyed when Dr Rahmani wrote back, encouraging me to keep my interest in the bird alive. I took his advice to heart, although I researched the ecology of the chinkara or the Indian gazelle, the state animal of Rajasthan, for my doctoral thesis. I stayed in touch with Dr Rahmani, keeping him updated of my interest in a research project on GIB conservation. In the winter of 2000, I was invited by Dr Rahmani to join him as a volunteer on a three-week survey on the GIB in western Rajasthan. I was elated. I packed my bags and took a bus to Bikaner to join the 10-member survey team under his leadership.

The next day, at 6.00 a.m. we were all in the field and started looking for evidence of the GIB in remote areas of the Bikaner district. On the first day, I learnt to identify and detect the signs of the Macqueen's bustard (better known as houbara in those days) and collected three feathers. One feather is still pinned on the board in my office and another inside the *Birds of Indian Subcontinent* (Oxford University Press, 1998) by Tim Inskipp, Richard Grimmett and Carol Inskipp. On the third day, while still in the Bikaner district, I spotted two large birds with long white neck, and I shouted in joy, asking Dr Rahmani if these were the GIBs. As he rushed towards me, the birds started to fly, and he confirmed my suspicion. These were my first two GIB sightings, and I was mesmerized by their size, wing span and the buzzing sound of their wings as they took flight over my head.

Midday sessions were well spent in nearby villages, where our team organized an awareness campaign, and I played a major role in translating into the local language almost everything that was written about GIB in the English and Hindi brochures that we carried. Dr Rahmani appreciated this and, over the next few days, he gave me the responsibility to translate all the awareness-generation sessions.

Our mornings and evenings were devoted to foot patrolling in the desert country to spot any evidence of the GIB or the Macqueen's bustard. These survey trips were tiring but very interesting. There was so much to learn from Dr Rahmani.

The Bird

In 2011, the International Union for Conservation of Nature (IUCN) listed the GIB as 'critically endangered'. It is a Schedule I protected species nationally under the Wild Life (Protection) Act, 1972. The GIB is one of the heaviest flying birds on the planet and is endemic to the Indian subcontinent. Males and females can be distinguished by size and the colour of their feathers. Adult males stand as tall as 122 cm and weigh 11–15 kg. Adult females reach around 92 cm and weigh 4–7 kg. The plumage of the GIB is mostly white and brown, with a darker black feather cap. Males can be distinguished from females due to their thicker neck and black eyebrows. It's a terrestrial bird with only three toes and roosts on the ground. During the breeding season, the adult males select elevated gravelly mounds (probably to become visible from far away) to display their attractive male plumage. They spend almost the whole day making deep humming sounds through their inflated gular sac or pouch. They fill up air in their gular sac, and walk gently to display and attract breeding females. Females lay a single egg on the bare ground and incubate alone. Chicks are precocial and walk and feed just after hatching. The breeding season generally coincides with the monsoons from mid-June to October-end. Occasionally, the macho, enticing males can be seen in cloudy weather in the winter too.

Historically, the GIB was distributed across the northwestern states, from Punjab, Uttar Pradesh to Odisha in the east and the entire Deccan Plateau up to Tamil Nadu. A bird of arid and semi-arid open grasslands, it used to be found in patches in as many as 11 states. Its stronghold was the Thar Desert in the northwest and the Deccan Plateau of peninsular India. Today, its population is confined mainly to western Rajasthan and the Rann of Kutch region of Gujarat.

After working with Dr Rahmani, I did many opportunistic

surveys in western Rajasthan for different wildlife species and, in 2006, I started a proper scientific expedition with my own team of friends cum field biologists. With two small grants in 2006 and 2010 from the Oriental Bird Club (UK), I did surveys for the GIB and other birds in Jaisalmer. It laid the foundation for all my community conservation work, which I am currently doing in the same landscape. During a survey in Jaisalmer, from a vantage point, on a single day, I saw 16 GIBs, including nine males in full courting display and one nest with a female keeping an eye on it. It is a sight I will not forget in my lifetime. Over the years, I have built a strong network of local friends, community volunteers and field biologists, who are constantly observing and monitoring many wildlife species with me.

Dr Gobind Sagar Bhardwaj, then chief conservator of forests (CCF) (Wildlife), Jodhpur division, and Mr Anoop K.R., deputy conservator of forests (DCF) and director, Desert National Park, helped me channelize my energies and gave full support to start an organized naturalist training programme for youth of the villages of the Desert National Park. This was organized from 2013 to 2016. I had many long discussions with both of them, in the field as well as in their offices, on the matter. This allowed youngsters to make some money as well as develop ownership of the ecosystem of their state bird. The forest department selected some 25 youth, and we (a team of half a dozen subject experts) were invited to train them in the field as well as in classrooms on nature-based rural entrepreneurship. A few of the more serious youngsters are currently working in the Jaisalmer district and escorting many national as well as international visitors interested in birding and landscape photography. It is truly heart-warming to see these tourism entrepreneurs doing well. They are well paid, respected by the tourists and have acquired a social status in their community.

I have received great support in all this from my wife, Dr Mamta Rawat, and other colleagues. Her non-government organization (NGO), the Ecology, Rural Development & Sustainability (ERDS) Foundation which currently works in the entire GIB distribution area of Jaisalmer, has helped in bringing enabling systems in place. The ERDS Foundation works on various community issues, but the GIB remains its central concern.

Community Involvement

Though I hail from western Rajasthan and am conversant with its culture, language and dialect, it took me a few years to make my people understand the value of these natural resources in their life and economy. In 2015, I stopped projecting myself as a scientist or an academician in front of the people in the GIB landscape. I became a part of them through frequent visits, regular meetings and personal interactions. The people of the desert areas are straightforward, and the local economy revolves around the vast landscape of the Thar Desert. It also serves as the pasture land for grazing their livestock—camel, sheep and goats. While it took me years to make them realize the value of the GIB, but within months, they understood that a reduction in pastureland would hamper their earning capacity and impact rural economics. I had to use a somewhat convoluted approach to convey that pasturelands are important for their livelihood and the existence of wildlife and the GIB.

In the last six years, I have expanded my work in the GIB landscape and picked up many community-centric issues. I campaigned to give legal status to the *orans*, the sacred groves of western Rajasthan. In the last two years, with help from Indian National Trust for Art and Cultural Heritage (INTACH) and ERDS Foundation, my team has documented more than 100 such sites. The local youth organized foot marches to district administration offices and submitted memorandums for recognition of oran lands in revenue records. In the last six years, most of the oran lands have been home to the GIB. Ironically, many of these oran landscapes are classified as a wasteland in the revenue records and earmarked as land banks for development work, such as the establishment of renewable energy parks.

Oran: The GIB Home

Oran is a sacred landscape delineated many generations, if not centuries, ago by the people of the area. Nobody knows the date when orans came into existence in western Rajasthan. Almost every oran has its own local deity, a small place of worship with waterbodies surrounded by the uncultivated land. People from the surrounding areas worship at the oran and follow the traditional customs. Every oran has its own history, surviving through stories and folk songs. There is no written law on the management of these oran lands. There are no gates or locks outside orans. The temple remains open, and no theft happens.

Uncultivated, these landscapes hold rich vegetation and are a repository of medicinal plants, herbs, shrubs and trees. This rich flora supports a large number of animals. Dense vegetation and abundant wildlife can be found in the Shree Degray Mataji Oran (Rasla–Sanwta), Shree Bhadariya Rai Oran (Bhadariya–Dholiya), Shree Dungar Peerji Oran (Mokla), all in Jaisalmer; and the Shree Viratra Mataji Oran (Chauhtan–Barmer). The oran differs from area to area and many of them figure in the revenue records as Khasra Oran and are properly numbered, while many do not figure in revenue records, for which there is a constant struggle between the local people and the revenue authorities. In 2018, the Supreme Court directed the Rajasthan government to designate and notify all orans/rudh/devbanis as deemed forests and to protect them. This order is yet to be implemented.

Overall, there is an ongoing loss of native biodiversity that affects local communities and long-ranging species like the GIB and chinkara in western Rajasthan.

The current challenge is how to save the existing habitat, where the GIB roams freely. The local communities are in full support to save these oran landscapes. If these can be saved from the so-called developmental projects, the future of the GIB can be assured.

Lessons and Learnings

In 20 years of fieldwork in the GIB landscape, I have seen the local extinction of this heaviest-flying bird from almost 80 per cent of its traditional home in the Thar Desert. In 1981, Rajasthan notified 3,124 sq. km of Barmer and Jaisalmer districts as the Desert National Park to conserve the biodiversity of the hot desert of India. Till 2006–2007, this area harboured the largest population of GIBs. After 2007, there was hardly any reported sighting of GIB from the Barmer part of the Desert National Park, which is almost equally divided into both districts. When all the GIB sightings, sourced from forest department records and reported by locals, are mapped up to 2010, it is evident that the GIB is not using the Barmer area. From 2010 to 2015, GIB sightings were largely restricted around Sam-Sudasari part of Desert National Park. The final notification of the surrounding areas of the national park is still awaited. With large landholdings in the park under the state revenue department or the local people, and no final notification of its boundaries, it is currently managed as the Desert Wildlife Sanctuary, although it is called the Desert National Park.

The present distribution of GIB in western Rajasthan is in two almost equal populations in and around the Sam-Sudasari area and around the Ramdeora-Pokhran field firing range. The Pokhran field firing range is under the control of the Indian

Army and is being used for combat training. The GIB breeds on both sides of Jaisalmer and, after the breeding season, roams the vast desert landscape dominated by local communities and used as pastureland but recorded in revenue records as wastelands. Surprisingly, till now, only 20 per cent of the area of GIB distribution is under the administrative control of the state forest department.

During this seasonal movement, these birds have to cross various renewable (wind and solar) energy project sites and their transmission lines. As per a long-term study by the Wildlife Institute of India (WII), around 15–18 GIBs die annually after collision with these high-power lines. We have documented seven GIB deaths from 2016 to 2022.

The current GIB conservation scenario is very complex. We have lost almost 90 per cent of the global population. Now, around 130 birds are roaming freely in five Indian states. Over 100 birds said to be in Rajasthan are found in Jaisalmer district and in only two locations. This is the only viable breeding population that has the potential to be revived. On an average, some 20 plus females are laying eggs annually. Since this is a K-selected species, it means that chicks spend about two years with the mother, forcing mama GIBs to lay eggs in alternate years.

Ex Situ Conservation: The GIB Hatchery Project

As the population of GIB and other bustard species, i.e. lesser florican and Bengal florican, was constantly decreasing in the country, in 2013, the Ministry of Environment and Forests (MoEF), which was later renamed the Ministry of Environment, Forest and Climate Change (MoEFCC), decided to initiate a long-term population recovery plan. A detailed guideline and action plan was prepared, and all range states were asked to implement it. The WII has been involved in a GIB population recovery project since 2014. It initiated landscape-level population estimation surveys and released annual population figures after a thorough grid-based survey and application of statistical models. In 2019, a tripartite agreement was signed between the Rajasthan government, the WII and the MoEFCC to expedite the conservation project and initiate captive breeding of the GIB.

The ex situ conservation cum hatchery unit was constructed in the Sam forest chowki of the Desert National Park.[1] A dedicated team of young researchers and veterinary doctors (trained by a team of scientists and experts of the International Fund for Houbara Conservation [IFHC], Abu Dhabi) have been stationed here since 2019, and they are collecting eggs from the field and artificially incubating them in the hatchery. Each and every chick is reared in full human exposure to prepare them for the next step of captive breeding. As per documents available in the public domain, a minimum of 25 such hand-reared chicks, known as the F1 generation, will be allowed to mate, and the next F2 generation will be taken for artificial insemination and other intricacies of the captive breeding programme. After a minimum of two generations, the chicks born can be released to augment the wild population. The time frame for the project is 25 years, from 2019 to 2044.

This goalpost is far away, and my apprehensions are about the continuing availability of the wild habitat. How can this ambitious project succeed if no habitat is left for the GIB?

As an independent researcher and consistent landscape-level observer, my main concern is about the conversion of natural landscapes into renewable energy projects. In the last three years, the pace of land conversion has surged in areas of GIB sighting. The state government should travel the extra mile to save its state bird. The majestic bird with just a few breeding females, which was struggling to survive, has fallen victim to the green and clean energy targets of the Government of India.

Ironically, the same government is engaged in a 25-year-long captive breeding and population recovery project!

My main concern is: where will these captive-bred birds be released after almost two decades? There is ambiguity in the promises on paper and actions on the ground. World over, renewable energy is being labelled as 'clean' energy, and our laws exempt it from mandatory environment impact assessment (EIA) studies. Being a desert ecosystem, western Rajasthan has hardly any notified forestland and only one protected area (PA), which it is still struggling to get notified as a national park. The process of land allotment and conversion in the name of green energy, correlated with the loss of pasture land for local communities and daily threats to their centuries-old sacred places have disturbed the local population. The commissioning of solar parks is being opposed in various places. Above all, the GIB is being neglected in its struggle for survival. A sorry fate indeed for a bird that once contented to be the national bird of India!

The Supreme Court Takes Notice

As a wildlife conservation biologist, working almost independently with the support of a few volunteers of the ERDS Foundation, I am extremely concerned about these developments in the GIB habitat. Between 2016 and 2019, I pleaded strongly to save this bird at every meeting I was invited to on GIB conservation by the WII, Rajasthan government and MoEFCC.

The PIL filed by Dr M.K. Ranjitsinh and others in the Supreme Court in 2019 is an important step in the GIB conservation movement.[2] It seeks to keep safe the entire GIB habitat (beyond the PA boundary) for bustard survival. After receiving the court-designated committee report, on 19 April 2021, two demarcated habitats were decided—the GIB 'priority' area and GIB 'potential' area. The GIB priority area is where the current GIB population roams freely, which includes the

Desert National Park. The GIB potential area is the entire GIB habitat where there has been sporadic sighting of GIB. The priority area was to have no new overhead power lines.

The seven recorded GIB deaths from 2017 to 2022 in Jaisalmer were just beneath the high-energy transmission lines. The WII landscape-level bird mortality survey in the entire GIB habitat showed that more than 80,000 bird deaths of all kinds and the 15–18 GIB deaths in a year were due to the power lines. The court also suggested that power lines in the potential area should be equipped with 'bird diverters'. The bird diverter is a light-reflecting device placed on wires of high-energy power lines so birds can detect these linear structures before coming too close and bypass them entirely. There are quite a few good examples in the world of the efficacy of these bird diverters. With these devices, the mortality of GIBs can be greatly reduced.

The court said that since the GIB is a long-ranging bird, a large area should be earmarked for its safety. This is a point of conflict with the state eager to push 'ease of doing business' in return for large sums of revenue promised by investors. On the other hand, it is a prime duty of the state (both Union and state government) to save the critically endangered bird, left with only one breeding population in Jaisalmer. This court decision is yet to be implemented on the ground in letter and spirit. In December 2021, a plea was filed jointly by the MoEFCC, Ministry of Power and the Ministry of New and Renewable Energy in the Supreme Court to give some sort of relaxation in the name of India's target to achieve installed renewable energy capacity (excluding large hydro) of 175 GW by 2022 and 450 GW by 2030. Jaisalmer is identified as one of the best sites for tapping solar and wind power.

Whenever there is a discussion about the survival of GIB, it is argued that India has made international commitments, including The Paris Agreement of 2015, for transition to non-fossil fuels and emission reduction. But India is also a signatory to the Convention on Migratory Species (CMS), and during the CMS Conference of Parties (COP13) meeting hosted by India in Gandhinagar in February 2020, the GIB was the mascot. With a lot of lobbying and negotiations, India was able to get this bird added into Appendix I for the conservation of its migratory population.[3] India has also signed a few more very important international agreements, like the Convention on Biological Diversity (CBD), and has the responsibility to protect this critically endangered bird as well as its habitat. So, India has international commitments that are not only limited to emission reduction but also towards the protection of migratory species and its own biological diversity!

It is very unfortunate that two good practices needed so much for a 'healthy' world, namely safeguarding threatened wildlife species and promoting renewable sources of energy, have come to grief at their point of intersection. This need not be, and measures can and must be found to prevent any further conflict.

GIB Extinction Must be Averted

This is a keystone species of the arid and semi-arid grasslands of the Indian subcontinent. Once found in 11 states, it is now barely visible in five, and among these five states, Rajasthan holds 100 per cent of the breeding and viable population. Scientific evidence shows that GIB populations saw a commendable revival in the 1980s and 1990s. Many range states took policy-level conservation measures and notified a series of PAs for the GIB. These included the Desert National Park (Rajasthan), Lala–Parjan Bustard Wildlife Sanctuary or Kutch Bustard Wildlife Sanctuary (Gujarat), Karera Wildlife Sanctuary and Ghatigaon Wildlife Sanctuary (Madhya Pradesh), Great Indian Bustard Sanctuary (Maharashtra), Ranebennur Wildlife

Sanctuary (Karnataka), and Rollapadu Wildlife Sanctuary (Andhra Pradesh). But the decline of its population did not stop, and now it faces extinction yet again.

According to the noted naturalist Dharmakumarsinhji, the population of the GIB was 1,269 in 1969. A rigorous landscape-level survey done by the WII in 2018 showed that this number had declined to 150, and in 2020, the Supreme Court was told by the WII it had dropped further to 130. More than 90 per cent of this population is in Jaisalmer. This was clearly alarming. There are just a few bustards in Maharashtra, Karnataka and Andhra Pradesh, and just four females in the Naliya area of Bhuj in Gujarat. Can states continue to turn a blind eye to the conservation of the GIB outside the Desert National Park?

The species was recategorized from 'endangered' to 'critically endangered' in 2011 by the IUCN, and since then, a decade has passed, but the conservation status of this magnificent flying bird still spells gloomy. Once, flocks of 20–30 individuals were a common sight in the non-breeding season. Now their sightings are very rare, except in Jaisalmer. The population can still recover if its habitat remains undisturbed. This is a big challenge in front of all of us. In an era of technology, scientific knowledge and a trained workforce, we cannot blame anyone else but ourselves if—God forbid—this magnificent flying creature goes extinct in front of our own eyes...

Notes

1. *Factual Report on the Great Indian Bustard Recovery Program*, MoEFCC, 11 July 2019, https://bit.ly/3o6Ngcc. Accessed on 13 July 2022.
2. *Dr M.K. Ranjitsinh and Others vs Union of India and Others*, Supreme Court of India, https://bit.ly/3yCqzBG. Accessed on 14 July 2022.

3. Government of the Republic of India, *Proposal for the Inclusion of the Great Indian Bustard (*Ardeotis Nigriceps*) in Appendix I of the Convention*, Convention on Migratory Species, 25 September 2019, https://bityl.co/D7KS. Accessed on 7 July 2022.

FOUR CONSERVANCIES SILENTLY PROTECTING WILDLIFE IN RAJASTHAN

ISHAN DHAR, DHARMENDRA KHANDAL AND ADITYA 'DICKY' SINGH

It is unusual to find successful wildlife conservation models outside of the purview of state forest departments in India. While narratives of local communities playing a crucial role in protection, such as the Bishnois, are ever-present in the discourse, rarely do we ever hear of private landowners contributing to the protection of biodiversity and the restoration of habitats.

However, there are four such cases in Rajasthan. In a more 'global' parlance, these small private properties might be considered 'conservancies'. Each parcel of land represents a different landscape type and economic model, and plays host to a diverse array of key species. Yet, there are some common denominators behind the overwhelming success of each of these examples. The diversity in ownership is also very significant, for they are owned by private citizens, ecotourism enterprises and community-run charitable organizations.

The importance of protecting small patches of habitat for the conservation of biodiversity is very well understood, especially in extensively modified landscapes such as those found in Rajasthan. In some areas where there has been significant habitat fragmentation, small pockets of habitat are all that remains, further necessitating their protection. In other cases, the small patches have an absence of the forces driving the extinction of species elsewhere, thus turning them into small semi-isolated biodiversity hotspots. They can also serve as nodal points for restoring species and entire landscapes by providing connectivity in highly modified environments.[1]

Discoveries on the Trail of a Man-Eater: The Badlav Conservancy and Karauli Gaushala

One morning in July 2019, just as an old woman was preparing to do her morning ablutions, a young male tiger, named T-104, killed her at the opening of a ravine in Kundera. T-104 then dragged her away to a nearby field and fed on her body briefly before he was tranquillized, radio-collared and moved back into the Ranthambore National Park by the forest department. Not long after this tragic episode, he was once again discovered outside the park. This time, without his radio collar, he spent days on a stretch of private land bordering the national park. The area had enough forest cover, access to natural prey and enough distance from human beings for a conflict tiger to localize without putting itself or any humans in any immediate danger. This land belongs to us, my wife Poonam Singh and I (Aditya Singh), which we bought in 2000. It was then 35 acres of denuded land abutting the Ranthambore National Park in the vicinity of the village called Badlav. The land was formerly owned by subsistence farmers who had given up on the land producing any crop of value. That very same year, I discovered evidence of the presence of a tiger on the purchased land.

Over the last 21 years, we have fenced the land, thus protecting it from grazing by marauding cattle, eradicated exotic flora, and even the invasive flora such as babul (*Acacia nilotica*) is beginning to die out on its own. The land, thus, slowly began to restore itself back to a quintessential example of the Aravalli landscape replete with its own waterholes, after some strategic relandscaping by us, which allowed the land to retain water for long periods of time. Ecologically speaking, the land is now an outward projection of the Ranthambore Tiger Reserve, which has acted as its 'seed bank', and the natural flora occurring in the reserve has slowly begun reclaiming the land with the natural dispersal of seeds over the years. Along with such species regeneration, the land also acts as an unofficial protective buffer area or protective layer for the reserve. The land now even has tigers visit it for considerable periods, especially during the summer months, as T-104 did.

The habitat is, therefore, unsurprisingly typical of the Ranthambore which is famous for its tigers and stunning landscapes, where history and natural history blend seamlessly. It is the best place for sighting tigers in the wild because it is the world's driest and hottest tiger habitat. Few water sources and sparse vegetation increase the chances of sighting tigers, making Ranthambore amongst the most popular destination on India's tiger tourism map. However, as tourism flourished and facilities catering to tourists, such as hotels, quickly developed far away from the peripheries of the reserve on stretches like Ranthambore Road, a tremendous opportunity to develop pastoral and agricultural lands bordering the reserve in a sustainable manner, like Badlav farm, where they could possibly benefit the tiger reserve, was irrevocably lost.

The forest type of Ranthambore is the tropical dry deciduous type that is dominated by dhonk (*Anogeissus pendula*) trees. It is, in fact, because dhonk is such perfect 'fodder' that Ranthambore comes under severe pressure from 250 pastoral villages, yet no less-damaging alternative was ever sought for these communities with any serious intent.

Along with fencing, a team of guards from the local community was also employed to ensure the protection of wildlife on the property. Besides tigers, leopards, nilgai, small mammals and birds are also routinely found on site. We (Aditya and Poonam) haven't initiated any ecotourism practices on this property yet, and therefore, it has not yielded us any financial returns.

Unfortunately, T-104's bloody trail of destruction did not end in the Badlav Conservancy. Despite being a known man-killer, T-104 was captured and released by the forest department after claiming a second victim in August 2019. He killed his third and final victim the following month in September, in Karauli, before he was finally captured and relegated to captivity for good. While the forest department cited the National Tiger Conservation Authority (NTCA) as the reason behind releasing T-104 the second time, this was likely to be a populist decision made from the fear of misguided online activism, the likes of which was seen when the male tiger T-24 was similarly rendered into captivity in 2015. However, this decision by the forest department cost at least two innocent lives and serves as a stark reminder of just how grave the consequences of populist decision-making in wildlife management can be.

Ironically, it is T-104 who led us to arguably our most astonishing example of habitat recovery. Astonishing because neither wildlife conservationists nor a scientist would normally associate a gaushala with the restoration of habitat! What is even more remarkable is that this parcel was completely denuded of vegetation because of illegal mining, and yet, had recovered within three to four years! The land was the site of an illegal stone quarry, and the entire layer of topsoil had been destroyed as the result of years of dynamite explosions. So, how on earth did a gaushala enable a landscape damaged by mining to recover so quickly to become a vibrant dhonk forest within such a short period of time?

The gaushala was discovered by the village wildlife volunteers of the non-governmental organization (NGO) Tiger Watch during the pursuit of the T-104 in Karauli. T-104 happened to stop and stay within the gaushala spanning a 5–6 sq. km stretch abutting the Kailadevi Wildlife Sanctuary that adjoins Ranthambore Tiger Reserve. The suitable cover the area provided, both in terms of tree cover and undergrowth, and the source of food in the form of cattle (of which he killed several), proved irresistible to the marauding tiger, which stayed on the gaushala land for several days. Thus, it served the same purpose for T-104 as the Badlav Conservancy once did earlier.

It was discovered that once the land was reconstituted as a gaushala some six years ago, the fodder-fed cattle slowly began to fertilize the land and also acted as seed dispersers, allowing the land to naturally restore itself to its original state by slowly providing the requisite amount of added biomass. Eventually, controlled grazing and a fair degree of protection allowed the progression of what appeared to be a miraculous case of habitat restoration in record time. Thus, this particular parcel of land has the potential to be a nodal point for not only species recovery but even landscape restoration, considering the degree of anthropogenic pressure on the Kailadevi Wildlife Sanctuary.

The neglected Kailadevi Wildlife Sanctuary is the main feature of the Vindhyan part of the Ranthambore Tiger Reserve. The sanctuary is mostly a combination of dangs or khos. The gorges are also perennial water sources for animals and Tiger Watch has ascertained that they have excellent potential to sustain growing populations of tigers. The dang, however, are also home to the Indian wolf (*Canis lupus pallipes)* and are among the finest locations to observe them in India.

This unintentional intervention also compels us to closely re-examine grazing as an activity. It should be noted that this gaushala does not allow lopping. Grazing alone does not appear to be inherently harmful to a landscape. Rather, it can also be a model for habitat restoration, particularly in areas where the land has been razed by highly destructive activities such as mining. The cattle need not necessarily be a permanent fixture in the post-recovery phase, as alternative uses for such lands can be sought. In addition, the presence of carnivores like leopards and a now-growing population of tigers in Kailadevi and Sarmathura (Dholpur district) also ensure that the numbers of cattle do not become unsustainable. In the nearby Kuno National Park in Madhya Pradesh, the population of feral cattle is actually on the decline, thanks to the depredation of calves by leopards.

Sanctum in the Desert: The Shri Krishna Samiti Gaushala

While the gaushala in Karauli has proven to be an innovative and effective way of restoring habitat that has undergone incredible environmental abuse in the form of mining and, by extension, the protection of biodiversity, there is another gaushala in Rajasthan, which has been doing the latter for a much longer time.

The Shri Samiti Gaushala in the town of Ramgarh Shekhawati in the Sikar district has protected a key desert ecosystem for 150 years. What is equally impressive is that this could be considered a local community-run intervention several years before 'community-led conservation' became a buzzword in environmental circles.

Surprisingly, the area is home to species like the desert cat (*Felis silvestris*) and desert fox (*Vulpes pusilla*). It is also a haven for migratory birds, particularly raptors, of which 20 species can be observed here. The area is particularly noted for the lagger falcon (*Falco jugger*) sightings in Rajasthan. The land also has the added distinction of being a herpetologist's delight, with both the red-spotted royal snake (*Spalerosophis arenarius*) and the Sindh awl-headed snake (*Lytorhyncus paradoxus*) occurring here.

The area is approximately 7–8 sq. km and is guarded by a group of cattle guards employed by the Shri Krishna Samiti, who do not follow a codified set of rules as such but an age-old unwritten understanding regarding just how grazing is to be conducted in the area. Buffalos are not permitted to graze, for instance, for they only have commercial value and not religious value like cows. As we saw earlier in Karauli, lopping is also strictly forbidden. The resulting flora to be found here is the kumtha (*Acacia Senegal*), rohida (*Prosopis cineraria*) and khejri (*Tecomella undulata*). Thus, the micromanagement of grazing rights has afforded this parcel of land the requisite degree of protection to serve as a habitat patch for some key desert species.

The biggest threat to this land is the ever-expanding town slowly starting to encircle it; however, equally valid is the strong civic sense of duty that some of the inhabitants harbour towards it.

Ramathra Fort Conservancy: Traditional Custodians in the Twenty-First Century

If the Ranthambore National Park is the tiger tourism capital of the world, and the main focus is the Ranthambore Tiger Reserve, the Kailadevi Wildlife Sanctuary is, in many ways, the poor cousin of the Ranthambore Tiger Reserve family. Neglected by tourists and authorities alike, it is only the most intrepid who ever dared to venture out here.

However, this sorry state of affairs might soon change because present on the fringes of the Kailadevi Wildlife Sanctuary is the Ramathra Fort in the village of Sapotara. The fort itself is now a burgeoning hospitality enterprise practising sustainable ecotourism, but crucially, approximately 100 bighas of land have been protected and slowly restored by the thakur cum proprietor, Ravi Rajpal Singh, and his young son, Uditchandra Pal Singh.

Starting with Thakur Brijendraraj Pal Singh, the family has protected this parcel of land for more than 20 years, which was initially completely denuded of vegetation with the exception of some old tamarind, neem, peepal and banyan trees. A process of natural regeneration ensued, although the family also took steps to remove invasive vilayati babul *(Prosopis juliflora)*, and Udit planted native trees back in 2020. Today, the area is dominated by dhonk and other indigenous flora, and some key species of fauna that can be observed on-site are the rusty-spotted cat (*Prionailurus rubiginosus*), the highly elusive caracal (*Caracal caracal*) and even the Indian wolf, for which the Kailadevi Wildlife Sanctuary is now becoming known. The nearby Kalisil wetland and an additional waterbody on-site are also a haven for migratory birds.

This begets the question: how did the family bring about such change in an area under so much pressure from grazers, illegal miners and other criminal enterprises?

While they did not fence the area to protect it from grazers, they put up a stone boundary to clearly demarcate it. In addition, they maintained two permanent guards in the early years who patrolled the area, and protected both the waterbody on-site and the Kalisil wetland. Today, Udit patrols the land himself and maintains a team of three guards to protect from illegal grazing and lopping. In addition, they also keep an eye out for illegal sand mining in the ravines abutting their property. Udit has also recently taken to fencing areas where illegal sand mining occurs and is now considering fencing the nearby Kalisil wetland facing recurring illegal encroachment.

Udit has only just begun to explore the tremendous ecotourism potential of this area. He has long taken a keen interest in the local biodiversity and documents all he can through still photography and opportunistic camera trapping. He has also been observing and habituating a couple of packs of Indian wolves from a 4x4 vehicle within their area. As of

2021, he has slowly begun making these experiences available as 'safaris' to guests lodged at the Ramathra Fort. We believe that this could be a future sustainable ecotourism option for the most neglected part of Ranthambore Tiger Reserve and encourage Udit's single-handed explorations in this direction.

Notes

1. Lindenmayer, David, 'Small Patches Make Critical Contributions to Biodiversity Conservation', *Proceedings of the National Academy of Sciences*, Vol. 116, No. 3, January 2019, pp. 717–19, https://doi.org/10.1073/pnas.1820169116. Accessed on 11 July 2022.

CONSERVATION CHAMPIONS

ANANDA BANERJEE

A tiger ambling by the lake with an old fort in the backdrop...a tigress and her cubs occupying a palace in ruins...a Stetson-wearing forest officer, and a hunting scene caught on film where a tiger is seen chasing a sambar into the water...

These visuals from Ranthambore captivated my adolescent mind in the 1980s. Some years later, while filliping through my favourite magazine, I found the forest officer again.

In May 1992, the *National Geographic* did a cover story titled 'India's Wildlife Dilemma', written by Geoffrey C. Ward, with photographs by Raghu Rai. The picture of Fateh Singh Rathore standing up from his jeep, as if in hypnotic conversation with two tiger cubs, amongst the ruins of a mosque struck a chord with me.

When I met Fateh Singh many years after that publication at his home in Sawai Madhopur, I couldn't recognize him for a few seconds. He was in a kurta-pajama, without his trademark Stetson-and-khaki outfit. By then, he had long retired from service, but as an honorary wildlife warden, he still visited his beloved tigers in Ranthambore National Park. And I was lucky to accompany him. On an overcast summer afternoon, we went into the forest; it was an experience just to listen to him explain how to read a forest, especially a particularly silent one with no animal or bird calls.

He stopped at a bend where he expected a tigress to cross, but nothing of that sort happened. Then soon, the heavens opened up; briefly, I remember we had a flat tire, which we fixed, and after the rain had stopped, we drove on towards the grasslands to see the mass congregation (which usually happens after a spell of rain) of cheetal. I still remember that visual clear as day—hundreds of spotted deer, one by one, shaking off the raindrops that had settled into their coats. Since those heady days in Ranthambore, where I spent some incredible times watching wildlife as a volunteer, much water has flowed in my life in wildlife conservation. I count myself extremely fortunate to have experienced such incredible natural history at such close quarters.

In 2020, India added 557 new species (407 new species and 150 new records) to its fauna and 267 new plant species, 202 are new to science.[1] The compilations (published in 2021) from the Zoological Survey of India (ZSI) and Botanical Survey of India (BSI), two of the oldest institutions in natural history, are something wondrous especially in context to our current epoch—the age of Anthropocene, an age where we, humans, have accelerated the natural rate of extinction in the natural world by several notches, chiefly through habitat destruction and alterations. The biennial *Living Planet Report* has been continuously raising the red flag on vanishing as well as in-peril species, and in its latest edition (2020) proclaims—'The population sizes of mammals, birds, fish, amphibians and reptiles have seen an alarming average drop of 68 per cent since 1970.'[2]

This decline is now referred to as the 'sixth extinction' by the scientific and wildlife conservation community. It is no secret that we are racing against time to get to know members of our natural world, and species are rapidly vanishing even before they can be described. This is more challenging in a mega-diverse country like India, with only 2 per cent of the global landmass, home to billions of people and livestock and yet home to only 7–8 per cent of the recorded world species. The newly discovered species has increased India's faunal tally to 102,718 species and 54,733 botanical species.

Despite all the challenges, India has success stories to flaunt, especially on keystone species. The last decade has witnessed substantial growth in the tiger, lion and great one-horned rhinoceros populations, plus a stable Asian elephant population.

Even though the Wild Life (Protection) Act (WLPA), 1972, has received a fair amount of criticism from a section of scientists and conservationists for either being elitist, or giving unlimited powers to a section of the bureaucracy, or based on pseudoscience, according to well-known ecologist Madhav Gadgil, the law must have done some things right amongst other sociocultural factors across India's diverse landscape. Without the WLPA, I can't fathom the state of wildlife we witness today. And it all started with a woman, a naturalist prime minister in Indira Gandhi.

But before we go further into change-makers and the WLPA story, for the past five decades, countless forest guards, fearless men and women, have devoted their lives to carrying out the idea of WLPA, in letter and spirit, 24/7, without a break for months and sometimes years. Many have lost their lives in the line of duty. Too many to mention in a book chapter. The same goes for several Indian Forest Service (IFS) officers who have made a difference in wildlife conservation and sometimes have gone beyond the call of duty. Whatever success we have to show to the world in the era of sixth extinction wouldn't have been possible without our frontline conservation heroes.

Much of our faunal knowledge was provided by two guidebooks. S.H. Prater's *Book of Indian Animals* (Oxford Universiy Press, 1948 [1st edn.]) and *The Handbook of the Birds of India and Pakistan* (Oxford University Press, 1969 [1st edn.]) by Dr Salim Ali, with S. Dillon Ripley. Vivek Menon changed everything (a range of colour photographs, graphics and an easy-on-the-eyes design) with *A Field Guide to Indian Mammals* (Dorling Kindersley, 2003, followed by an updated version in 2014), which became the first comprehensive guide that attempted to cover all mammal species in India. Likewise, *Birds of the Indian Subcontinent* (Oxford University Press, 1998 [1st edn.]) by Richard Grimmett, Tim Inskipp and Carol Inskipp took birdwatching to new heights.

Even before her entry into the political world, Indira Gandhi had a deep abiding interest in nature, especially birdlife. She was one of the founding members of the Delhi Bird Watching Society in the 1950s. Soon after she took office in 1966, the well-being of wildlife (and forest) became one of her major preoccupations, as seen in her letters and speeches. In the same year, her government offered the Ninth General Assembly of the International Union for Conservation of Nature (IUCN) to host the tenth edition in New Delhi in 1969.

The year 1969 was a momentous one in the history of nature conservation in India. This was the year when the groundwork for the WLPA was set, and the concern regarding the decline of tiger populations led to an inclusive conservation programme being set up to save the tiger from further shikar and going extinct. This was the year Mrs Gandhi reconstituted the Indian Board of Wildlife (IBWL) and put Dr Karan Singh at the helm of affairs. This was also the year the lion became our national animal, inspired by the national symbol—the lion capital at Sarnath. The deliberations in IBWL enforced the idea of a uniform law on wildlife protection in the country. The IBWL came into existence in 1952. The 1950s and 1960s saw a series of articles in the *Journal of the Bombay Natural History Society (JBNHS)* from the noted naturalist and tea-planter E.P. Gee advocating for a wildlife protection law and inviolate protected areas (PAs) for wildlife conservation. In 1972, the tiger replaced the lion as the national animal. Dr Karan Singh (encouraged by his family nickname 'Tiger') was instrumental in this change as he argued the pan-India presence of the tiger vis-à-vis the presence of lions in just one corner of Gujarat.

Indira Gandhi's frequent correspondence, especially with Dr Salim Ali, on matters of wildlife made her more determined to act. In a letter dated 30 April 1969, to Agriculture Minister Jagjivan Ram (whose portfolio included forest and wildlife), Mrs Gandhi said, 'I have been greatly concerned at the progressive decimation of our wildlife. From all that I read and hear, the situation appears to be much more serious than official circles are prepared to admit.'[3] It wasn't only the big mammals like lions and tigers; she was equally concerned about the blackbuck and the sangai. Her letters to members of the Cabinet and chief ministers throughout her career are testimony of the political will we so often hear for the conservation and protection of species.

The IUCN's Tenth General Assembly in New Delhi (24 November–1 December 1969) brought together a diverse group of wildlife enthusiasts and conservationists. There were royals, politicians, administrators, game wardens, members of the IFS, representatives of non-governmental organizations (NGOs), scientists, educationists, journalists, nature photographers, and advertising and marketing professionals. The attendees list from India even had a farmer. These formed the founding fathers of the wildlife conservation movement in India.

The organizing committee of the General Assembly included R.C. Soni (chairman), K.S. Sankhala (secretary), P. Barua, G.K. Bora, S.S. Buit, Mrs K. Chatterjee, Zafar Futehally, Mrs Usha Ganguli, S.A. Hejmadi, Peter F.R. Jackson, R.D. Joshi, R.C. Kaushik, M. Krishnan, K.L. Lahiri, Dr R.N. Misra, K.N. Mishra, K.K. Nair, D. Nanjundappa, G. Naqushband, K. Narayan Pillai, Kamala Prasad, T.N. Srivastava, S.N. Tulsiani and M.L. Widhani.

There was an honorary committee comprising Dr Salim Ali, F.C. Badhwar, S. Chakravarti, K.K. Das, K.S. Dharmakumarsimhji, Hans Raj Gupta, Hari Singh, Dr D.S. Kothari, His Highness

Maharaja of Nabha, His Highness Maharaja of Sandur, B.N. Maheshwari, J.C. Mathur, Ashok Mitra, Dr Nagendra Singh, P. Pant, B.R. Patel, C.R. Ranganathan, S.K. Roy, Dr H. Santapau, Dr B.R. Seshachar, R.C. Soni and B. Venkatappaiah.

Some other notable attendees included J.C. Daniel (curator, Bombay Natural History Society [BNHS]), Humayun Abdulali (BNHS), Dr M.K. Ranjitsinh (collector, Mandla, Madhya Pradesh), Maharaja Fatehsinghrao Gaekwad of Baroda, Anne Wright, Hari Dang (Doon School), Y.H. Ghorpade and Billy Arjan Singh.

Today, much of the conservation-related deliberations still flow from the declaration at the Tenth IUCN General Assembly, 1969. Back then, the members also took cognizance of 'the growing threat to the environment caused by pollution' and:

> [T]hat economic development depends entirely on the utilization of natural resources,that this utilization is carried out often with little attention to the needs of renewal... that, because of this, much of the earth once well-watered and productive is now impoverished and degraded, that once abundant plant, animals and scenic resources have been ravaged, that therefore the attainment of a high quality of living for all mankind now depends upon the conservation and restoration of these dwindling resources, and finally that the natural resources of the world are a heritage on which the survival of future generations must depend[.][4]

There were deliberations on the declining lion population in Gir and encroachments in the lion habitats. And the tiger was in grave danger from 'licensed hunting, indiscriminate use of crop protection guns, commercial hunting, poisoning, burning of breeding cover, destruction of habitat, and biotic activity such as grazing, and the fur and skin trade.'

Shikar was still in vogue in the 1960s. Various estimates of that time revealed that tiger numbers were decreasing rapidly as guns became more sophisticated and jeeps with searchlights made further access into the wilderness easy. Organizing hunts for foreign guests was an economic activity, and a matter of foreign exchange earning. But by then, the wanton destruction of wildlife and forest had converted many royals to root for wildlife protection. Billy Arjan Singh, in an interview with Bittu Sahgal, founder-editor, *Sanctuary Asia*, and ardent advocate of the natural world explained:

> The tiger was slipping away from us that sport hunting was a sinful, hypocritical act opposed to all civilised human thought. No one has the right to be entertained by murder. Sadly the virus of sport killing runs deep in the human psyche and wild predators like wolves, tigers, leopards and sharks continue to pay the price for human blood lust that condones killing with the use of telescopic sights, automatic weapons and even helicopters. Yes, I took on the outfitters of the day. They tried every dirty trick in the book to coerce the Indian government to let them carry on their bloody business when tiger shikar was banned in 1969-70. They spoke sanctimoniously then about conservation but took extra money for guaranteed kills. They were an unscrupulous lot and India is well rid of them.[5]

Billy and his residence 'Tiger Haven', on the edge of the Dudhwa National Park and Tiger Reserve, is a part of conservation folklore. Hailing from the royal family of Kapurthala, hunter-turned-conservationist Billy Arjan Singh was the first to reintroduce tigers and leopards from captivity into the wild. In 1973, Billy reintroduced an orphaned male leopard cub named Prince. And to provide Prince with companionship, he subsequently raised two orphaned female leopard cubs, Harriet and Juliette. Later, in 1976, Indira Gandhi helped him to acquire a female tiger cub from the Twycross Zoo, Leicestershire, England, which he reintroduced in Dudhwa. This was Tara, the tigress that drew considerable controversy from a section of foresters and conservation practitioners of the time.

The 1969 meeting was also not just about the status of tigers or lions. The gathering took note of the decline of smaller wild cats:

> While continued and widespread concern has been aroused over the precarious state of many of the larger wild mammals, resulting in many field studies of such mammals, and whereas there is up to now practically no sound knowledge available on the status of many smaller felid species, and many of these are still ruthlessly exterminated as 'vermin' and/or overexploited for the fur trade, special attention needs to be given to the following species which are either very rare or overexploited.[6]

From an Indian perspective, they were marbled cat (*Felis marmorata*), the Himalayan golden cat (*Felis temmincki tristis*), the fishing cat (*Felis viverrina*), Pallas's cat (*Felis manul*), the caracal (*Felis caracal*) and the clouded leopard (*Neofelis nebulosa*).

The events of 1969 flowed into 1972. The task to draft the WLPA fell on Dr M.K. Ranjitsinh, civil servant and member of the royal family of Wankaner, Gujarat. On 9 September 1972, Parliament passed the WLPA to protect wild animals, birds and plants. This was also the centenary year of the establishment of Yellowstone National Park, United States of America, as the first national park in the world. The celebration bolstered other countries to follow suit, boosted by the first United Nations Conference on the Human Environment in Stockholm, where Indira Gandhi was the only head of state to attend along with the host, Swedish Prime Minister Sven Olof Joachim Palme.

It took a few years to implement the WLPA on the ground; as Billy mentioned, clandestine shikar continued, but the political will of the day soon put an end to it. This year, 1972, also saw India's first official tiger count—1,827 tigers. It was led by IFS officer Saroj Raj Choudhury, the proponent of the pugmark methodology, which was used for this count, and was the go-to method for the next 35 years for Project Tiger. Like Billy, Choudhury and his companion became a household name in Odisha and other parts of the country with their 'domesticated' tigress Khairi. Even as an adult, the tigress lived in the same household; the story is well documented in the book *Khairi: The Beloved Tigress* (Natraj Publishers, 2003).

In later years, the methodology was more misused to inflate tiger numbers than in the way that Choudhury originally intended. It drew severe criticism from the conservation community as unscientific. The poaching debacle in Sariska, Rajasthan, that led to a complete depletion of tigers in the reserve put an end to the over-reliance on the pugmark system. In 2006, under the new National Tiger Conservation Authority (NTCA) led by Dr Rajesh Gopal, the camera-trap technique to capture and identify individual tigers as shown by Dr K. Ullas Karanth in Nagarhole was finally inducted into the census methodology.

India's conservation narrative is largely centred around the tiger. And the fortunes of other species solely depended on the tiger by the logic 'if you save the tiger, you save the tiger forest and the other species which live down the food chain'. And the flag of the striped cat flew high with a star cast of tiger defenders like Saroj Raj Choudhary, Kailash Sankhala, H.S. Panwar, P.K. Sen, Fateh Singh Rathore, Rajesh Gopal, Valmik Thapar, Dr K. Ullas Karanth, Ashok Kumar, Belinda Wright and Dr Raghu Chundawat, to mention a few.

Among these stars, Dr Karanth had the most unusual career graph—from odd factory jobs to selling tractors and farm machinery, being a tobacco farmer to one of the world's top tiger specialists/scientists. In an interview with yours truly, Dr Karanth said:

> While I was pursuing engineering, my biggest inspiration to chart a career in wildlife came from George Schaller. In college, I read Schaller's article in *Life* magazine and later, *The Deer And The Tiger*, his detailed account of the ecology and behaviour of Bengal tigers and four species of ungulates on which they prey in India's Kanha National Park. This inspired me to pursue wildlife biology and science. I didn't want to be a tour guide or anything else. So, I started trying to get out of the engineering profession and become a biologist like Schaller, but it was easier said than done. There was no way I could get into a wildlife school in the US, as the cost was too high and I didn't have the right undergraduate degree. After passing out of college, I did odd factory jobs, sold tractors and power tillers, and rode all over Karnataka on a motorcycle and still was not satisfied, I bought a tobacco farm in 1976 not very far from Nagarhole so I could spend a lot more time in the wilderness.

Others were also concerned with the status of other species and debunking myths. And there is no better person to start with than the exploits of Dr A.J.T. Johnsingh. He is known to be independent India's first wildlife scientist. Dr Johnsingh went on to study wild dogs, one of the most misunderstood animals of that time. In peninsular India, sportsman and naturalist E.G. Phythian Adams (popularly known as Python Adams), representing the Nilgiri Game Association (NGA), called the dhole a 'perfect swine' in the *JBNHS* of 1949. 'Except for his handsome appearance, the wild dog has not a single redeeming feature, and no effort, fair or foul, should be spared to destroy these pests of the jungle,' wrote Adams. 'A virtual war was declared on this animal,' wrote naturalist E.R.C. Davidar in his book *Whispers from the Wild: Writings by E.R.C. Davidar* (Penguin, 2012).

Davidar himself was an early advocate of wildlife

conservation, although he became interested in wildlife through hunting. He was associated with the Nilgiri Planter's Association (NPA) and became concerned about the status of the Nilgiri tahr. In 1975, Davidar's survey in the Western Ghats (published in the *JBHNS*) put the mountain goat population at around 2,200.

For long, the scientific community had to depend on anecdotal tales of dholes—mainly from British officers in colonial India—and many myths surrounded the species until Dr A.J.T. Johnsingh's path-breaking study of the species in Bandipur Tiger Reserve in Karnataka between 1976 and 1978. The study disclosed that dholes are not bloodthirsty as portrayed; instead, they are extremely social and cooperative, living in organized packs. When a pack is not hunting, the dholes are sleeping or at play, bonding socially, sharpening their hunting skills and establishing rank.

Among the many myths that were woven around the dhole was one that said it attacked people running away from it. In contrast, Dr Johnsingh observed a pack of nine dholes emerging from the thicket in his direction in Bandipur. When the pack was 50 metres away, he decided to see their reaction and ran in full view towards a climbable tree. Instead of attacking him, the dholes turned back and ran into the bushes. Dholes are extremely shy of people, and when he approached them, even when they were on a fresh kill, they growled and ran away. At the den site, the mother dhole ran away with a growl, even with the den-bound pups around.

The same year saw another wildlife survey in Rushikulya beach, Odisha, where during the night of *arribada*, Prof. B.C. Choudhury (who, along with Dr Johnsingh, can be credited for training several batches of fine wildlife biologists at the WII, Dehradun) went scampering around the length of the beach, marking olive ridley turtles with a bucket of paint and a brush. Today, the Students Sea Turtle Conservation Network (SSTCN) remains the longest-running voluntary conservation initiative that mainly runs off the efforts of students who have been walking the beaches of Chennai since 1987 to conserve and create awareness about the endangered olive ridley sea turtle. The SSTCN nurtured several conservationists, and amongst them, Kartik Shanker and Shekar Dattatri continue to educate us on matters of herpetology and marine conservation. And the man who played a key role in starting the turtle walks was none other than Romulus Whitaker, best known for his work on snakes (notably the king cobra) and crocodiles. Whitaker founded the Madras Crocodile Bank Trust (MCBT), the Agumbe Rainforest Research Station (ARRS) and the Andaman and Nicobar Environment Team (ANET). In an interview with Kartik Shanker, Whitaker said:[7]

> We collected all of 11 nests in the first year. Over the next few years, we rescued about 20,000 ridley eggs from poachers and dogs. We released more than 10,000 hatchings and it made us all feel real good. "This is conservation action," we thought, as we patted ourselves on the back. In later years, when we learned about temperature sex determination, we realised our approach should have been a bit more scientific... I think the work we started back in the early 1970s has had a positive effect on sea turtle conservation in India, mostly by waking us all up to the plight of these wonderful but beleaguered creatures. By protecting the breeding base of India's sea turtle population, by waking up people all along India's coast to the problems facing turtles we've seen a lot of dedicated young biologists and naturalists getting seriously involved. I do believe all these efforts have helped save our sea turtles and it's very encouraging to see that the interest persists and that the turtle walks and outreach to coastal villages are still going strong!

Dr M.K. Ranjitsinh, who drafted the WLPA, often lamented that we have been myopic as a nation. While we have protected charismatic species like the tiger and the rhinoceros, we have been not so good at protecting important ecosystems outside tiger reserves, like grasslands and wetlands.

In the 1960s, when Dr Ranjitsinh, who later became India's first director of wildlife preservation, visited the Corbett National Park, a zone inside the park—the grasslands of Dhikala—was dotted with hog deer, which was the principal prey of the tiger, as it vastly outnumbered the spotted deer or chital in population. Unfortunately, today the number has dwindled, which is a sad reflection of the present state of wildlife conservation in a prime tiger habitat.

In Corbett National Park, the decline of the hog deer began with the submergence of a large part of the grasslands with the building of a dam on the Ramganga River in 1974. Some of the best grasslands, including the Buxarchaur and Berichaur, adjoining Dhikala, were submerged. Today, the Dhikalachaur is bordered by the river on one side and a sal forest on the other three, leaving the hog deer trapped within its limits. Similar submergence will happen in the Panna Tiger Reserve—which has seen a remarkable recovery in the big cat population—with the Ken-Betwa river interlinking project, and we can't even fathom the loss of biodiversity in the coming days.

'We follow this old method of burning grasslands for better crop, but haven't spared much thought for animals such as the hog deer, pygmy hog, hispid hare, Assam tortoise, birds such as the Bengal florican, jungle fowl and black partridges, which breed in grasslands and reptiles that can't move fast enough to escape the fire,' says conservation biologist Goutam Narayan[8], credited for successfully rewilding the elusive and endangered pygmy hog, the world's smallest and rarest wild pig, after successfully captive breeding in Assam. This was a species that E.P. Gee, in his book *The Wildlife of India*, thought India had lost. The 1971 rediscovery was credited to another tea planter, J. Tessier-Yandell, who found pygmy hogs being sold in a tea garden market near the Bornadi Wildlife Sanctuary in northern Assam before it disappeared again until Narayan started his conservation programme in the mid-1990s.

Dr Ranjitsinh also laments the decline of the great Indian bustard (GIB), a bird now locally extinct from almost 90 per cent of its former range. The GIB was once a runner for the title of national bird, and he fears that it will be the first species to be declared extinct unless urgent conservation measures are put in place. 'Once known as the king of grasslands, the great indian bustard is now a BPL [below poverty line] species,' according to Dr Asad Rahmani, former director of the BNHS, referring to it being found only in the poorest districts of India. Dr Rahmani has been working on bustards for almost four decades and has seen how the population has declined drastically from around 1,500 birds in the early mid 1980s. And not just the GIB but also the Bengal florican and the lesser florican populations have declined rapidly due to habitat mismanagement.

Dr Rahmani has a chapter on Dr Salim Ali in this book. We recently met at his home in Lucknow, where he narrated some of his interactions with Dr Ali, especially on declining bird populations, 'Whenever Salim Ali shared his old experiences, particularly from Bharatpur, he used to mention the unimaginable number of waterfowl. Many a times sky got darkened by the flight of wintering waterfowl.' But those numbers have drastically reduced over time for various reasons. However, in these times, I can relate to what the great ornithologist was saying through my own experience of watching the en masse migration of Amur falcons in the Nagaland skyline, again because one woman took the lead and stopped hunting. The WLPA came to the aid of Bano Haralu, who championed the cause of the species as well as community pride to turn things around within a year—a remarkable achievement in our conservation history. May her tribe grow!

To present an unfinished list of people in wildlife conservation here are some notable names of wildlifers of the yore that I can recall:

Forest Officers: Saroj Raj Choudhury, Kailash Sankhla, J.J. Dutta, S. Debroy, Kamal Naidu, Fateh Singh Rathore, P.M. Lad, Mir Inayatullah, V.B. Saharia, V.B. Singh, M.K. Appaya, Pushp Kumar, S.P. Shahi, S.A. Hejmadi, A.S. Negi, M.G. Gogate.

Others: Salim Ali, S. Dillon Ripley, E.P. Gee, Humayun Abdulali, Zafar Futehally, 'Billy' Arjan Singh, Duleep Matthai, Fatehsingh Rao Gaekwad, Rishad Naoroji, K.S. Dharmakumarsinhji, Y.R. Ghorpade, E.R.C. Davidar, J.C. Daniel, Anne Wright, Hari Dang, S.P. Godrej, Sally Walker, Ashok Kumar, C.D. Krishnegowda, Reuben David, J.H. Desai.

Here, I have just been able to mention a few names that have stuck with me through the ages. Surely, there are many, many more...

Notes

1. *Animal Discoveries 2020*, Zoological Survey of India, June 2021, https://bit.ly/3aHR68V. Accessed on 7 July 2022.
2. Almond, Rosamunde, et al. (eds.), *Living Planet Report 2020: Bending the Curve of Biodiversity Loss*, WWF and Zoological Society of London, 2020, https://bityl.co/DAh8. Accessed on 11 July 2022.
3. Quoted in Ramesh, Jairam, *Indira Gandhi: A Life in Nature*, Simon & Schuster, 2017.
4. Futehally, Zafar, '10th General Assembly and 11th Technical Meeting of the Inter-National Union for Conservation of Nature and Natural Resources', *Journal of the Bombay Natural History Society*, Vol. 67, No. 1, April 1970, pp. 30–39, https://bityl.co/DAh1. Accessed on 11 July 2022.
5. Sahgal, Bittu, 'Meet Billy Arjan Singh', *Sanctuary Asia*, Vol. 20, No. 9, September 2000, https://bityl.co/DAh2. Accessed on 11 July 2022.

6. *Tenth General Assembly: Volume II Proceedings and Summary of Business*, IUCN and UNESCO, 1970, https://bityl.co/DAfq. Accessed on 7 July 2022.
7. Shanker, Kartik, 'The Journey of Sea Turtle Conservation in India: An Interview with Romulus Whitaker', *Current Conservation*, No. 6.2, 13 June 2012, https://bit.ly/3z5D8XC. Accessed on 14 July 2022.
8. Personal communication with the author.

NGOS IN WILDLIFE CONSERVATION

MANOJ KUMAR MISRA

Chornai was an intriguing name. Actually, it was Choti that met Badi before they merged themselves into Hasdeo. All three are names of streams that once used to be free as a bird. I loved them and spent some memorable time amidst them. But unknown to them, my time spent with them was for a purpose not very honorable. I was part of a team that came with a death sentence for at least two of them—this is a regret that I will take to my grave.

The year was 1982; as a new recruit in the Indian Forest Service (IFS), I assisted the Divisional Forest Officer (DFO) in marking trees for felling so that a reservoir could engulf the treeless space. That very reservoir, today, stands behind the Bango Dam on the river Hasdeo.

My introduction to the legal aspect of my job came not with Wild Life (Protection) Act (WLPA), 1972, but with the newly enacted law to protect forests, namely the Forest (Conservation) Act (FCA), 1980. Contractors busy raising initial structures for the dam were flouting the new law with impunity, breaking land without any prior approval from the central government, which the FCA had mandated. Work came to a halt briefly, but the political economy associated with the dam soon overwhelmed the requirements of ecology and the law. Soon, I got posted out on promotion. But the mayhem with tree clearance for a reservoir made me resolve—never again!

Soon, in mid-1984, I applied for and joined training in

wildlife management at the Wildlife Institute of India (WII), Dehradun. I was doubly motivated. First, that a wildlife-trained status might ensure that I never again need to handle tree felling as part of my job, while the second was more personal—newly married and with a baby on the way, training in Dehradun, my hometown, for almost a year was more than welcome.

My introduction and exposure to non-governmental organizations (NGOs) came at the WII. In those early days, three organizations stood out—the World Wide Fund for Nature (WWF) and the International Union for Conservation of Nature (IUCN; then called International Union for Conservation of Nature and Natural Resources, and later, briefly, as the World Conservation Union) were reputedly 'international'; and the 'national' organization that boasted of Dr Salim Ali, the famous Birdman of India, was the Bombay Natural History Society (BNHS) based in Bombay (now Mumbai).

The IUCN did not have an office in India till 2007. It was known most for its 'Red Data Book', a list of wildlife species in need of priority conservation action and the various 'commissions' in the form of a body of experts in different species and related matters.

The WWF was known most for its advocacy and education work. It was a kind of nursery for many budding conservationists. Many known wildlife experts and conservationists in the country, some with graying hair today, would fondly recall cutting their baby teeth in the company of stalwarts like Duleep Matthai, who ran a small WWF office out of a garage in Delhi. It was initially headquartered in Bombay. I had little inkling that my own path would cross with the WWF in a major way in the future.

During our wildlife training, we spent some 10 days at the famous Bharatpur Bird Sanctuary (now known as the Keoladeo Ghana National Park). In 1981, its status had been upgraded to that of a national park, and the law requiring that 'no grazing was to be permitted' in a national park turned around 7,000 buffaloes and cows, the traditional primary consumers as grazers in the area, into persona non grata. That was also the time when Dr V.S. Vijayan and his wife, Lalitha, were halfway through their decade-long (1980–1990) research and ecological monitoring project of the national park for the BNHS. On 7 November 1982, nine villagers, all of whom were trying to enter the park with their cattle for grazing, were shot dead by the police. The discourse around cattle grazing in a man-made wetland like Bharatpur was obviously a hot topic and a management priority; as such, it attracted numerous researchers. We learnt from the Vijayan couple about the charms, challenges and vicissitudes of wildlife research, and their initial findings that perhaps the strict ban on cattle grazing in Bharatpur had been an ecological mistake.

The BNHS, courtesy of Dr Salim Ali, in the post-Independence era, has been at the forefront of several conservation initiatives in the country. It was founded in 1883 by eight nature-loving residents of Bombay, two of whom were Indians. Today, it has grown into one of the most well-known nature research, education and advocacy non-government-affiliated institutions in the country. Its collection of wildlife specimens, an extremely rich library and two regular publications, namely the *Journal of the Bombay Natural History Society (JBNHS)* and the *Hornbill*, has made it known and respected all over the country and beyond. The association of committed conservationists such as S.H. Prater, E.P. Gee, Dr Salim Ali, Humayun Abdulali, Zafar R. Futehally, J.C. Daniel and Dr Asad Rahmani, to name but a few, has contributed towards this organization's unrivalled reputation. Two of its publications, namely S.H. Prater's *Book of Indian Animals* (Oxford Universiy Press, 1948 [1st edn.]) and *The Book of Indian Birds* (BNHS, 1941), have achieved cult status.

Our stay at the Keoladeo Ghana National Park at Bharatpur was suddenly cut short due to the assassination of Prime Minister Indira Gandhi on 31 October 1984. We rushed back to Dehradun through largely deserted roads and a Delhi marred by anti-Sikh riots.

In January 1985, my father introduced me to the Dehradun-based Wildlife Preservation Society of India (WPSI), which has since been renamed the Wildlife Preservation Society (WPS). He had become an ordinary member and carried home a copy of its quarterly journal *Chital*. Its office was at the famous Astley Hall, and my father wished me to contribute articles to its newsletter.

Initially named the Wildlife Preservation Society of Northern India, it was established on 13 April 1958 in Dehradun with His Highness Maharaja Pratap Singh of Nabha as its founder-president. In 1960, it became the WPSI, and much later, in 2017, the WPS. The WPS claims the privilege of having two former presidents of India, namely V.V. Giri and Fakhruddin Ali Ahmed, as its patrons and E.P. Gee and Dr Salim Ali as its honorary members. *Chital*, a quarterly journal, has remained its mouthpiece and its most visible ambassador.

Post wildlife training, I was posted as the director of Madhav National Park at Shivpuri (Madhya Pradesh) in June 1985. The assignment brought challenges and pleasures galore. Each day was a learning experience amongst the plants and animals that constituted the forests of predominantly kardhai/dhonk (*Anogeissus pendula*). How a dry- and drab-looking summertime habitat overnight turns verdant as if by magic with just a hint of monsoon showers is a sight to behold and cherish.

The new year (1986) had just begun. As I entered my office after an early morning visit to the park, my attention was drawn to a small magazine with a glazed black-and-white cover sitting on my desk. The cover boasted of a majestic tiger, and the magazine's title—*Zoo's Print*—sat emboldened as its fitting crown with a proud cheetah profile within the two OOs. Edited by Sally Walker, it was a potpourri of wildlife articles from both zoos and the wilds. It turned out to be the inaugural issue of a publication that a Mysore-based NGO called the Zoo Outreach Organisation (ZOO) had started. Sally was the secretary of the organization.

Only a few months before, a staff member had handed me an orphan hyena cub. We had hand-reared it, but once it grew old enough to survive on its own, it was kept in a small cage at the 'Ladies Club' (a Scindia-period guest house in the park). It used to roam around during the day and spend its night within the safety of the cage, but one evening, it failed to return. A search in the morning found it inside a python not too far from the Ladies Club building. I wrote a brief, poignant tale of our time with the cub and sent it to Sally Walker. It was duly carried in the next issue of *Zoo's Print*. This started my long association with Sally and her wonderful organization. Sally is now no more, but ZOO continues to grow from strength to strength, now in its thirty-sixth year. ZOO has fallen into the capable and experienced hands of Sally's protégé—Sanjay Molur.

Started in 1985, ZOO was established by Sally Walker, an American citizen living in India by choice. A chance visit in 1984 to the zoo at Mysore opened for Sally the doors of a lifelong mission. In her own words: 'I wanted to do something to help zoos improve their image, upgrade their management and enhance their educational potential.' There would be no knowledgeable wildlife person within and outside of the country that wouldn't vouch that the Sally-led ZOO has indeed succeeded in helping zoos accomplish all the three objectives it set for itself and much more![1]

In 1987, I proceeded on secondment to the Government of India (GoI) as an instructor at the Central Forest Rangers College, (CFRC) Chandrapur (Maharastra). It was the year when the Asian waterbird census was first held. One of the birds that we saw and counted in the wetlands around Chandrapur was the saras crane. My eagerness to know more about cranes, in general, and saras, in particular, put me in touch with Prakash Gole, who, at the time, was heading the Ecological Society at Pune.

Ecological Society is a Pune-based NGO set up in 1982 by a group of nature enthusiasts with an objective to further ecological research and education. Its founding members, among others, included Prakash Gole and Dr Swati Gole. With a mission to promote ecological understanding of nature conservation, it conducts an innovative 10-month postgraduate programme in 'sustainable management of natural resources and nature conservation'. It proposes to create a 'Nature University', which will spawn scientists and researchers who practice an ecological approach to finding solutions afflicting the planet and the human race.[2]

While at Chandrapur, meeting Dr Prakash Amte and Dr Mandakini Amte at their ashram at Hemalkasa in the Gadchiroli district of east Maharastra was an honour. Son and daughter-in-law of the well-known social worker Baba Amte, in 1973, they started a medical facility at Hemalkasa in a remote forest enclave to meet the health needs of the local Madia Gond tribal community. A chance possession of an orphan monkey started their acquisition of more orphan wild animals gifted by the tribals to the ashram, called Lok Biradari Prakalp. When I visited sometime in 1988, all kinds of wild animals were housed there. It was a fantastic sight to find Dr Prakash and his six-year-old daughter entering the holding room of a leopard without any fear or concern. 'Love conquers all' was his mantra. The process is on to convert the menagerie, now called the Animal Ark, into a proper zoo, under the guidance of the Central Zoo Authority (CZA).

I often accompanied my range forest officer trainees on field trips to different parts of the country. During one such trip to Madras (now Chennai), we visited the famous Madras Crocodile Bank Trust (MCBT). Set up as a society in 1976 by the legendry herpetologist Romulus Whitaker and his then-wife Zai, it started as a support system for the Irula snake catchers' community, who had lost their traditional means of sustenance after the ban imposed on the export of snake skins from India, following the promulgation of the WLPA. In 2003, a Centre for Herpetology was added to the mandate and name of the MCBT.

With a mission 'to promote the conservation of reptiles and amphibians and their habitats through education, scientific research and captive breeding', the MCBT and Centre for Herpetology is India's leading centre on herpetology. Its fieldwork is spread over the Andaman and Nicobar Islands (Andaman and Nicobar Environment Team [ANET]), Agumbe rainforest (Agumbe Rainforest Research Station [ARRS]), Western Ghats and Gharial Ecology Project, and river Chambal. Education and awareness-building activities at MCBT are one of its most significant contributions to wildlife conservation.[3]

To determine how many tigers are left in India has been a challenging task at least since the founding of the Project Tiger in 1973. The pugmark census technique propounded by Saroj Raj Choudhury and followed by most PAs in India, came under severe scrutiny in the 1980s. This was led by Dr K. Ullas Karanth, who, in 1988, established the India office of the US-based Wildlife Conservation Society (WCS). He promoted the use of the camera trap methodology for estimating the populations of large mammals, which has now become standard practice.

WCS India, with a goal 'to protect and conserve India's natural environment, its flora and fauna, and in particular the preservation of wildlife and wild places', has its programme themes spread over carnivore and herbivore ecology and conservation; counter wildlife trafficking; livelihood support; eastern ghats and Telengana; Western Ghats; human-wildlife interactions; human dimensions network; marine and species like elephant, turtle, great Indian bustard and dhole.[4]

Back in Bhopal in 1991, I took charge as the director of Van Vihar National Park, a wilderness area cum modern zoo almost in the heart of the city, next to the famous Upper Lake. In partnership with Giridhar A. Kinhal, an IFS batchmate, a society called the Forum For Forestry Furtherance (4F) was constituted with an objective to spread the message of forest, wildlife and environment conservation among fellow foresters as well as schoolchildren in and around the city of Bhopal. We devoted almost all our spare time to activities geared at meeting the 4F objectives. Among other activities, the 'nature camps' that we organized for the schoolchildren were the most popular. In 1993, I attended a three-month-long international environmental education course at the famous zoo at Jersey in the Channel Islands (UK) and brought home several learnings that came in handy during these nature camps.

Prachi Mehta was a resource person at a 4F nature camp held in the Bori forests. She was engaged in researching birds in Bori as a PhD scholar at the WII and became an instant hit with the nature camp participants. Later, in association with Jayant Kulkarni, a former forester and her partner in life, she set up the Wildlife Research and Conservation Society (WRCS) in Pune.

The WRCS was established in 2005 to conserve wildlife and biodiversity based on scientific principles and information. Currently, the NGO is focusing on tiger conservation in Melghat, the study of forest owlet, human-elephant conflict and the conservation of private forests and corridors for large carnivores in the Western Ghats. Working closely with the forest department, the WRCS believes that wildlife conservation and long-term sustainability depend on the involvement of the local community.

In 1993, on being promoted as a conservator of forests (CF), I shifted to the Indian Institute of Forest Management (IIFM) in Bhopal, as its administrative officer. From 18–21 October 1993, a Population and Habitat Viability Analysis (PHVA) workshop by the ZOO, in partnership with the Gujarat Forest Department, for the Asiatic lion (*Panthera leo persica*) was held in Baroda, Gujarat. On the agenda was identifying a suitable site for creating a second home for the Asiatic lion, which was then restricted to a single population in the famous Gir National Park in Gujarat. My participation in the workshop helped identify Kuno National Park in northwest Madhya Pradesh as the most promising of the four sites under consideration. This was on account of my first-hand knowledge about the habitat and prey conditions in the sanctuary; it was part of my official and technical jurisdiction as the director at Madhav National Park, Shivpuri. Later, in 1995, as CF (Wildlife) in the office of the Chief Wildlife Warden (CWLW), Madhya Pradesh, it fell to my lot to prepare a 20-year lion reintroduction plan for Kuno under the guidance of R.C. Sharma, the then CWLW.

The 1990s, in India were, in many ways, a watershed decade. It started in 1991 with two almost paradoxical developments. India opened up its economy, bidding goodbye to the 'mixed' pattern of economic activity whence the public sector and private sector coexisted in an uneasy marriage, giving India an epithet of an 'elephant' unwilling to move to a western-style free market system where the private sector and free enterprise receive preference over the public sector for a faster rate of economic growth.

At the same time, a conservation-oriented WLPA underwent a significant revision in 1991 to skew it firmly towards protection, with the deletion of few provisions in chapters III and IV that permitted limited hunting and use of wildlife. A large number of PAs, in the form of national parks and sanctuaries, were created, and enforcement action against erstwhile legitimate wildlife use and practices became the order of the day. Some professions and practices like traditional hunting and taxidermy became illegal overnight, so did the trade of common wildlife items like ivory, skins, furs, horns, antlers, etc.

Soon enough, the two developments had to either clash or collude, and they did so in the form of underground wildlife trade. Professional hunting tribes and willing conduits became easy tools in the hand of illegal wildlife trade mafias out to make a fast buck. After all, in an open economy, making money legally or illegally comes easy. This resulted in the wildlife revival bandwagon of 1970s and 1980s, exemplified in Project Tiger director, Dr H.S. Panwar's 1982 article 'What to Do When You Have Succeeded' marking the completion of 10 years of Project Tiger, receiving a rude and shocking jolt within the next decade.

Tiger and leopard skins, bones and claws began to be seized all over, beginning with the big one at Majnu ka Tila, a Tibetan refugee colony in Delhi, on 30 August and 1 September 1993.[5] A tiger crisis, which could potentially translate into a wildlife crisis, began brewing, and with each new seizure, people began to doubt the veracity of the tiger numbers in the country as claimed by the authorities. This renewed focus on threatened wildlife and the need for its protection spawned many NGOs focused on tiger and wildlife protection and revival.

Trade Record Analysis of Flora and Fauna in Commerce

(TRAFFIC) India at World Wide Fund for Nature-India (WWF-India) was one of them. TRAFFIC India is part of the global TRAFFIC network engaged in the study and monitoring of domestic and international trade in wildlife items, with its headquarters at Cambridge, UK. Mentored and started by Ashok Kumar, a charismatic individual, TRAFFIC India was behind many of the initial enforcement breakthroughs, including the one at Majnu ka Tila in 1993, where 287 kg of tiger bones, eight tiger skins, 43 leopard skins and more than 100 skins of other endangered animals, including foxes, snakes and crocodiles, were seized.[6] It became worrisome for all when these wildlife seizures revealed international linkages.

I lost my father in early 1996. This required my presence in or close to Dehradun, where my mother was now alone. After performing my father's last rites, I was at the New Delhi railway station on my way back to Bhopal, having failed to identify any position vacant for deputation in Dehradun that I could have applied for. A stranger suddenly accosted me at the railway platform bookshop and asked, 'Has Khushwant Singh's latest book on women in his life been published'?

I looked askance at the gentlemen and replied, 'No!'

Gazing long at my face, he forgot all about his interest in Khushwant Singh or his book and declared, 'Your life is going to change.' I was taken aback at this intrusion and declaration but laughed it off. But what a soothsayer he turned out to be! Although what the connection to Khushwant Singh and his book was—I have never stopped wondering.

Kishore Rao, a senior colleague posted as a deputy inspector general (DIG) (Forests), at the Ministry of Environment and Forests at Delhi, whose acquaintance I had made during trips made in 1995 to finalize the Government of India-financed lion reintroduction project at Kuno, informed me of a possible position at the WWF-India office in New Delhi. He asked that I meet Samar Singh, the secretary-general, for more information. In short, I joined the WWF-India secretariat as the new director, TRAFFIC India, in mid-1996. I had firmly entered the world of wildlife NGOs.

Life at WWF and TRAFFIC was a sharp and educative change from the one I experienced until then within the state bureaucratic system. But that is another story for another time.

I soon learnt that my entry into WWF-India had followed sudden organizational changes and was not without internal heartburn. Ashok Kumar, the founder-director of TRAFFIC India, had left in a huff, and Vivek Menon, his brilliant deputy at TRAFFIC, had followed suit. Ashok Kumar went on to first help Belinda Wright run her newly formed WPSI and later co-found the Wildlife Trust of India (WTI) with Vivek, who now runs it with aplomb.

Belinda Wright came to wildlife protection from a career in wildlife filming for the BBC and National Geographic. This included the National Geographic's Emmy Award-winning film *Land of the Tiger*. In 1994, she founded WPSI with a mission 'to bring new focus and energy to tackle the growing wildlife crisis in India'.[7]

The WPSI, with a focus on combating illegal trade in wildlife, especially the tiger, provides support and information to government authorities; maintains a wildlife crime database; organizes enforcement training workshops; assists prosecution of poachers; researches and publishes reports; and supports field-based conservation, research and community support projects.

The WII, Dehradun, has produced a large number of outstanding wildlife scientists. Two of them, Charudutt Mishra and Dr M.D. Madhusudan set up the Nature Conservation Foundation (NCF) India, in 1996. Based in Mysore (Karnataka), the NCF's goal is 'to contribute to the knowledge and conservation of India's unique wildlife heritage with innovative research and imaginative solutions'.[8]

With a vision of 'a world in which nature and society flourish together', NCF India's programmes are spread over the eastern Himalayas, high altitudes, oceans and coasts, Western Ghats, cranes and wetlands, education and public engagements and PhD and conservation leadership.[9]

After his stint with TRAFFIC India, Vivek freelanced as a wildlife researcher for few years, including a year in Africa. Then, in 1998, he founded the WTI with a vision 'to secure the natural heritage of India'. The WTI, as an organization, prioritizes an interesting and exciting approach, a sort of hybrid between animal protection and welfare, called animal conservation. This uniqueness is evident in the projects that WTI is implementing at 40 locations in 23 states.

WTI activities are spread over themes like wild aid, wild rescue, species recovery, protected area recovery, conflict mitigation, enforcement and law, wild lands, natural heritage campaigns, and right of passage. WTI works closely with various government agencies, in particular, the forest and wildlife departments of various states.

P.K. Sen joined as director, Project Tiger, in New Delhi in 1996, the same year I joined the WWF. So, it was inevitable that our paths would cross. This was also when the tiger crisis engulfed the nation, and Sen, true to his wont, never desisted from calling a spade a spade. After his retirement in 2002, he first joined WWF-India to handle its tiger conservation work and later became director of the Ranthambore Foundation.[10]

Ranthambore Foundation was started in 1987 by the well-known tiger advocate Valmik Thapar 'to "integrate locals with the greater cause of protecting the tiger and its ecosystem"'. The foundation has focused on the healthcare of tribals in and around Ranthambore Tiger Reserve, environmental education, and tribal and local art. Ranthambore School of Art is based in Sawai Madhopur and raises income for the foundation and the local artists. It publishes *TigerLink* as its newsletter.[11]

Fateh Singh Rathore, the celebrated founder director of the Ranthambore Tiger Reserve, joined a few of his friends to start Tiger Watch, an NGO, in 1997. Its main objective was to combat poaching and habitat encroachment in the Ranthambore Tiger Reserve.

Key activities of Tiger Watch include anti-poaching, poaching community reform, village wildlife volunteers, capacity-building, and research and conservation awareness. Its volunteers are spread over 50 villages surrounding the Ranthambore Tiger Reserve. Activities of Tiger Watch complement the forest department in the efficient management of the Ranthambore landscape.

Rajat Bhargava, a staff member at TRAFFIC, was a bird trade expert. He had a wide network of friends and acquaintances in the city of Delhi. One of them was Geeta Sheshamani of Friendicoes, an animal welfare organization. Geeta and Kartick Satyanarayan had, in 1995, started a new enterprise called Wildlife SOS, aimed primarily at eradicating the practice of 'dancing bears'. It wasn't easy work, but persistence paid off, and today, Wildlife SOS, with a chapter in the UK and the USA, is an organization that 'aggressively battles illegal animal trade and poaching, promotes habitat protection, and the rescue, treatment and return of injured wildlife.[12]

In 2001, while I was still with WWF-India, my cadre state, Madhya Pradesh, was bifurcated to create the new state of Chhattisgarh. As is the norm, a few officers from the original state get allocated to the newly formed state. I was among a few officers of the Madhya Pradesh cadre of IFS who went to Chhattisgarh. In June 2001, I completed my five-year deputation tenure at WWF-India and joined my duties at Raipur (Chhattisgarh). Led by forces challenging to define even in hindsight, I was back in Delhi by November 2001, having opted for voluntary retirement from the IFS.

In Delhi, on my return, a small NGO named the PEACE Institute Charitable Trust was started in 2003. A couple of field projects were taken up. One such work for the WII involved assessing the country's protection aspects of Natural World Heritage Sites. This took me to the Kaziranga National Park in Assam, where I learnt about Aaranyak, a Guwahati-based regional NGO. Started in 1989 as a weekend nature club, it has since established itself as a prominent NGO in northeast India.

With a mission 'to foster conservation of biodiversity in northeast India through research, environmental education, capacity building and advocacy for legal and policy reform to usher a new era of ecological security', Aaranyak carries out its activities on avifauna research and conservation; conservation and livelihood; environmental education and capacity-building; geospatial technology and application; legal and advocacy; media production and communication; species research and conservation; water, climate and hazard; and wildlife genetics.[13]

Registered in 2002, the Wildlife Conservation Trust (WCT) is the newest large wildlife NGO in the country. Established by Hemendra Kothari, a former president of the Bombay Stock Exchange, Mumbai-based WCT is today active in and around 160 protected areas with an all-India presence.

Founded to safeguard India's life-giving ecosystems in a holistic, sustainable manner, the WCT recognizes the interconnectedness between people and ecosystems, and uses a 360-degree approach to conservation by placing equal emphasis on both forest and wildlife conservation and community development. It works closely with forest departments across the country to fortify on-ground protection by training and equipping frontline forest staff. Through partnerships with NGOs, the trust is attempting to strengthen public education systems, provide alternative livelihood options to rural youth and make healthcare accessible to people living in and around India's forests. The idea is simple—secure, key wildernesses to safeguard wildlife, people and rivers, and mitigate climate change.

There are large numbers of NGOs in the country that support conservation of wildlife, among their other activities. Few of them are: Centre for Science and Environment (CSE), Delhi; Indian National Trust for Art and Cultural Heritage (INTACH), Delhi; People For Animals (PFA), Delhi; Samrakshan Trust, Delhi; Ashoka Trust for Research In Ecology and the Environment (ATREE), Bengaluru; Centre for Ecological Studies at the Indian Institute of Science (IISc), Bengaluru; National Centre for Biological Sciences, Tata Institute of Fundamental Research (TIFR), Bengaluru; Kalpvriksh, Pune; Bombay Environmental Action Group (BEAG), Mumbai; Goa Foundation, Goa; Orissa Environmental Society, Bhubaneswar; Ladakh Ecological Development Group (LEDeG), Leh; Madras Naturalists Society, Chennai; Assam Science Society, Guwahati; Kerala Sasthra Sahitya Parishad, Thrissur, Kerala, etc.

I have often wondered why NGOs are needed when government departments exist to do the job. By 'job', I mean to do all that which ensures that the rule of law remains paramount in a republic. The legislature makes laws to further the mandate provided by the Constitution. Laws are made actionable by rules and regulations and are implemented by the state. Quite a simple arithmetic!

But if it was this simple, then why did the national tiger crisis of 1990s and beyond lead to local tiger extinctions in at least two tiger reserves, namely Sariska and Panna?

Obviously, even with all the good intentions, many aspects of the 'job' fall between the two stools, and then if the rule of law is to reign supreme, somebody has to do that part of the job on which the State—on account of its own shortcomings—fails to deliver. Here come the NGOs and their legitimate role. Time and again, NGOs have, through sustained research, both academic and action, innovative ideas and focused action filled the gap. NGOs lack the reach of the State, while the State lacks sustained pursuance of a cause, at which NGOs excel.

May this equation and complementarities last long, and wildlife law, whenever updated, make space for this relationship to flourish.

Notes

1. 'Genesis and History', Zoo Outreach Organization, https://bit.ly/3acKSgR. Accessed on 4 July 2022.
2. 'Who We Are', Ecological Society, https://bit.ly/3bSYizi. Accessed on 4 July 2022.
3. The Madras Crocodile Bank Trust & Centre for Herpetology, https://bit.ly/3AlyRAs. Accessed on 4 July 2022.
4. 'About Us', WCS-India, https://bit.ly/3ybCO8d. Accessed on 4 July 2022.
5. 'Signs of Hope for Tigers and Rhinos', *Down to Earth*, 30 September 1993, https://bit.ly/3yF1NlL. Accessed on 4 July 2022.
6. Ibid.
7. WPSI-Wildlife Protection Society of India - About Us', WPSI, https://bit.ly/3og8tAw. Accessed on 18 July 2022.

8. 'About Us', Nature Conservation Foundation, https://bit.ly/3zfPRr2. Accessed on 18 July 2022.
9. Nature Conservation Foundation - India, https://bit.ly/3OJLIkb. Accessed on 4 July 2022.
10. Bindra, Prerna Singh, 'PK Sen: A Large-Hearted Gentleman', Conservation India, 31 May 2021, https://bit.ly/3Rc3hej. Accessed on 4 July 2022.
11. Ghose, Anindita, 'Ranthambore Foundation | Call from the Wild', *Mint*, 21 October 2011, https://bit.ly/3nCW4GB. Accessed on 4 July 2022.
12. 'Our Approach to Saving Wildlife', Wildlife SOS, https://bit.ly/3unAolz. Accessed on 4 July 2022.
13. 'Aaranyak: Mission Statement', https://bit.ly/3bNtgse. Accessed on 4 July 2022.

WLPA IN A CLIMATE-ALTERED INDIA

NIVEDITA KHANDEKAR

Two years before the Wild Life (Protection) Act, 1972, came into being, in 1970, somewhere in the erstwhile eastern Madhya Pradesh, Dr Dharmendra Prasad, honorary secretary of the district archaeology unit, had discovered a site that is now known as the Ghughua Fossil Park.

It is located in today's Dindori district, some 75 km from Jabalpur. It has a fascinating collection of priceless plant fossils dating back 65 million years, right when it was the Gondwana supercontinent. It has rare palm and eucalyptus fossils apart from the variety of fossils of plants, trees, climbers, fruits, flowers and even dicotyledons.

A small site exhibition tells the visitor about what possibly might have happened those many aeons ago. During my visit to the place in 2015, I could quickly relate to the circumstances that had led to the formation of fossils.

An extreme climate event in that era was singularly responsible for bringing forth the change in the landscape. A massive volcanic eruption had shook the land, almost instantly putting everything under the cover of the molten lava. Once that cooled down, it led to a complete transformation of life in the area.

One thing was obvious: such a site offers a unique peek into the knowledge gaps that possibly exist vis-à-vis changes in climatic conditions, extreme climatic events, natural disaster and the earth's natural history. One gets to imagine what kind of changes occurred over a short span of time because of the volcanic eruption, a sort of fast-forward glimpse of what changing climate can achieve over a long duration.

This January 2022, I was reminded of that visit in 2015 as I watched the visuals of the colossal volcanic eruption in Tonga in the Pacific. A United Nations' release had described that the volcanic eruption was the largest recorded in 30 years. A huge, 20-km-high mushroom cloud of smoke and ash was followed by a tsunami, and the eruption was heard as far away as Australia and New Zealand, causing tsunami warnings across the Pacific.

Soon after it, Dr Zeke Hausfather (@hausfath), climate scientist and Intergovernmental Panel on Climate Change (IPCC) author, took to Twitter to give a detailed account of what could this eruption mean. 'We do not know how much cooling SO_2 it has put in the stratosphere (data will come in later today), but this is the effect a Pinatubo-sized volcano would have on temperatures today,' he said and shared a graphic showing a steep dip in the projected warming in next few years.[1]

Taken together, Ghughua and Tonga remind us of the oft-repeated principle in palaeontology, archaeology and even in history: 'looking back to look into the future'. Simply put, the events of the past that have unfolded over the centuries give us clues to the future, the manner in which things would unfold in the near and far term.

As per the latest IPCC Sixth Assessment Report (Working Group II [AR6 WGII]), *Climate Change 2022: Impacts, Adaptation and Vulnerability,* biodiversity loss, degradation, and damage to and transformation of ecosystems are already key risks for every region due to past global warming and will continue to escalate with every increment of global warming.[2]

While there have been projections about what may or may not go extinct, *State of the World's Trees*, September 2021, mentions that 18 per cent of the trees, i.e. 469 species, face the threat of extinction in India.[3]

The State of India's Birds Report 2020, which measured the abundance and distribution of 867 bird species, concluded:

> Of the 261 species for which long-term trends could be determined, 52% have declined since the year 2000, with 22% declining strongly. In all, 43% of species showed a long-term trend that was stable and 5% showed an increasing trend. Current annual trends could be estimated for 146 species. Of these, nearly 80% are declining, with almost 50% declining strongly. Just over 6% are stable and 14% increasing.[4]

Before that, in 2019, *The Hindu* had reported four species of fauna and 18 species of flora had gone extinct in India in the past few centuries.[5] It quoted a reply to a question in the Lok Sabha.

The reasons are many, including habitat loss, which is only going to be aggravated in the times of climate change.

What All Comprises Wildlife?

It may sound juvenile to raise this question here. But to my mind, this clarity is important, as perceptions matter as much as definitions. While there are certain textbook definitions, for the layperson, it is just the animals out there in the wild—animals, including mammals, reptiles, amphibians, marine species and birds. Needless to add, even when most people associate wildlife with just animals, all kinds of plants are very much part of the wildlife. The National Board for Wildlife (NBWL) does deal with cases where trees are to be felled for a linear project, where certain habitat destruction can cause problems for a species.

Environmentalists, therefore, offer a broader view, and it gels well with the larger understanding of the term *jeev shrishti* as understood by millions of Indians. In that broader view, wildlife would refer to any and all living beings—plants, shrubs, animals, birds, insects, fungi, everything—thriving even in areas that are off-limits for humans or, generally, where humans would not live.

Very rightly, the existing WLPA gives a clear definition: 'wild animal' means any animal specified in schedules I to IV and found wild in nature; and 'wildlife' includes any animal, aquatic, or land vegetation, which forms part of any habitat.[6]

Interestingly, the two are not separate but intricately interlinked, dependent on each other and thriving because of and not independent of each other. Again, as mentioned in the Indian scriptures: *jeevo jeevasya jeevanam*. In the journey of evolution, the species evolve together, fighting each other and helping each other.

An example much prevalent across India, well almost, is that of the weed lantana (*Lantana camara*). It came in as an exotic hedge species with pretty flowers. Now, thanks to the impact of climate change leading to the weakening of ecosystemic resilience, an invasive like lantana will only grow further, capturing a far larger area aided by the increasing temperatures. Needless to add, lantana's invasion would come at the cost of native species of plants and suitable habitats for animals.

In their study 'Modelling the potential risk zone of lantana invasion and response to climate change in India', a team of researchers have established how lantana while unable to penetrate through the intact native virgin forest, was abundantly distributed along agricultural lands and in open, disturbed forest areas, restricting the regeneration and extension of native species.[7]

As I said above, it is a clear case of *jeevo jeevasya jeevanam*—the survival of the fittest. The virgin forest was stronger, it defended its turf. In other places, the lantana has managed to survive and even expand its territory.

It is believed that climate change impact is going to be most evident across the Himalayan belt. Let us look at two examples from its two ends.

Arunachal and Ladakh

One of the top biodiversity-rich states is the northeastern state of Arunachal Pradesh, nestled in the eastern Himalayas. It has about 20 per cent species of the country's fauna, about 4,500 species of flowering plants, 400 species of pteridophytes, 23 species of conifers, 35 species of bamboos, 20 species of canes, 52 species of rhododendrons and more than 500 species of orchids. Two national parks and 11 wildlife sanctuaries constitute the PA network of the state, covering 11.68 per cent of its geographical area. Beyond this, large areas fall under community forests.

I have been visiting Arunachal Pradesh regularly since 2011 (it was the year when I spent a whole month in eastern Arunachal Pradesh pursuing the Rural Reporting Fellowship offered by the Centre for the Study of Developing Societies [CSDS]). It is one state that has offered both positive and negative examples when it comes to the conservation of biodiversity.

Let me start with the latest, which, unfortunately, is the negative part, and take you to my field trip from 2016 to highlight the positive that fills my heart with joy and pride.

In January 2022, the *India State of Forest Report 2021* brought out a dismal picture of the Indian forests, especially in northeast India. In the case of Arunachal Pradesh, the report showed that the total forest cover (that within and outside the recorded forest area) is 66,430.67 sq. km.[8] As per the 2019 report, the forest cover was 66,687.78 sq. km; the *India State of Forest Report 2017* said the total forest cover was 66,964 sq. km, while the 2015 report said the total forest cover was 67,248 sq. km. The trend of decreasing forest cover could not be more blatant.[9]

Arunachal Pradesh is entirely a tribal state, meaning that, for centuries, the forests have been the mainstay for the livelihoods of local people. At the turn of the last century, when exposure to the outside world began to increase, there was an inevitable change. Now, over the years, practices such as *jhum* have increased owing to the increase in tribal population, which, in turn, puts pressure on the forests consistently. Add to it the devil named development.

Of the total, only five districts in Arunachal Pradesh showed positive change, while the rest were negatively impacted according to the *India State of Forest Report 2021*. Of the latter, the Lower Dibang Valley, Dibang Valley, Lohit and Anjaw have seen the worst negative trend, the same areas that I have been visiting so often to report and witness the massive destruction of thick-trunk trees with large canopies. For these districts the forest cover has been going down constantly, year after year, and this is happening in almost all categories—the very dense, moderate and open forest.

For Lohit and Anjaw, most of the forest that has fallen prey to destruction are right next to the Kamlang Tiger Reserve. The scale at which the connecting corridors are being summarily chopped off—be it for agriculture or for growing opium, the fact remains that the timber is finding its way to the illegal market—it would not be a surprise that not just the tiger, the flagship species, but the other species too start walking away from the area.

Who is responsible? The trader who buys and takes away the timber comes from outside. The middlemen that come and buy opium are from outside. But who does the legwork? Who fells the trees? Who grows the *kani* there?

It is against this gloomy backdrop that I recall two examples wherein the community is leading by example. One is a pan-Arunachal Pradesh example, and the second is from the westernmost district of Tawang.

Hunting has been a common practice for centuries across Arunachal Pradesh, but earlier, it was strictly need-based, which would mean no direct threat to the wildlife. As man progressed, as need changed to greed, hunting increased, and with the easy availability of air guns, it skyrocketed, not just for meat but for a game that led to poaching.

Air guns do not require any licence, and scores of people hunt birds and smaller animals using these airguns across Arunachal Pradesh, unaware of the biodiversity loss. Most of the ownership of the land rests with the tribal communities, effectively leaving a very small area under the forest department. It renders much of the wildlife-related laws ineffective.

The state's environment minister, Mama Natung, thought of bringing about a change. In March 2021, to be precise, he publicly appealed to the people of Arunachal Pradesh to surrender their airguns.

With the help of a non-governmental organization (NGO), Natung first started the awareness drive. What started as an off-beat attempt has now succeeded in a full-fledged programme. Over 2,000 airguns and about 500 rifles were surrendered by year end, and Natung and the officials from the forest department were hopeful of more.

If it was Mama Natung who came forth to appeal to his community and others to drop the airguns; in Tawang's case, the community, on its own, decided not to kill certain animals and fell trees from certain areas.

It may sound unbelievably incredible, but it is true.

Tawang is the westernmost district of Arunachal Pradesh, abutting Bhutan. Towards the northernmost part, in the Pangchen Valley, are the last two civilian villages, Lumpo and Muchut, inhabited by the Monpa community that has been taking vital steps to save the red panda.

Listed as 'vulnerable' in the IUCN Red List of Threatened Species and also under the Schedule I of the WLPA, the red pandas in India live in the eastern Himalayas only. They prefer the deciduous and coniferous forest mixed with bamboo undergrowth at approximately 7,000 feet to 14,000 feet.

The two remotest villages are not connected with the central power grid, and perched at such high altitude they experience a harsh winter. Naturally, people extensively used firewood for cooking and heating. About 20 years ago, WWF-India started working with the community and made them realize that felling jungles around them—and at times, even in far-off places too—would mean habitat destruction for the red panda.

Slowly but firmly, the community was convinced and initiated a conservation programme in 2005. Even at the cost of increasing their troubles, the community took it upon themselves to save the fragile habitat and, thus, the red panda. They had the earlier example of how the snow leopard once sighted in their area had gone missing due to the loss of habitat.

The core zone of the red panda and the buffer zone were mapped for the entire Pangchen area, and the people themselves decided to abstain from killing any animals and felling any trees. They even started patrolling in their designated areas twice a year. This definitely helped bring down poaching. The two villages were entirely involved in the process, and the listing of biodiversity from the area was displayed prominently. They also imposed a fine of ₹10,000 for the violator for collecting firewood timber from the buffer zone. Unlike the typical sarkari conservation schemes, this has been a success! Not a single fine was imposed, as the community members religiously abide by their commitments.

With such an approach, we do not have a doubt that the community, the forest and the red panda will face any problems in years to come, climate change impact notwithstanding.

Across to the extreme west side, beyond the Himalayas in the Ladakh region, changing climatic conditions have already started playing havoc. It is not just the quality of the pastureland that is declining fast; for some residents, it has had a direct livelihood impact, as the health of the livestock is on the decline.

Ladakh depends on its snow/precipitation in winters, but precisely, that is what is on the decline. Among the most impacted are the livestock rearers and owners. With every passing year, the pastures are drying, and grazing animals need to travel further and further. The snowline going higher up is indeed a cause of anxiety.[10]

Karma Sonam is a field manager with the Bengaluru-based Nature Conservation Foundation (NCF). I have known him since 2010 and enthusiastically listen to his tales from the field. He speaks of a simple, direct equation. The changing precipitation and temperature pattern in Ladakh mean that the pasturelands have declined in quality and quantity over the decades. As a result, there is a decline in livestock and wild animals dependent on pastures and the animals up the food chain.

'What happens if the top predator vanishes from the scene? Or for that matter its numbers decline?' Karma poses a question and answers himself: 'Imbalance—if we look at the overall impact due to climate change, it has meant fewer options for the animals, for the communities dependent on them and for nature itself.'

The WLPA, in its current form, fails to help Karma. But it is not just Ladakh where the problem lies.

The Wildlife Act

A write-up about species in *The Third Pole* in November 2020 quoted Abi T. Vanak, senior fellow at the Ashoka Trust for Research in Ecology and the Environment (ATREE), who said the WLPA is not designed to help the endangered species in any way except prevent poaching. 'The law doesn't outline what needs to be done to revive the species,' he said.[11]

A slow but steady manifestation can be seen in the heart of central India, which is an incredibly rich biodiverse forest. Former forester from Maharashtra, Maruti Chitampalli, has spent decades tending to the forests and writing books about jungles, in the process, documenting vital processes and introducing many of them to lay readers.

Chitampalli talks of how devrais and vanrais (sacred groves) that were in the middle of a settlement with various plants had waterbodies within. Over the years, rampant tree felling has led to a complete decline in the dense vegetation, for which these sacred groves were known. That, in turn, prompts the wild animals to come out and become a potential threat to humans and also liable to be harmed by humans. Taking the same thread further, Chitampalli suggests ensuring food and water for the animals to reduce human–animal conflict (HAC). If that is sufficiently available within the forest, there won't be any reason for such conflicts. Simple? Well, yes—and no!

Chitampalli told me of two different aspects. One is the lantana spreading across jungles with a detrimental effect, which has not been removed. Another, he tells, about *nallah bunding* that led to water percolation and waterbodies formation, practices that led to ample availability of water and avoided wild animals from coming out.

Brihad Samhita is an ancient text that Chitampalli refers to; there is a chapter that talks about how much rainfall will be received in a given circumstance; where and how a crow builds its nest, whether in the east direction or west. So, the trees need to be protected. Forget the old trees in the jungle—new officers come and plant ornamental trees in their bungalows. The old ones are felled or destroyed. The ancient needs to be preserved!

The former Indian Forest Service (IFS) officer-turned-author of books on jungles further asserts the importance of having more trees that are directly beneficial to the wildlife. For instance, the rapid decline in old trees everywhere—in cities, in villages, on farmlands along the bunds. 'These massive canopies not just harbour hundreds of birds but also protect the village in case of thunderstorms. With the trees gone missing, the existence of birds is threatened. Another habitat that both communities and the governments have neglected is the waterbodies, the lakes. Hundreds of waterbodies are infested with the weed *Ipomoea*,' a worried Chitampalli told me.[12]

This is a common sight across waterbodies in the Bhandara and Gondia districts of Maharashtra, and I have seen hundreds of village ponds infested with *Ipomea* eating into the pond's body, trapping filth, including plastic, and, then, generally leading to a decline in the health of the waterbody—neglected, left to dry and destroyed. Irrigation, fisheries and forest department all carry out their own schemes, not coordinating with each other and leaving the community out of the conservation work.

Land ownership determines the fate, determines the action that would likely be taken and, ultimately, the future of that waterbody. If a waterbody is inside a recorded forest, reserved, protected or within a categorized parcel of land, then the forest laws are applicable. But if the waterbody is even adjacent to the forest but outside, the revenue department may or may not invoke forest laws to protect it.

'These water holes need to be protected under the wildlife act. Animals need water, so the water sources need to be protected. In fact, the whole ecosystem needs to be protected,' the 90-year-plus Chitampalli said.

Suddenly, it makes sense to have the entire ecosystem protected under the provisions of the WLPA. The IPCC reports have time and again warned of dire consequences if the world continues with a business-as-usual attitude. What will happen to the resident bird or animal if the host habitat is to perish?

And then Chitampalli makes a drastic suggestion. The ecosystem, for wild animals, also includes Adivasis, the tribal communities that have had a symbiotic relationship with the forests throughout the centuries. 'In view of the threats to the jungles and their livelihoods, their habitats...in the name of national parks, sanctuaries, or game reserves, Adivasis are uprooted. So, they need to be brought under the purview of Wildlife Act for protecting the local ecology,' he suggested.

Wild sans Humans—Impossible?

Maruti Chitampalli is clearly not alone in making such a drastic suggestion. Wildlife—and, by extension, the forest—without humans is an idea that has not gone down well with activists too. I remember the bitter criticism that a beautifully picturized film, complete with mesmerizing drone shots, named *Wild Karnataka* had received when it was released in January 2020.

In fact, Nitin D. Rai from ATREE in Bangalore protested in writing in *The Science Wire*. The heading itself indicated that he wanted to take the subject head-on: '"Wild Karnataka" Is Beautiful to Behold but Embraces an Idea That Deserved to Die'.[13] Nitin highlighted that the 'visually stunning technical masterpiece had ignored the humans that made the wilderness what it is'. 'Wild Karnataka ignores the history of humans in Karnataka's forests, implying that this place is no place for people. It is worth checking who exactly benefits from this idea and what the consequences of this film could be for the people who live in this wilderness,' he wrote.

This seemed to echo exactly what I heard from Leo Saldanha of Bengaluru's Environment Support Group (ESG). 'A forest devoid of humans is antithetical,' he told me. According to Leo, Adivasis were the greatest protectors of this planet and, today, they are thrown out of the forest. The Scheduled Tribes and Other Traditional Forestdwellers (Recognition of Forest Rights) Act, 2006, also known as the Forest Rights Act (FRA), 2006, has not been implemented well. In fact, he is very clear—those who protected the forest, protected the wildlife. Needless to add, a look at the physical map of India overlapped with tribal-dominated areas makes it amply clear where the densely forested areas are, and who has protected those till now.

The Way Forward

While a lot of thought has gone into the conservation practices that are needed and the measures needed for protecting wildlife, my mind goes back to the past to think about the future. Lot of us are aware of a Sanskrit shloka, which is conventionally believed to be remembering the five great female characters from mythology.

Ahilya Draupadi Seeta Tara Mandodari Tatha |
Panchakam Na Smarenityam Mahapataknashanam ||

Sanskrit scholar Pradnya Deshpande from Nagpur has derived a totally different meaning from this shloka. She has termed Ahilya as soil that has never been plowed; Draupadi as land that can witness double sowing; Seeta as white soil that is most natural; Tara is wetland, reflecting the stars above; and Mandodari is a land that produces ample crop without any effort.

Thus, Pradnya Deshpande says that healthy soil is essential for good produce and for raising forests, both a must for human survival. Plus, the ground is home to numerous organisms. Protecting our soil in a climate-altered India cannot be overstated. Soil being the most critical sequester of carbon on earth only adds to the point already made.

Taking that point forward, I would say, the old Sanskrit shloka can be incorporated as essential duties under the WLPA. Protecting the soil will form the basis of protection of forests, wetlands and, in turn, the wildlife—that can be a valuable action plan to combat the changing climate.

Notes

1. Zeke Hausfather [@hausfath], *Twitter*, 15 January 2022, https://twtr.in/3K7j. Accessed on 7 July 2022.
2. *Climate Change 2022: Impacts, Adaptation and Vulnerability*, IPCC, p. 14, https://bityl.co/D7Mt. Accessed on 7 July 2022.
3. *State of the World's Trees*, Botanic Gardens Conservation International, September 2021, https://bityl.co/D7N8. Accessed on 7 July 2022.
4. Eapen, Nikhil, 'Indian Government Misleads Parliament on Wildlife Decline', The Third Pole, 9 November 2020, https://bityl.co/D7NA. Accessed on 7 July 2022.
5. Singh, Shiv Sahay, 'Vanishing Wildlife: 22 Species Have Gone Extinct in India', *The Hindu*, 30 July 2019, https://bityl.co/D7Or. Accessed on 7 July 2022.
6. *The Wild Life (Protection) Act, 1972*, Parliament of India, https://bit.ly/3mPOtnO. Accessed on 15 June 2022.
7. Tiwari, Sharad, et al., 'Modelling the Potential Risk Zone of *Lantana Camara* Invasion and Response to Climate Change in Eastern India', *Ecological Processes*, Vol. 11, No. 1, January 2022, p. 10, https://doi.org/10.1186/s13717-021-00354-w. Accessed on 7 July 2022.
8. *India State of Forest Report 2021*, Forest Survey of India, MoEFCC, 2022, https://bityl.co/D7Qa. Accessed on 7 July 2022.
9. *India State of Forest Report 2015*, Forest Survey of India, MoEFCC, 2015, https://bityl.co/D7RW. Accessed on 7 July 2022; *India State of Forest Report 2017*, Forest Survey of India, MoEFCC, 2017, https://bityl.co/D7RS. Accessed on 7 July 2022; *India State of Forest Report 2019*, Forest Survey of India, MoEFCC, 2019, https://bityl.co/D7RN. Accessed on 7 July 2022; *India State of Forest Report 2021*, Forest Survey of India, MoEFCC, 2022, https://bityl.co/D7Qa. Accessed on 7 July 2022.
10. Wani, Riyaz, 'Climate Change, Border Tensions, Destroy the Habitat of the Pashmina Goat', The Third Pole, 4 February 2021, https://bityl.co/D7NC. Accessed on 7 July 2022.

11. Eapen, Nikhil, 'Indian Government Misleads Parliament on Wildlife Decline', The Third Pole, 9 November 2020, https://bityl.co/D7NA. Accessed on 7 July 2022.
12. Personal interview with Maruti Chitampalli in November 2021.
13. Rai, Nitin D., '"Wild Karnataka" Is Beautiful to Behold but Embraces an Idea That Deserved to Die', *The Wire Science*, 31/1/2020 ed., https://bityl.co/D7Si. Accessed on 7 July 2022.

LOOKING INTO THE CRYSTAL BALL: WLPA OF 2072

NEHA SINHA

Imagine this...

Under a crystal-clear blue sky, you are looking at a green expanse of water. The water reflects shrubby growth on its banks, and lush floating plants shine from its expanse. An inky shadow falls upon your cheeks—a bird-like flying animal shrieks as it glides across the sky. Behind the shrubbery is a long, sinuous neck belonging to a giant but peaceful-looking herbivore. A sudden tremor breaks the peace—a predator is on the prowl, and every dinosaur is now alert.

This is possibly how a typical scene with flying pterodactyls and meat-eating dinosaurs looked like millions of years ago as they occupied their marshy ecosystems untouched by the human hand.

Today, the human hand is all-pervasive. Roads cut through forests, wires slice the sky, trains thunder between fragile forest corridors, irrigation projects threaten to drown tiger reserves and solar farms bisect the desert. This is why laws that enable some places to remain wild, unarranged by us, are so important. The Wild Life (Protection) Act (WLPA), 1972, and The Environment (Protection) Act (EPA), 1986, when read together, place wild animals on a certain pedestal. Overall, wild animals are legally safe from being hunted. Broadly speaking, areas set aside for the purpose of conservation are supposed to have minimum intervention.

Yet, 50 years since the WLPA was passed, wild animals are not as safe as they should be. In my adulthood, I have watched the common become uncommon, and the list of rarities grows larger than my imagination. Those big-sized *mithus*, Alexandrine parakeets with their shrill, excited calls and red thumbprint marks on their wings, are now 'Near Threatened' as per the International Union for Conservation of Nature (IUCN) Red List. So is the woolly-necked stork, once so commonly found in rural areas that birdwatchers did not consider the bird to be a real 'sighting'. Wildlife with their most important breeding grounds in India—the great Indian bustard (GIB), the Ganges River dolphin, the Indian skimmer, the Bengal florican, to take just a few examples—have the ground (or waters) shifting from beneath their feet, hanging precariously from their last strongholds. The last wild population of Asiatic lions is in India, but the domestic politics of Gujarat ensures lions have no safe habitat in any other state of India despite a 2013 Supreme Court verdict on this issue. I also wonder if the wild creatures that are still common—the black-winged stilts in roadside slips of water, common mynas pecking at footpaths, small Indian mongoose foraging in cities, migratory black-eared kites hovering in our skies, will soon slip away from our lives.

Linear projects—roads, railways, canals, electricity lines—are some of the most significant threats to wildlife and habitat today. Threats to individual animals are also mounting—electrocution of flying birds and animals (both residents, like the GIB, and migratory visitors, like the steppe eagle), death by roads and railways (leopards, tigers, snakes, elephants), poaching (all the big cats, elephants and rhinoceros), revenge (tigers and leopards, for eating livestock, and nilgai, wild boar and elephants, for eating crops) and accidental poisoning (*Gyps* vultures). Large-scale loss of breeding areas may also hinder future reproductive success.

But can this change? I believe planning for the future can help us achieve some conservation goals. The last 50 years have shown us what we can gain (and lose) for unspeaking but ever-present Nature. The next 50 years will be even tougher than the last half-century. At the United Nations Climate Change Conference (COP26) in Glasgow, in 2021, India said it will achieve a net-zero economy by 2070. This means we will have a furious pace of growth till the middle of the century before we plateau and taper off our emissions. We are already headed in this direction. In 2022, changes have been proposed in our entire suite of environmental legislation—The Biological Diversity Act, 2002, the WLPA of 1972, and the Forest (Conservation) Act (FCA) of 1980. There are moves to decriminalize the provisions of The Water (Prevention and Control of Pollution) Act, 1974, Air (Prevention and Control of Pollution) Act, 1981, and the Environment (Protection) Act, 1986. Most of the changes are geared towards the 'ease of doing business' and concessions for the industry. Ironically and at the same time, we are facing the spectre of climate change—cyclones, forest fires, floods, unseasonal rainfall, longer heat spells and rainfall in places that are unused to and unprepared for it (such as Ladakh, parts of the Himalayan regions, etc.). Generally speaking, wildlife responds to changing climates by attempting to move towards more favourable regions. For animals on mountains in a heating region, this often means moving up the slope, which leads to undue pressure on the habitat and the danger of displacing other animals. And at the end of the slope, there is only a sheer drop.

What a WLPA of the Future Could Look Like

From the age of the dinosaurs, let us move our gaze towards other ancient habitats in the future.

In the National Capital Region, a city hums and moves; in the backdrop, an old, time-worn ridge of rocks is gripped by dhau saplings. Migratory flycatchers move between native trees and city parks. In the eyeline are foreign tulip plants and native semal trees. On the same latitude, westwards, a gritty expanse of sand meets the eye.

At first, there is nothing to see in the Thar Desert of India 50 years from now. And then, you start seeing perfectly camouflaged wildlife amidst dunes and scrub. The signs of a desert fox. Roheda trees in the blurry distance and spiny acacias with their root claws deep in the soil are launch pads and sanctuaries for little creatures. The booming call of a GIB reverberates in the air. A kestrel cocks its head from its branch. A greater spotted eagle flies in the clear sky. You can turn your head and see the sun-browned land in every direction and an endless, uninterrupted yellow-blue sky. Is something missing, you wonder? Where are the wires and wire posts? Where are the dazzling solar panels hungrily drinking up the sun?

You realize then that there are no wires in the sky. The desert area is a breeding ground for species like desert fox, the GIB, the blackbuck, the chinkara, all of whom are part of a habitat unimpeded by huge solar and wind farms and their servants-in-attendance, electric wires.

In the last 50 years of the WLPA, we have managed to establish the idea that wild animals have some rights—the right to live and not be hunted. Perhaps the correct descriptor is that animals have the right to not be hunted indiscriminately. In the next 50 years, we should be able to respond adequately to the 2014 Jallikattu judgement in the case of Animal Welfare Board of India vs A. Nagaraja. It said: 'Animal has also honour and dignity which it cannot be arbitrarily deprived of and its rights and privacy have to be respected and protected from unlawful attacks.'[1]

It also has the following observation:

> Article 21 of the Constitution, while safeguarding the rights of humans, protects life and the word 'life' has been given an expanded definition and any disturbance from the basic environment which includes all forms of life, including animal life, which are necessary for human life, fall within the meaning of Article 21 of the Constitution. So far as animals are concerned, in our view, 'life' means something more than mere survival or existence or instrumental value for human beings, but to lead a life with some intrinsic worth, honour and dignity.

In the current WLPA, it is important to understand how animals can be hunted as 'vermin'. The purpose of the schedules of the Act is to prohibit hunting wild animals and provide conditions for the scheduled animal to be declared vermin.[2]

The WLPA 1972 defines hunting as follows:

> '[H]unting', with its grammatical variations and cognate expressions, includes,—
>
> [(a) killing or poisoning of any wild animal or captive animal and every attempt to do so;
>
> (b) capturing, coursing, snaring, trapping, driving or baiting any wild or captive animal and every attempt to do so;]
>
> (c) injuring or destroying or taking any part of the body of any such animal or, in the case of wild birds or reptiles, damaging the eggs of such birds or reptiles, or disturbing the eggs or nests of such birds or reptiles.[3]

On prohibition of hunting of Scheduled animals the WLPA says: 'Prohibition of hunting.—No person shall hunt any wild animal specified in Schedules I, II, III and IV except as provided under section 11 and section 12.'

The WLPA 1972 has the following clauses for declaration of vermin:

> 11 (a) the Chief Wild Life Warden may, if he is satisfied that any wild animal specified in Schedule I has *become dangerous to human life* [emphasis added] or is so disabled or diseased as to be beyond recovery, by Order in writing and stating the reasons therefore, permit any person to hunt such animal or cause such animal to be hunted;
>
> 11 (b) the Chief Wild Life Warden or the authorised officer may, if he is satisfied that any wild animal specified in Schedule II, Schedule III, or Schedule IV, has *become dangerous to human life or to property (including standing crops on any land)* [emphasis added] or is so disabled or diseased as to be beyond recovery, by order in writing and stating the reasons there for, permit any person to hunt [such animal or group of animals in a specified area or cause such animal or group of animals in that specified area to be hunted].

The 1972 WLPA, thus, allowed threatened animals to be hunted if they became dangerous to human life. Generally, less threatened animals (found in Schedule II) could be hunted if they became dangerous to human life or property.

The proposed 2021 amendment seeks to make the process of vermin declaration even easier, with a suggestion that any animal in Schedule II could be declared vermin (thus indicating a less common animal in the Schedule like a jungle cat would be at par with the more common animals in Schedule II, like the wild pig).

Sadly, the declarations of vermin have been political decisions based on hyperlocal perceptions of damage and distress. Declaration of vermin and the killing of nilgai, rhesus macaques, wild pig, etc., have not solved root causes of human–wildlife conflict (HWC). If animals are raiding crops because they don't have good habitat to forage in, the answer is to provide better habitat and timely compensation for losses. With the reality of global warming, which threatens both wildlife and livelihoods, this becomes even more urgent.

In the WLPA of the future that I wish for, vermin declaration should be made following scientific assessments and an understanding of baseline populations. The idea of population estimations should go beyond species like tigers and co-predators (counted every four years in the all-India tiger estimations). In the future WLPA, animals at the centre of the conflict should be counted, and their needs accounted for. Let us not forget that even 50 years before the 1972 WLPA, the tiger was considered vermin and hunted as such. In the future, some animals should have expanded ranges—generalist species, such as the Indian crow, may benefit from global warming. But niche specialists like frogs or salamanders, which are point endemics, might suffer.

This brings us to the next important change in the future WLPA that is required. This includes looking at ecosystems as things that need to be assessed, rated in terms of importance and endangerment, and protected through the schedules of the WLPA.

Thus, Schedule I of the 2072 WLPA may look like:

i. tiger;
ii. GIB;
iii. Indian skimmers and riverine sandy island ecosystems;
iv. Bengal florican and wet grasslands;
v. inter-tidal mudflats and their suites of species;
vi. coastal plateaus;
vii. coral atolls; and
viii. a particular tree that has an above-ordinary number of beehives or is a breeding site of suites of several species and more.

In the image that I evoked at the beginning of this section, why was the desert seemingly untouched? For one, it was no more referred to as 'wasteland' or 'barren land'. Like the desert, the Aravalli Range will be managed for what it really is—an ancient ridge of rocks and slopes, with thorny, tough, survivor-spirited trees and plants. It will not be managed as a Miyawaki forest or seen as a lesser cousin of tropical moist forest with scant canopy cover. Not only will the WLPA of the future expand its scope with ecosystem types, it will also have decadal assessments of the schedules—both species and ecosystems.

There should also be a change in how wild animals are accorded rights, and their lives should not be snatched from them without science as an ally. Secondly, their habitats should be ranked and protected in schedules. We now come to the third change: actively assessing threats to wildlife and ecosystems.

In this regard, the looming threat of invasive alien species is an important issue to be tackled. Invasive alien species are species that are not native to India. To understand the threats they pose, they need to be studied, assessed and stopped at the native ecosystem level, because even an *Indian* species can be invasive in another part of India. An Indian crow is very, very unwelcome and very, very invasive in the Andaman and Nicobar islands.

The definition of 2072's WLPA should be:

> 'invasive alien species' means a species of animal or plant which is not native to an ecosystem and whose introduction or spread may threaten or adversely impact wild life or its habitat, also including domestic predators like dogs and cats as appropriate.

If the WLPA is planned like this, India would look like the following.

The desert is protected as a desert, not as a degraded, ugly forest. Rock faces are protected on coasts, and rock ridges through cities and highways are left alone. They become a breeding site for *Gyps* vultures. The building of overpasses for cars, not animals, means that elephant herds, gaur, rhinoceros and chital can move across highways safely. Rope bridges are made for macaques. There is a department in the environment ministry that looks at the success of mitigation implementation measures.

The Panna landscape in Central India flourishes and becomes part of a vibrant necklace of tiger reserves because the Ken-Betwa River interlink project is scrapped. Gujarat still does not give lions to MP, but both Gujarat and Goa on the Western parts of India establish tiger reserves and work towards functional tiger connectivity with other forests where tigers roar. Northeast India has lush moist forests that are prospected for recording their biodiversity, not oil palm plantations.

Occasionally, people are able to see the world's fastest land animal, the cheetah, and one of the world's heaviest flying birds, the great Indian bustard, together. In 2022, the cheetah was brought in, but because the grassland was placed in Schedule I of the WLPA, more grasslands were brought under the ambit of local conservation. Communities will work hand in hand with conservation—they create their own people's biodiversity registers and keep their own records of bird sightings and threats to birds. The GIB has since expanded its current range from Thar and Kutch, and is seen in larger parts of Central India, Maharashtra and Deccan. Black cotton soil is well complemented with tawny cheetah spots and GIB browns.

There is a conversation on the personhood of animals, ecosystem features and plants. Some plants, such as big trees that hold many beehives and individual trees of extraordinary size, age or impact on the ecosystem, are considered entities that need parens patriae. Rivers are given the right to life, and, thus, the right to flow. Himalayan mountains are also considered entities. They are not blasted for road widening—instead, steel braces are used to extend the width and stability of roads. Carrying capacity studies of fragile areas are deeply intertwined with the idea of personhood—a mountain is not seen as a person just because it is a large mountain. It is treated as a legal entity with the right of refusal of how many people it has to encounter, gleaned through studies on its carrying capacity.

All these actions should be done not just to safeguard these places but also with the understanding that ecosystems can only provide optimal ecosystem services when they are managed as their most true, resilient and ecologically sound versions.

The Final Act

I don't want you thinking everything is hunky-dory in the WLPA of 2072. The Sixth Assessment Report of the Intergovernmental Panel on Climate Change (IPCC) has found something we are already experiencing—that India is among a global hotspot of human vulnerability. Our country will likely face flooded coastal areas, biodiversity loss, decline of fish on coasts, rainfall variability and drought. Miseries will be compounded as climate change causes cascading losses. When bundled with developmental challenges, the losses are unspeakable for both wildlife and humanity. I think this makes the task of having newer, more appropriate ways of protecting wildlife much more urgent. Tragically, the Ministry of Environment, Forest and Climate Change (MoEFCC) seems to be surrendering its mandate—for example, it has tied up with the power ministry to state electric lines can't be taken underground in Thar Desert. This is even though the Supreme Court directed for the lines to be taken underground because critically endangered GIBs collide with them and die. If the MoEFCC does not speak for wildlife and the unbroken wildlife habitat, then I am afraid we will only see birds in cages, not in skies free of wires.

Surely, we will lose many species to both the development-at-any-cost, ease-of-doing-business wheel and also to climate change. Perhaps exciting diversity may be the first to go—in a place where we saw 50 kinds of birds and 15 kinds of mammals, we may see half or one third of that. This will be robbing our future generations of the chance to be moved by the chorus of crickets in the monsoons, the whirring-flap of flying fox bats overhead at dusk, the stardust-like slow blinking of fireflies in long wild grass, the metronome call of barbets at the beginning of summer, cranes standing at attention in our fields, the slink of a jackal in a city park, the cautious leap of a jungle cat in a scrub land, the beauty of a plateau covered in purple flowers that bloom only in their own time. In order to progress both as a great nation and as a sustainable one, we must plan ahead. Having a science-led, morally driven, eco-centric WLPA can help us more than hinder us.

India's wildlife deserves this approach many times over. So does the habitat the wildlife lives in. If the river did not need a legal guardian, if it could speak, perhaps it would gurgle and bubble this truth to us, in a language that we could understand.

Notes

1. 'Animal Welfare Board Of India vs A. Nagaraja & Ors on 7 May, 2014', iKanoon, 7 May 2014, p. 193, https://bityl.co/DAcq. Accessed on 15 June 2022.

2. In the 2021 proposed amendment, there is 'rationalization' of schedules—these have been reduced to schedules I and II as opposed to Schedule I–IV in the principal Act.
3. *The Wild Life (Protection) Act, 1972*, Parliament of India, https://bit.ly/3mPOtnO. Accessed on 15 June 2022.

ACKNOWLEDGMENTS

Any creative work, least of all putting together a book and getting it published is a collective effort, where family members, friends and colleagues, sometimes even strangers (with ideas), play a part.

This book, an anthology really, could not have become a reality if people, many of them colleagues and friends of long standing and few brief and new acquaintances had not readily agreed to become a part of it. I can't thank them enough for sharing their life and work experiences, learnings and lessons, and putting up with my frequent reminders and often, short submission time frame for their tales. I just wish to tell all the contributors that it is *our* book.

In particular I am obliged to Ananda Banerjee, Neha Sinha, Raman Khanna and Usha Rai for helping me sort things out when the going seemed somewhat overwhelming. I am also thankful to my niece, Saumya Mishra, for her keen perusal of portions of the early manuscript and making useful inputs from a young reader's point of view. Sudha Mohan is thanked for her expert help in arranging the book into a shape in which it could be shared with the publisher.

My sister, Shraddha Bakshi and brother-in-law, Lieutenant General (Retd.) Ashwini Kumar Bakshi, are thanked for looking after and nursing me back to health when the dreaded malignancy caught up with me. But for that help I wonder if I could have found enough energy and strength to work on this book.

Senior commissioning editor, Rudra Narayan Sharma; deputy managing editor, Nishtha Kapil and editorial assistant, Soumya

Rampal at Rupa Publications are thanked for their professional inputs and for making the book happen in time. I am grateful to Kapish Mehra, managing director, Rupa Publications, for finding merit in the one pager of a concept note for this book, and later, taking personal interest in its production.

Finally, I would like to thank my mother, Dr Padma Siddhesh, for several things, most of all, looking after me as only a mother can while the book was under preparation.

ABOUT THE CONTRIBUTORS

Aditya 'Dicky' Singh, with a background in sciences and a bachelor's degree in engineering, joined the Indian Civil Service and worked there till finally deciding that his interests and calling lay in working with wildlife. He has lived in Ranthambore since early 1998, working on various wildlife documentaries, photography and conservation projects.

Ananda Banerjee is an award-winning environmental journalist, author and artist. Ananda has been part of several leading organizations—NGOs and national media—to give voice to important environmental issues through his research, writing and artwork. His ability to popularize data, research, science and developmental issues through research, writing and design has won him several prestigious awards. He co-founded the environmental law quarterly magazine *Paryavidhi* and has been instrumental in the production of several periodicals, e.g., *Tiger Link*, *Stripes* and *GTF News*. For more, visit https://anandabanerjee.com/.

Anjali Bhartari has spent the last 25 years working on the management of natural and cultural heritage sites. She works with communities and stakeholders through interpretation, outreach, publications, training and capacity-building. Her projects include the UNESCO World Heritage Site of Nalanda, Corbett Tiger Reserve, Rajaji Tiger Reserve, Jim Corbett Heritage Village and several museums. She has authored five books on natural and built heritage and its conservation, and several communication materials. She is pursuing her PhD in 'community involvement in conservation reserves' in Uttarakhand.

Aparajita Datta is a scientist at the Nature Conservation Foundation, leading the Eastern Himalaya programme. She studies hornbills, plant–animal interactions and human impact on wildlife, and works with local communities for conservation. She has carried out surveys that led to discoveries of new mammal species. She has written books for children and a field guide to the trees of Arunachal. She is the co-chair of the International Union for Conservation of Nature Species Survival Commission Hornbill Specialist Group. When not in the field, she finds peace and joy in watching and photographing birds and trees in the city. She enjoys writing and occasionally updates her blog.

Arvind Kumar Jha, an Indian Forest Service (IFS) officer, worked in the forest, tribal development and water conservation departments of Maharashtra; and as regional deputy director (Wildlife) in the Government of India. He retired as principal chief conservator of forests and director general (Social Forestry). Author of four books and 45 articles, he works on conservation and legal aspects of forestry, wildlife, biodiversity, tribal development and spiritual ecology. He is also founder trustee of the Global Enviro-Legal Services Foundation; he is on the board of advisors, Sacred Groves, which is a community interest company in the United Kingdom; member, Maharashtra and Goa Bar Council; and senior legal advisor to the Environment Law Defence Firm, New Delhi.

Asad R. Rahmani is the former director of the Bombay Natural History Society. His work focuses on birds, particularly bustards, cranes, storks and ecosystems such as grasslands and wetlands. He has written more than 160 peer-reviewed research papers, numerous reports, hundreds of articles, book reviews and editorials. He has authored or co-authored 26 books.

Bhuvana Balaji has a master's in development, with eight years of experience working as a trainer and facilitator, along with content and curriculum design, product design, participatory communication and design, research, journalism, photography, documentary filmmaking, and organizational development. Her core areas of work have been gender, menstrual health, sexual and reproductive health, the political economy of food, and environmental justice.

Dharmendra Khandal has served as a conservation biologist with Tiger Watch since 2003. His work with Tiger Watch has involved pioneering groundbreaking initiatives in proactive anti-poaching, the monitoring of wildlife and scientific research. He has also forged new frontiers in the world of community-based conservation through the Village Wildlife Volunteer programme in the Ranthambore Tiger Reserve. Dr Khandal is also the co-author of *Unexplored Ranthambhore* (2018), a first-of-its-kind book on the canids and striped hyenas in Ranthambore.

Faiyaz Ahmad Khudsar is a trained environmental and wildlife biologist with over 20 years of field experience. His area of interest is ecological restoration and wildlife research. He carried out long-term biological research at the Kuno National Park for his PhD. Widely published, including a book on Kuno Wildlife Sanctuary, he is a recipient of the Carl Zeiss Award for Excellence in Wildlife Conservation. He is associated with the Delhi biodiversity parks, a joint collaborative programme of the Delhi Development Authority (DDA) and the Centre for Environmental Management of Degraded Ecosystems (CEMDE), University of Delhi.

Ghazala Shahabuddin is an ecologist with a special interest in studying anthropogenic impacts on wildlife and ecosystems at various spatial and temporal scales. Since 1994, she has carried out numerous studies on the effects of land-use change, biomass extraction and habitat fragmentation on forest bird diversity in the Aravalli Hills, Western Ghats and Kumaon Himalayas. She has also published extensively on wildlife policy and politics in India. Her book *Conservation at the Crossroads* (Permanent Black and New India Foundation, 2010) examines conservation strategies in India. She is currently a visiting professor at Ashoka University, Haryana, and a scientist-affiliate with Wildlife Conservation Society (WCS), India.

Harbhajan Singh Pabla is a former chief wildlife warden (CWLW) of Madhya Pradesh. A proponent of active wildlife management, Pabla has led the reintroduction of several locally extinct species. He believes that wildlife conservation has limited scope purely as an ecological and moral pursuit, and must fit into the country's economic planning for sustainable success. According to him, hunting and tourism are natural corollaries of the conservation of wildlife. He considers India's current wildlife conservation approach rather aimless and has authored four rather unusual books to illustrate his vision. He has worked as a consultant in Sri Lanka, Bangladesh and Nepal.

H.S. Panwar considers he is amongst the few survivors a bygone age of foresters who identified their professional life with wildlife conservation. A member of the Indian Forest Service, Panwar was founder-director of Kanha Tiger Reserve, where he served for 12 years; director of Project Tiger and founder-director of the Wildlife Institute of India. In a pioneering role in the period of foundational wildlife management in India, he took the gauntlet and succeeded. Both Kanha and WII were founded on a visionary perspective by grooming competent and cause-inspired teams. Honoured by the President of India with the Padma Bhushan (2013), he is also a recipient of the WWF-International Duke of Edinburgh Conservation Medal (2002), International Union for Conservation of Nature Fred M. Packard Award (1996) and the Ministry of Environment and Forests inaugural Wildlife Conservation Medal (1998).

Ishan Dhar became associated with Tiger Watch when the village wildlife volunteer programme first expanded in 2015 and has been an active participant in Tiger Watch conservation interventions ever since. Since April 2021, he has served as communications manager for the organization. He has also served on Tiger Watch's board of directors since 2017, the youngest individual to do so. He has co-authored a book on the village wildlife volunteer programme titled *Wildlife Warriors* (Tiger Watch), along with multiple research articles in journals and the electronic and print media.

Ishan Kukreti is an environmental journalist based out of New Delhi. He has written extensively on environmental and developmental issues ranging from forest governance to energy and climate change within a framework of political ecology. His reporting adds a human lens to the broader debates around environmental policies and problems. His stories have been used as evidence in court cases at all levels of the Indian judiciary and to raise questions in the Indian parliament and state assemblies.

Joanna Van Gruisen is from the UK but has lived in the subcontinent since the late 1970s. She came to India in 1981 to make wildlife documentaries and has lived here ever since. An early pioneer of wildlife photography in India, she has been part of the conservation scene for several decades, filming, photographing, writing, researching and editing. She presently lives in Madhya Pradesh, where she co-runs a small eco-lodge and is active in sustainable tourism fields and local nature projects.

Koustubh Sharma has been involved in active research and conservation since 2001. Presently associated with the Snow Leopard Trust as its assistant director of Conservation Policy and Partnerships, he has been deputed since 2014 in Bishkek (Kyrgyzstan) as the International coordinator of the Global Snow Leopard & Ecosystems Protection Program. Post a master's degree in physics, he obtained PhD (2006) in wildlife zoology from Mumbai University based on the first detailed study of the four-horned antelope while working with the Bombay Natural History Society (BNHS). His professional interests include population ecology, conservation biology, policy, data visualization and technology.

Lala Aswini Kumar Singh is a lifelong wildlife researcher with many pioneering contributions to the conservation of crocodiles, tiger, elephant and their ecological associates. He has worked in the river basins of Mahanadi, Chambal and Similipal, and his PhD thesis is on the gharial crocodile. Two of his books, one each on the crocodile and the elephant, are available in eight international languages. Widely published, Lala A.K. Singh has authored several popular science articles and a book on the crocodile in the local language of Odisha state. Honoured by many national and international organizations, in 2013, he received the State Biju Patnaik Award from the government of Odisha. After superannuation in 2010 as senior research officer (SRO), he is based in Bhubaneswar, working as an independent researcher and editor-reviewer of scientific journals.

Manoj Kumar Misra is a former member of the Indian Forest Service. He has a postgraduate diploma in wildlife management from the Wildlife Institute of India, Dehradun. During government service, he managed protected areas, was a trainer and researched forestry and wildlife. Before seeking voluntary retirement from government service, he headed Trade Record Analysis of Flora and Fauna in Commerce (TRAFFIC) India in World Wide Fund for Nature-India (WWF-India). Since retirement, he has devoted himself to better understanding and advocating for the rejuvenation of our country's rivers. Presently, he is the convener of Yamuna Jiye Abhiyaan, a civil society campaign for the rejuvenation of the river Yamuna and is on the steering committee of India Rivers Forum (IRF) and the Forum for Policy Dialogues on Water Conflicts in India.

Nayana Udayashankar has a degree in law with several years of experience working in the field of environmental justice. For the last five years, she has critically examined tourism from a development lens and advocated for the rights of local communities in the tourism context. Drawing from her strength of knowing and understanding the law, her work focuses on democratizing decision-making with respect to environmental governance, particularly in tourism areas.

Neha Sinha is a conservation biologist and an author interested particularly in the destiny of wilful wild animals that crisscross our lives and the intersection of politics and the environment. She heads Conservation and Policy at the Bombay Natural History Society (BNHS) and is the author of the critically acclaimed *Wild and Wilful: Tales of 15 Iconic Indian Species* (2021).

Nivedita Khandekar is an associate editor with IANS, India's largest news agency. Based in Delhi, she writes on environmental, developmental and agricultural issues. She has travelled extensively across India, the Himalayas being her favourite destination, for reporting from the remotest areas. Calling herself a 'socially sensitized reporter', she endeavours to put forth the voice of the unheard or lesser heard people. She has earlier worked with *Hindustan Times* and the Press Trust of India and, during her stint as an independent, regularly wrote for multiple prestigious news organizations. She has won reporting fellowships, travel grants and awards too. She can be reached at nivedita_him@rediffmail.com.

Prerna Singh Bindra has been at the forefront of the battle to conserve India's wildlife for over a decade. She was a member of India's National Board for Wildlife and its core standing committee (2010–2013) and also served on Uttarakhand's State Board for Wildlife. She is particularly interested in protecting wildlife habitats, strategies to mainstream conservation concerns and developing a robust nature ethic in society. She has co-edited *Wild Treasures: Reflections on Natural World Heritage Sites in Asia*, published by the Wildlife Institute of India in 2019. She is the author of the critically acclaimed book *The Vanishing: India's Wildlife Crisis* (2017). She went back to college after two decades and is currently doing her PhD at the University of Cambridge. She is dogs' best friend, reveres trees and has a soft spot for elephants.

R. Sreenivasa Murthy is a former member of the Indian Forest Service. He was the team leader that revived the Panna tigers from zero to 34 between 2009 and 2015. He followed the path of 'Tiger Conservation with People's Support' at Panna. Cambodia is following the Panna model of tiger reintroduction, and he visited Cambodia to share his experiences and expertise. He is a recipient of World Wide Fund for Nature-India (WWF-India) and Pacific Asia Travel Association (PATA) Bagh Mitra Award (2011), Royal Bank of Scotland (RBS) Earth Hero award (2015), Madhya Pradesh Gaurav Samman and Chief Minister Excellence Award of the Madhya Pradesh government in 2016.

Rabindra Kumar Singh, an officer of the Indian Forest Service, has been the chief wildlife warden (CWLW), Chhattisgarh, and retired as the principal chief conservator of forests (PCCF) and head of forest force (HOFF) there. He has a wide administrative and teaching-cum-training experience, including placements at the Indian Institute of Forest Management, Bhopal (Madhya Pradesh), and the State Institute of Rural Development, Raipur (Chhattisgarh). He has chaired and been a member of various state- and national-level committees. Presently, R.K. Singh is a member of the Central Zoo Authority (CZA). He is widely published and has produced more than 20 films for teaching and educational purposes.

Ritwick Dutta is an environmental lawyer and co-founder of Legal Initiative for Forest and Environment (LIFE), a public interest environmental law group. In 2021, LIFE was conferred the Right Livelihood Award, also called the 'Alternative Nobel', for its contribution to using the law to protect the environment. Ritwick is an Ashoka Fellow and a fellow at the Right Livelihood College, Bonn. He has authored and edited over 13 books on environmental laws. Besides litigation, he is a regular writer in leading journals and newspapers, and a speaker in universities and training institutions.

Saket Badola is a postgraduate in veterinary sciences and is a member of the Indian Forest Service. Due to his passion for wildlife management, he completed the advanced postgraduate diploma in wildlife management from Wildlife Institue of India, Dehradun, and went on to serve as divisional forest officer in the Upper Yamuna Forest Division, Uttarkashi and Mussoorie forest divisions. He also managed the Corbett Tiger Reserve as deputy director. He has worked as the country head of Trade Record Analysis of Flora and Fauna in Commerce (TRAFFIC) in India on deputation with World Wide Fund for Nature-India (WWF-India) and held the additional responsibility of the secretary-general in the Central IFS Association. Presently he is the director, Rajaji National Park, Uttarakhand.

Sharad Gaur is a biologist with a conservation career spanning more than 42 years. Holding a master's degree in zoology, he worked with World Wide Fund for Nature-India (WWF-India), Wildlife Institute of India (WII), Dehradun, and Centre for Environment Education (CEE) retiring in 2018 as Scientist-G (senior programme director). As a visiting lecturer, he also taught photography to postgraduate students at the Mass Communications Research Centre, Jamia Millia, New Delhi. He is now a freelance consultant and also undertakes high-end digitization and restoration of images (negatives and slides in several formats).

Stella James studied law and has worked for about a decade on environmental justice. Her work and interests are interdisciplinary, and she aims to find creative ways in which different knowledge systems can come together to center local communities on conservation. She has worked on the rights of Adivasi communities in Odisha around mining, in Lakshadweep on changing fisheries and in Tamil Nadu on the impacts of coastal tourism. Stella is deeply interested in storytelling and believes that we best understand the world through the stories we tell ourselves and each other.

Sudha Ramen is a member of the Indian Forest Service (2013, Tamil Nadu). Presently posted at the State Planning Commission, she has, in the past, served as district forest officer (DFO), Thiruvannamalai, and deputy director/curator at the Arignar Anna Zoological Park, Chennai. She is a biomedical engineer with work experience at Wipro. Her interests are in finding IT solutions to governance issues. *Tamil Nadu Treepedia*, an encyclopedia for tree planting, and the *Vandalur Zoo* mobile app are some of her works. She has received the Dr Kalam Innovation in Governance Award (2019) and Prani Mitra Award (2020). She is a passionate artist with interests in watercolour, mandala and zentangling art.

Suhas Kumar retired as principal chief conservator of forests from the Madhya Pradesh forest department. He is a trained wildlife manager, a law graduate and a PhD in the field of ecotourism. He was the director of Pench National Park for five years during its formative period. He headed the Wildlife Extension faculty at the Wildlife Institute of India, Dehradun, from 1990 to 1996, and contributed to the growth of its training and publishing capabilities. Two-thirds of his 35 years in the Indian Forest Service was spent managing, supervising and guiding the management and training of officers and staff in national parks, sanctuaries and tiger reserves of the state.

Sumit Dookia has been researching wildlife for more than 20 years. With a PhD in the ecology of chinkara in western

Rajasthan, his work experience includes the Zoological Survey of India (Jodhpur), Wildlife Institute of India (Dehradun), Bombay Natural History Society (Mumbai), Government Lohia College (Churu) and presently faculty at the Guru Gobind Singh Indraprastha University, Delhi. He works very closely with the local communities and has been instrumental in the declaration of Guda Bishnoi (Jodhpur) and Gogelao (Nagaur) as conservation reserves. Widely published, he is running a GIB community conservation programme in coordination and support of the Ecology, Rural Development & Sustainability (ERDS) Foundation in Jaisalmer, Rajasthan.

Suresh Chandra Sharma is a former Indian Forest Service officer of Uttar Pradesh Cadre. He worked for the Government of India as joint director (Wildlife) in the Ministry of Environment and Forests (1987–1992), founder member secretary, Central Zoo Authority (1993–1998); additional director general of forests (Wildlife) in the Ministry of Environment and Forests (1998–2002). He was involved in the drafting of the 1991 and 2002 amendments to the Wild Life (Protection) Act; launch of National Wildlife Action Plan, 2002; the constitution of Central Zoo Authority; schemes like Project Elephant and 'Eco-Development in Areas Around National Park and Wildlife Sanctuaries'. He has been felicitated with the Dr. Salim Ali & Dr. Sankhala Fellowship Award to Wildlife Personnel Doing Research Work. Post retirement he spent one term on the National Board for Wildlife and chaired several committees set up by the Supreme Court of India. He also carried out the planning and evaluation of zoos for more than a decade.

Usha Rai is a veteran journalist (*Times of India*; *The Indian Express*; *Hindustan Times* and Press Institute of India) of over 40 years of standing. She has worked with World Wide Fund for Nature-India tiger cell. She has covered the Bruntland Commission's public hearing on sustainable development, the Rio Earth Summit, and various social and environmental movements in India like the Narmada Bachao Andolan and the Right to Information movement. She is a recipient of the Chameli Devi Jain Award for Outstanding Women Mediaperson, FAO/Science Writers Award for her article on forest rights and tribals, the Media India Award for a series of articles on school education in Delhi and the Dayawati Modi Streeshakti Samman as a woman journalist. Presently, she is a media consultant and freelance journalist focusing on education, health, the environment and women's issues.

Vinod Kumar Uniyal is a former member of the Indian Forest Service. He has a master's in Botany, a postgraduate diploma in wildlife management and an MPhil in human ecology. He has served in various capacities in the Kerala forest department, retiring in 2015 as principal chief conservator of forests. A field person to the core, he is known for his contributions to the scientific planning of protected areas and for involving local communities in protected area management. He is also an experienced teacher, initially a college lecturer and, later, a faculty on deputation to the Wildlife Institute of India. Widely travelled, he now lives in Dehradun.

Vishwas B. Sawarkar has had a long tenure in the forest department of Maharastra. A member of the Indian Forest Service, Sawarkar is highly experienced and is well known in the field of wildlife conservation. He joined as a faculty member at the Wildlife Institute of India, Dehradun, and retired as its director. In 1983, he received the Government of India's Award for Outstanding Service rendered to Project Tiger. He was a visiting faculty (1984–1985) at the Colorado State University, Fort Collins, USA, and the United Nations Food and Agriculture Organization (FAO) Consultant (1994–1995) to Sri Lanka for training wildlife management professionals. Presently, he is a member of the National Board of Wildlife;

trustee, Ecological Society, Pune; and chairman, Wildlife Research and Conservation Society, Pune, amongst many other professional associations.

GLOSSARY

Adda	Place for informal hanging out
Akhand shikar	Uninterrupted hunt
Akka	Honorific for older women
Anna	Honorific for older men
Badi	Elder
Bandh	Strike
Bigha	A traditional metric for measuring land area which varies by location
Chaur	Grassland in a forest opening
Chhak	Road crossing
Chhoti	Little, also used as an endearing term for younger siblings/children
Dal	Group
Dang	Vindhyan plateau top
Deh	A pool of water
Elakkadai	Auction house
Elam	Auction
Gaja	Elephant
Gaon burra	Village senior
Gaushala	A shelter for homeless cows
Ghada	Pitcher-like structure astride the snout of male gharial
Gond	Glue
Hanka	Animal drive by humans
Hasti vanas	Elephant sanctuaries
Idli	South Indian rice cake

Jal	Water
Jameen	Land
Jeevo jeevasya Jeevanam	Living things are interconnected to each other.
Jhum	Shifting cultivation
Kaka	Term of endearment for one's son
Kani	Opium
Kawadi	Assistant to the mahout
Kho	Vindhyan gorge
Kos	A unit of distance measurement; 1 kos equals 1.8 miles.
Kuladaivam	Deity associated with a particular village/clan/family
Kumki	Trained captive elephants that are used in human–elephant conflict management and capture of wild elephants
Kutcha	Temporary (made of mud)
Makhna	Tuskless male elephant
Mashal	Fire torch
Mitra	Friend
Muniasami	Name of the deity in Nallathanni island
Nallah bunding	Putting up a small barrier across a stream.
Pal payasam	A flavourful dessert made with milk and green gram or rice, usually sweetened with jiggery
Pancha	Independent witness
Panchnama	Document drawn by 5 independent persons
Paradh	Hunting
Pataur	Local name for a hut in Saharia tribal dialect
Poonkavanam	Sacred forest
Purana	Old
Quila	Fort
Sadya	An elaborate vegetarian noon meal

Seha	Locations where sudden and deep waterfalls have formed localized cliffs, gorges and secure caves.
Shikar khelna	Playing the game of hunting
Smriti	Remembrance
Suraj ko diya dikhana	Showing (or rather, comparing) a lamp to the sun
Talaab	Pond
Thakur	A hereditary title for traditional landowners
Theevu	Island
Van	Forest
Vayal	Marshy lands

INDEX